New York Architecture

1970–1990

New York Architecture

1970–1990

Edited by
Heinrich Klotz
with Luminita Sabau

Essays by Douglas Davis, Kenneth Frampton,
Christian Norberg-Schulz, Walter Prigge/Hans-Peter Schwarz,
Michael Sorkin and Robert A. M. Stern

Prestel

First published in German in conjunction with the exhibition
'New York Architektur 1970 – 1990' shown at the Deutsches Architekturmuseum,
Frankfurt am Main (1989).

Cover illustration: (front): The Stubbins Associates, Citicorp Center, page 224
(back): Kevin Roche John Dinkeloo and Associates, J. P. Morgan Headquarters, page 212

Endpapers: Manhattan, Island, N.Y., view from the south, 1985,
© Steve Proehl, The Image Bank

Frontispiece: Manhattan, N.Y., view from the east, 1988,
© Andrea Pistolesi, The Image Bank

Distributed in continental Europe and Japan by Prestel-Verlag,
Verlegerdienst München GmbH & Co KG,
Gutenbergstrasse 1, D-8031 Gilching, Federal Republic of Germany
Tel. (81 05) 21 10, Telefax (81 05) 55 20

Distributed in the United Kingdom, Ireland and all other countries by
Thames & Hudson Limited, 30 – 34 Bloomsbury Street,
London WC1B 3QP, England

Distributed in the United States and Canada
by Rizzoli International Publications, Inc.,
300 Park Avenue South, New York, NY 10010

Designed by Dietmar Rautner
Typeset by Max Vornehm, Munich, in Olivier light
Offset Lithography by Reinhold Kölbl Repro GmbH, Munich,
and GEWA-Repro GmbH, Gerlinger und Wagner, Munich
Printed and bound by Passavia Druckerei GmbH, Passau
Printed in the Federal Republic of Germany

ISBN 3-7913-0923-4 (German edition)
ISBN 3-7913-0989-7 (English edition)

Contents

Buildings and Projects outside New York   263

Appendix

Heinrich Klotz

Introduction

Over the past thirty years New York has not been the creative center of American architecture. Major American architects such as Robert Venturi and Frank Gehry have their offices in other parts of the country; with his prestigious address in Princeton even Michael Graves can be counted only in a limited sense as part of the New York scene. Bob Stern had already studied in New Haven at Yale University when he ventured into the world metropolis at the same time as the "New York Whites" was formed as a group of architects, with Graves, Peter Eisenman, Richard Meier and Gwathmey/Siegel. Today, they are among the most important architects in the country. However, during that period of radical change in the early sixties they were not well known. New York made a name for itself relatively late (this was also true of Chicago) during the incubation period of Post-Modernism and for a long time hung onto the outgoing ideas of ageing Modernism. Together with the director of the Cooper Union School, John Hejduk, and the Austrian Raimund Abraham, who teaches at the same school, those architects appeared on the scene that lent the New York "Le Corbusierism" another dimension and led the way into the realms of a fictional narrative architecture. The SITE group has in a completely different way intensified this tendency to re-semanticize architecture and with their BEST stores spread throughout the country, developed in competition with Graves and Greenberg, they have introduced new architectural ideas. Philip Johnson has dominated the scene for many years; with his wit and intelligence he has kept New York in permanent suspense. Johnson is *the* New York architect, the incarnation of all New York architecture which has hardly ever been original but has nevertheless absorbed and digested everything conceivable.

The world metropolis was not particularly creative in the field of architecture, but nevertheless invented the skyscraper and produced the Rockefeller Center. Together with the Chrysler Building and the Empire State Building, New York has made these fairly eclectic but nevertheless most beautiful high-rise buildings possible. It was here that the grid was spiritualized in its last conclusive stage as the basic shape of American urban planning, and that the Brooklyn Bridge was built. The pertinent ideas were indeed conceived elsewhere earlier, but first resulted in a clear form in New York.

Frank Lloyd Wright and Mies van der Rohe, Gropius, Breuer and SOM like almost all major post-war architecture offices have not been based in New York, but nevertheless have built there some of the most important buildings of Modernism: Guggenheim, Seagram, Pan Am, Whitney and the Lever House.

New York has brought the ideas for many of its most prestigious buildings from outside the city. Just as abruptly as the high-rise architecture of the glass-grid container broke into the city, it was equally abruptly – almost without warning – swamped by Post-Modernism. Again it was Philip Johnson who with his AT&T Building did not actually start anything new, but built the first Post-Modernist skyscraper amidst the glass containers of Late Modernism.

In New York it is clear to the expert on architecture that the innovation of styles and inventions of forms cannot be the beginning and end of architectural history. The needle-pointed Woolworth Building of 1913 is a late product of the Neo-Gothic – and indeed the first genuine tower high-rise building, *the* skyscraper. And Johnson's AT&T Building is typologicalle new, a building with "faccia" with face. New York is not the city of new styles but of innovative typology. The Rockefeller Center is not the first Art-Deco work of art but it is the first "skyscraper center" of a city. Up until then there were only *individual* skyscrapers.

New York is the one city that literally allows us to speak of nothing but architecture. Trees are something special here. And yet Central Park is there to remind New Yorkers of nature. The architecture of New York permits, as no other place does, the emotive question as to what nature really is. In no other place are the two poles so provocatively placed opposite one another: Nature – Architecture.

As inhabitants of this city people can seem, to be quite unnatural. As determinants of architecture they are nevertheless at its mercy, especially when in their cars. As pedestrians they still always belong to that humane region restricted to the perspective of the first ten to twelve floors. Above that setback forms mandated by the Zoning Law slip out of sight; people have created their own field of vision. They don't see right up to the top, they don't see the incredible violence of those stacked-up floors. The height itself is a relative value that people may have in their heads, but not in their sight. It is only from a great distance that the skyline is to be seen in its full splendor.

The people of New York can only be seen in relation to the architecture. A person on Madison Avenue is a special person. This is also true of the people in the Bronx where the confrontation with architecture changes into a relationship of aggression. Here, too, New York is unique: not even the downtown demolition squads from St. Louis have known the same violence in town demolition as it exists in the Bronx. It is no longer necessary to simulate cultural decline.

Here films about the end of the world are shot entirely without backdrops. The reality is the end, whether real or fictitious there's no difference!

And yet New York has proved that it is capable of regeneration. Deserted parts of the city as in Downtown around Bleecker Street, Houston Street, Greene and Broome Street are once more desirable places of residence. The cast iron warehouses, built since 1850 in Lower Manhattan, have gradually been decaying since the end of the last war and provide an early example of a miserably dying city. Indeed, the first cast iron building by James Bogardus was pulled down without any consideration for it as a historical monument; it had to give way to Yamasaki's smooth twin tower World Trade Center. New York destroys itself continually; equally it continually regenerates itself. Today the "iron town" of Lower Manhattan, where the prefabricated metal columns march in a continuous band around the blocks of buildings, has become a residential quarter with a special local color.

In New York architecture plays such a visible role that architects should – so one believes – play a special role too. But, however, Philip Johnson is hardly in the same league as Woody Allen. The degree of popularity of the architects is – as elsewhere – relatively low. Even with his Seagram Building Mies van der Rohe did not acquire that general notoriety typical of the giants of the fine arts. Only Frank Lloyd Wright, who never seriously involved himself with New York, enjoys the exotic patriarchal recognition of having his own postal stamp. His Guggenheim Museum is indeed the most famous New York building after the Empire State, the Chrysler, the Rockefeller Center and St. Patrick's Cathedral. An architect like Raymond Hood, who built the Radiator Building and the "McGraw-Hill," the first skyscraper of New York Modernism, has indeed remained unknown even to some experts on architecture. If Helmut Jahn actually ever does build that new part of town for Donald Trump, he might become the talk of the town. Slowly, architects are again beginning to awaken interest, after having for some time been unrecognizable behind the anonymity of the grid-façades with their Container architecture of the late fifties and sixties. Today a furious drive for individuality has arisen as a sort of counter-blow, which in their urge to find a distinguished address has brought the architects out of their anonymity. But even now the new onslaught seems already to be subsiding, for the degree of individuality levels out not only with monotony but also with variety.

While elsewhere the family house is usually the first commission for a young architect, in New York it is the private suites and the rooms and offices of medium-sized companies that have the honor of becoming the important initial works of many a New York architect. A little known beginner such as Steven Holl has with his small design shop (cf. p. 148) attracted the interest of his colleagues. With the design of a private apartment in Lower Manhattan (cf. p. 128) the well-known architecture critic of the "New York Times," Joseph Giovannini, has not only acknowledged

his preference for the term "Deconstructionism," actually invented by him, but at the same time has been accepted again into the guild of practicing architects in New York with this his first work. Nonetheless, he has clearly contradicted the towering figure of Philip Johnson and made him aware who was to be thanked for his "inspirations" for the Deconstructivism exhibition at the Museum of Modern Art.

Michael Sorkin, too, who writes elsewhere in this publication, is an architect who would prefer to build, but who has indeed won considerable recognition as a journalist. As one of the sharper members of the left-liberal "Village Voice" he has denied himself the dazzling exterior of New York. He is the personification of criticism, has a love-hate relationship with New York, is a critic of its forms and suffers because of the social conditions existing in Moloch's town.

Douglas Davis also belongs to the writing team of New York journalism; as architectural critic of "Newsweek" he has bared his teeth to the over-extravagant Post-Modernist New York skyscraper architecture and was one of the first to speak up for a new "Vision of Modernism."

As Dean of the Architecture Faculty of Columbia University Kenneth Frampton for many years held the leading role in New York architectural criticism. His convictions have found expression in the encouragement of the "white New Yorker;" he was not able to get anything out of Post-Modernism. When he took on his university post he replaced Bob Stern; it was almost equivalent to a symbolic ritual for a change in views. He found an appropriate successor to himself in the Swiss Bernard Tschumi.

New York has proved anew to be a bastion of modern tradition even if the Post-Modernist style is being built everywhere. Michael Graves in Princeton and Robert Venturi in Philadelphia are the opponents knocking at the gates of New York and to whom Bob Stern also can be counted. Stern's office meanwhile has become one of the largest in New York. Only a few years ago he was still a postmodern outsider and a newcomer, today he has become one of the most desired architects for country houses. Stern is one of the finest experts on New York architectural history. He knows precisely to which historical period his architecture refers. His buildings have become reconstructions that incorporate the original historical quotation in an unfamiliar setting. With Allan Greenberg, Stern is the personification of Historicism in today's battle for architectural direction. The criticisms he subjects the newly established Deconstructivism to are as harsh as the judgments he himself had to suffer because of his uncompromising commitment to historical Post-Modernism.

Christian Norberg-Schulz, like Kenneth Frampton, is an architectural theoretician and historian. With him a European takes the floor as if he were a New Yorker.

We gratefully thank all of them for their co-operation. Finally, we are indebted to Peter Pran who is head of the New York office of Ellerbe Becket; his good offices and his untiring energy were an essential part of the driving forces that allowed this exhibition to take place with its accompanying publication.

Luminita Sabau

Foreword

Twenty years after the first attempts to define the features of so-called Post-Modernist architecture, and amidst the "Deconstructivist" discussion, the basic concepts are still missing with which the urban complexity and architectural variety of New York may be summarized.

The world metropolis is, as far as its architectural history is concerned, ahistorical, since, in the beginning, most historical building styles were taken up almost at the same time and given the same importance. In less than eighty years, between 1850[1] and 1930, almost all architectural styles throughout history were represented on the New York street grid. Under the comprehensive term "American Renaissance" we find at the same time Doric and Ionic temples, Gothic and Baroque palaces or churches. This "Cast-Iron Classicism," assimilating architectural history in quick succession, defines the character of the initial phase of New York architecture. And because the buildings of this epoch have never acquired the authority of the monuments which developed historically, they became the "costly stopgap." It was Henry James who said that a story is only good until a better one is told and that skyscrapers are only the non plus ultra of economic inventive genius until another page is turned.

And that is what happened. Until the laws for the protection of historical monuments were introduced in the sixties, buildings were pulled down and new ones put up according to requirements, taste and whim.

And so a picture developed of the city which was characterized by change and by the "simultaneity of the non-simultaneous." On this basis, after the short-lived absolutism of Modernism in New York, a fruitful pluralism could develop in particular over the last twenty years.

The exhibition in Frankfurt and the accompanying publication record the salient features and the turning points of "New York Architecture" over the past two decades.

Especially after the economic collapse of the city at the beginning of the seventies,[2] which coincided with the decline of "Modernism," and the ensuing newly won economic vitality, the starting point was created for forming new architectural symbols of this reality. It is not intended to present a documentation of the "American dream;" rather, the selection of the projects presented should make clear the essential characteristics of development during this period. There has therefore been no stringing together of "highlights," rather the symptomatic and the exemplary is presented, but sometimes using as examples lesser known projects.

Because of the theme to be presented and the wealth of material, we have decided to give a polarized overview, which excludes an all-encompassing exhibition in which each aspect is represented equally.

The more thoroughly we discussed this theme, the more important it seemed to us to give up the narrowly drawn topographical limits. Many of the projects developed outside New York can fill a gap in the presentation of New York's architecture. Often enough, it was here that architects were first confronted with commissions that could hardly be carried out in New York because of the complex financial structure of its building industry. And just as we had to make this detour to show certain aspects of contemporary New York architecture, we also wish to emphasize that actual building in this city is not nor ever can be identical to the projects presented here.

We hope all the more then that this publication will provide a visual aid to New York architecture, while at the same time looking at it from a critical distance but also with understanding.

The range of the projects includes residential and office high-rise buildings, public buildings, museums, social welfare buildings, hospitals, as well as commercial buildings, interior installations, or conceptual projects. In addition, we have included important competition designs like those for the J. F. Kennedy Airport, Times Square, Columbus Circle, for the Guggenheim, Whitney and Brooklyn museums.

In the projects we selected various architectural conceptions came to light. Almost all characteristic directions for the period from 1970 to 1989 are represented.

The present-day generation of well-established architects almost without exception underwent a change from the stance of Modernism to the associative Post Modernism. This happened either explicitly with the help of historical quotes (Robert A. M. Stern, Michael Graves, Roche/Dinkeloo) or through the adoption of classical typology (Kohn Pedersen Fox, Murphy/Jahn, Cesar Pelli).

Only a few still strive for the aesthetic continuity of Modernism. Their norms are not strictly followed, however. With the integration of constructivist elements a new architectonic expression and a new three-dimensionality has developed (Peter Pran/Carlos Zapata, Emilio Ambasz).

The younger generation sees itself especially bound to the positions of Constructivism and Early Modernism. However, the strict use of forms has been relaxed to a large

---

1 In 1853 Central Park was laid out; this and the grid regulation of 1811 became the fundamental urban principles of New York.
2 In 1974 the city was insolvent.

extent. The morphology of this language is still "modern" or "constructivist." The composition of the elements presupposes, however, a "Post-Modernist syntax" that removes the severity from the rigorousness of the architectonic statement thus creating scope for fantasy (UKZ, George Ranalli, New York Architects, Diller + Scofidio).

Could it possibly be that the first sign of a reconciliation of today's intentions lies in the results obtained at the beginning of the century? In any case, seen this way the designs included in this book present a possible outlook for the architecture of the outgoing century. We regret that the architectural office of Burgee and Johnson has not taken part in this exhibition. However, we believe that other buildings as, for example, "425 Lexington Avenue" (see p. 162), give expression to the views intended with the AT&T Building. All the more pleasant and stimulating were the encounters with the younger architects. We would like to mention Tod Williams/Billie Tsien and Elizabeth Diller + Ricardo Scofidio as being representative of them.

In order to underscore the overview character of this publication, we have presented the projects in alphabetical order of the architectural offices and/or the architects themselves. Nevertheless, we would like the reader to look at these projects in an urban context. For this purpose, we have added a detailed city plan. We would like to apologize if not all projects are shown with consideration to the privacy of the inhabitants.

That this first fairly comprehensive overview of the architecture of New York in the seventies and eighties has been made possible is due to the architects and those who placed this extensive material at our disposition.

Essays

Robert A. M. Stern

Building the World's Capital

America was the first nation to grow up wholly in the Modern age and thus it is not surprising that its leading city, New York, became the Modern city par excellence. New York's wealth, influence and irrepressible energy render it unique; while it is virtually the only world-class city that is not a national capital, it is the world's capital. The richness and complexity of its architecture and urbanism define an essentially commercial, man-made environment with all the monumentality of the great capital cities of the past and the seeming inevitability of a force of nature (fig. 1).

The Beginnings

In 1625, detailed plans were drawn up by the Dutch West India Company for New Amsterdam, a five-pointed fortification to be built at the tip of Manhattan Island in the New World (fig. 2). But the ambitious scheme had little to do with the harsh realities of life in the colony and the city was never realized as drawn. Instead, a much smaller fort, protecting only a few buildings required for defense and the trading company's operations, was built at the island's tip and the adjacent town developed without an overall plan. Streets, laid out as needed over time and as a matter of convenience, were lined with buildings erected in typical Dutch styles of the day. Even more quintessentially Dutch than the architecture was the decision to run a canal from the East River into the center of the village. In addition to the Hudson and East rivers, two principal thoroughfares running northward would become the essential lifelines connecting New Amsterdam with the rest of the Dutch colony and with the colonies adjoining: Broadway running from the settlement at Manhattan's southern tip north to outlying farms, and the Bouwerie which would continue as the Boston Post Road. North of New Amsterdam were other Dutch settlements on Manhattan Island including Bossen Bouwerie and Haarlem (fig. 3).

In 1664, Dutch rule gave way to English. With the exception of a brief interval when the Dutch regained control in 1673–74, the English remained in charge until the Revolutionary War. The transformation of the Dutch village of New Amsterdam into the English town of New York was more clearly reflected by changes in the community's political, rather than physical structure, although Dutch architecture

1   Titan City Exhibition, 1925, Wanamaker's Department Store. Banner of New York skyline past to future by Willy Pogany. *Wanamaker's, Tercentenary Pictorial Pageant of New York*. Local History. New York Public Library.

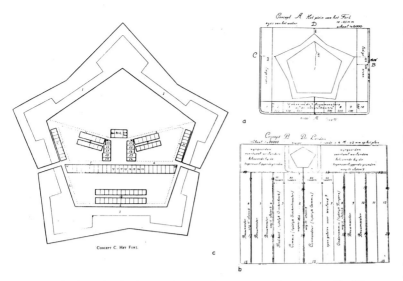

2   Dutch plans for the fort and town of New Amsterdam, 1625. Olin Library, Cornell University. Photo: Robert A. M. Stern Architects.

was gradually replaced by the dominant English Georgian style. The English incorporated the city and replaced the dictatorial municipal government of the Dutch with a rather more democratic organization. In 1696, the city's charter was amended to give the municipality control over all of Manhattan Island and to grant the city exclusive ownership of property not yet privately owned, as well as of land occupied by public buildings and roads. Additionally, the revised charter stipulated that the city owned the island's shoreline between low and high water marks, establishing the framework for the system of municipal piers and wharfs which would prove critical in the exploitation of the city's greatest natural resource, a majestic harbor.

While changes instituted by the English were pivotal in shaping the city's future development, the immediate pat-

terns of physical growth remained largely the same as they had been under Dutch control. A Dutch tobacco plantation located north of New Amsterdam and called Bossen Bouwerie (Farm in the Woods) was, however, radically transformed into a town, named Greenwich, which had a more distinctly English character. In the early nineteenth century, when "Village" was added to its name, Greenwich became a suburb that attracted thousands of New Yorkers seeking refuge from smallpox and yellow fever epidemics.

New York's history is as much one of crisis and decline as it is of growth and prosperity. The Revolutionary War period marked the first of New York's recurring cycles of decline: British military occupation curtailed normal business activities; major fires in 1776 and 1778 destroyed much of the city; and by 1783 the city's population was reduced by half. Despite serving as the new nation's capital from 1789 to 1790, New York remained decidedly provincial throughout the early years of the Republic. Symptomatic was the construction of the elegant French-inspired City Hall, completed in 1811 (fig. 4). The 1802 competition for the building's design was won by the French-born architect Joseph F. Mangin and New York's first native-born architect, John McComb, Jr. The new City Hall had been built because the existing building, completed on Wall Street in 1700, seemed neither large enough nor grand enough, despite a remodeling by Pierre L'Enfant in 1789. Nevertheless, the usually sagacious Mayor DeWitt Clinton was so insecure about New York's future that he ordered that Newark brownstone be substituted for Massachusetts white marble on the new building's rear facade, arguing that the cost-cutting measure would not be noticed since so few people lived above Chambers Street or were likely to in the future.

3   Plan of New Amsterdam, 1660. Stokes Collection, New York Public Library.

5   The Commissioners' Plan of New York City, 1811. New-York Historical Society. Photo: Robert A. M. Stern Architects.

A Metropolis Develops

By the second decade of the nineteenth century the city once again took possession of itself and prospered. The year 1811 was pivotal in the city's history; just as the south-facing City Hall was being completed, the city fathers began to come to grips with the island's larger destiny to its north. In 1811 a board of commissioners appointed four years earlier to lay out streets and public squares proposed to grid Manhattan Island with comparatively narrow, closely spaced, numbered east-west streets crossed by generously proportioned but widely spaced north-south avenues, extending to 155th Street, far beyond the limits ever imagined by the city's founders (fig. 5). The resulting blocks were broken up into 25-foot wide, 100-foot deep building lots with no rear alleys, dooming the city's streets in perpetuity to a ragtag mix of ceremony and services, elegance and garbage. Furthermore, no effort was made to zone particular areas for particular uses: land use was left to the influence of geography (industry would naturally cluster near the rivers) and private entrepreneurship (fashion would cluster along the high ground of the island's spine at Fifth Avenue which happened to be as far from the industrializing waterfront as one could get). Though the plan, which stood in marked contrast to the largely haphazard patterns of previous development practice, met with opposition from those who thought it interfered with individual rights, the court upheld it. The Commissioner's Plan was a businessman's dream, facilitating easy land subdivision and convenient access. To realize the relentless gridiron of streets, Manhattan's hillsides would be leveled, her forests cleared and shorelines altered through landfill. Similarly, this regular gridiron of streets heightened the impact of one of Manhattan's greatest "natural" amenities, its superb, clear light, captured in seemingly endless corridor-like streets slicing between rows of buildings, no matter how tall or densely massed.

In 1796, John Fitch, who nine years earlier had launched the nation's first steamboat, tested the first screw-propeller craft on the Collect Pond, a small, nearly stagnant body of water in lower Manhattan that was soon filled in. One of the people aboard was Robert Fulton, whose "Treatise on the Improvement of Canal Navigation" (1796) focused national attention on the need for water transportation systems. In 1807, Fulton, having acquired the necessary financial backing from Robert R. Livingston, cashed in on twenty years of experimentation with steamboats. Fulton's "Clermont" successfully plied the waters of the Hudson River from New York to Albany in thirty-two hours and soon he and Livingston monopolized steamboat operations in New York, which were of critical importance in connecting Manhattan Island to the surrounding region.

Ideally situated at the mouth of the Hudson River, New York is the United States' northern-most, all-year-round Atlantic Ocean port. Its role as the country's principal port was greatly enhanced by the completion in 1825 of the Erie Canal. Vigorously promoted by DeWitt Clinton, ten-term mayor of New York City and three-term governor of the state, the canal and adjacent water routes linked the city to

4   City Hall, City Hall Park between Broadway and Park Row. Joseph F. Mangin and John McComb, Jr., 1811. View north from City Hall Park. Photo: Robert A. M. Stern Architects.

6   View of Broome Street between Wooster and Greene streets showing cast-iron loft buildings. View northeast. Photo: Robert A. M. Stern Arch.

the entire Great Lakes region, giving New York a critical role in the opening of the West. The city's status as a transportation hub was further solidified in 1853 with the formation of the New York Central Railroad through the consolidation of ten lines connecting New York and Buffalo.

By the middle of the nineteenth century, in response to requirements for warehouse space, the city's architects and builders began to make imaginative use of innovations in building technology to create one of America's first distinct architectural building types; the cast-iron loft building (fig. 6). New York's loft buildings were a typically American blend of realism and idealism: cast-iron structural framing not only made larger interior spaces with fewer columns than ever before possible, but more remarkably still, builders and architects began to explore cast-iron as a cladding material, creating a new Classicism of metal, transforming utilitarian buildings into mercantile palaces. In 1857, when the first passenger elevator with a safety device was installed in J. P. Gaynor's modular, cast-iron-paneled Haughwout Store, architecture was at last free from the constraints of leg power and from the upward limits of masonry construction – and New York's architecture came into its own.

From the point of view of economics and politics, the Civil War was New York's first great moment on the national stage; for fifty years a transportation hub, now it was the leading city in terms of both manufacturing and finance. New York financiers largely controlled national production

and trade, including the South's principal source of livelihood, the cotton business. Abolitionism was fiercely supported in New York and thus, motivated by both practical and idealistic considerations, New Yorkers strongly backed the war effort. The business community insisted, however, that only a short conflict could be tolerated economically and after a year of warfare, popular support for the war effort began to weaken. In July, 1863, following the enactment of the nation's first mandatory military conscription, called the draft, New York underwent four days of riots that cost the city between one-and-a-half- and five-million dollars in property loss and more than one hundred buildings destroyed by fire; according to conservative estimates two thousand people were killed in the Draft Riots. While ultimately New York's sacrifices to the war were great, with the city contributing 400 million dollars and losing more than 10 per cent of its population, it emerged economically stronger and more important then ever before. At the war's inception, New York had been suffering from a recession; by the war's end the city's economy was booming.

While industrialization fueled the city's growth, it was also widely viewed as a threat to the public health as well as to traditional morality and aesthetics. Frederick Law Olmsted and Calvert Vaux's pioneering design for Central Park (1853; fig. 7) introduced 840 acres of open landscape into Manhattan's otherwise virtually unbroken gridiron plan as it transformed a squalid area of swamps and shanty towns into a man-made arcadia. Brilliantly synthesizing naturalistic landscaping and technologically advanced planning, which included the ingenious submersion of traverse roads below grade to minimize the presence of traffic, Central Park exerted a profound and lasting influence not only on New York City, but on American urbanism in general. Central Park combined dollars-and-cents realism with social idealism; a village green rendered at metropolitan scale, it at once increased the value of the surrounding real estate as it served up a slice of nature to New Yorkers of all classes. For affluent New Yorkers who lived at its periphery, particularly on Fifth Avenue, it was a grand front lawn; for the working man, it was an easily accessible bit of the countryside. Olmsted succinctly stated his democratic goals, noting that visitors to the park reflected "an evident glee at the prospect of coming together, all classes largely represented, with a common purpose … each individual adding by his mere presence to the pleasure of all others, all helping to the greater happiness of each … poor and rich, young and old, Jew and Gentile."[1]

After the Civil War, though not the nation's political capital, New York began to function and conceive of itself as such in most ways, largely by virtue of its wealth and its relationships to Europe, which were both cultural and commercial. In the afterglow of the Civil War, New York emerged as a truly metropolitan city, a complex geographic and social entity that supplied the same services and benefits as the nation as a whole. The city was perceived not merely as an economic reality, but as the highest representation

CENTRAL PARK.

of cultured life and for many observers, the embodiment of national beliefs and aspirations – as well as national material and social success. It also represented the collapse of critical aspects of the American dream: the end of Jeffersonian agrarianism and the rise of an ethnically heterogeneous urbanism.

New York was the first city to aggressively capitalize on major technological advances of the 1870s and 1880s: the Bell Telephone Company opened its first exchange in New York in March, 1876, Thomas Edison began to provide the city with electricity in 1882. The magnitude of these innovations was paralleled by a tremendous growth in human resources resulting from the waves of immigration which touched its shores between 1880 and the First World War.

Many immigrants chose to remain in the city, where they combined with the native stock to give New York the cosmopolitan character that was, and remains, its most obvious distinction.

The city's diverse ethnic and cultural composition was celebrated by the completion of the French sculptor Frederic Auguste Bartholdi's colossal Statue of Liberty on Bedloe's Island in New York Harbor in 1886. A gift to the nation from the French people, the statue, funded through private contributions, contained an iron framework designed by the French engineer, Alexandre Gustave Eiffel. Based on a likeness of the sculptor's mother, it stood on a monumental pedestal designed by Richard Morris Hunt that was inscribed with Emma Lazarus's ambiguously patronizing

8 Brooklyn Bridge. John A. Roebling and Washington Roebling, 1867–83. View looking west from Brooklyn. Municipal Archives of the City of New York.

sonnet including the famous lines: "Give me your tired, your poor, /Your huddled masses yearning to breathe free, /The wretched refuse of your teeming shore..." The statue came to symbolize not only the national commitment to liberty, but, particularly to the millions of immigrants pouring through Ellis Island, New York's role as a gateway to the New World.

Eclecticism

Except for the repetitious rows of brownstones, late nineteenth-century New York urbanism was rather motley, its landscape one of independent monuments, the greatest of which was the Brooklyn Bridge (fig. 8). The bridge transformed New Yorkers' sense of their city's geography, linking New York, which was on Manhattan Island, to the independent city of Brooklyn, on Long Island. Founded as the village of Breuckelen, meaning "broken land," by the Dutch in 1646, Brooklyn had grown as Manhattan's somewhat dependent sister city. In the nineteenth century, Brooklyn Heights, located on a bluff high above the East River, developed into the nation's first suburb, as workers daily commuted from Wall Street in lower Manhattan aboard Robert Fulton's ferry service, established in 1814. The completion of the Brooklyn Bridge in 1883 was as important for New York as the opening of the transcontinental railroad in 1869 had been for the nation as a whole. Providing the island city with its first direct connection to a major land mass, the bridge tied together the two cities of Brooklyn and New York and opened up a vast area for residential development close to the business and governmental center of lower Manhattan. The bridge, designed by John A. Roebling, a Prussian-born farmer who invented the wire rope that made its extraordinary leap across the East River possible, constituted an unprecedented technological feat. At 1595 1/2 feet long, it was

the world's longest suspension bridge, supported by four cables cumulatively containing 14,060 miles of wire. A week after Roebling's plans for the bridge were approved, his foot was crushed by a boat docking at Fulton Ferry and three weeks later he died of the ensuing tetanus. His son, Washington A. Roebling, oversaw construction which lasted fourteen years. Ironically, the younger Roebling suffered from "caisson disease," also known as "the bends;" his wife, Emily, served as a liaison between him and the workers, while he watched the progress through a telescope from his house in Brooklyn Heights.

The bridge was more than an effective artery of commerce or a stupendous work of engineering, it was a great work of art whose poetry resided in its ability to soar free of its context and be seen as an object of veneration, a paean to physical and emotional freedom, a secular cathedral with a roadway nave threaded through aspirational Gothic gateway-piers. In *Specimen Days*, 1882–83, Walt Whitman celebrated the "grand obelisk-like towers of the bridge on either side, in haze, yet plainly defined, giant brothers, twain, throwing free graceful interlinking loops high across the tumbled, tumultuous current below."[2] Since Whitman, the bridge has continually inspired artists and writers as varied as Joseph Stella, John Marin, Paul Strand, Vladimir Mayakovsky, Hart Crane, Maxwell Anderson, Thomas Wolfe and Arthur Miller. In his book, *Sticks and Stones* of 1924, the architectural critic Lewis Mumford noted: "Beyond any other aspect of New York, I think, the Brooklyn Bridge has been a source of joy and inspiration to the artist... All that the age had just cause for pride in – its advances in science, its skill in handling iron, its personal heroism in the face of dangerous industrial processes, its willingness to attempt the untried and the impossible – came to a head in the Brooklyn Bridge."[3]

Architecturally, the era was defined by its eclecticism. In 1893 John F. Sprague somewhat simplistically observed in

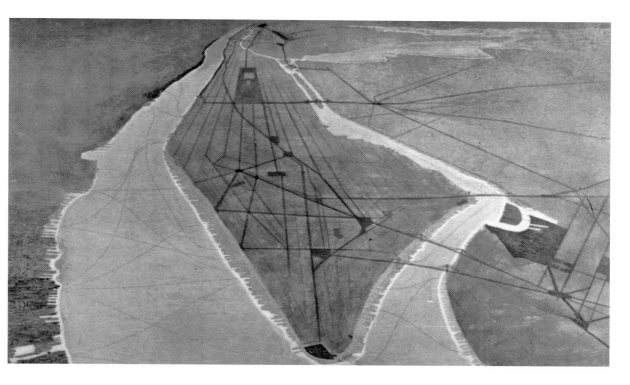

New York the Metropolis that the variety of the city's architecture was attributable to the diversity of the nationalities who "stay long enough to leave some impression of their manners and customs. Hence, with a great, throbbing, ever increasing, cosmopolitan population and a

conglomeration of races and ideas, a diversity in the architecture is a natural result."[4]

The era's eclecticism could be vividly seen in the designs of several major religious buildings (fig. 9). In 1868, the city's Protestant hegemony was challenged by the completion of Temple Emanu-El on Fifth Avenue. Designed by Leopold Eidlitz and Henry Fernbach, it housed the city's most affluent Jewish congregation. Stylistically, it sought to establish an appropriate identity for New York's Jews, exhibiting an orientalizing tendency in its flamboyant synthesis of Gothic and Saracenic motifs. St. Patrick's, a Roman Catholic cathedral also located on Fifth Avenue, was first designed by James Renwick, Jr. in 1850 but not completed until 1888 (fig. 10). It, too, announced the rising status of an American minority, Roman Catholics, in general, and in particular, the Irish. The city's Anglo-Protestant establishment reacted to these developments by proposing the construction of an immense, metropolitan cathedral to be built on a high, rocky outcropping that would crown the cliffs of Morningside Park and lord it over the rapidly expanding city. In 1888, as St. Patrick's was being completed, a design competition for the Cathedral of St. John the Divine was held; the wide diversity of proposed styles and the eclecticism of individual entries, epitomizing the era stylistically, more significantly reflected the establishment's heroic attempts to reconcile traditional church architecture with the unique situation of New York. The winning entry, designed by Heins & LaFarge, was, despite the somewhat Norman Romanesque character of its facades, a rather astylar design, as seemed appropriate to the nondenominational spirit of the undertaking. It also stood in stark contrast to the more ethnically specific stylistic vocabulary selected by the Jews and the Irish Catholics. The Protestant cathedral is still under construction today.

Despite the ambitions of these religious monuments, however, the principal symbols of the era were secular.

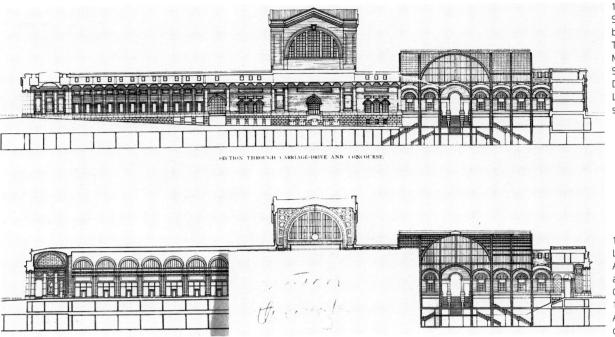

SECTION THROUGH CARRIAGE-DRIVE AND CONCOURSE.

13 Pennsylvania Station, Seventh to Eighth avenues between Thirty-first and Thirty-third streets. McKim, Mead & White, 1904–1910. Section through Carriage Drive and Concourse. Avery Library, Columbia University.

15 New York Public Library, west side of Fifth Avenue between Fortieth and Forty-second streets. Carrère & Hastings, 1897–1911. View from Fifth Avenue. New-York Historical Society.

Stanford White's Madison Square Garden, completed in 1890, was a pleasure palace realized at an unprecedented scale, combining restaurants, theaters and a hall for horse shows (fig. 11). The building's complex interior spaces were wrapped in a regular exterior that gave little hint of what was contained within. Although the building, which was dominated by a tower evocative of the Giralda in Seville, used classical architectural elements in a highly eclectic manner, its importance as an early example of the so-called American Renaissance cannot be underestimated. The Garden's bold scale and carefully designed relationship to Madison Square established a dialogue between the realm of private business and entertainment with the public realm of civic life that would become a standard of measure for all important civic undertakings in the future.

City Beautiful

When the nation fully entered into its Imperial Age in the final decade of the nineteenth century, marked by territorial expansion abroad – the acquisition of protectorates in the Caribbean and South Pacific – so too did its leading city, annexing whole sections of the mainland and joining with its sister city Brooklyn to form Greater New York in 1898. At the same time, New Yorkers, faced with the consequences of virtually uncontrolled growth, developed a new sensitivity to their environment. When New York lost out to Chicago as the site of the celebration honoring the four-hundredth anniversary of Columbus's discovery of America – what would become the World's Columbian Exposition of 1893 – New Yorkers vigorously set out to rebuild their city as a glorious, permanent representation of its role as the epitome of American achievement during the age of American imperialism. The public began to demand that each new major work of architecture go beyond utilitarianism and carry with it a sense of responsibility toward the expression of public purpose and the

embellishment of the public realm, synthesizing the high Roman-inspired Classicism of the American Renaissance and the complex set of ambitions for beautiful and logical cities that came together under the banner of the City Beautiful movement.

A fierce nostalgia for the social and architectural decorum of the nation's Colonial and early Republican past fostered a revival of Classical architecture and urbanism.

14 Pennsylvania Station, Seventh to Eighth avenues between Thirty-first and Thirty-third streets. McKim, Mead & White, 1904–1910. Waiting Room. New-York Historical Society. Photo: Robert A. M. Stern Architects.

In the face of an economically weakening and socially volatile Europe, America arrogantly and jingoistically regarded itself as the last best hope for Western civilization. The sense that the twentieth century would belong to America was shared even by some Europeans, including the English Prime Minister William Gladstone who was said to have observed that "Europe may already see in North America an immediate successor in the march of civilization."[5] The Classical revival was not only a response to new wealth but also went to the roots of American architectural values, reflecting Thomas Jefferson's taste and his dreams of democratic empire.

Where other American cities such as Cleveland and Chicago rebuilt whole sections in accord with the City Beautiful model fostered by the success of the ensemble of Classical buildings surrounding the Court of Honor at the Chicago Fair, New York characteristically contented itself with isolated monuments. But in 1904–07, an attempt was made to reconceive New York's plan in ideal terms when the New York City Improvement Commission was formed to carve a series of monumental, axially-organized public spaces out of the intractable city grid (fig. 12). The commission's goals were largely aesthetic; architectural ensembles were to be created at key points in the city while the remainder of the urban fabric was left to develop under the forces of real estate speculation. Although the 1907 city plan ultimately had little effect on the city's appearance, New York's architects for the first time succeeded in demonstrating that it was possible to work within the framework of capitalism to foster a monumental urban vision.

McKim, Mead & White's extraordinarily integrative design for Pennsylvania Station created not only an efficient transportation facility, but a convincing monument for the railroad and a grand gateway to the city it served. Completed in 1910, the building reflected McKim's belief in the continuity of Classical form (fig. 13). Electrification allowed McKim to transform the characteristic symbol of the station's nineteenth-century predecessors, the vast, glazed shed, into a concourse in which natural light bathed passengers as they descended to the trains a level below. McKim juxtaposed the glazed concourse with a classical waiting room loosely based on the Baths of Caracalla in Rome (fig. 14).

Carrère & Hastings's New York Public Library, completed in 1911, gave the city a great library open to the public that would surpass those already established in Chicago and Boston (fig. 15). Designed in a robust, Modern French style, the building emphatically demonstrated the style's applicability to the design of grandly conceived and functionally rational public buildings. The first important building in New York to provide its own monumental setting within the densely developed city fabric, the library was set back from its bounding streets to provide for landscaped terraces and broad steps that stood in sharp contrast to the brownstone character of the surrounding neighborhood and the Victorian naturalism of Bryant Park immediately behind.

As realized between 1893 and 1913, McKim, Mead & White's master plan for Columbia University established a carefully modulated architectural ensemble that represented in miniature form the urban ideals of the City Beautiful movements and rendered lithic the plaster and lath scenography of Chicago's World's Columbian Exposition (fig. 16). The plan called for tightly defined courtyards between near-identical classroom buildings, juxtaposed with grand vistas culminating in monumental buildings. The principal focus of the plan was McKim's Low Memorial Library, a restrained but inventive Classical building, based on a Greek-cross plan, carrying a low dome, that was entered through an imposing Ionic entrance colonnade. The crowning element of the Acropolis-like campus situated high on Morningside Heights, which, by 1900, it shared with the Cathedral of St. John the Divine and other

17 Columbia University, Broadway and Amsterdam Avenue between 114th and 120th streets. McKim, Mead & White, 1893–1913. A view from 116th Street showing McKim's Low Library and the dome of Howells & Stoke's St. Paul's Chapel. Museum of the City of New York.

16 Columbia University, Broadway and Amsterdam Avenue between 114th and 120th streets. McKim, Mead & White, 1893–1913. The top of the plan represents the original 1893 masterplan; the lower half was added in 1903. Avery Library, Columbia University.

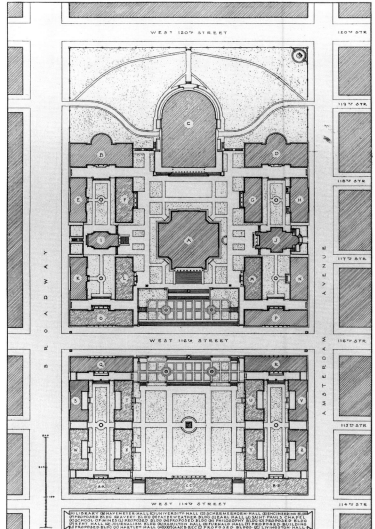

important institutions, Low library was elevated on three tiers of stairs that formed a remarkably expansive plaza (fig. 17).

A vision of the city as a collection of classically inspired monuments to corporate and private wealth in the service of civic glory was further enhanced by the construction of numerous social club buildings. Two clubs by McKim, Mead & White epitomized the type. The Metropolitan Club, designed by Stanford White and completed in 1894, was a rather chaste Classical building distinguished by a ceremonial entry court screened by a splendid gateway (fig. 18). Inside, an opulent marble hall rose all the way through the clubhouse like a palazzo "cortile" that had been closed in and covered in luxurious materials. Completed six years later in 1900, the University Club, designed by Charles McKim, was a boldly detailed vertical palazzo that exuded confidence. McKim drew from a variety of sources; references to Florentine palazzos such as those of the Strozzi and Medici, the Sienese Palazzo Spannochi, and the Bolognese Palazzo Bocchi and Albergate were used together with quotations from other Classical, Mannerist and Baroque sources in a composition that established a strong identity of its own. The facade was embellished with the escutcheons of the new aristocracy – the aristocracy of learning as each shield carved with the name of an honored and established American university.

Housing

At the same time that New York was becoming a city defined by remarkable works of monumental architecture, its housing stock remained undistinguished, with increas-

ing numbers of its citizens inadequately housed. Tenements, multiple dwellings for the working class, had begun to appear in the 1830s, but the middle class was slow to give up the ideal of individual townhouse living, despite arguments that they were widely accepted in sophisticated cities like Paris. The principal objection to the apartment house appears to have been social: whereas in Paris,

18 Metropolitan Club, northeast corner of Fifth Avenue and Sixtieth Street. McKim, Mead & White, 1894. A view from Grand Army Plaza that shows, to the left, Richard Morris Hunt's Elbridge Gerry mansion. Photo: Byron Museum of the City of New York.

19 Stuyvesant Apartments, 142 East Eighteenth Street. Richard Morris Hunt, 1869. View from the northwest. Photo: Charles von Urban, courtesy of the Museum of the City of New York.

families from different social strata mixed in a single apartment building, prevailing social conventions established social hierarchies which minimized contact between residents; but in ethnically diverse and more democratic New York, only money defined class — money not only didn't guarantee "breeding," it might be made by undesirable foreign minorities. Yet the growth of the island's population and the congestion it then generated on the overtaxed streets, encouraged ever-greater concentration in the more central areas. High-density, multi-family housing became a necessity by the 1870s. Significantly, the first

architect to realize a "socially acceptable" apartment house was Richard Morris Hunt, the first American to attend the Ecole des Beaux-Arts in Paris. Hunt's Stuyvesant Apartments, built in 1869 at 142 East 18th, initiated a new category of tenement, initially described as a "French flat," and later as an "apartment house" (fig. 19). Although significantly inferior to contemporary French apartment houses in both the luxury of its appointments and the rationalism of its plan, the Stuyvesant, which was intended to house society bachelors, did initiate a reconsideration of how affluent New Yorkers would live. While there was compara-

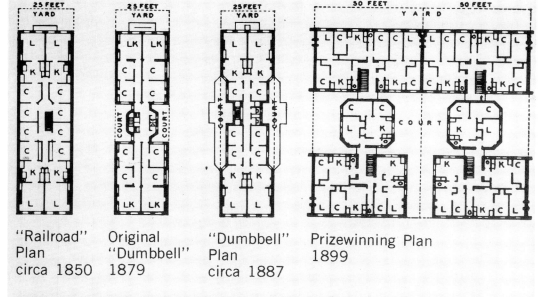

20 Evolution of the typical New York tenement apartment plan. The "New Law" of 1901 was based on the requirements of an 1899 design competition held by the Charity Organization Society; the prize-winning plan is shown at far right. Arthur B. Gallion and Simon Eisner, *The Urban Pattern*, 3rd ed. (New York: D. Van Nostrand Company, 1975).

"Railroad" Plan circa 1850

Original "Dumbbell" 1879

"Dumbbell" Plan circa 1887

Prizewinning Plan 1899

TENEMENTS OF THE INDUSTRIAL CITY

tively little apartment-house construction for the middle and upper classes in the 1880s and 1890s, owing as much to the instability of the national economy as to the failure of the new typology to gain more than a toehold of acceptance, working-class tenements proliferated, often bringing slum conditions with them. The tenement-house type, first codified by the guidelines established in the Tenement House Law of 1867, was modified in 1879 to ensure the reforms introduced in what came to be known as the "dumbbell" type, which called for a narrow airshaft between adjoining buildings; further reforms were instituted by the so-called New Law of 1901 (fig. 20).

The Skyline

As the country discovered an invigorated sense of national cultural identity and pride in the decades following its centennial, New York began to develop the skyline that would become its architectural signature. In 1875, Richard Upjohn's 284-foot Gothic-style Trinity Church, built in 1846, was still the city's tallest building, dominating the city much as a cathedral did in a medieval town (fig. 21). But in that year, Richard Morris Hunt's Tribune Building presaged a new era when it rose 260 feet; although still shorter than Trinity Church, it was the city's tallest commercial building to date and ushered in the time when the scale of Manhattan would be radically altered by tall buildings, soon called skyscrapers, and the commercial nature of the city was at last given its full architectural expression in a building type that powerfully asserted corporate pride. In contrast to New York's earlier cast-iron loft buildings and the utilitarian

in-fill office palazzi built after Chicago's fire of 1871, these towering, skyscraping buildings were as much celebratory monuments as utilitarian facilities. While it was not until 1892 that George B. Post's Pulitzer Building thrust its mass higher than Trinity Church, the formal lessons of traditional church design already had been learned by the architects of tall buildings. Height was important but of far greater interest were a striking silhouette, a permanent independence of form, and an inspirational quality. It was not the innovative technology or mere height that made a tall building a successful skyscraper; a true skyscraper had to be a proud tower, a fully modeled form, rising from a decisive base to an equally decisive pinnacle-like conclusion at its top. Louis Sullivan, the great Chicago architect, understood the symbolic possibilities of articulating a building's height, rather than just its mass. For Sullivan, a skyscraper had to be "every inch a proud and soaring thing."[6] Yet, Sullivan was never able to see his vision fully realized, even in his one New York building, the Bayard Building (1898), which was an infill building, not a skyscraper (fig. 22).

It was not a New York architect, but a Chicagoan, Daniel H. Burnham, who, in 1902, first propelled the New York skyscraper into that realm of functioning poetics it had been struggling toward for a quarter century. Burnham's Flatiron Building (1902) was the first to come close to the ideal skyscraper – a tower stacking floor upon floor of neutral loft space, yet standing forever free from its context to function as a campanile (fig. 23). The building brilliantly exploited an accident of New York's street plan: the very prominent but irregular triangular site caused by the intersection of the Colonial road, Broadway, and the gridiron of the city's 1811

21   1884 view of Manhattan from Brooklyn Bridge showing steeple of Trinity Church (Richard Upjohn, 1846). New-York Historical Society. Photo: Robert A. M. Stern Architects.

22   Bayard Building, 65 Bleecker Street. Louis H. Sullivan and L. P. Smith, 1897. An 1897 view looking east on Bleecker Street. Avery Library, Columbia University.

23   Fuller Building, Twenty-third Street between Broadway and Fifth Avenue. D. H. Burnham & Co., 1903. View looking south from the intersection of Broadway and Fifth Avenue. New-York Historical Society.

plan. The site was surrounded by streets and faced Madison Square Park, insuring that it would be permanently free of encumbrances on all sides. Officially called the Fuller Building after the prominent firm of building contractors who built and owned it, the name "Flatiron Building" was a joking reference to the building's shape.

The Flatiron Building revolutionized the institution of the office building, transforming it from a mere real estate venture into an advertisement for its patron and a permanent symbol of corporate pride. Quickly becoming the sensation of its time, the Flatiron Building joined the Statue of Liberty and the Brooklyn Bridge as a premiere postcard

24   View of Madison Square looking south. To the left, on the southeast corner of Madison Avenue and Twenty-fourth Street, is the Metropolitan Life Tower (1909) by Napoleon Le Brun & Sons, next to the Metropolitan Life Building (Napoleon Le Brun & Sons, 1892) and across Twenty-fourth Street from Madison Square Presbyterian Church (McKim, Mead & White, 1906). To the right, at the intersection of Broadway and Fifth Avenue, is the Fuller Building (D. H. Burnham & Co., 1903). Avery Library, Columbia University.

souvenir of the city. For photographer Alfred Stieglitz, it was "like the bow of a monster ocean steamer – a picture of a new America still in the making."[7]

The twenty-two-story Flatiron Building became an instant challenge to the Metropolitan LIfe Insurance Company's ten-story office building (1893) across the street. After the financial collapse of 1893, insurance companies sought to regain the public's confidence through architecture that symbolized enduring stability. Giver this need for stability for the Metropolitan Life Tower (1909), the architect Napoleon Le Brun chose a strange model: the campanile of Venice's St. Mark's Cathedral – which had collapsed

seven years before. Le Brun seized the campanile icon from ruin and rebuilt it at much larger scale, rendering it "useful" by wrapping its facades around a fifty-one-story filing cabinet full of office workers (fig. 24).

Completed in 1908, Ernest Flagg's Singer Tower encapsulated the emerging base-tower form of the ideal skyscraper and foreshadowed the zoning ordinances which would be adopted after World War I. Flagg, who had first argued against and refused to design buildings over one hundred feet tall, devised a six-hundred-foot-high tower to surmount the ten-story Singer Headquarters Building he had completed nine years earlier. The tower was a slender lattice of steel, with a skin of glass and metal panels stretched between corners sheathed in brick and limestone, crowned by a spectacularly mansarded rooftop lantern (fig. 25).

In the Woolworth Building (1913) Cass Gilbert created what the popular reverend S. Parkes Cadman dubbed a "Cathedral of Commerce"[8] (fig. 26). Like a church, it was built on the nickels and dimes of its parishioners, except that Woolworth's flock dropped their money into chain-store cash registers rather than church collection plates. Frank Woolworth was determined to build the most beautiful, the grandest, the biggest, but above all the tallest building in the world. His bankers refused to finance the project, and his builder, Louis J. Horowitz, president of the Thompson-Starrett Company, predicted a financial nightmare of unrented office space. But Woolworth went ahead anyway. He could do without bankers: he paid for the building with thirteen million dollars cash. Those who had said that Woolworth would squander his fortune must have stood in amazement on its opening night in 1913 when eighty thousand light bulbs, switched on by a signal from President Wilson in the White House, made it blazingly clear that Frank Woolworth had created an authentic symbol of his time.

Era of Skyscrapers

Following World War I, New York began to pursue new goals, abandoning the high-toned aestheticism of the fin-de-siècle City Beautiful movement for a more pragmatic, realistic approach to urban growth in an era of skyscrapers and mass communication. The previous era's largely failed but nonetheless heroic attempt to order the sprawling horizontal city according to Classical principals gave way to a new set of problems and goals for the rapidly emerging vertical city. Idealism was tempered with more realism than in the immediate past. The new generation took as one of its principal tasks the improvement of the living conditions of the citizen of modest means, as dramatically reflected in the Multiple Dwelling Law of 1929 which ended the tenement-house era, and the large-scale housing projects of Andrew Jackson Thomas and Clarence Stein, as well as federally funded public housing projects. It also undertook to ameliorate the congestion of cities.

The long term consequences of unrestricted skyscraper building were brought into sharp focus in 1915 with the completion of Graham, Anderson, Probst and White's behemoth Equitable Building. Occupying a site only slightly

28/29   Study for Maximum Mass Permitted by the 1916 New York City Building Zoning Resolution, Stage Four. Rendering by Hugh Ferriss based on a diagram by Harvey Wiley Corbett, 1922. Cooper-Hewitt Museum. – Fig. 29 (see left) "The Finished Building," following the four stages of the Study for Maximum Mass Permitted by the 1916 New York City Building Zoning Resolution. Rendering by Hugh Ferriss of a design by Harvey Wiley Corbett, 1925. Edwin Avery Park, *New Backgrounds for a New Age* (New York: Harcourt, Brace, 1927) Avery Library, Columbia University.

THE HECKSCHER BUILDING.
TH ON FIFTH AVENUE FROM 63T STREET

30 Heckscher Building, southwest corner of Fifty-seventh Street and Fifth Avenue. Warren & Wetmore, 1922. View from Fifth Avenue and Sixty-third Street. The Cornelius Vanderbilt II House (Richard Morris Hunt, 1879–83; George B. Post, 1892), stands directly in front of the Heckscher Building; the Plaza Hotel (Henry J. Hardenbergh, 1907) is to the right. Photo: Byron. Museum of the City of New York.

31 Proposal to Increase Street Capacity, developed by the Advisory Committee of Architects of the Regional Plan of New York and its Environs, 1923. Rendering by Hugh Ferriss, included in the Titan City exhibition, 1925. Photograph in Drawings Collection, Avery Library, Columbia University.

32 *Just Imagine*, 1930. Film still. Art directors, Stephen Cooson and Ralph Hammeras; directors, Buddy DeSylva, Lew Brown, Ray Henderson, and David Butler. Photo: Arts. New York Public Library.

33 Two Park Avenue Building, between East Thirty-second and East Thirty-third streets. Buchman & Kahn, 1926–27. View from the southeast showing the Vanderbilt Hotel (Warren & Wetmore, 1912) on the right. Photo: Wurts. Museum of the City of New York.

34 Barclay-Vesey Building. View from the northwest across West Street. The Hudson Terminal (Clinton & Russell, 1908) is in the left background. Photo: American Telephone and Telegraph Photo Center.

larger than an acre, the H-shaped structure rose forty stories straight up from the building line without a single setback to contain 1,200,000 square feet or forty-five acres of enclosed space (fig. 27). Visually overpowering its neighbors, the building transformed the surrounding streets into preternaturally dark canyons. In 1916 New York was sufficiently concerned about the threat posed by tall buildings that it enacted the nation's first zoning law in an attempt to encourage the best features of the skyscraper city – freestanding towers. Recognizing that a tall office block deprived its neighbors of light and air, and consequently tenants, the new law required upper stories to be set back in calculated stages. Above the setbacks, a tower could rise to any height if it occupied no more than a quarter of its site (figs. 28, 29).

The Heckscher Building, designed by Warren and Wetmore and erected in 1921, was the first skyscraper to be built under the new zoning (fig. 30). Whitney Warren's initial scheme called for a twenty-two-story slab set on a nine-story base, with no transition between. The final massing was somewhat subtler; while the base was still capped by a strongly horizontal cornice, the slab acquired projecting wings below and a richly decorated octagonal crown with a steeply tiled roof rising to a gilt weathercock. Although the Heckscher Building was a rather awkward first essay in the new skyscraper form, it nonetheless reassured even the most suspicious observer that the new law could produce fine architecture as well as substantial profits.

Hugh Ferriss was the Piranesi of post-zoning skyscraper metropolitanism. For the Regional Plan of New York and its Environs, he illustrated a proposal to create a multi-level city separating pedestrian and vehicular traffic (fig. 31); with Harvey Wiley Corbett, he drew a city of freestanding towers; for Raymond Hood he sketched skyscraper apartment houses that formed the towers of bridges spanning New York's rivers. In drawing upon drawing, Ferriss poured forth a vision of a new Babylon of massive office pyramids and towers, spires, and needles bathed in sunlight by day and incandescent with electricity by night. Ferriss's vision was thrilling but also terrifying; his ideal city, described in his book *The Metropolis of Tomorrow* (1929), featured thousand-foot towers, but they were at least set at wide intervals. Such a vision was truly futuristic: even in the mid-1920s, the average building height in New York was six stories.

Newspapers, magazines, and films carried the message of the new skyscraper world to virtually every corner of the

31

32 33 34

globe. Fritz Lang on a visit to New York, in 1924, thrilled to its reality and returned to Germany to create his film "Metropolis." The sophomorically lighthearted movie musical, "Just Imagine," 1930, portrayed New York in 1980 as a nine-level city containing 200-story skyscrapers between which ordinary citizens flew in their private planes (fig. 32). But New York's romance with the skyscraper was not only apparent in books and movies; it could be seen on the streets as well. Among the most innovative and skillful New York skyscraper architects to create the new poetics of skyscraper pragmatism were three, Ely Jacques Kahn, Ralph Walker and Raymond Hood, who as well were among the first architects to achieve the status of celebrities.

Kahn elevated the industrial loft building and the ordinary, speculative office building to unprecedented levels of artistic achievement. In numerous commissions, Kahn created finely modeled, setback compositions that often incorporated inventive, vividly polychromed decorative motifs both externally, as on the facades of Two Park Avenue (1927; fig. 33) and internally, as in the lobby of the Film Center Building (1929).

Ralph Walker's pioneering Barclay-Vesey Building (1926), composed of an eighteen-story base that supported a fourteen-story tower, brilliantly solved the complex massing problems imposed by the 1916 zoning law and an irregularly shaped site, as well as the programmatic requirements of an office building and switching station for the New York Telephone Company (fig. 34). The facade combined a wide variety of stylistic references to strike a

fine balance between tradition and modernity. Completed in 1931, the Irving Trust Building was a forty-nine story columnar tower and Walker's only true skyscraper (fig. 35). The building's steel facade was wrapped in grooved stone facades. The tower vacillated between seeming as if it were draped in weightless rippling curtains and resembling a work of nature, slowly shaped by erosion rather than by human hands or machine blades. Inside, a three-story-high banking room covered in red and gold Venetian glass mosaic was one of the era's most dramatic interior spaces, while a top-floor observation lounge was distinguished by walls covered in fabric decorated with an American Indian war bonnet motif (fig. 36), as well as by dizzying views in all directions.

Raymond Hood was the era's quintessential New York skyscraper architect. Educated at Brown University, the Massachusetts Institute of Technology and the Ecole des Beaux-Arts, Hood eked out a living largely by designing decorative radiator covers for the American Radiator Company until, at the age of forty-one, he and his former classmate at the Ecole, John Mead Howells – the son of the famous editor and writer – entered the international competition for the Chicago Tribune Tower and won. As a result of his success, Hood's former employer, the American Radiator Company, then hired him to design a skyscraper to serve as its New York headquarters. The building, completed in 1924, powerfully reflected Hood's understanding that the true symbolic function of a skyscraper was to advertize the corporation it housed (fig. 37). Hood's deci-

sion to sheath the building in black brick enhanced the building's sense of mass. He reasoned that windows, normally seen as a monotonous pattern of black voids in the walls of towers clad in lighter materials, would virtually disappear when framed by black brick, allowing the building to be seen as a solid monument. Yet Hood lightened the building's dark monumentality by gilding the top with gold. During the day, the golden pinnacles and crown glittered above the stark black brick shaft, while at night the crest glowed with light, suggesting to some observers that Hood intended the design as a symbol of the furnaces and radiators sold by its owner.

Howells & Hood followed their Tribune collaboration with a design for the offices and printing plant of the New York Daily News (1930). America's first mass-circulation tabloid, the News was led by Captain Joseph Medill Patterson, a campaigning populist and first cousin of Colonel McCormick of the Chicago Tribune. The Daily News Building's alternating pattern of vertical windows and brick piers was Gothic in spirit, yet Hood eliminated the decorative crown and chose instead to carry his unadorned ribbed cliffs from the sidewalk to the sky, justifying his design on functionalist grounds although he valued the walls' sweep of unending verticality enough to extend the facade ten feet beyond the upper story to hide the building's ungainly rooftop services.

Hood avoided applied ornament except for a narrow band at street level and a striking two-story-high granite frontispiece at the entrance that depicted the grandeur of

35 Irving Trust Building. One Wall Street, southeast corner of Broadway. Voorhees, Gmelin and Walker, 1929–31. View from the northwest across Broadway. The American Surety Building (Bruce Price, 1894–95) is to the left and Trinity Church (Richard Upjohn, 1846) is to the right. Photo: Underhill. Museum of the City of New York.

36 Irving Trust Building, One Wall Street, southeast corner of Broadway, Voorhees, Gmelin and Walker, 1929–31. Observation Lounge. Photo: Nyholm & Lincoln. Haines, Lundberg & Waehler.

37 American Radiator Building, 40 West Fortieth Street between Fifth and Sixth avenues. Raymond Hood, 1924. View from the north. American Standard, Inc.

38 McGraw-Hill Building, 330 West Forty-second Street between Eighth and Ninth avenues. Raymond Hood, Godley & Fouilhoux, 1931. View from the northeast. Photo: Wurts. Museum of the City of New York.

37

the skyscraper city of New York (with the News Building at the center). In the middle of the building's glistening black entrance lobby, like the control tower of a Buck Rogers spaceship keeping pace with the earth itself, Hood placed an enormous globe, fifty feet in diameter, which told the time of day around the world to remind visitors that the scope of the News went beyond the skyscraper city to include the entire planet.

For the publishers McGraw-Hill, Hood did an abrupt about-face, exchanging the verticality of his former designs for one with horizontal bands of windows and blue-green tile, a move that was immediately seen as an embrace of European Modernism. More to the point, it showed both Hood's restless eclecticism and his commercial pragmatism. The McGraw-Hill Building (1932; fig. 38) was an ideally flexible loft for the widely divergent functions of a large publishing and printing operation, and its glazed terra-cotta skin was easy to maintain. But Hood also recognized the complexity of the skyscraper tower's "function." The building's color and the sign at the top – the owner's name wittily emblazoned in Broadway capitals – were calculated efforts at shock value, which, along with the crest's tombstone massing, dismayed architectural critics but succeeded as corporate advertising.

The World's Tallest Building

So intoxicated with skyscrapers had New York become by the late 1920s that the city's developers and architects waged a dizzying race for height. H. Craig Severance's Bank of the Manhattan Company Building (1929) on Wall Street and William Van Alen's Chrysler Building (1930; fig. 39) in midtown jostled for position as the world's tallest building. When Severance and Van Alen, who had recently dissolved

39 Chrysler Building. William Van Alen, 1930. View east showing the Hotel Commodore (Warren & Wetmore, 1919) in the foreground, the Chanin Building on the right, and Tudor City (Fred F. French Company, H. Douglas Ives, 1925–28), visible in the background between the Chrysler and Chanin buildings. Photo: Wurts. Museum of the City of New York.

40 Empire State Building, 350 Fifth Avenue between Thirty-third and Thirty-fourth streets. Shreve, Lamb & Harmon, 1931. View from the south showing 500 Fifth Avenue in the background. Photo: Wurts. Museum of the City of New York.

their architectural partnership, each announced that his new building would be the tallest, the competition became a bitter and widely publicized personal rivalry. Walter Chrysler ordered Van Alen to shorten his design by ten floors, but during construction he recognized the potential publicity value of sheer height and reversed his decision, adding more floors, only to discover that Severance, working in association with Yasuo Matsui, had added a lantern atop their design and just to be sure, were proposing to top it off with a 500-foot flagpole as well. But Van Alen, determined to capture the title of "world's tallest," had the last word by hiding a 185-foot spire, which he called the "vertex,"[9] within the building's fire shaft until Severance completed his seventy-one-story, 927-foot-high building and then lifting it into place, topping his building out at 1,048 feet above street level. He later recalled, "The signal was given and the spire gradually emerged from the top of the dome like a butterfly from its cocoon, and in about ninety minutes was securely riveted in position, the highest piece of stationary steel in the world."[10] But height is not the principal feature of the Chrysler Building: it is a twentieth-century cathedral dedicated to the worship of automobiles

and transportation. At the thirty-first floor, four enormous winged radiator caps cornered a frieze of steel hubcaps and running boards rendered in black brick. At the sixty-first floor, four chrome eagle-gargoyles, monstrously over-scaled versions of the hood ornaments on Chrysler's cars, hovered over the traffic in the streets below. Inside the building, which was entered through great coffin-like portals framed in polished black Georgia marble, an elegantly detailed lobby contained a mural portraying the history of transportation.

Just as soon as Chrysler captured the height prize, it was immediately challenged by the Empire State Building (fig. 40). Conceived in boomtime but built after the stock market crash, in 1930–31, it rose on the site of the first Waldorf-Astoria Hotel, once New York's most fashionable meeting place. Constructed at a record-breaking pace in thirteen months, the Empire State Building soared past the Chrysler Building to 1,250 feet. Given the collapsed economy, the owners were aware that their building was likely to remain the world's tallest for a long while to come: To make sure, they insisted that the building be topped with a 200-foot mooring mast for dirigibles, an impractical feat of

41   Rockefeller Center, Fifth to Sixth Avenue between West Forty-eighth and West Fifty-first streets. Associates Architects, 1931–40. Rendering of view from the east by John Wenrich, 1932. Museum of the City of New York.

43   Rockefeller Center, Fifth to Sixth Avenue between West Forty-eighth and West Fifty-first streets. Associated Architects, 1931–40. View from 8–10 East Forty-ninth Street of RCA Building. Photo: Gottscho-Schleisner. Museum of the City of New York.

42   Proposed Rockefeller Center, Fifth to Sixth Avenue between West Forty-eighth and West Fifty-first streets. Associated Architects, 1931. Model of 1931 proposal. *Pencil Points*, Avery Library, Columbia University.

aeronautics that was put to the test of reality only twice, in September 1931.

Shreve, Lamb & Harmon's Empire State design, a paradigm of symmetrical massing, was remarkable for its central shaft, 725 feet of unvarying fenestration and wall that contemporary critic Douglas Haskell described as having "something positively brutal in the monotony, but something inevitable and hypnotic too." Haskell theorized that the Empire State Building was exciting because of its contradictions: "It was caught at the exact moment of transition – between metal and stone, between the ideal 'of monumental mass' and that of airy volume, between handicraft and machine design."[11]

The Metropolitan City

With Rockefeller Center, the skyscraper reached its apogee, not merely as a distinct building type but as a means for shaping monumental urban spaces (fig. 41). Rockefeller Center was first conceived as a cultural center in the booming 1920s but was realized as a commercial venture during the Depression. As designed by Raymond Hood and a team of architects including Wallace K. Harrison, Rockefeller Center transposed the grandeur of traditional civic centers to the purposes of corporate capitalism. Many of Hood's proposals for Rockefeller Center never went further than beautiful renderings: skywalks between towers connecting rooftop gardens, which recalled his and Ferriss's visions of skyscraper cities as the modern version of the hanging gardens of Babylon; a low elliptical tower, which was lampooned by newspaper critics as an oil can symbolic of the source of Rockefeller's fortune (fig. 42). Yet Rockefeller Center as built was the manifestation of the dream Hood shared with the prophetic artists of the 1920s: a city of proud towers defining great urban spaces, of vibrant congestion disciplined to the order of Classical composition. It was a city within the city,

44 *Swing Time*, 1936. Film still. Art director, Van Nest Polglase; director, George Stevens. Photo: Arts. New York Public Library.

one which symbolically encompassed the world through its statue of Atlas in front of the International Building, its array of national flags, and the French and British Empire Buildings, separated by a garden wittily named after the Channel that lies between. The Center's composition was balanced around the central spine of the Channel Gardens and a sunken plaza, and the soaring slab-like shaft of the seventy-story RCA Building (fig. 43) that rose like a great pylon – a sliver of ceremonial axiality cleft between as much hollowed-out masonry as corporate greed could get away with. The sunken plaza was a garden restaurant in summer and an ice-skating rink in winter. At the top of the RCA Building was the Rainbow Room, the magnificent mirrored drinking, dining, and dancing palace that was the real-life inspiration for the celluloid settings of countless musical supper clubs, most notably the ones in which Fred Astaire and Ginger Rogers danced in "Swing Time" (fig. 44).

While Rockefeller Center was a monument to the metropolitan ideal, the vast network of highways and parkways that Robert Moses built surrounding and radiating out from New York proved to be the metropolitan city's undoing. As New York's State Park Commissioner, Moses stretched his job description to a magnitude rivaling that of a president. Recognizing the potential impact of the automobile on patterns of development, he decided in the 1920s that he would orchestrate the transformation of New York from a nineteenth-century metropolis into a twentieth-century megalopolis. America's middle class had acquired the automobiles that would allow them to spread out beyond the dense inner city. Moses would give them places to go and the roads to get them there. The linchpin of his parks proposal was Jones Beach, a magnificent public playground only 25 miles from Times Square that would become a Lido for New York's motoring middle class.

In addition to extending parkways into the suburban areas of Westchester County and Long Island, Moses used a second approach for his highway system; he would "belt" Manhattan, Brooklyn, and Queens with a system of circumferential highways united in turn with the parkway systems, to link the city and the suburbs in a way that had never been done before, virtually surrendering the city to the region. Moses literally paved the way for the transformation of suburban villages and open countryside into the virtually endless suburban sprawl that shifted development away from the city in the post-World-War II era, when New York was swiftly changed from a clearly defined and unified metropolis to the principal but not exclusive focus of a megalopolitan entity whose boundaries went far beyond those of a traditional city to constitute a regional urbanism stretching from Washington, D. C. to Boston, Massachusetts.

The International Style

At the same time, the post-World War II period saw International Style Modernism become the principal architectural expression of corporate America, which would assume a

45 Lever House, 390 Park Avenue. Skidmore, Owings & Merrill, 1952. View northeast. Photo: Robert A. M. Stern Architects.

46 Seagram Building, 375 Park Avenue. Ludwig Mies van der Rohe and Philip Johnson, 1958. View from the northwest showing Waldorf-Astoria Hotel (Shultze & Weaver, 1931) in background. Photo: Robert A. M. Stern Architects.

47 World Trade Center Towers, between Church, Vesey, West and Liberty streets. Minoru Yamasaki & Associates and Emery Roth & Sons, 1974. Photo: Robert A. M. Stern Architects.

primary role as client and patron. As the individual entrepreneur was transformed into the corporate man in the gray flannel suit, so the city's instantly identifiable "cathedrals of commerce" were challenged, and in some cases replaced by anonymous glass-and-steel boxes. A few office buildings rose above self-constraining anonymity to become landmarks: Skidmore, Owings & Merrill's glass-wrapped Lever House (1952; fig. 45), which rejected traditional urbanistic values by lifting itself above a street-level plaza and turning its slender curtain-wall volume perpendicular to Park Avenue; and Mies van der Rohe and Philip Johnson's Seagram Building (1958; fig. 46), whose glass and bronze mass was as solid seeming as Lever House was evanescent. But these were exceptions, as the skyscraper type, distinguished by a traditional composition of base, middle and top, gave way to the "hi-rise" extrusion, powerfully exemplified by Skidmore, Owings & Merrill's One Chase Manhattan Plaza (1960), and their 140 Broadway

48   View of west side of Sixth Avenue, looking northwest from West Forty-seventh Street. Photo: Robert A. M. Stern Architects.

49   CBS Building, 51 West Fifty-second Street, southeast corner of Fifty-second Street and Sixth Avenue. Eero Saarinen & Associates, 1965. Photo: Robert A. M. Stern Architects.

50   Kips Bay Plaza, East Thirtieth to East Thirty-third streets, First to Second avenues. I. M. Pei. & Partners, 1961. Photo: Robert A. M. Stern Architects.

(1967). The reversion of the campanile skyscraper type into the vertical tall building container was nowhere more clearly shown than by the destruction of Ernest Flagg's remarkable Singer Building of 1908 to make way for Skidmore, Owings & Merrill's behemoth, fifty-four-story One Liberty Plaza building of 1972. The collapse of the iconic skyscraper type is best represented in Minoru Yamasaki's twin, 110-story World Trade Center towers of 1974 (fig. 47).

While many of the International Style buildings erected during the 1940s and 1950s challenged traditional urbanism by being set back from the street on broad plazas or built on landscaped sites that negated the city's street grid entirely, it was not until the ratification of the Zoning Law of 1960–61, the first major revision of zoning in New York since 1916, that the erosion of the wall of the city's streets was virtually mandated by law. The old zoning ordinance encouraging set-back buildings was abandoned in favor of regulations that encouraged unmodulated, independently spaced skyscraper tower slabs rising from

51   Riverbend, Fifth Avenue, 138th to 142nd streets. Davis, Brody & Associates, 1967. View east across the Harlem River. Photo: Robert A. M. Stern Architects.

52   Lincoln Center for the Performing Arts, Broadway to Amsterdam Avenue, Sixty-second to Sixty-sixth street. Max Abramovitz, Philip Johnson and Richard Foster, Eero Saarinen & Associates, Skidmore, Owings & Merrill, Wallace K. Harrison and Pietro Belluschi, with Eduardo Catalano and Westermann & Miller, 1962 – 68. View west showing the New York State Theater (Philip Johnson and Richard Foster, 1964) on the left and the Metropolitan Opera House (Wallace K. Harrison, 1966) on the right. Photo: Robert A. M. Stern Architects.

plazas. The wholesale rebuilding of Sixth Avenue, ceremoniously renamed the Avenue of the Americas, resulted in near identical bland-box towers rising from broad, lifeless plazas (fig. 48) that went a long way toward eradicating the city's traditional spatial hierarchies and opening for reconsideration and rejection, age-old concepts of urban scale and texture. As rebuilt, Sixth Avenue epitomized the bland, anonymous, meretriciously constructed environments that were exalted by their proponents as up-to-date, functional and technologically advanced. Only Eero Saarinen's CBS Building (1966; fig. 49), located on Sixth Avenue between Fifty-first and Fifty-second streets, stood apart. Like its neighbors, the building adopted an abstract composition and rejected traditional urbanistic values, but

it mocked the surrounding, seemingly tinny, glass-and-metal boxes with somber and elegant dark granite facades. Taken as a whole, the new Sixth Avenue represented the epitome of non-place urbanism that was brilliantly castigated by Norman Mailer as constituting "the empty landscape of psychosis."[12]

At the same time, amidst a tremendous apartment house boom, there was a general diminution of quality in the city's housing stock. The term "luxury," when used in reference to housing, became more a reference to a building's location than either to its level of accommodation or its external expression. Boxy rooms, low ceilings, detailless construction inside and out brought the level of private sector housing down to that of the public housing projects that were just built to "clean up" the slums. There were, however, a few significant projects, all built with government assistance, though most were built for the middle class. I. M. Pei's Kips Bay Plaza (1961; fig. 50), the city's first housing project built under the federally assisted Title I urban renewal project, was distinguished by its reinforced concrete, grid-pattern facades as was Pei's subsequent University Village of 1966 at New York University where three towers were placed on spacious grounds and overlooked a large-scale sculpture, Portrait of Sylvette, by Pablo Picasso. Davis, Brody & Associates' sociologically enlightened if coarsely detailed Riverbend (1967; fig. 51) and their sculpturally modeled Waterside (1974) were among the few projects to break out of the mold of the typical anonymous slab or tower form.

The Cultural City

While the post-war years witnessed many building schemes that were urbanistically destructive, including numerous Corbusian "tower-in-the-park" social housing projects, the city's civic identity was bolstered by the advent of one major cultural complex that realized, albeit with a compromised, even confused aesthetic, the

urbanistic and cultural goals of the City Beautiful movement of more than fifty years before. The Lincoln Center for the Performing Arts, catalyzed by Robert Moses and John D. Rockefeller, III, and designed by a team of architects including Wallace Harrison, Max Abramovitz and Philip Johnson, was an up-dated version of the World's Columbian Exposition held in Chicago, with travertine-clad buildings arranged around a fair-like Court of Honor (fig. 52). The theater building, designed by the iconoclastic Eero Saarinen playing the role of Louis Sullivan, was set off to a side court. But Lincoln Center's plan lacked the rigor of its predecessor and the constituent buildings, neither convincingly Classical nor Modernist, lacked the variety that comes from a rich vocabulary of details. The complex's architects and sponsors were never completely comfortable with the scheme and, in an effort to fully achieve the spirit of the City Beautiful movement, suggested that it be connected to Central Park by means of a tree-lined mall, a proposal that was at first greeted positively by the municipal government but then widely attacked as the public came to realize the essential banality of the idea. As built, Lincoln Center was, however, despite its architectural and urbanistic shortcomings, a bold attempt to create a cohesive collection of buildings and a decisive affirmation of the enduring appeal of city life even in an era of extraordinary suburbanization.

The postwar years were also a fertile period for the construction of art museums, which have come to be regarded by some as twentieth century churches. Two additions by Philip Johnson in 1951 and 1964 to Philip L. Goodwin and Edward Durell Stone's pioneering Museum of Modern Art (1939) framed the original building's Corbusier-inspired facades with unique architectural identities derived from the postwar work of Mies van der Rohe. In contrast, the master plan for the reorganization and

expansion of the grandly Classical Metropolitan Museum of Art, (principally designed by R. M. Hunt and McKim, Mead & White) devised by Kevin Roche, John Dinkeloo and Associates, called for a decisive change in stylistic direction. Cavernous glass-enclosed pavilions were grafted on

55 Solomon R. Guggenheim Museum, 1071 Fifth Avenue, between Eighty-eighth and Eighty-ninth streets. Frank Lloyd Wright, 1959. View northeast. Photo: Robert A. M. Stern Architects.

56 Whitney Museum of American Art, 945 Madison Avenue, southeast corner of Seventy-fifth Street. Marcel Breuer and Hamilton Smith, 1966. Photo: Robert A. M. Stern Architects.

to the museum's existing structures to create a behemoth art warehouse amidst Central Park's arcadia (figs. 53, 54).

The era's most architecturally significant museum was the Solomon R. Guggenheim Museum, which Frank Lloyd Wright began to design in 1942 and which was completed seventeen years later (fig. 55). The architect's only building in Manhattan, it was daring and highly controversial from the start, an intensely personal, sculptural comparison shoehorned into an ordered urban context. At once brilliantly set off by, and at odds with its surroundings, the building struck some observers as more appropriately placed in Central Park, rather than across from it. Inside, a soaring, monumental space was encircled by a continuous, spiraling ramp that contained the museum's principal exhibition space.

As designed by Marcel Breuer and completed in 1966, the Whitney Museum ignored its Madison Avenue neighbors, a striking inverted ziggurat built of gray granite and pierced by trapezoidal bay windows (fig. 56). Literally standing the city's traditional setback building form on its head, the museum was progressively cantilevered out over itself. The sculpture garden was placed in a moat along the principal street front, partially protected from the elements but still visible to passersby; a canopy-covered bridge led over the garden to the main entrance.

The Turning Point

While the postwar era began with the rise of the city's fortunes amidst an economy finally recovered from the Depression and refueled by the war effort, it can be said to have ended in 1975, the nadir of the city's history in terms of both its economy and sense of self. "Ford to New York: Drop Dead." So ran the *Daily News* headline reporting the federal government's refusal to bail the city out of its fiscal crisis in 1975. With New York teetering on the brink of default, the rest of the nation seemed unmoved, perhaps even gleeful.

But just when the nation appeared content to watch the city expire, not so much with a bang as with a whimper,

New York rallied. Typically, ballyhoo preceded real growth. The summer of 1976, with New York hosting elaborate Bicentennial celebrations and the National Democratic Convention, marked a turning point in New York's ability to convince the rest of the country that not only was it not dead, it was also not hopelessly corrupt or cynical – that in fact, New York was as American as the stars and stripes.

New York's optimism was not, however, merely a matter of hype or imagination. A new city government, under the leadership of Mayor Edward I. Koch, elected in the fall of 1977, drastically cut back services in order to balance the books. Soon, real economic changes stimulated a turn-around of the city's fortunes. Though the city's economic future was far from certain, demographers began to observe a trend toward the reverse migration of affluent surburbanites back into the inner city. All at once, it seemed, residential neighborhoods throughout the city, particularly in Manhattan and Brooklyn, took on new luster: run-down Columbus Avenue transformed itself into a sophisticated promenade of fashionable boutiques and restaurants; what had been known alternately as Gowanus or Red Hook or just plain South Brooklyn became Cobble Hill; and a new word was coined: gentrification.

While the city was renewing itself as a place to live, it was as a place to work that a newly energized New York was most fully realized. After decades in which bland, curtain-walled high-rises dominated the skyline, turning the moun-tain range of soaring towers from the 1920s and 1930s into a mesa of flat-topped mediocrity, the skyscraper reas-serted itself as the preeminent architectural symbol of municipal pride. Hugh Stubbins's Citicorp Building marked the critical turning point. The first major corporate sky-scraper to be built since the recession of the early 1970s abruptly ended the building boom of the 1960s, its con-struction between 1976 and 1978 began as an act of faith in the city's capacity to rise from its own ashes. As built, however, Citicorp's attitude to the city was, at best, wary; the building's obsessive internalization of services was a frankly anti-urban gesture. Ground-level stores turned their backs on the street and faced an interior court which, although a lively gathering place, functioned more like a suburban mall than an active participant in the urban drama. St. Peter's Church sold its site to the bank with the promise of a new building as a part of the new complex. As rebuilt, St. Peter's Church was overwhelmed by the swag-gering sixty-story-high, aluminum-clad tower which rose above it on four 127-foot-high legs, a reiteration of an old story of New York real estate, wherein Mammon, not God, triumphs. Citicorp's unornamented, contextually undif-ferentiated, slick, thin-skinned, strip-windowed facades reflected what was by the late 1970s a traditional Modern-ist approach. Even the building's great ski slope-like diagonally pitched roof, conceived of as part of a solar heating system that was ultimately scrapped because of technical problems, and then for a while intended as apartments, was never fully considered for the highest destiny it was in fact to enjoy as a bold, skyline-enhancing,

57   AT&T Building, 550 Madison Avenue, Fifty-fifth to Fifty-sixth streets. Philip Johnson and John Burgee, 1984. View east on Fifty-fifth Street. Photo: Robert A. M. Stern Architects.

corporate advertisement, a symbol for Citicorp and for New York's rebirth.

The AT&T Building (1978–84; fig. 57), though smaller, went much further toward exhibiting the major tendencies of architecture that began to emerge in the late 1960s – the tendencies that are by now widely known as "postmodern-ist" – tendencies that at the basic level mandated an architecture which resumes its traditional responsibility to go beyond functional accommodation and constructional reality toward the representation and enhancement of traditional civic values and ideals. Whereas the designer of Citicorp seems to have created a skyscraper icon almost by inadvertence, Philip Johnson and John Burgee set out deliberately to create a symbolically charged corporate monument that would pick up where the skyscrapers of the golden age of the 1920s left off. Restoring a sense of narrative to the architecture of the city, AT&T pointed the way toward a renewed vision of New York as a man-made mountain range of symbolic towers. A Modernist slab cloaked in traditional forms, the AT&T Building was ordered as a column with a base, shaft, and capital. With its pedimented top, AT&T recalled the aspirational quality that had characterized an earlier generation's swaggering skyscraper designs. And while the management of AT&T eschewed as undignified the life-giving commercialism of Citicorp's shopping mall, its grandly scaled street-level loggia nonetheless provided a sheltered space for brown-bagging New Yorkers to enjoy their lunch breaks.

Suddenly, designer-architecture was big news in a way it had not been since the glory days of the late 1920s. Philip Johnson glowered from *Time*'s January 8, 1979 cover clutching a model of AT&T and the developer Donald Trump propelled himself into the media limelight with a tower of such stupendous vulgarity that only hard-core puritans could not but secretly love it. The developer George Klein was the first in New York to bring a regular line of boutique-scaled "designer buildings" to the speculative market, carving out a special niche for his Park Tower Realty Corporation by erecting a series of relatively small office buildings that, by virtue of their individuality – personality one is tempted to say – contribute a measure of richness and variety to the streetscape virtually absent in the postwar Modernist era which preferred to wrap its typical buildings in the architectural equivalent of plain vanilla. It is said that Klein was inspired by the Texas developer Gerald Hines who has been credited with updating the spirit of the 1920s iconic skyscraper into the more personality-oriented "signature building." Hines has only recently brought his talents to New York where his firm is responsible for two buildings completed in 1987, Johnson and Burgee's oval tower, 53rd and Third (fig. 58), popularly known as the "Lipstick Building," and Kevin Roche, John Dinkeloo and Associates' E. F. Hutton Building on Fifty-third Street between Fifth and Sixth avenues.

While most people welcome the new buildings as alternatives to the blandness of the postwar era, the price for that variety of shape, richness of surface and amenity has often as not been bonuses offered by the city to developers, bonuses that permit additional height or mass or both, bonuses which have raised questions about density and the city's capacity to absorb the crowds these buildings bring with them. As welcome as the current building boom may be in both artistic and economic terms, the overriding concern has become density: is New York simply overbuilding itself? While this question will, and no doubt should be rigorously investigated and debated, it raises another question: is congestion itself a problem? In the 1920s, architects such as Harvey Wiley Corbett celebrated what has come to be known as the "cult of congestion," arguing that it was a principal ingredient in New York's vital urbanism. The challenge, he argued, was not to limit high-density development but to find effective methods of adapting traditional urbanism to the new scale. That challenge is as important today at it was sixty years ago.

Times Square, New York

The city's continual evolution – including the processes of improvement, decline, and revival – is nowhere more apparent than in Times Square and on Forty-second Street between Seventh and Eighth avenues.[13] Today the area is a troubled, but vital district, once identified in the popular imagination with glamourous night life and with the current

58   53rd at Third, 885 Third Avenue. John Burgee Architects with Philip Johnson, 1986. View from the southwest. Photo: Greg Murphey, courtesy of John Burgee Architects with Philip Johnson.

reality of the mythology of pornography and crime. As late as the 1820s, the area consisted of farms and open countryside owned by a few families. In 1825, John L. Norton, the owner of the area's most successful farm, known as the Hermitage, and a founder of the City National Bank, ceded part of his land to the city at a price of ten dollars for the purpose of creating a public thoroughfare: Forty-second Street. In 1836, the street was officially opened by Mayor C. W. Lawrence, who invited New Yorkers, most of whom lived and worked below Twenty-third Street, to "move up and enjoy the pure, clean air." By 1866, though still the hinterlands, the street was reachable from downtown by six horsecar lines and further served by the Weehawken Ferry that docked at the street's Hudson River terminus. Cornelius Vanderbilt early on understood the economic consequences of the city's enormous northward expansion and Forty-second Street's destiny as a transportation hub; in 1871, having seized control of the ten railroads that connected New York and Buffalo, Vanderbilt completed the first Grand Central depot at Forty-second Street and Fourth Avenue. Seven years later, the construction of the Third and Sixth Avenue elevated railways secured Forty-second Street's status as a transportation center. Despite these improvements, Forty-second Street was not quite an urban paradise: there were garbage dumps and shanty towns, particularly on the East Side, and cattle was driven

across it from the Hudson River docks to the slaughter houses along First Avenue.

By the 1890s, Longacre Square, where Forty-second Street, Broadway and Seventh Avenue come together, was a stable, if not fashionable residential neighborhood. Neat rows of brownstones, two churches and a library lined Forty-second Street between Seventh and Eighth avenues. But commerce was moving steadily northward and in 1898, Oscar Hammerstein decided to build his Victoria Theater at the northwest corner of Seventh Avenue and Forty-second Street, making it the most northern outpost of the entertainment Rialto which then stretched along Broadway between Fourteenth and Fortieth streets. In 1904, the subway reached Longacre Square; the same year, the intersection was renamed Times Square when the *New York Times* completed its tower, designed by Eidlitz & MacKenzie, at Forty-second Street and Broadway. The area soon emerged as the city's "New Rialto," with a remarkably dense concentration of theaters and roof gardens, as well as many other buildings to house theater-related activites. Previously, the city's theaters had been gas lit, poorly ventilated and contained exits largely unregulated by building codes; not surprisingly, the theaters experienced a series of disastrous fires in the 1880s.

The new theaters were safer, primarily because they were electrically lit. Architects soon discovered the almost limitless potential of electric and neon light for advertisement and nighttime decor (fig. 59). The result, widely recognized by 1910, was the transformation of Broadway into the Great White Way. Not only did the signs shine brightly on Broad-

way, but the world's greatest "stars" lit up the street in entertainments that collectively were distinguished by their excellence and perhaps as importantly, by their enormous variety, from the most high hat to the most lowbrow. The area also contained fashionable restaurants, including the sumptuous Murray's Roman Gardens, perhaps the first theme restaurant ever. In 1919, when Prohibition stopped the champagne from flowing in these elegant watering holes, Times Square and Forty-second Street were at their peak; despite the subsequent disappearance of fine dining and cabaret, the area managed to hold on to its glamour.

During the 1920s, while remaining a key asset in the city's rich cultural bank account, the area began to take on a more democratic aspect than it had previously when it catered principally to the "carriage trade." Murray's was replaced by Hubert's Museum, better known as the Flea Circus. The "museum," which remained in operation for more than forty years, featured a permanent human freak show, an electronic shooting range and numerous other attractions. It became fashionable for theatergoers in evening clothes to stop by and listen to Grover Cleveland Alexander lecture on baseball or hear Professor William Heckler play the harmonica while on his forearm he fed trained fleas named Caesar, Napoleon, Cousin Charlie and Peaches. One waggish observer commented that over the years Hubert's didn't change along with the neighborhood because it had been fully deteriorated from the beginning. Still, it added strongly to the street's new democratic ambience.

60 View of west side of Broadway between West Forty-seventh and West Forty-eighth streets, ca. 1937. New York Public Library.

61 Victory Theater, 209 West Forty-second Street, between Seventh and Eighth avenues. J. B. McElfatrick & Co., 1900. Museum of the city of New York.

The birth of "talkies" in the late 1920s and the subsequent advent of the Depression transformed the New York theater world. True, throughout the 1920s, "legitimate" theaters had shown movies to stay open between plays, but by the early 1930s, many of the area's theaters, and particularly those on Forty-second Street, had discontinued live performances entirely or played burlesque exclusively. Forty-second Street was ideally suited to attract the movie-going public. The street's superb accessibility was augmented in 1918 by the extension of the IRT subway line south of Times Square along Seventh Avenue and in 1923 by the construction of a line along Broadway that formed part of the newly organized BMT line. In 1932, the municipally-sponsored IND subway line was completed along Eighth Avenue and five years later, in 1937, the completion of the Lincoln Tunnel's first tube underneath the Hudson River opened up Forty-second Street to New Jersey suburbanites. In the late 1930s, so rich was Forty-second Street, in its mix of entertainments and patrons, that Cecil Beaton, the English author, photographer, costume designer and bon vivant could accurately proclaim that its appeal was "universal" (fig. 60).

Throughout the area's nearly century-long history as an entertainment center, the architecture of its theaters played an important role in establishing its ambience. Theaters that featured dramatic productions, such as the Victory, designed by J. B. McElfatrick & Co. and completed in 1900, were built with high ideals for an elevated theatrical art reflected in the dignity and energy of their architectural character (fig. 61). Theaters specializing in musical comedy fare, such as Herts & Tallant's New Amsterdam of 1903, further entertained playgoers with spectacularly opulent fantasy decor (fig. 62). After World War I, a new theater type evolved which, with wider and shallower houses, cantilevered balconies, and streamlined backstage

62 New Amsterdam Theater, 214 West Forty-second Street, between Seventh and Eighth avenues. Herts & Tallant, 1903. New-York Historical Society.

facilities, competed for audiences by appealing to their creature comforts as well as their growing critical awareness of professional theater. This type of theater, exemplified by the Times Square designed by Eugene DeRosa and completed in 1920, was actually designed to show motion pictures as well. In the 1930s and '40s, those parts of the theater devoted to live entertainment decayed. Changes were cosmetic, such as new signs and marquees, or destructive, such as box seating removed for wide-screen projection.

The Second World War brought hordes of servicemen on leave into the Times Square area like the eager sailors vividly portrayed in *On The Town*; for many servicemen, a visit to Times Square provided their most memorable, and perhaps their only opportunity to get a taste of the Big Apple's glamour. In the postwar era, the rise of television and the general emphasis on domestic family life that accompanied widespread suburbanization conspired to drain the street of much of its life. Nonetheless, the area remained active and the construction of the Port Authority Bus Terminal in 1950 further reinforced Forty-second Street's traditional role as a transportation hub. By the 1970s, despite the continued presence of numerous live-production theaters in the area, Times Square and Forty-second Street had significantly declined.

Numerous large-scale office and mixed use projects currently under construction or on the boards, including four mammoth, mansarded towers designed by Philip Johnson and John Burgee, will no doubt radically change the appearance and character of Times Square and Forty-second Street. At the same time, the 42nd Street Development Project, a collaborative effort of the New York State Urban Development Corporation and the City of New York Public Development Corporation, proposes to return the blight-ridden block of West Forty-second Street between Seventh and Eighth avenues to the world-renowned, popular entertainment district it was before.[14] In addition to calling for the construction of office towers, a wholesale mart and a hotel, the plan mandates the acquisition and renovation of nine important theaters on the street. Studies made by the author and Hardy Holzman Pfeiffer Associates have documented the theaters' current conditions and suggested potential uses; while not presenting a final design, the interim report suggests how the street would look should one or another of a series of alternative strategies for the restoration of the theaters and the reconstruction of their adjacencies be undertaken. The future of Forty-second Street hangs in the balance and with it the hope for the city as well: can the renewed city be a place for all, a true urban democracy, or will it only thrive as a middle-class haven from the blight of the slums and the banalities of the suburbia?

A Rich Architectural Future

Perhaps the explosive New York of the 1980s is more difficult to comprehend and cope with than the stagnant New York of the 1970s, but it is also truer to itself. Before the Second World War, most New Yorkers believed that a new building going up would be better, not merely bigger, than the one coming down; in the decades following the war

63 Demonstration against destruction of Pennsylvania Station (McKim, Mead & White, 1910). The three picketers in front are, from left to right: Aline Saarinen, Philip Johnson, and Mrs. Bliss Parkinson. August 2, 1962. "Architectural Forum," Avery Library, Columbia University. Photo: Robert A. M. Stern Architects.

much of the city was rebuilt in an arrogantly anti-historical, anti-urban manner, with countless bland, placeless, glass-and-metal boxes giving us good reason to lose the faith. The tragic loss in 1963 of McKim, Mead & White's Pennsylvania Station (1910) shocked us into recognizing the need to protect our architectural past and gave rise to the public protest movement that culminated in the passage of the Landmarks Preservation Law two years later. At the same time, the fate of another of New York's greatest architectural monuments, Grand Central Terminal (1913) designed by Reed & Stem and Warren & Wetmore was uncertain. Grand Central's capacious concourse, deemed a waste of space, was threatened with demolition. Its designation as a landmark by the New York City Landmarks Preservation Commission in 1967 was challenged by real estate interests, who took the case all the way to the Supreme Court, which ruled in favor of preservation. Today hundreds of individual buildings and scores of historic districts have been designated as landmarks, though the need to cast the protective net still wider remains. Now that we have in large measure rediscovered the importance of saving our architectural heritage, we must find the courage to believe in our own ability to create a rich architectural future and a truly diverse, representative democratic urbanism – once again creating monuments that both reflect and define the spirit of a continually changing New York.

Notes

This essay was written with the help of Thomas Mellins. Many of the ideas contained within have been discussed in greater detail in Robert A. M. Stern, Gregory Gilmartin and John Massengale, *New York 1900: Metropolitan Architecture and Urbanism 1890–1915* (New York: Rizzoli, 1983) and Robert A. M. Stern, Gregory Gilmartin and Thomas Mellins, *New York 1930: Architecture and Urbanism, Between the Two World Wars* (New York: Rizzoli, 1987).

1 Frederick Law Olmsted, "Public Parks and the Enlargement of Towns," *American Social Science Association* (Cambridge, Massachusetts: Riverside Press, 1870): pp. 1–36.

2 Walt Whitman, *Specimen Days & Collect* (Philadelphia: Rees Welsh, 1882–83): p. 116.

3 Lewis Mumford, *Sticks and Stones: A Study of American Architecture and Civilization* (New York: Bom and Liveright, 1924), p. 116.

4 John F. Sprague, *New York the Metropolis* (New York: The New York Recorder, 1893), p. 36.

5 Robert Kerr, Supplement to James Ferguson, *History of the Modern Styles of Architecture*, 3rd ed. (London, 1891), p. 373; quoted in Richard Guy Wilson, "The Great Civilization," in *The American Renaissance: 1876–1917* (New York: Pantheon, 1979), p. 13.

6 Louis H. Sullivan, "The Tall Office Building Artistically Considered," first published in *Lippincott's* 57 (March 1896): pp. 403–9; reprinted in Sullivan, *Kindergarten Chats and Other Writings* (New York: George Wittenborn, 1947), p. 206.

7 Alfred Stieglitz, as quoted in Dorothy Norman, *Alfred Stieglitz: An American Seer* (New York: Aperture, 1973), p. 45.

8 S. Parkes Cadman in *The Cathedral of Commerce: The Woolworth Building, New York* (New York: Broadway, Park Place, 1917; 1921), introduction.

9 William Van Alen quoted in Donald Martin Reynolds, *The Architecture of New York City: Histories and Views of Important Structures, Sites and Symbols* (New York: Macmillan, 1984), p. 235.

10 William Van Alen, "The Structure and Metal Work of the Chrysler Building," *Architectural Forum* 53 (October 1930): pp. 493–98.

11 Douglas Haskell, "The Empire State Building," *Creative Art* 8 (April 1931): pp. 242–44.

12 Norman Mailer, "Mailer vs. Scully," *Architectural Forum* 120 (April 1964): pp. 96–7.

13 The following discussion was prepared as part of *Forty-second Street: Glorious Past, Fabulous Future*, exhibition catalogue (Forty-second Street Development Corporation, 1988).

14 For further discussion, see Robert A. M. Stern Architects, Brannigan-Lorelli Associates, Robert E. Meadows, *Study of Apollo, Lyric, Selwyn and Times Square Theaters and Related Infill Parcels*, prepared for the New York State Urban Development Corporation and the New York City Public Development Corporation, October, 1988.

Kenneth Frampton

New York's Narcosis

Reflections from an Archimedean Point

The merchandizing apparatus, of which many designers are now members operates more to create want than to satisfy wants that are already active. Consumers are trained to "want" that to which they are most continually exposed. Wants do not originate in some vague realms of the consumer's personality; they are formed by an elaborate apparatus of jingle and fashion, of persuasion and fraud. They are shaped by the cultural apparatus and the society of which it is a part. They do not grow and change as the consumer's sensibilities are enlarged; they are created and they are changed by the process by which they are satisfied and by which old satisfactions are made unsatisfactory. Moreover, the very canons of taste and judgment are also managed by fashion. The formula is: to make people ashamed of last year's model; to hook up self-esteem itself with the purchasing of this year's model to create a panic for status, and hence a panic of self-evaluation, and to connect its relief with the consumption of specified commodities.

C. Wright Mills, "The Man in the Middle"
International Design Conference, Aspen, Colorado, 1958

The self-criticism of Modernism grows out of but is not the same thing as the criticism of the Enlightenment. The Enlightenment criticized from the outside, the way criticism in its more accepted sense does; Modernism criticizes from the inside, through the procedures themselves of that which is being criticized. It seems natural that this kind of criticism should have appeared first in philosophy, which is critical by definition, but as the nineteenth century wore on it made itself felt in many other fields. A more rational justification began to be demanded of every formal social activity, and "Kantian" self-criticism was called on eventually to meet and interpret this demand in areas that lay far from philosophy.

Clement Greenberg, "Modernist Painting"
Art & Literature, Spring, 1961

The assertion that there is a need for art is largely ideological. People can do without art if they have to. This statement holds objectively as well as subjectively in terms of the psychological household of the consumer (who has no trouble changing his tastes in response to changes in his existence provided they are piecemeal). In a society that teaches its members not to think beyond themselves, anything that transcends the material reproduction of life is ultimately useless. And that includes art, even though society makes every effort to pound the notion of art's usefulness into their heads. At a time when, absurdly enough, material penury continues, when barbarism reproduces itself on an expanding scale and when the threat of total destruction is ever present – at such a time any phenomenon that shows no concern for the preservation of life takes on a silly appearance . . . Theodor Adorno, Aesthetic Theory, 1970

The so-called battle of the Whites, the Silvers and the Grays, that is to say, the famous Los Angeles debate between the East Coast Neo-Modern Purists, the Californian High-Tech Minimalists and the one time purveyors of the Neo-Shingle pastiche, has long since been superseded by the general reactionary triumph of Postmodernism, the so-called "end of prohibition" as the Venice Biennale of 1980 was to characterize the phenomenon.

Among corporate firms of New York, few have remained immune to the blandishments of this quasi-historicist revival, along with all the media ballyhoo that has attended its ascendancy. In retrospect, Helmut Jahn's "popular mechanism" of the late 1970s and Philip Johnson's AT&T building of 1982 may now be seen as precursors, for in recent years, Jahn has succeeded in installing his Neo-Art Deco "Wurlitzers" in Midtown Manhattan while Johnson has built and occupied his own monstrous "lipstick" skyscraper

with his inimitable mixture of audacity and bad taste. Other large firms such as Kohn Pedersen Fox have followed the same supposedly popular "rappel à l'ordre." As a result, one is witness to a historicizing jamboree in which the anti-modern architectural establishment and the nouveau riche developers have found their common ground, irrespective of whether it is Johnson and George Klein in Times Square or Cesar Pelli and Olympia & York in Battery Park City. One has to go back to Pelli's Museum of Modern Art Tower or Kevin Roche's first building at UN Plaza to find the last minimalist high-rise buildings of quality to be erected in New York. It is sobering to have to recognize that these once promising talents from Argentina and Ireland have since become mesmerized by their own worldly success as their current production would indicate since it displays little of that tectonic precision that characterized their early work.

On balance, this catholic survey of recent New York architecture seems to be about something else, although the shifting reactionary taste has left its mark all over the place so that one can hardly regard this show as a "salon des refusés." Thus, in attempting an assessment, one has to bear in mind that in architecture, as in other professional fields, Manhattan is largely made up of a handful of fashionable corporate firms, a few passing plan factories, together with a large number of struggling one to five-man practices of varying calibre. Unlike in the so-called Sunbelt, a successful, cultivated, middle-level public client is conspicuous by its absence. Even a modest enlightened developer is hard to find around here and it is significant, to say the least, that not even an architect of Richard Meier's stature has been able to make it with the property moguls of this city. Here, in Trumpville, an appalling level of post-modern "schlock" seems to rule. Thus, one is either an architectural tycoon or an architectural street fighter, although from time to time someone breaks through and produces quality, middle-range work for a while, without becoming artistically corrupt or going to the wall. Despite the reassuring pluralist aura, one cannot entirely dispel the feeling that this show has been contrived to pay a discrete homage to these committed marginal practices. And so, the questions arise as to who are they and what they have done and even more pointedly, what is it, if anything, that makes their output representative of New York?

It is surely a sign of our multi-national, jet-setting times that while most of the architects included in this show have practiced sometime in New York and indeed still continue to do so, many now have their base of operations elsewhere. The emigré German architect Helmut Jahn from the Chicago firm of Murphy/Jahn is a case in point, for while he has successfully transplanted his Neo-Art Deco megaliths to New York (see 425 Lexington Avenue), and while he has aspired to even greater glory on the Upper West Side with his mega-skyscraper projected for Donald Trump's Television City, the firm of which he is now the design partner remains ensconced in Chicago. The French architect, José Oubrerie, and the North Carolinian architect, Harry Wolf, exhibit a similar level of "nomadism" since they have both recently stopped in New York on their ways to somewhere else, with Oubrerie becoming the dean of the school at Lexington, Kentucky, and Wolf shifting to the West Coast to serve as chief designer in Ellerbe Beckett, LA. And while they have both either built or projected works close to or in New York and have, moreover, taught at Columbia University, their finest achievements to date lie farther afield; namely, Oubrerie's French Cultural Institute in Damascus and Wolf's NCNB bank in Tampa. Obviously, Manhattan has always been an island of emigrés, but not perhaps with the same accelerating reciprocity as one sees today, with all its multiple internal and external migrations, not only of talent but also of capital, as insurance profits, laundered drug money and Japanese corporations compete with unprecedented voracity for a piece of the Big Apple.

Thus, the question becomes what patterns, if any, may one discern in the multifarious works exhibited here? By way of response, I would like to suggest that we may roughly divide the works of the fifty odd firms included in the exhibition into a taxonomy that not only relates to their superficial appearance but also to their ideological affinities. Moreover, one should try to discern different forms of practice within the same apparent style. At the same time, one needs to note how many well-established New York firms seem to oscillate today between rival ideological and expressive poles. Thus, while many of these firms were to make their debut with Minimalist architecture of high quality, to wit, Edward Larrabee Barnes, I. M. Pei, Cesar Pelli, Kevin Roche, etc., today they all display a strange instability despite their inclination towards some form of gratifying traditional expression. This loss of a stable house style and method finds itself replicated over even shorter cycles in the case of the younger corporate firms. Thus, Kohn Pedersen Fox have yet to equal the compelling elegance and plastic energy of their No. 1 Wacker Drive, Chicago, of 1979, even if their more recent work and, above all, their projected high-rise for Frankfurt appears to be assuming a new energy, wherein an assembly of cluster-towers is reinforced by counter-pointed rhythmic fenestration and by an articulate spatial outline of cantilevered cornices. This is surely the most arresting commercial building to come out of KPF since their first work on Wacker Drive so that one cannot help wondering what the intervening pastiche manner has been about. Thus, it would seem that the current preoccupation with style as an a priori rather than an end is the fundamental malaise of our time, irrespective of whether the overriding paradigm is traditional or otherwise. Professionalism in se is obviously not the issue, for the dilemma turns on the intrinsic inner quality of the work rather than on the way in which it is executed.

In this regard, it is distressing to note how a purist like Barnes began to falter after his audaciously cantilevered IBM slab, poised at the corner of 57th and Madison; a building that was so evidently superior to Johnson's adjacent AT & T tower, despite Barnes's willfull manipulation of the structure. Fashion aside, any comparison between these two high-rises serves only too well to reveal the superficiality of Postmodern historicism, for where Johnson combines a noisy and windy street-front peristyle with an equally graceless galleria to the rear, Barnes contrives to accommodate an elegant, air-conditioned, bamboo-planted winter garden-cum-cafe terrace to one side of his slab. The unqualified success of this last, that is to say, its provision of urban elegance and tranquility amid appalling densities of urban noise and dirt, makes the empty failure in his ill-proportioned and awkwardly planned Equitable Tower of 1986 all the more disturbing. A similar unevenness is to be found everywhere today in American corporate practices, from offices such as the New York branch of SOM that has so far failed to find a convincing modus operandi after the retirement of Gordon Bunshaft, to Murphy/Jahn who have attempted to return to the modernist fold in their United Air Lines terminal for O'Hare Airport and in their recent proposal for Times Square. This oscillating malaise has extended even to I. M. Pei and Partners, where an architect of such exceptional calibre as James Ingo Freed seems to have moved uneasily in his recent work, between the high-tech Minimalism of his Jacob Javits Convention Center and the oddly historicizing syntax of his Holocaust Museum projected for Washington. By the side of these corporate mood swings we may set other New York practices that for reasons of fashionable acceptability, seem to have opted categorically for historical pastiche, be it classical, Art Deco or Neo-Palladian. Into this loose category one may place a wide variety of firms, ranging from "tycoon" houses such as Robert Stern, Der Scutt or Swanke Hayden Connell, to more modest practices such as Voorsanger & Mills, Agrest & Gandelsonas or Kliment & Halsband.

In a class on their own and yet distinct from each other, one has to recognize the Neo-Corbusian line that runs through the separate works of José Oubrerie, Michael Fieldman and Richard Meier, although Meier's recent Bridgeport development is so inflected as to undermine the brilliantly luminous syntax from which the office made its name and by which Fieldman has been felicitously influenced; see Fieldman's recent hospital work. And while Meier stands as the unrivaled architect laureate of his generation, having received in addition to numerous national and international honors, the ultimate accolade of the much coveted Getty commission, he has yet to produce a work of such tight proportional rhythm and spatial interpretation as Oubrerie's French Cultural Institute in Damascus.

On the other side of the modernist spectrum, so to speak, one has to note that Gwathmey/Siegel have veered back towards Minimalism in their recent public undertakings, see their Guggenheim Museum extension, etc., even if their earlier upper middle-class houses were obviously inspired by Le Corbusier.

Wolf's NCNB Tampa complex is equally committed to Minimalism though it is altogether more articulate and rhythmically considered in terms of tectonic detail and proportional control. While its essentially Platonic order comprises a cylinder and two cubes, it is at the same time a subtly contextual work. The basis of this last derives from the link established between the proportions of the tower and the angle of incidence of the river as it runs into the city grid. At the same time the whole complex depends for its stature as a landmark and a civic amenity on its provision of a large public park, designed in collaboration with Dan Kiley. This feature serves as the most concrete link between the high-rise tower and the overall urban structure. The civic intention of this park is notably less suburban than the greensward part sub-terranean complexes that Emilio Ambasz has projected over recent years. Wolf's ability to exploit a large, free-standing work as a device for re-reading the surrounding fabric is equally evident in his Williamsburg Bridge proposal on which he worked with Ove Arup & Partners, engineers, and with Michael Fieldman & Partners, architects.

If it is possible to identify a single critical approach that is somehow typical of New York today, one would venture to suggest that it manifests itself as a Neo-Constructivist genre, that, in all its various modes, is as distinct from the so-called International Style of the forties and fifties as it is removed from the New Monumentality of Kahn, Saarinen, Stone and Rudolph, that once served as the received manner of the Pax Americana. At the same time, this Neo-Constructivist mode is equally distinguishable from the Post-Miesian "mirror-glass" Minimalism of the 70s.

For all the current implications as to their similar post-Derrida "deconstructive" attitude and method, what Bernard Tschumi and Peter Eisenman have most in common is a propensity for distorted volumetric assemblies and a penchant for a dynamically splayed structural rhetoric. This last attribute is shared in different ways by the smaller Neo-Constructivist offices. Thus, while Eisenman's preoccupations are more intellectually hermetic and "de-constructively" denser than those of any other New York practice, one has perhaps to turn to the more marginal Neo-Constructivists to find a freer and more fortuitously inventive approach to the various contextual issues that now attend tectonic form. It is thus worth commenting on the work of three such practices in order to reveal something of this Neo-Constructivist sensibility as it has recently emerged on the New York scene.

Primary among these firms, in terms of wit and craftsmanship, is the practice of Steven Holl Architects, above all, for their recent entry in the limited competition for an extension to the American Library in Berlin. Aside

from his capacity to take a received type and exfoliate its form so as to create a more critical and open assembly (see his Berkowitz-Ogdis house of 1987), Holl has made much of the craft-oriented "running" through his tactile use of contrasting materials. This self-conscious, Scarpa-like approach is rapidly becoming the touchstone of New York Neo-Constructivism. Holl's Cohen apartment and his GIADA showroom display, to an equal degree, his extremely sensitive use of tinted polished plaster and lacquered copper sheet, although an equally expressive use of metal may be found in the work of Henry Smith-Miller and Lawrie Hawkinson (see their Wooster Street art gallery) or in the burnished aluminum and glass interiors designed by Sulan Kolatan and William MacDonald. Kolatan and MacDonald's most sophisticated project to date is undoubtedly their hypothetical interior for an actor/dancer wherein elaborated structural furnishings are used to create what one might call a hyper-existential environment. This proposal epitomizes the more sophisticated, one might even say mannered, aspects of Neo-Constructivism. Moreover, the implicit metropolitan narcissism could be applied, I feel, with little change to a great deal of current New York work. This much can be sensed in their description that seems to oscillate between narcissism of the client and the solipsism of the architect.

The Actor's Apartment was designed with the intent of expressing both "program and content" as a function of its occupant's life-style. It represents a "critical speculation" on metropolitan living using the actor/dancer as a departure point in order to describe an architecture which responds to the current human condition created through changing "cultural demands/desires," and the ever increasing need for individual space. ... The two primary constituent elements of the space, the "window-wall" and the "mirror-wall," extend the space optically and metaphorically by providing a link to the exterior world, the city, and by suggesting another world beyond the mirrors. The ambiguity introduced by the mirrors operates on yet another level: in the apartment the actual and virtual worlds which together determine the existence of the actor/dancer coincide. The two spaces adjacent to the central space are the "Bed" and "Bath" which are considered as subsidiary to the activities of this space and are to be used in ritual preparation for the daily performance. This ensemble creates a realm in which the distinction between actor and spectator is obscured, so that, situated between two worlds, the actor is performing for a most private audience, himself.

This introspective, solipsistic mode, so characteristic of New York, is close to the structurally oriented, metaphysical ethos emanating from Cooper Union, that is to say, to a line that extends from John Hejduk and Raimund Abraham through to the brilliantly, self-reflexive Neo-Duchampian work of Elizabeth Diller and Rick Scofidio; above all perhaps to their ironic theatrical setting entitled "A Delay in Glass," based on themes drawn from Duchamp's Large Glass.

A quite different constructivist order prevails in the firm of Ellerbe Beckett, New York, where up until recently Peter Pran and Carlo Zapata have jointly striven to transform the output of a large architectural conglomerate. They have brought to this daunting task a retrospective taste for Suprematism but, as with other adherents of the Neo-Constructivist genre, they have tried to transform this received syntax into a new synthetic order based in part on Platonic solids (see their Oslo newspaper building), and in part on operational vectors, see their architectural school projected for Minneapolis and their air terminal proposal for JFK, New York. Aside from its swirling operational dynamism at grade, the Pran/Zapata terminal clearly attempts to reassert the drama and romance of flight and to express once again its triumphant dynamism as in Eero Saarinen's famous TWA terminal of 1962.

A number of other New York practices could perhaps be subsumed under this rubric of Neo-Constructivism, including the stridently gridded Manhattan Hotel recently completed to the designs of Rafael Viñoly and, at the other end of the spectrum, the subversively structuralist designs of Neil Denari. An equally constructivist tendency can be detected in the work of Pascal Quintard-Hoffstein and in the more metallic pieces designed by the firm New York Architects (Frank Lupo and Dan Rowen), whose big media-screen projected for the Times Square competition of 1985 was surely as constructivist as Raimund Abraham's brilliant cinematic tower proposed for the site. This comparison leads one to regret the absence of Abraham's work from this exhibition, since he has been, without doubt, one of the most fertile architects on the New York scene, influencing figures as diverse as Giuliano Fiorenzoli on the one hand, and Diller and Scofidio on the other. Mention also has to be made of the Franco-American "constructivist" genre evident in the recent work of John Keenen and Terence Riley; above all, their garden pavilion projected for Lambertville wherein one may readily detect shades of Jean Prouvé and Paul Nelson. Finally, one has to acknowledge the presence of a kind of crypto-structuralism as this appears, say, in Tod Williams and Billie Tsien's Feinberg Hall for Princeton of 1987 or in UKZ's Knee Residence, New Jersey, of the same date. In all this it is somewhat surprising that only one architect among those represented here could be considered a Rationalist in the Northern Italian sense. I am alluding to the work of Livio Dimitriu who has been directly influenced by the typology and the design methodology of Mario Botta.

One cannot conclude this appraisal without remarking on the specific background from which this exhibition derives, for the curatorial origin of this show stems in part from two successive AIA New York Chapter, Unbuilt Projects Awards juries held in December 1985 and 1986 respectively wherein the jurors included, on two separate occasions, Thomas Beeby, Mario Botta, Douglas Davis, Heinrich Klotz, Elizabeth Plater-Zyberk, Jean Pierre Estrampes, Hans Hollein, Eric Moss, Christian Norberg-Schulz and Werner Seligman. I had the privilege of serving as a juror on both occasions and part of the work that surfaced as a result of our deliberations was to be reassembled, with additional materials, in an exhibition that was staged in Enna in Sicily in February 1987. The traveling exhibition and catalogue "New York Architects" was first jointly conceived in 1987 by Livio Dimitriu of New York and Pasquale Culotta of Palermo. A second volume, by Livio Dimitriu, bearing this title was published in 1988 by USA Books, New York.

We may look to this present exhibition for a redressing of the imbalances that unavoidably arose in the substance of the Enna exhibition and indeed Heinrich Klotz has widened the scope of the selection so as to include many factions that had been hitherto unrepresented. Klotz has, of course, been an aficionado of the American scene for many years, certainly since the appearance of his provocative book *Conversations with Architects* (1969), not to mention his Postmodern Architecture exhibition staged at the DAM in Frankfurt in 1986, that naturally embodied an implicit accolade for the American Postmodern initiative.

Three further formative events on the New York scene require comment. The first of these was the initiative taken by the critic Douglas Davis in staging his Modern Redux show at the Gray Art Gallery, New York, in March 1986; a show in which he attempted to re-assert the validity of a reformulated modern architecture as opposed to the then prevailing American taste of pastiche Postmodernism. This exhibition was polemically supported by Davis's essay, "Late Postmodern: The End of Style," published in *Art in America* in June 1987, a text that took issue with Robert Stern's anti-modern, pro-historicist, TV series of 1985, entitled "Pride of Place."

The second dissenting incident worthy of comment was Michael Sorkin's ambivalent attack on the "Kleinpolitik," lying behind the Museum of Modern Art's Deconstructivist Architecture exhibition that was staged in the summer of the following year, an attack that appeared some eight months before the show in the "Village Voice" newspaper. Sorkin's broadside was an attempt to uncover and undermine Philip Johnson's return to critical patronage by proxy, as it were. Sorkin was to argue that Johnson was once again seeking to impose the vagaries of his taste by institutional dicta, exploiting the Museum of Modern Art as a propaganda vehicle, as he had done in his Modern Architecture exhibition of 1932. Sorkin accompanied his critique with accusations of curatorial plagiarism and then went on to take issue with Johnson's co-curator, Mark Wigley.

Whether one likes it or not, the Deconstructivist architecture show has been the most significant New York event to address architecture over the past decade and it is perhaps worth mentioning that, with the exception of Tschumi and Eisenman, none of the aforementioned local works were to anticipate the polemical rupture to be presented by Johnson and Wigley in their "deconstructivist" anthology. Naturally, it is of the utmost relevance that this show was international rather than national in its constitution, despite the emphasis placed on the spirit, if not the letter of New York's "panoramic delirium;" evident, let us say, in Rem Koolhaas's waterfront proposal and in Zaha Hadid's winning entry for the Hong Kong Peak competition. This widening of the scope brought to the forefront an arguably different, late-modern sensibility, that to Wigley's credit, he has been the first to acknowledge.

It is difficult to say how de-Constructivist architecture will eventually be read against the wider historical scene although we must surely recognize Wigley's critical claim and his characterization of the rupture, as a conscious deformation of the received modern architecture from within. Wigley has the temerity to see this "violated perfection" (to use the phrase coined by Aaron Betsky), as consummating, so to speak, the radical perspectives opened up by such artists as Kasimir Malevich and Vladimir Tatlin. In his catalogue essay he argues that the early Soviet Constructivist architects compromised the post-Cubist, plastic deformations of pre-Revolutionary Russian avant-garde. Wigley's assertion that the post-Revolutionary architects were corrupted by the purity of the modern movement is surely a somewhat prejudiced and reductive reading of pre-Stalinist Soviet architecture. It is also an interpretation that willfully ignores the wide ranging, more "organic" aspects of the modern movement to which the Russian work was distinctly related (Aalto, Scharoun, et al.). Moreover, it is far from clear that today's Deconstructivist architects are in any way immune to the pitfalls of aestheticism. On the strength of the MOMA exhibition alone, it would be hard to deny this aporia, particularly given the strong aesthetic drive that is evidently the prime impulse behind much of the work. In many instances, as in the case of Daniel Libeskind's canted mega-slab for Berlin, we have to take the programmatic attributes of the proposal entirely on faith, since in this instance, it is hard to imagine the project being realized as an acceptable piece of public housing. Equally dubious is Wigley's contention that by imparting a structural or volumetric frisson to the formal investigations of the Russian avant-garde these will, so to speak, be restored to their historical lost radical socialist destiny. The fact is that the "disturbed" architectural object, to use Wigley's phrase, guarantees very little as far as our late modern, post avant-garde predicament is concerned. It is sobering, to say the least, that not a single vestige of the social appears to lie at the heart of any of the "de-constructed" projects exhibited at the Museum of Modern Art. Moreover, Wigley's metaphorical allusion to a pathological but apparently desirable infection of form (as he delicately puts it: "to remove the parasite would be to kill the host") would seem, somewhat perversely, to recognize the inherently auto-destructive nature of late-modern society and with it, its largely degenerate urban culture and modus vivendi. This is particularly the case in New York where some 50,000 people are homeless, 600,000 are addicted to crack, where school children are armed and where the municipal government spent five hundred million dollars in

a single year, in a largely ineffective effort to suppress narcotics. One cannot help wondering how much housing stock could have been built instead of this panoptic potlach, given the political will to do so. Obviously, architecture cannot be made to answer for societal aberrations such as these but, nevertheless, in the face of such a reality, how can one possibly assert the new-found capacity of Deconstructive architecture to transcend the alleged conservatism of the early Soviet architectural avant garde?

At the same time, there is no doubt as to the break made by Deconstructivist architecture, its capacity that is, to wring the familiar from the unfamiliar, its feeling for estrangement or its ability to effect subtle erasures, displacements and displays of an all too scintillating formal brilliance. Nor can we dispute the breadth of this phenomenon, that is to say, how it has emerged as a kind of universal mode, evident throughout the transatlantic world; from the Mecano Group in Holland to Michel Bourdeau in France, from Miralles and Pinos in Spain to Formalhaut in Germany. However, the ultimate intent behind all this is modernist rather than avant-gardist. It is this, perhaps, that compromises the supposed radicalism from within, for the modernist aim, as Greenberg reminds us, is to entrench a given practice deeper within its own solipsistic certainty rather than to engage the world outside itself. While this strategy may well serve the field of fine art, in architecture it is essentially a dead end, for architecture, in the last analysis, cannot separate itself from the life-world. However much Wigley may evoke the act of building and the supposedly carthetic fusion of theory and practice, we remain impotent without the socially committed client and, as we have seen, it is just this last that is so patently absent in a city like New York. Surely, our engagement would be generally more focused, if, as I have suggested elsewhere, we were to commit our selves to a critically ontological architecture wherein the disjunctions derive from concrete transformations and their contingent conditions rather than from abstract speculation and where, to paraphrase Alvaro Siza, the architect is called upon to transform reality rather than to invent form. In the meantime Deconstructivist architecture, as exhibited at the Museum of Modern Art, serves to give new currency to the living practice of architecture rather them to legitimize the mask of historicizing pastiche.

Douglas Davis

New York in the Next Century

Fragments from a Post-Post-Modern Diary

Flying from New York to San Antonio, Texas, late in 1988. A single event reminds me this day of a fact apparently unknown to most architects and certainly every critic, historian, or theorist of architecture in my country: the twentieth century, for all intents and purposes, is over... This means, among other things, that the oversimplified polarities that have acted as hinges for our discourse in architecture and in art (new vs. old, traditional vs. avant-garde, "modern" vs. almost everything, the heavy industrial techniques of mass production vs. hand-held crafts, metal vs. stone) are as outmoded as they increasingly seem to be in politics... I'm prompted in this direction when I buy a tabloid on the way to my flight and read that Mikhail Gorbachev, who had just proposed a half-million-man reduction in his armed forces, is returning to the U.S.S.R. to attend the victims of the earthquake in Armenia. But more to the point, he and his colleagues are welcoming American aid, in the form of doctors, medicine, equipment, for the first time. Does this mean the Cold War has melted to the point where it is no longer solid – that is, no longer a polar hinge for our discourse on the world? Good God! What a loss... I am not sure we can sustain the loss of the Ugly Russian, for it leaves us conceptually naked, without the usual catch-words and phrases to shape our thinking... And this reminds me of the architecture of New York, the city I have chosen to make my emigré home, for almost twenty years... No matter where one looks, skill, intelligence, savvy, and money abound; every single style and trend flourishes; in the clubs, parties, and seminars frequented by architects, the face of the nation is noticeably altered, here with a dab of lipstick, there with a right to the jaw; whether the activists working in the city live there, like John Hejduk, James Polshek, Charles Gwathmey, Steven Holl, Tod Williams, Bart Voorsanger, and Peter Pran, or invade from abroad, like Bernard Tschumi (Paris and Geneva), Zaha Hadid (London), Helmut Jahn (Chicago), Cesar Pelli (New Haven), Robert Venturi (Philadelphia), Frank Gehry (Los Angeles), Mario Botta (Switzerland), or Emilio Ambasz (the world), the summa codex that is "New York Architecture" bestrides the world... And yet, and yet, it seems curiously abstract and disembodied, without stylistic homogeneity, or, worse, purpose. Everyone feels it, senses the vast difference between this shot-gun period and its comparatively serene predecessors, the *Skyscraper Moderne* of the late twenties and thirties, the High Corporate Modern of the fifties and sixties, the Revivalist Post-Modernity of the seventies. Each of us assails in one form or another the thin-skinned stylistic eclecticism of the eighties, while acknowledging its raw vitality. Indeed, it is precisely this vitality that alone makes New York architecture worth considering as the centuries shift gears.

Insofar as the vigor in New York is genuine, generated by the city's hugely competitive internal combustion engine, which whets fine minds and imaginations to a jagged point, it is meritorious. Insofar as the energy is simply responsive bravado, forced upon the city's architects from the outside, by conceptual and political and strategic forces rooted in the old century... it is tragically mistaken... a signpost for final decay and death... As I near Texas, I am not sure which fate is truly ours.

In New York, the architectural "cafe society" shares intellectual values not on the basis of agreements on particular stylistic directions in architecture, but more on the level of strategy at the level of the kind of personal style which is needed to engage the public eye. Also involved is a highly visible exclusivity which is reminiscent of the tradition of the salon and the private club. This demeanour represents an aspect of the issue of style in architecture which Schapiro referred to as "style" in quotes: as a "value term" or a desirable quality which a person or thing can be said to have or lack.
Richard Plunz and Kenneth Kaplan,
"Precis" (Journal of the Columbia University Graduate School of Architecture), 1984

Certainly the devastating essay written by Richard Plunz and Kenneth Kaplan in 1984 is essentially correct. It is in fact a working assumption that is widely held, by virtually every architect or critic with whom I worked and talked in the years when I practiced architectural criticism as a weekly trade, or craft. Rarely admitted or written about on any serious level, this attitude toward Style as style is central to the understanding of New York now. From the outside, the alliances that link architects as superficially unlike each other as Philip Johnson, Frank Gehry, Peter Eisenman, Richard Meier, and Michael Graves are contradictory. Each man appears to practice a manner of making and thinking about shelter and decoration that opposes the work of his colleagues. With the sole exception of Johnson, who freely admits that he changes styles with the weather, each man lectures, writes, and propounds his convictions with intense conviction. In at least two cases – Gehry and Meier – the surface style has been both rigorous and consistent. What links them all, as Plunz and Kaplan see, is tactical strategy, as well as a drive to embrace the larger audience beyond the client and the architectural press. The point I want to make here is neither moralistic nor critical. The point is that "style" in New York at the end of the old century is bereft of ideology, if we mean by "ideology" a shared set of convictions about the higher goal of living, or working.

Style, now, is technique, a means to an end that is entirely pragmatic, roughly akin to information processing.

Let me quickly add that the means is often highly qualified by personal need, manner, and tastes. Architects like Gehry, Meier, Emilio Ambasz, and Steven Holl are clearly committed to a well-defined palette of forms, as well as working methods. John Hejduk is perhaps an even stronger example of a practice primarily motivated by a personal vision, as deliberately executed as an artist draws or chisels (Hejduk works alone before his drafting table in the Bronx, removed from even the semblance of an office). The results are five bodies of work that radiate contrasting sets of inner convictions. Certainly, for my taste, they are among the finest architects practicing in the United States today. But in no case is any of these men or women driven by an "ideology" in the high, grand sense. We look in vain into their work for a signal as to the meaning of the life we live or the direction of the society we inhabit, beyond a well-defined mannerism (Gehry's buildings exude a liberating aura of casual eccentricity; Meier's homes and office buildings are precise and radiant, like a sun setting across a still pond). When Style degenerates into style, motivated at its best by subjective passion, architecture gives up its role as a signifier. The New York Style is a set of styles without meaning or content.

We are witnessing the emergence of this New Class... to which work has none of the older connotation of pain, fatigue, or other mental or physical discomfort... Prestige is... one of the most important sources of satisfaction associated with this kind of work... The overwhelming qualification (for the New Class) is education. Any individual whose adolescent situation is such that sufficient time and money is invested in his preparation... can be a member... In the early nineteenth century... it consisted only of a handful of educators and clerics... It could not have numbered more than a few thousand individuals. Now... undoubtedly in the millions.
John Kenneth Galbraith, *The Affluent Society*, (1958)

In "The Affluent Society," Galbraith announced for the first time the arrival of an immense new class that neither Marx nor Adam Smith ever figured into their sweeping forecasts. His "New Class" theory, which insisted on the radical distinction between our society, where education for the first time is widely shared, and all previous societies, where it was limited, for a time dominated social thinking. Daniel Bell's equally influential "The Coming of Post-Industrial Society," which confirmed with relentless precision many of Galbraith's hypotheses, particularly the rise in status of the Idea – as opposed to the product, or commodity – shared this premise. In the past decade, blinded by what appears to be a conversion by the body politic to a fundamentalist capitalist ethic, this seismic change in the audience for architecture has been ignored. But I here proclaim it to be the critical social event of our time.

Further, the lust for cultural certification, for prestige, for a theoretical or critical foundation on which my home or office tower can rest, is the reason why we are drowning in New York-based labels. It is no accident that two Americans, Robert A.M. Stern and Charles Jencks, largely invented and propagated "Post-Modernism." Instinctively, they sensed the hunger of the New Class. For ideas limned in labels.

More surely than any comparable practice in the world, New York architecture at the end of the last century became the labeled idea incarnate. What was demanded by clients and critics of all stripes was a handy conceptual context, not a craft, and certainly not usage or comfort. We might think of this period, to borrow a note from Stern & Jencks, as Early Post-Industrial Architecture ("Post-Modern" is thus simply a subset of this larger category). Stunned, overwhelmed, and certainly overimpressed by the words that poured from the Post-Modern word processor, the Early New Class neglected to search for deeper meaning, or utility.

Certainly in the end the fate of Stern and Jencks will be carefully, lovingly extricated from the verbal webs they have wound around the buildings they reared or praised. In the new century, Post-Modernism will be properly placed and evaluated as a low-grade retrogression of the dominant themes in the old century. But let no man think this means *the label* is of no importance. In the lowest, most practical sense, it can affect and modify the built environment if it acts as a persuasive agent, in the manner of "Early Post-Modern" (roughly dating from Venturi's "Complexity and Contradiction," in 1966, through 1984–88), or "Late Post-Modern," when the first concerted responses began to occur.*

In the highest sense, *the label* might yet link the new century with verbal signifiers that respond to the kind of lives we lead (mobile; secular; white-collar; inundated with free, fast-moving media and information; desperately short on grace, charm, dignity) and the fateful decisions we must make (to heat or cool the arms race; to cleanse or continue to contaminate the air and water; to bear or not bear children). In the new century, a decade can accomplish what used to occur in a century. Gorbachev's UN speech, transmitted instantly to every corner of the Earth, is an example close at hand. At this moment, *the label* can drive a decade.

Returning from San Antonio to New York even later in 1988. I go there to see the arcadian glass-walled earth berms of the Louise Halsell Botanical Center, designed by Emilio Ambasz, whose plight – he carries, like certain of his colleagues, no label – inspires me. What is required is to find organizing epithets for the developing synthesis of attitudes that rejects the constraints of historical recall – the notion (which one might label "Late Post-Modern") that every building must gratuitously refer to the past whether its site, use, or material require it or not. This new position needs a signifier, or at least a set of related signifiers.

---

* These include buildings, like Norman Foster's Hong Kong Bank; exhibitions like those organized by Heinrich Klotz and myself in the same year of 1986 (an ocean apart) that called for a fresh look at the "modern" movement; developing bodies of work by younger architects acting beyond revivalism (Ambasz, Holl, Tschumi, Botta, Hadid, Pran, Gwathmey & Siegel); the 1984 issue of "Precis;" the growing influence on students exerted by older architects like Aldo Rossi and Luis Baragan; and the widespread revulsion for built (as opposed to drawn) Post-Modern skyscrapers, shopping centers, and pseudo-suburban developments; and, finally, the decision made by Philip Johnson to join with Peter Eisenman and others in mounting "De-Constructive Architecture," a loosely managed exhibition at the Museum of Modern Art in the summer of 1988 that pronounced – by implication, if not example – the end of the counter-revolution.

And so I did it! As I flew back to my adopted city I wrote out a list of works by New York architects and designers that seem to me to be transcribing a new line, beginning back in the grooves dug during the heroic early modern years but snaking out around High Corporate Modern, then swerving once more, this time to the left of the decaying fortress reared in the middle of the road by Stern, Jencks, etc. one decade ago, breaking free into the unmarked wood beyond. As for "The Label"... it turns out to be more than one label, though each is clearly linked to the other by its common lust to move on, into new building types, materials, sites, and methods. By no means did any of the works I committed to paper betray a robotic aversion to the past, in the manner normally attributed by the Post-Modernists to party-line Modernists (who are rarely named). Rather, they confidently make use of the past... where required by meaning or purpose.

And so here they are, labeled to the core, completed as the left wing dips toward LaGuardia Airport:

Classical Avant-Garde (brash, atypical, late industrial):
Emilio Ambasz, N14 Engine, Cummins Corporation
James Freed/I. M. Pei, Javits Convention Center
Kohn Pedersen Fox, 333 North Wacker Drive, Chicago
Richard Meier, Bronx Developmental Center

Neo-Modern (abstract but lyrical; new methods and materials):
Ambasz, MAFA Tower
Meier, Hartford Seminary, Hartford, Connecticut
Meier, High Museum, Atlanta
Mario Botta, ICF Showroom
Cesar Pelli, World Financial Center

De-Constructive Modern (radical asymmetry):
Peter Eisenman, Long Beach Museum, California
Pran & Zapata, New Hartford City Hall, Hartford, Connecticut
Pran & Zapata, University of Minnesota Architecture School
    Auditorium

Modern Redux/Modern Two (site-specific; past-specific; user-oriented; new methods, novel uses):
Peter Eisenman, Ohio State University Art Center
Gwathmey & Siegel, Guggenheim Museum extension
Steven Holl, Cohen Apartment
Holl, Bridge Houses
Holl, GIADA Showroom
James Stewart Polshek, 500 Park Avenue Tower
Polshek and Arata Isozaki, Brooklyn Museum plan
Pran & Zapata, 233 Park Avenue South
Pran & Zapata, AA/NW Terminal, JFK Airport
Diller & Scofidio, Gate, Battery Park
SITE, Theater for the New City
SITE, Laurie Mallet Residence
Bernard Tschumi, Loft in Manhattan
Bart Voorsanger, Vacant Lots Competition
Tod Williams & Billie Tsien, Whitney Museum (Downtown)

Nostalgia Modern (recalls specific 20th-century types, heroes):
Arquitectonica, South Ferry Plaza
Hardy Holzman Pfeiffer, Rainbow Room renovation
Murphy/Jahn, 750 Lexington Avenue
OMA, Projects from "Delirious New York"
Polshek, Carnegie Hall renovation
Kevin Roche John Dinkeloo & Associates, Ford Foundation Headquarters Vignelli Associates, Studio

Down with art. Long live technics... The collective art of the present is constructive life.   Program of the Productivist Group, Moscow (1920)

Returned to New York, nearing 1989. I re-read the polemics mounted in the 1920s simply to demonstrate again to myself how different we now are. The Productivist group included the artist and photographer Alexander Rodchenko, his wife, the brilliant painter and designer, Vavara Stepanova, and most of all V. Tatlin, the painter-sculptor-architect whose infamous leaning metal tower, "Monument for the Third International" (1921), was recalled over and over in the Museum of Modern Art's "De-Constructive Architecture" exhibition. The Productivists were easily the most radical of the many modernist groups that formed in the 1920s to chart a fresh, clean path away from revivalism, eclecticism, and what they felt to be the corrupting influence of the past. But their conviction that art, architecture, and life leveraged each other – that no esthetic act could escape moral or functional consequences – was widely shared.

Further. I have recently returned from the U.S.S.R., from a first-hand tour of those magnificent, doomed early modern buildings. More of them still stand than we dare to know, in Leningrad, in Tallinn, in cities far beyond Moscow. Nearly always badly built and woefully proportioned, they nonetheless stand as a testament to an architecture that attempted to mold itself as a symbol of evolution. *No, we refuse to go back*, these spartan, clean-limbed schools, theaters, and clubs say. *Something is beyond that needs a new expression. Let us wipe the slate clean*.

We cannot put it exactly this way anymore. But certainly we can agree that the future is ahead not behind us; further, that we can't completely predict it any more than we could have predicted Gorbachev's behaviour five years ago or – three decades back in time – the prolongation of the life cycle, the rise of the economic independence of women, or the levitating motorless train now on the track in Japan (powered by semi-conducting magnets). If we cannot find yet the ideology that can anchor our architecture, we can at least begin to indicate in our forms, our interiors, our façades that new questions ought to be asked now, if not answered. To simply continue to supply the old answers – the Corinthian columns, the Gothic spires, the marble floors – will violate our deepest convictions about ourselves and our destiny. In its poised uncertainty, in its persistent attempt to break one rigid mold after another, New York architecture at the end of the old century unintentionally heralds the next.

Michael Sorkin

Ciao Manhattan

When I was a boy, my father and I used to go clamming. Standing ankle deep in the seaside mud, we'd scrape for cherrystones, filling a pail. Because my father was the sole eater, we'd only take a few dozen each trip. Our catch was nonetheless regulated by game wardens who patrolled the beach, empowered to command the rejection of young clams, to preserve the population. The medium of inspection was a brass ring: any clam small enough to pass through had to be thrown back.

The idea of a "New York Architecture" also invites a brass ring. As with those Cape Cod clams, something's needed to define the consumable population, some principle of exclusion and inclusion. What principle yields this bucket-full? Here's what I gather: this is a show comprised mainly of work done in or near New York City, mainly by architects from the more or less respectable category (the higher hacks are admitted but not the unselfconscious toilers who make most of the cityscape) who mainly practice in or near New York City. This ring has a dimension, but it's elastic, happy to let pass quite a few mussels and oysters (not to mention sharks).

But the elastic ring may be a necessity, given the organizing trope. "New York Architecture" is a classification without an obvious basis just at the moment. Sure, there are possibilities: region, type, history, metaphysic but none's really the throat grabbing, noose-tight category that invents the subject. Of course, this might be a very canny position. If there's a consciousness that's emblematic of current New Yorkism, it lies in the comingling of anxiety and hype. "If you can make it there, you can make it anywhere" is the mantra of empty struggle elevated to credo.

New York, capital of capital, exults proprietorship über alles. Forms have always followed. At its origin, Manhattan parsed itself with bold irrevocability by self-imposing America's premier grid, a primal mapping of property relations. Special conditions sprang, eventually, from the confrontation with anomaly, the grid's dissipation at the island's heroic edges: Central Park, the rectilinear eye of the storm; the rivers - Hudson, East, and the concrete flow of Broadway, those great skewers of the orthogonal; and the twisted by-ways of Dutch downtown, the ever tugging seat of the irrational, lying wait.

Up through this skein pushed the bar graph of value, extruding architecture. And, within it, flourished the roiling ecology of the neighborhoods, New York's greatest accomplishment, the manufactories of both assimilation and diversity. Our architectural inventions were narrower: the scaling up of the party-walled domicile as it marched towards the cliffs of densification, from rowhouse to tene-

ment to block-sharing and then block-filling apartment house. Then we made the skyscraper, never mind other claims at origin. This was omega, a form which rapidly rose and exhausted itself, cycling in less than one hundred years into autoparasitism.

There are also further, urbanist, claims on the genius loci, a little less indigenous. That the municipality housed millions in its projects, however Voisinoid. That Olmsted and Moses, their ancestors and heirs, built mighty roads and bridges, covered acres with parkland, provided sites of recreation for millions. That the town generated complicit climax forms, hard-edged avenues, zoning-fired set-back profiles, and the whole lexicon of unexpected juxtapositions that resulted from uneven development, continuous immigration, and anything goes.

But now, it's pretty much over. Exhausted by this activity, riven irrevocably into two cultures, the town's become historic and indifferent, done with fresh ideas. Sure, sure, we're an old city, densely built and filled with compacts about what's supposed to be. And, sure, points transpacific seem destined to become capitals of the twenty-first century (never mind that it's not many years off that cities will be not simply indistinguishable but continuous). But the central fact remains: whatever individual activity is stimulated by mad synapsing Manahatta, whatever flights this pituitary city goads, the renunciation of the New has become the central fact of construction even as the excluding cycle of publicly assisted greed squeezes our well of variety dry.

Consider Battery Park City, The Third Manhattan, the current urbanist paradigm of our municipal Mussolinis. Initiated during the Rockefeller regency, the site's an invention, a real estate speculator's wet dream, land created out of nothing. It's landfill in the Hudson River, adjacent to Wall Street, where a commercial risorgimento in the nineteen sixties is officially credited to Nelson's brother David, lion of the Chase Manhattan, whose new bank building was the first big "prestige" project the area had seen in years. Following on, Battery Park City was the administrative creature of a Moses-like public authority, able to raise its own funds and create its own agenda, freed from the niggling restrictions of the normal public bureaucracy.

The first schemes were thundering, heroic, pyrotechnical, megastructure: vast waterside plazas, edged by gigantic architecture. But the fashion for such excess was waning and a new idea came to take its place. Battery Park City would be a careful recapitulation of the spirit of New York, a perfected version of its native forms. The basis, naturally, would be the street grid and the site was duly platted and subdivided into developable parcels. Public spaces – most prominently a waterside promenade – were laid out. Finally, an aesthetic code was imposed which sought to distill the essentials of the "classical" New York Apartment House: brick construction, articulation of the base, a bit of decoration, etc. Whatever one thinks of the results (and there are highs and lows), the point is that the mode is now characteristic. Retrieval has become both the consequential initiatory and corroborating act.

Due east of Battery Park City, just on the other side of the island is the so-called South Street Seaport. Occupying old buildings from the former Fulton Fish Market, newly constructed pavilions in the manner of the old, and a series of recycled smaller structures from the last century, and arrogating the aura provided by an adjacent maritime museum, the South Street Seaport is the Rouse Corporation's New York outpost. Like its kith in Boston and Baltimore, it's a retail zone, a miasma of boutiques meant to suck in yuppies and tourists, in the guise of offering a slice of history. It's also a machine for differentiating a consumer population.

One of the more striking sights of a pleasant summery afternoon in New York City is that of the citizenry of Battery Park City sunning themselves on the riverside promenade and in the several tiny parks and plazas located among the apartment buildings. It's halcyon, an urban idyll, an activity that should be the minimum right of every city dweller. What strikes, though, is the utter homogeneity of the tanning population. Like South Street Seaport, Battery Park City is, effectively, a demographic instrument, an urban magnet for young, visibly fit, largely childless, almost entirely white, professionals.

It isn't simply the fact of the enclave, or the proximity to Wall Street that sustains this, it's the architecture. The applique of gentility (here expanded to include a minimum urbanism) is the designated domain of this population, whether in their postmodernized office buildings, their genially cloned downtown restaurants, or their marginally enlivened domiciles. Make no mistake: this isn't the heart of darkness exactly. It's just that it displaces something, that it's yet another factory of hyperreality.

Significantly, uptown, a nearly identical drama is being enacted. There, on the West Side, also along the river Donald Trump – rapacity incarnate – has acquired the largest hunk of undeveloped land remaining in Manhattan, a former railroad yard. Trump proposes to erect a condominium Xanadu, originally called Television City (after a major tenant he was hoping to seduce) and now more frankly Trump City. The original plans were drawn up by Helmut Jahn and featured a gross phalanx of towers (including one meant to be the world's tallest) sitting on a massive podium. A deafening public outcry forced a re-do and Trump turned to the same architects who had produced the (much lauded) Battery Park City scheme.

The expectation, of course, was that they would produce a plan sufficiently rich in the signifiers of "historic" urbanism (of which the Jahn scheme was so aggressively bereft) to allay the fears of the public, especially those in the immediate neighborhood, forced to share already dysfunctional transportation and other strained services with a huge new population. The scheme is presently in doubt, in some measure, it seems, because of the impossibility of packaging the densities desired in a semblance of "traditional" scale. But it's the operation that's the key. And, indeed, it's recently been repeated once again, a few short blocks from the Trump site at Columbus Circle where an aggressively large (if perfectly legal according to existing zoning) scheme by the hapless Moshe Safdie for an office and apartment complex was thrown out by an approval desperate developer in favor of a marginally smaller version from Skidmore Owings and Merrill, done up in the current version of good taste, camouflage offered in lieu of meaningful urbanism.

The city, then, is afflicted by a plague of semiosis, a St. Vitus dance of occlusive signification. Architecture has been devalued by its real proprietors to the level of Madison Avenue: a certain cleverness will do for the endless repackagings that drive the architectural economy. The real issues are territorial: by what means and by what time can the homogenizing up-scaling be pressed into every corner of Manhattan? This is the developer version of Manifest Destiny, the assertion that it's the natural right of white folks to occupy all of the island. Localizations of development, surges within discernible boundaries, are merely the medium for the run-up in real estate values. Like the policy of "Strategic Hamlets" that guided the failed latifundianization of the Vietnamese countryside during our late imperial adventure there, the mentality of carve and conquer is relentless in Manhattan.

Another conquest. Times Square is our historic epicenter, comingling our essences – dynamism, variety, vulgarity, art, pleasure, sleaze, corruption, publicity, anonymity, promise, and change without end. Immemorially, this free-fire zone of self-expression has simultaneously constituted liberation and threat, a place at once exalted and loathed. Times Square has, in every conceivable sense of the word, been irregular. A theater of behavior beyond bounds, it has also been a setting for architecture outside of conventional discipline. As the premier slashing of the grid by irregularizing Broadway, it liberates an archipelago of sites and conditions for the jostling colonization of stressed-out activity.

The self-sustaining ecology of Times Square – the mash of costumers, pimps, actors, theatrical agents, three card Monte players, hoteliers, pin-ball artists, ticket scalpers, porno exhibitors, barkeeps, pizza vendors, tourists – is the place where the grid of rationality that seeks to structure the city according to the routines of consolidated profit simply breaks down, a compendium of everything and everyone the system doesn't desire. Scarcely a surprise, then, that the greatest barrage of municipal and developer firepower laid down in the past ten years has fallen on Times Square, an enormous and successful effort to expunge Anathema.

Two major prongs to the attack. First, a quasi-public development authority – like that at Battery Park City – was consecrated to do in 42nd Street with a suite of enormous new buildings and the conversion of a block's worth of "historic" low-priced movie houses (magnets for the undesired poor) into "legitimate" theaters. The centerpiece of the scheme is an overbearing clutch of kitschy Mansardic towers from the office of the arch-hack himself, Philip Johnson. Although this awful project attracted enormous amounts of flak from the public, it turned out to be simply drawing fire from an even larger initiative.

While debate over 42nd Street raged, a change in zoning regulations provided a windfall for developers not simply there but all over the area. To stimulate the transformation, the city offered builders the opportunity to construct towers within a so-called "special district" which were substantially larger than those permitted under normal limits. This inducement proved, of course, irresistible: the area is now a forest of girders and form-work.

As with the much vaunted Battery Park City design guidelines, the authorities have tried to take the sting out of this enormous transformation by promulgating a set of obligatory decorative standards for the new buildings on the old square. It's the forest for the trees syndrome again, as if the "messy vitality" of the original could be reduced to a question of signage. Nevertheless, this is exactly what has been done, another menu for another banquet of empty signifiers. Each of the new buildings is obliged to tattoo its bulk with advertising and other supergraphic media, reducing a complex ecology to a matter of decor. Soon, the square will be converted to an office canyon, flashing its neon incitements back and forth across the maw.

The proper name for all of this is "gentrification." Now, gentrification amasses a number of qualities. First, it inevitably displaces, it's about expropriation, one class making a move on another. But it's also about reoccupation. Space must be recast, reacculturated. What distinguishes gentrification from the old model "urban renewal" is that while the latter loves effacement the former thrives on the digestion of the old aura, a parasite. Its claim, though, is to restore, to reinscribe eradicated ingredients. In Manhattan, the gentrifier's beau-ideal is the loft and Soho (always a new name) its ancestral home.

Contemplate the archetypal loft. It's a void, as undifferentiated as possible and the bigger the better, the magnitude of the capture signalling its raw consequence. The primal loft always asserts that it has been emptied, stripped bare of the particulars of its previous occupation. Its floors have been sanded smooth and sealed with urethane. Its walls have been sprayed a spotless uniform white. Its ghosts have been exorcised.

What's left, the certifying relic texture, is architecture, those cast iron columns, tin ceilings and grandly scaled windows and rooms. There's an adequate certification of historic detail and the sure knowledge that such extensive space is itself historic, unrealizable afresh under current conditions. And the walls hold art. Like the geometric

baubles in the plazas in front of our old international style skyscrapers or the flashing signs of brave new Times Square, the art validates the space. On the Lower East Side of Manhattan, the Thermopylae of gentrification, the shock troops for the erasure of the poor were the art galleries. The irony lies in the fact that these lofts, galleries, and boutiques are by and large the only commissions available to talent in town these days.

Official architectural culture knows the city according to a narrowing set of standards, the contractions of consumer pluralism and its dedication to producing endless things which are merely distinguishable. This architecture has as its only agenda the production of strategies for telling it apart. The city is, at once, both shopping mall and museum, a distinction which is itself continually effaced in American culture as museums become appendages to their gift shops and stingless art has no ambition beyond ornament: the Museum of Modern Art rebuilds itself in the image of a shopping mall. Battery Park City is peppered with easy-access art. And so it goes.

In the climate of today, architecture's only substantial claim in New York is as a "Landmark." Indeed, the absence of sanction for any other constructive value has transformed the municipal Landmarks agency into a virtual rump planning department, the planners having relinquished authority to the developers. But landmarking is a very frail bulwark, finally answerable only to staid historical routines: unfortunately you can't landmark people's lives. Nor, it seems, are we even able to adequately revere our best buildings. The narcissistic trashing of the Guggenheim and Whitney Museums by two of the architects included in this show registers the low ebb.

The simple fact of the matter is this. New York is no longer a center for the building of serious architecture. Sure, talents burn bright in this irresistible city, small projects by underutilized talents abound, the airports and fax lines are jammed by would-be consumers of what we make. But, casting memory back, it's hard to discern just what our last really distinguished building was. My own candidate for the door closer is Roche's Ford Foundation. It's certainly a rich example of the culture of the end of the line. The philanthropic arm of the nation's premier industry, arguably the one which has brought our cities to their knees by its hammerlock on the convenience of mobility. The foundation occupies a beautifully crafted, sumptuous cathedral from which funds are disbursed to further American charity's favorite aims: education, the arts, small ameliorations of the lots of various colonized peoples, at home, and – especially – abroad, gentrification with global reach.

The parti is also apt to an ecology that's run its course. A fragment of nature is sustained like an art object in its climate controlled museum. From the offices flanking Ford's court the city, viewed through the foliage, is softened, converted to modernism's great vision of greening compatibility. But it's false, of course. On the other side of the glass lies unbreathable air and a population obliged to spend its nights sleeping over grates in the sidewalk.

Christian Norberg-Schulz

The Prospects of Pluralism

The excitement caused by New York is first of all due to its "newness." Here everything we used to believe about cities is turned upside-down. We used to believe that a city consists of buildings that have a similar character and therefore belong together (even a large city such as Paris is like that). We also used to believe that a city is gathered around a square which offers a sense of "arrival" (for instance, the Campo in Siena). And we used to believe that a city ought to possess certain dominant landmarks which represent public values; a cathedral, a city hall, a castle (in Florence there is the saying that only those who were born in the shadow of the "cupolone" are real Florentines!).

In New York every building stands by itself. Hardly any takes its neighbor into consideration, and standing there it does not know what might happen next to it the following day. Classical, Gothic, Art Deco, and Modern; they are all different, and do not constitute a "family," in the sense of traditional urbanism. And where is the piazza? Washington Square, perhaps, but even there you do not settle down and say: "Now I am in New York." The landmarks, finally, are no longer public. Rather than being a cathedral or city hall, they are "nodes of activity," and are named after persons and corporations: Woolworth, Chrysler, RCA and AT & T. And they do not gather a "civitas" around them. Standing by themselves, they do not have to look alike, and do not have to offer any "interpretation" of the general, built fabric. In New York similarity is the exception rather than the rule.

New York has always been like that. Walt Whitman dedicated songs to the "great, democratic island city" and Henry James praised its "unspeakable power." Maxim Gorki was shocked by its "bulky, ponderous buildings" that "tower gloomily and drearily," but Leon Trotsky recognized it as "the fullest expression of our modern age." The theorist of the modern city, Le Corbusier, called New York a "catastrophe," but added that "it is a beautiful catastrophe." A disaster indeed if we believe in traditional urban values. But beautiful, because it expresses our own "open world." Thus, the key to New York is the "beauty of openness." Here freedom and opportunity have become manifest as a city, a city that lives and changes, and still somehow remains the same, because it remains "open." Beyond that quality, however, it expresses the possibilities of openness, or, in other words, the prospects of pluralism.

New York is the first pluralistic city. Receiving immigrants from the whole world, it could not find a simple identity. All the newcomers wanted to participate with their wishes, ideals, and memories. All of them had to stand up for themselves. Certainly, some communities did result from this process of meeting and mixing: the Jewish Lower East Side, the German Yorkville, "Little Italy," and black Harlem. But these were "islands of meaning" within the encompassing openness, rather than settlements in the traditional sense. Like the major buildings, they were alone, or rather, together in a sense unknown to the cities of the past. A comparison with Rome illustrates the point. Rome has also been a meeting-place throughout history, but its exceptionally strong "genius loci" transformed all newcomers into Romans, and the city preserved its "eternal" identity. New York, on the contrary, does not transform people, it rather leaves them free. It is therefore wrong to call it a "melting pot;" rather, it is a "boiling pot" (Thomas E. Dewey). As such it is truly pluralistic, and as such it is "the fullest expression of our modern age."

But are not all American cities like that? Not really. Boston possesses a distinct local character, as do Chicago, New Orleans, and San Francisco. Pluralistic phenomena are certainly present, and are lately becoming more evident, but still we visit these cities to experience their local flavor; the "nordic" Classicism of Boston, the explicit Modernism of Chicago, the visual music of New Orleans, and the colorful fantasies of San Francisco. New York we visit to experience "everything," and thereby to get an injection of vitality you cannot have anywhere else. Paul Goldberger made the point when he wrote: "New York has always wanted to be all things to all people, and in a surprising amount of time it has succeeded."

Although it is different, New York is an American city. The American city in general is distinguished by "openness,"and New York indeed possesses the gridiron plan which is the primary manifestation of this quality. In addition to the spatial openness of other cities, however, New York exhibits a more pronounced "openness of content." This characteristic does not necessarily make it more "American," but certainly more "modern." Chicago has been called "the most American city," because it developed a new architecture expressing the spatial openness of the frontier, that is, of America as a new world to be conquered by going ever further toward the West. Today the spatial openness of the frontier is a past stage, and we have to face a situation of openness as to content. This aspect of American civilization was always there potentially, but it did not come to the fore until after the Civil War, when the semistatic patterns of early colonization broke down to be substituted by a society characterized by a "free play of forces." Hence pluralism has superseded the melting pot, and New York has become more "modern" than ever. Perhaps this is what Thomas Paine had in mind when he wrote that America is "destined to be the primitive and precious model of what is to change the condition of man over the globe."

And here we return to our point of departure: New York is a new kind of city, and as such "the fullest expression of our modern age." In fact, many cities all over the world are today developing similar characteristics. Frankfurt is certainly a case, but even a "provincial" capital city like Olso is starting to move in the same direction. The obvious reason is the new Pluralism that is becoming increasingly normal. In most places the population is no longer of one color, and the media make us participate daily in the life of the entire globe. As a consequence, the old world of integrated "ethnic domains" breaks down, and we experience a new situation, where bits and fragments of the most various origin come together and intermingle. That is, everywhere we experience the kind of condition that has distinguished New York for more than two hundred years.

When the ethnic domains break down, the forms they have generated are freed from their immediate relationship to a locality and a particular social structure. They become signs of memories rather than concrete facts, and as such they may be transferred to another place. We could also say that our world is becoming increasingly artificial. To some, this implies that it becomes false and meaningless, and therefore devoid of any stability and identity. To understand this problem, we must take a closer look at the "precious model" of New York.

Is New York, as a human environment, meaningless and false? Our immediate experience seems to contradict such a conclusion. When Walt Whitman wrote that Manhattan "seems to rise with tall spires, glistering in sunshine, with such New World atmosphere, vista and action," his perception was certainly meaningful, and Le Corbusier's catastrophe could not have been "beautiful" if it had been a mere fake. Rem Kolhaas makes the point, saying that "Manhattan has consistently inspired in its beholders ecstasy about architecture." I myself experienced that ecstasy upon arriving in New York by sea in 1952. The breathtaking cluster of skyscrapers on Lower Manhattan, the stretch of the infinite avenues running toward the north, and the canyonlike streets crossing the island, as if they had been cut through by the course of the sun. An overwhelming sense of something rather than nothing, and something that could be followed into an inexhaustible richness of detail. In general, the experience consisted in the recognition of quality. The forms certainly had the most diverse origin, but even in their new context they were meaningful, perhaps even better than the originals!

How is this possible? How can bits and fragments brought along from somewhere else make up a significant whole? It can only happen if forms preserve their meaning when transferred to a new place, and when the "whole" that they constitute is of a new kind. I have already mentioned that the forms encountered in New York are Classical, Gothic, Art Deco, and Modern and I could add many

more designations. But is not a Greek column meaningful only in a Greek context, and a Gothic arch only as part of a Medieval structure? History proves the contrary. We do not have to go to America to see that the Classical column makes sense "everywhere." From Khartoum to Helsinki it "works," and the same holds true for most historical forms, although not all of them may possess the same capacity for adaptation. "Adaptation" is here a crucial word; it says that forms are new as well as old; that is, they possess general meanings which have to be interpreted over and over again, in accordance with the local and temporal circumstances. Classical forms have a particularly great capacity for adaptation, evidently because they express memories of a very high generality.

Trapped in their particular traditions, Europeans have not been able to understand the true nature of architectural Pluralism. Thus the pioneers of the Modern movement rejected all historical forms because they "belonged" to other epochs, and wanted to re-invent architecture from zero. The development of twentieth century architecture has proved the futility of this endeavor and for some time it left us mute and blind. Americans, however, not possessing a tradition of their own, had to recover "the first principles of the art" (Thomas Jefferson), and they found these principles in history rather than in the abstract "visual fundamentals" taught at the Bauhaus. History, in fact, has always been a major preoccupation of American architects, not because they needed a "cultural alibi" (the words are Giedion's), but because they wanted to understand what architecture is all about. The use of past forms as a means of expression is called eclecticism, and American architecture illustrates the eclectic nature of our field.

New York is the eclectic city par excellence. Here every building stands by itself and wants to be something. That is, it wants to possess quality. The word "quality" stems from the Latin "qualis," "of what kind." To possess quality therefore implies that something is something rather than nothing, and a thing distinguished by quality is something that is fully itself. Evidently buildings that stand "alone" have a stronger need for quality than buildings which are supported by a related environment. American builders and architects have recognized this fact from the very outset, aiming at the realization of forms with a pronounced figural and typological value. The pluralism of the American environment is therefore the result of embellishments on a ground of "first principles," or, we might say, the result of a meaningful use of the "language or architecture."

This also holds true for New York architecture. Today the iron fronts of the SoHo district represent the oldest manifestation of New York Pluralism. Daniel D. Badger's catalogue of cast-iron architecture from 1865 illustrates its expressive possibilities: "Iron is capable of all forms of architectural beauty. It must be evident that whatever architectural forms can be carved or wrought in wood or stone, or other materials, can also be faithfully reproduced in iron." Pluralism of expression was thus a conscious aim, and the models shown here have many sources. Classical

Roman, Renaissance, and Gothic designs abound, and the elevation of a "Grain Building" is rather Modern in its extended repetition of equal bays. Whereas the historical reminiscences endow the buildings with a sense of dignity which celebrates the achievement of the individual owner, the "open" iron structure expresses the opportunities of the New World. Although the SoHo buildings come as close as anything in the United States to a "family" of related members, each unit still stands by itself, expressing a distinct identity of its own. The experience of the district around Lower Broadway is therefore one of continuous discovery and enchantment.

With the rise of the skyscraper, New York Pluralism entered a new phase of exuberant expression. Now the problem is not primarily the façade in relation to the street, but how the building rises and terminates toward the sky. Evidently Classical forms do not lend themselves easily to the articulation of tall structures, and as a consequence the Gothic was used. Rather than the subdued Gothic we find in Chicago buildings, such as the Fisher and the Reliance, New York Gothic is outspoken and picturesque. The Woolworth Building (Cass Gilbert, 1913) does not exploit the Gothic idiom to gain a "cultural alibi," but to interpret the ascension of the high-rise structure. It thereby reveals hidden potentials of the style. In other words, the Woolworth Building proves that the Gothic is a "language," capable of meaningful new expressions. (That the Classical style also possesses "new" capacities, had been demonstrated by Thomas Jefferson over a hundred years before.)

The rise of the New York skyscraper culminated with the splendidly picturesque Chrysler Building by William van Alen (1928–30). Here the energies of the Gothic have been abstracted into electrifying Art Deco patterns, which at the top terminate in a series of superimposed fanlike arches that seem to express the meeting of the built structure with the rays of the sun. The Aurora motif of Art Nouveau is thus given a fantastic architectural interpretation. After more than half a century, the Chrysler Building still stands out as the most characteristic landmark of New York City. Its "top" marks the skyline with its distinct figural quality, and the "lonely" skyscraper thus becomes part of a new Pluralistic totality.

The Art Deco architecture of New York represents a decisive step in liberating architectural eclecticism from too direct citation. Here the "first principles of the art" are recovered as new interpretations of the acts of standing, rising, and receiving the light of the sky. The details are both new and old, such as the winged radiator caps at the 30th floor of the Chrysler Building, which recall Gothic gargoyles and thereby express a dream that is romantic in a double sense. When Robert Venturi many years later advocated an architecture of "inclusion," he thus adopted the principal endeavor of American architecture.

After World War II, the international style introduced different aims. In spite of its architectural qualities, the Lever House (SOM, Gordon Bunshaft, 1952) does not really belong to the New York scene. Not only did it present the reflecting surface as a substitute for distinct figural form, it also interrupted the continuity of the street, a point to which I shall return later. Does not the concept of Pluralism, however, also comprise buildings of this kind? It certainly does, as long as they remain few in number. When they become the rule, Pluralism dies and monotony takes over, as is proved by the recent series of glass boxes on Park and Seventh Avenues. The distinctive top is lost as well, and with it the skyline as a manifestation of American enterprise. The only means of expression now becomes sheer height, and the two towers of the World Trade Center do not really convince us that "big is beautiful." (The banality of the glass box may, however, to a certain extent be overcome by subtle detailing and proportions, as is proved by the Seagram Building by Mies van der Rohe and Philip Johnson, 1958.)

The revival of figurative architecture was started by Philip Johnson and John Burgee with the AT & T Building on Madison Avenue (1979–84). Here the qualities of standing, rising, and terminating are recovered, as well as a meaningful relationship to the shopping street in front. The architects themselves define the aim as "the design of a building that would communicate the essence of one of the greatest business institutions in the world," that is, an "attempt to define the architectural qualities that made New York 'New York,'" and the means were "classical composition, masonry cladding with superb detailing, and dramatically articulated rooflines."

The AT & T Building caused much embarrassment among Late-modern architects, and the harsh criticism directed against its eclectic forms makes a general change in attitude manifest. That is, the traditional Pluralistic liberalism of New York architects has given way to a narrow-minded, "exclusive" approach, which does not allow for any freedom of choice. It was against this attitude that Robert Venturi directed his attack when he advocated "a complex and contradictory architecture based on the richness and ambiguity of modern experience." Unfortunately, his message has not been properly understood, and after the failure of Late-modernism, the New York scene has split into competing currents, each negating the value of the other. What was a positive and vital openness, has thus become negative "deconstruction."

The fashionable term "deconstruction" well describes the present crisis. Rather than being a manifestation of Pluralism, Deconstructionism (or "Deconstructivism") maintains that any meaningful expression is impossible, and that the task of the architect is to make designs that "mean nothing" (Bernard Tschumi). The point of departure is a rejection of the Modernist dream of a new unity based on an "esprit nouveau," and hence it is related to the criticism advanced by Venturi. But the conclusions are different. Whereas Pluralism recognizes that life means choosing between values, Deconstructionism negates any value whatsoever. Thus it betrays the traditional American belief in freedom and progress, and reduces the richness and ambiguity of modern experience to a nihilistic game of visual narcotics.

Since the MOMA recently dedicated an exhibition to "Deconstructivist Architecture," the trend deserves a further comment. What is "deconstructed" by architects like Tschumi, Hadid, Eisenman, and Coop Himmelblau, are the sterile forms of Late-modernism, and certainly not the types and principles of past styles, which rather are negated through absence. The result is not an architecture that means "nothing," but an architecture that repeats the poor contents of Late-modernism. Poverty of content is in both cases due to the use of "nameless" elements, that is, "forms" that cannot be assigned any reality. The introduction of memories of Soviet Constructivism, however, offers an echo of industrial iconography, and thus implies a return to an obsolete belief in the machine. (Adding a flavor of the computer, Peter Eisenman advances a further step toward total alienation.) Deconstructionism also expresses a wish to resume certain beginnings of Modern architecture. Also this endeavor, however, has to fail, owing to the present need for meaningful images and symbols.

Although Deconstructionism does not belong to Pluralism, a limited number of such works could represent a contribution to a varied and complex environment. The contribution, however, would not consist of a new interpretation of the "first principles" of architecture, but of something contrary that makes these principles stand forth more clearly in other, authentic works of architecture.

My criticism of Deconstructionism implies that the various manifestations of Pluralism have a common basis. Robert A. M. Stern makes the point by saying: "To be an architect is to possess an individual voice speaking a generally understood language of form," and he asserts further that what the architect says "presents an opportunity to affirm and reestablish the inherent order of things." Before the advent of Modernism, New York architects certainly possessed individual voices, and they also spoke a generally understood language of forms, a language that was capable of grasping the inherent order of things. That was the basis for our perception of the city as a meaningful, varied, and fascinating place which expresses the richness and ambiguity of modern experience. What, then, is this common "language"?

In general, a language serves to express "something," and the meaning of any something consists in its relation to the inherent order of things. It is not possible to discuss this philosophical problem in any detail here; just let me assert that the kind of "order" primarily related to architecture is the way things "are" in space. An indication of what this means is offered by Kästner's statement: "Also those who no longer believe in Heaven and Hell, must, however, understand the difference between up and down." A thing is thus characterized by its standing, rising, extending, opening, and closing. If we relate these properties to human actions such as departure, arrival, meeting, and withdrawal, we may comprehend the "order" expressed by the language of architecture. The structures in question are evidently "inherent" or atemporal as well as temporal. The atemporal structures or "archetypes" are never expressed as such, but are subject to ever new temporal interpretations. However, I have already suggested that certain forms, such as the "Classical," possess archetypal properties, a fact that is proved by their continual appearance throughout history. Forms possessing archetypal properties are "nameable objects," to borrow a term of Leon Krier's. A nameable object is distinguished as something that can be recognized and remembered. In general, the world of man consists of nameable objects. "Where word breaks off no thing may be," Stefan George wrote.

Although the nature of the language of architecture is revealed in certain places and at certain times, its basic forms do not lose their meaning when they are transferred to a new context. That is, they are new as well as old, and thereby endow the circumstantial situation with general human memories. Hence the situation may be experienced as a meaningful moment in history. Since the very beginning, American architecture has been based on "old" forms which are used in new contexts. Many Europeans have condemned this approach as a superficial and "false" eclecticism. But, again, why is the use of Classical forms more convincing in Helsinki or Edinburgh than in Boston or New York? Evidently eclecticism is not a question of the use of memories as such, but rather of a more or less meaningful employment of "known" linguistic elements. Needless to say, any language may be used to express nonsense.

"Old forms in a new context" – the word "context" today means an open and dynamic world. Its basic spatial manifestation is the "plan libre," and, as we know, this concept is mainly an American one, starting with "Chicago construction" and gaining its grammar in the prairie houses of Frank Lloyd Wright. Wright was fully aware, however, that his plans were also "old," offering a "deeper sense of reality." On the urban scale, the free plan becomes the gridiron. The grid is certainly an old form, but in its American interpretation it becomes an essay in openness and dynamism. It is, in fact, the grid which allows for Pluralism, particularly its New York variety.

The American grid extends infinitely. Its constituent is the open street, that is, a street without definite ends. The open street expresses modern man's role as "homo viator" and thus it offers a new interpretation of an archetypal existential structure. To function as an open form the street has to possess continuity or simple linear coherence. Modern buildings such as the Lever House and the Seagram do not respect this demand, and manifest a lack of understanding of the grid. The same holds true for certain more recent projects, where superimposed patterns "deconstruct" the grid, creating chaos rather than freedom. The grid is not a straightjacket. The basic idea behind its formation was to offer everybody equal opportunities, and its openness is an expression of freedom.

As such the grid is simple, and it ought to be simple. When it interacts with the given topography, however, "surprises" occur which reveal a new relationship between man and nature, a relation of counterpoint rather than embedment. In New York the "surprises" are particularly fascinating owing to the given island situation. Cutting across the island, the streets disclose the natural conditions, illuminating "something" that was always there in a new, meaningful way.

Within the grid, buildings and spaces (such as Central Park and Rockefeller Center) stand by themselves as "islands of meaning." The island of meaning is the constituent of the open city, substituting the meeting-place of the piazza and the monumental landmark of the historical town. To become an island of meaning, a building has to possess a distinct top which acts in the cityscape, and an interior space which serves as a point of repose in the streetscape. Ever since the Rookery Building in Chicago (1886–87), American buildings have been centered to a large extent on lobbies that relate to the grid. Evidently the lesson of the "plan libre" may be utilized in their planning, as well as the Postmodern definition of paths and nodes by means of such figural motifs as the pediment and aedicula. A successful example of this development of the free plan is offered by Bart Voorsanger's Graduate Business School Library at New York University (1983).

To act as such, an island of meaning demands architectural quality. Quality depends, as has been suggested above, on the use of a commonly understood language of form. Inspired by Louis Kahn's and Robert Venturi's pioneering efforts, numerous American architects have contributed to a revival of quality during the last decade, and the New York scene is gradually freeing itself from the deadly grip of Late-modernism. This is not the place to separate the sheep from the goats, but I may indicate that what I have in mind is a building like 70 East 55th Street by Kohn Pedersen Fox rather than the superficial "splendor" of the Trump Tower and its likes. In general, Pluralism is back, and with it the "beauty of openness."

What, then, is the lesson of New York Pluralism and what are its prospects? The history of New York architecture tells us that, in an open world of bits and fragments, language comes to play a fundamental, coordinative role. A commonly understood language of form is today the only means of obtaining mutual understanding between users, and, in a figurative sense, between buildings. And it is also the only means to endow the pluralistic world with meaning. A fragment (of something remembered or imagined) becomes an island of meaning only when it possesses the quality of significant discourse. The new kind of "wholes" that are made up of such islands are not systematically organized unities, but collections of separate parts, within an open infrastructure. What they have in common is a basic language of form. This language is based on "first principles" and may therefore cope with the particular memories of each group of users. It supersedes the practices of locally rooted production, although in most places adaptation to natural conditions and habitual forms is still necessary.

The open, pluralistic world has come to stay. Until now it has been a primarily American phenomenon; today it is gaining global actuality. Small New Yorks are appearing everywhere, and eclecticism is becoming the main characteristic of contemporary experience. As a "precious model," New York shows us that this state of affairs makes sense, is beautiful, because its many voices speak about man's being in space together with the nameable things that constitute the inherent order of the world.

Walter Prigge / Hans-Peter Schwarz

New York

Deconstruction of a Cityscape
A Collage

Bernard Tschumi

THE
MANHATTAN
TRANSCRIPTS

MT 1
THE PARK

'They found the Transcripts by accident. Just one little tap and the wall split open, revealing a lifetime's worth of metropolitan pleasures – pleasures that they had no intention of giving up. So when she threatened to run and tell the authorities, they had no alternative but to stop her. And that's when the second accident occurred – the accident of murder . . . . They had to get out of the Park – quick. But one was tracked, by enemies he didn't know – and didn't even see – until it was too late. THE PARK.'

"Places and people, justice and the law are losing all sense of moderation and limitation, in a way which constitutes a political parallel to the crisis of the concept of dimension and which exhibits a strange analogy with the theory of fractals which has recently emerged in physics."

In his aptly titled essay "The Critical Space," Paul Virilio outlines the scenario for what he calls the "catastrophic state," a post-industrial and transpolitical state founded on the threat of the apocalypse, rather than on hostility to its enemies or its economic rivals. The inspiration for this vision stems not from the conglomerations of people and architecture in the so-called Third World, which are scarcely recognizable as cities, but from New York, the cityscape which, like no other, has shaped the twentieth-century image of the city.

"Time, rather than space, is being populated," Virilio claims, and Bernard Tschumi's "Manhattan Transcripts" attempt to pursue the trail of precisely these populations. In a manner analogous to the investigation of an everyday crime, they reconstruct the structure of relationships which, according to Virilio, has long since become a "world beyond," virtually indistinguishable from the space of quantum mechanics.

It goes without saying that Tschumi's aim is not merely to replicate the generally accepted field theory which states that distant forces have an effect without requiring a medium; however, his diagrams constitute what is perhaps the most direct approach that we have to the transarchitectural phenomenon of New York.

Tschumi's primary interest is not in the statics of architectural forms, but in the dynamics of action in space and time. Architecture becomes mobile; urban planning loses its stability; space is nothing more than the anamorphosis of a threshold.

Rem Koolhaas's "Delirious New York," a work which resembles the psycho- analysis of an urban organism and which uses techniques related, in formal terms at least, to the critical paranoia of Dali, is located on this side of that threshold. "City of the Captive Globe" combines historical palimpsests and contemporary postulates in a pamphlet whose intention is to criticize architecture, but which at the same time transcends such criticism.

The isolation, shown here, of the block structures – the caricatured emblem of Manhattan and the metaphorical plateau for the architectural monument – also reveals the area in which urban analysis is primarily interested: the space between the monuments, the free or empty spaces in which a vision of something new might arise; the secret places where the city is in decline, where industry is dying; the places which, for the time being, have been forgotten (Leon/ Wohlhage). New York has a considerable number of these places, such as the Bronx and the Lower East Side; and it is here that a

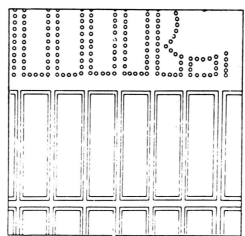

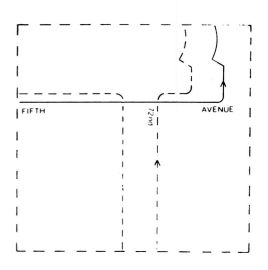

FIFTH   72nd   AVENUE

heightened sense of their-significance could emerge. Admittedly, there is at present little evidence of such a form of interest in the city. The importance accorded to the city's most obvious architectural monument, the skyscraper, is a sign of the inability of urban planners to come to terms with the phenomenon of New York. The series of lost battles against the architectural monument begins with the 1916 Zoning Act, which was revised in 1961, and extends to the 1982 planning law regulating building in midtown Manhattan, between 33rd and 60th Street; and as this exhibition and catalogue demonstrate, the struggle still continues.

However, the city in general and New York in particular are made up of a wide variety of structures, in which architecture is by no means the sole determining factor. Deconstruction is the prime architectural instrument for analyzing this network of relationships, for revealing the various levels of meaning, for finding out what New York really is.

"Today and in the near future, the important thing is not the form of cities but the shaping of their decay. It is only via the revolutionary process of erasure, through the creation of liberated zones, in which all the laws of architecture are suspended, that one of the most intractable problems of urban life can be solved: the problem of the conflict between program and content" (Rem Koolhaas).

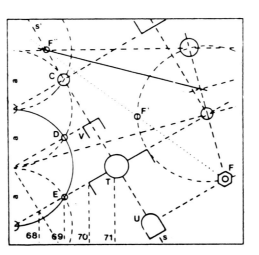

The City of the Captive Globe

Religion in ruins, **(1):** the conservative rituals of the church are replaced in Manhattan by mutant accommodations for a "thousand new religions."

Architecture in the process of reproducing itself, **(2):** perhaps this was a subconscious portrait of O.M. Ungers' architecture that is generated by an unstoppable impulse of continuous transformation, reinterpretation and regeneration.

Le Corbusier's Plan Voisin, **(3):** two towers in grass. This turned out later to be the actual model of Rockefeller Center where 5 high-rise towers were implanted in an artificial "park" on the 10th storey roofs of the lower blocks, so that one of the "layers" of the Center is the European City of CIAM and the Athens Charter.

The Cabinet of Dr. Caligari, **(4):** the Expressionist movie that takes place in the mind of a patient in a mental asylum. Manhattan's architecture is equally the outcome of such manias, but of such a multitude and of such undeniable reality that their cumulative effect is a new form of sanity.

The Waldorf-Astoria Hotel, **(5):** a characteristic – (which had been just grasped at the time) of Manhattan's architecture – and in principle of all architecture whose volume reaches beyond a certain "critical mass" – is that there can be no direct relationship between interior and exterior. The richness and variety of their internal activities – often contradictory – is such that it cannot be represented on any facade. Buildings such as the Waldorf-Astoria Hotel are the resultant of two distinct architectures: the serene exterior is a monolithic sculpture that, through its size alone, *has* to be a monument, not to a particular cause or ideal, but a monument that symbolises nothing but its own existence – an auto-monument. Inside though, there "rages" a deliberately skin-deep form of interior design, whose continuous iconographic transfigurations accommodate the volatile changes in manner, fashions and values which is the essence of the Metropolis.

Homage to Mies, **(6):** the discredit – in the 70s – of an architecture of such originality, sensuousness, extravagance, permissiveness and the liberating potential as that of Mies van der Rohe is a tragically self-destructive example of the self-induced amnesia and illiteracy that now threaten architecture.

Dali's "Architectural Angelus," 1933, **(7):** two formless blobs, of an unspecified white substance, that support each other through their very spinelessness. For Dali such shapeless blobs – shapeless like concrete before the insertion of reinforcements – represent the volatile substance of paranoic speculations that need the crutches of our rational underpinnings to be established as more solid paranoid-critical realities on the face of the earth, where they form a new category of pseudo-facts that exist like spies in the world: the more unnoticed their existence, the better they can devote themselves to a society's ultimate collapse. Such strictly rational "reinforcements" applied to irrational desires have the not-so-secret intention "of discrediting completely the world of reality," something they have in common with Manhattan's architecture.

Ivan Leonidov's Ministry of Heavy Industry, **(8):** in 1933 the purist Constructivism of Leonidov confronted itself with the doctrine of Socialist Realism on an historically loaded site along Red Square – a cluster of three towers explicitly engages the iconographies of the local context – the golden domes, St. Basil's Cathedral, the Kremlin walls, Lenin's mausoleum – in an early example of a modern architecture that constructs a viable relationship with history.

El Lissitsky's orator's stand, **(9):** the forward thrust of the beam reinforces the movement of the "progressive" speaker – Lenin – always pointing forward (although in many different directions).

Outdoors indoor, **(10):** before the actual discovery of existing examples in Manhattan such as the interior golfcourse in the Downtown Athletic Club, this block represents the intuition that, in the Metropolis, nature could only be preserved *inside* buildings – displayed as a taxidermist preservation – where its life functions are actually supported by complex technical apparatus.

Architecton of Malevitch, **(11):** in the early 20s Malevitch and his UNOVIS Atelier in Vitebsk produced a series of architectural models that display a striking parallelism with the forms that would emerge *later* in Manhattan through the imposition of the Zoning Law. They were an "architectural forecast" (equivalent of weather forecast) without scale, location, programme, occupants, to be realised by later civilisations (now?).

RCA building, Rockefeller Center, 1933, **(12):** the first Manhattan skyscraper planned according to the principles of European functionalism, with the penetration of daylight as the dominant parameter. But its apparent modernity is contradicted by the irrational spectacles – such as the high-kicking Rockettes in the purple glare of the synthetic sunset – that take place within the building's base. The Rockefeller Center = several superimposed projects/ideologies that coexist at the same address.

Homage to Superstudio, **(13):** in the late 60s Superstudio offered one of the few inspiring and stimulating models of the retrieval of a modern tradition applied to a new sensibility. (Next to the Berlin Wall, their *Continuous Monument* was an obvious inspiration for *Exodus*.)

Trylon and Perisphere, **(14):** the theme exhibit of the 1939 World's Fair designed by Wallace

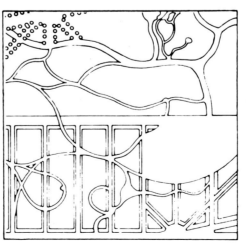

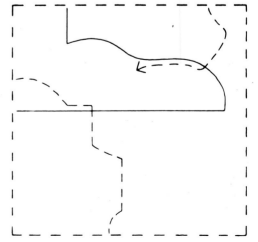

Harrison. As it turned out later, the interior of the sphere contained "Democracity": a Le Corbusier-inspired "Metropolis of the future," i.e. towers in grass – an *anti-Manhattan*. "This is not a city of canyons and gasoline fumes, it is one of simple functional buildings – most of them low – all of them surrounded by green vegetation and clean air..." The exhibit marked the death of Manhattanism.   *Rem Koolhaas*

Rem Koolhaas, Zoe Zenghelis
Office for Metropolitan Architecture
"The City of the Captive Globe"

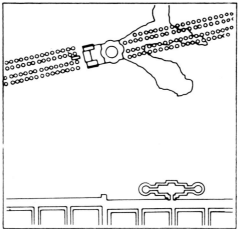

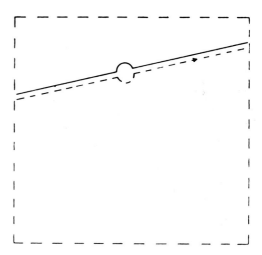

Walter Prigge
"The City of the Captive Globe", Collage 1979

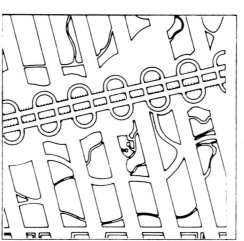
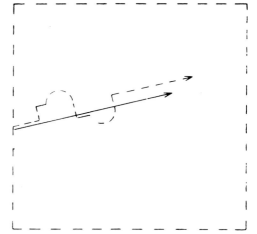

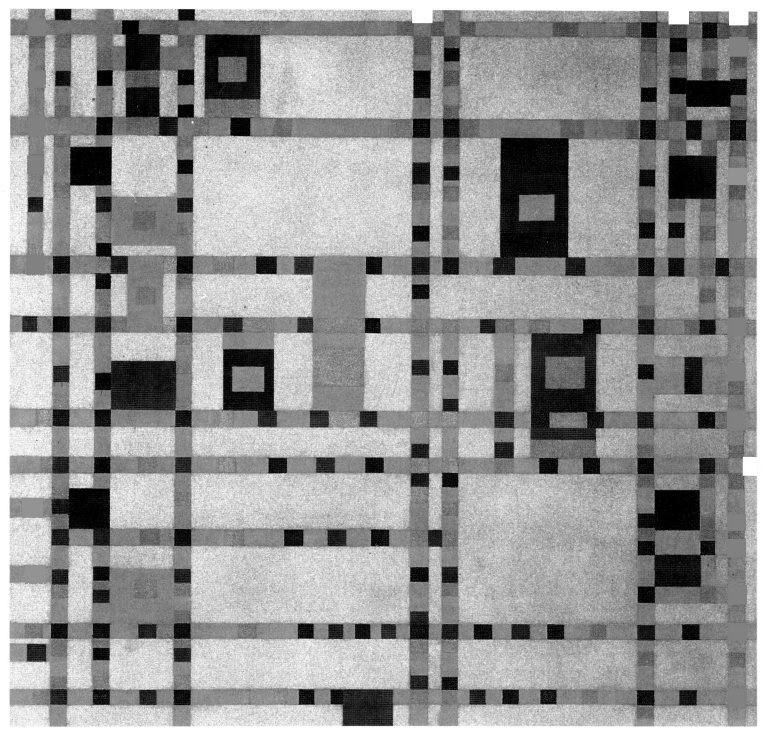

Piet Mondrian, Broadway Boogie Woogie, 1942/43,
The Museum of Modern Art, New York

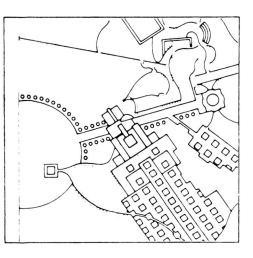

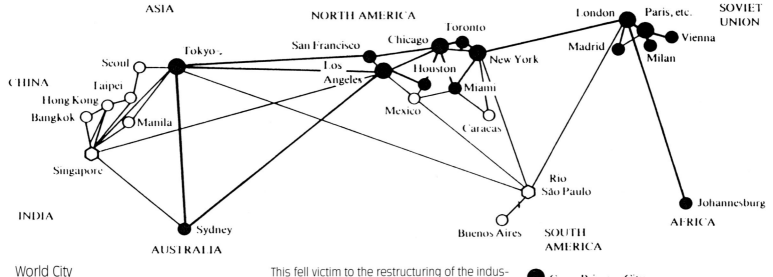

Core: Primary City.
Semi-periphery: Primary City.
Core: Secondary City.
Semi-periphery: Secondary City.
——— Linkages between core cities.
——— All other linkages.

John Friedmann

World City

"My short-sighted European gaze looked in vain in New York for a point of rest where it might have lingered. For New York is a city for the far-sighted; nothing affords a point of rest to the gaze except the vanishing point. And so my gaze met only space. It slid along whole street blocks and got lost, held by nothing, on the misty horizon" (Jean-Paul Sartre). It is the huge space of this urban landscape that spontaneously creates the concept of the city. New York is the metropolis per se. Nowhere else does such a view so penetratingly represent the image of modern society. The spaciousness of New York, and the Manhattan skyline, identify the city with the tertiary center, and establish New York as the capital city of the twentieth century.

The present boom in Manhattan is leaving behind the dangers of the seventies – the threatened collapse of New York, regarded as the "crisis of the city" worldwide – and replenishing the myth of this city as the "World City" on the basis of the development of the last two decades. Paradigmatically, this has been the decline of Manhattan as an industrial center with wealth derived from the old textile industry (the notorious immigrants' "sweatshops" that still dominate many parts of Manhattan today).

This fell victim to the restructuring of the industrial centers within America, with their shift to the sunbelt. Equally paradigmatically, there has been the rise of New York as a financial center in the network of the world cities of the eighties. The World Trade and World Financial Center are symbols of the incorporation of New York in the tertiary restructuring of the world market economies, in which new industrial zones have also appeared on the international maps.

The construction of capital factories like Battery Park City, the technological renovation of the stock exchange and the connection of this and other "intelligent buildings" to the teleport are characteristic of the international trend in redevelopment projects. With their detailed economic utilization of space these have little of the historical poetry of the patterns and the zoning laws (as South Ferry Plaza has nothing of the charm of the Statue of Liberty).

The current zoning maps of the city administration, which underline their political role in the growth strategy, lay down the figures on space utilization and building heights, that can be handled flexibly within the appropriate limits that economize with the sky. The sky planes that have to be calculated lay down maximum utilization lines determined by the sun's rays. These can be shifted upwards with planning gifts (investors build public theaters, open atria, sub-

way connections etc.) or the purchase of the neighbor's air column now usual in many projects (at market prices).

The latest boom in urban growth that has come from Manhattan and the corporations of the finance capital is the expression of the economic pressure of the post-Ford restructuring of the international division of labor and it is pulling the other parts of New York into a vehement dynamic of change, in which the urban spaces and their relations are being restructured to the pattern of the world cities. Peripherization and centralization of areas and the restructuring of the population are opposite movements in one and the same city. In particular, this means the upgrading and downgrading of residential areas, with the appropriate social polarization of poverty and wealth, and the self-organization of those affected, with support for their self-help projects from the municipal administration, appears to be the only way out.

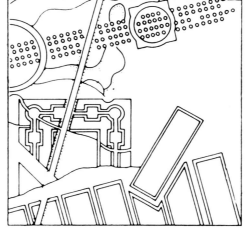

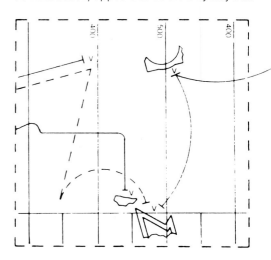

Amann/Schikora/Zierold
King Kong Kunstkabinett Munich/Frankfurt
From: "Die Sinne suchen ihre Heimat"
(The Senses Look for Home)

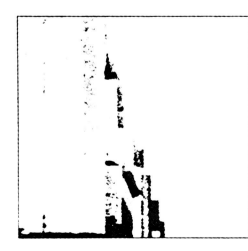

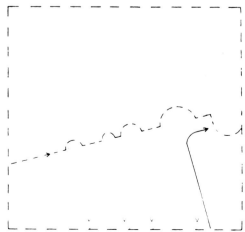

Entry into the Promised Land:
Sweatshops

My father, deep in his Sunday nap on the living room couch, toward whose kindly face I looked up from the floor as to a bison, an albino buffalo that blinked softly at my loudest outcries and moved in measured pace when everyone else was rushing around hysterically, had arrived in New York all alone from the middle of Poland before his seventh birthday. Nowadays he had a National and a chauffeur waiting for him at the curb to take him downtown to the Seventh Avenue garment district every morning. Such a transformation had nothing strange, nothing even noteworthy about it then, nor would it for many years to come, life being accepted as an endless unfolding, a kind of scroll whose message was surprise and mostly good news.

Logically, I suppose, Isidore's lone-boy trip across Europe and the ocean should have evoked all kinds of negative feelings in us, like outrage at the parents who had left him behind, or resentment toward the three brothers and three sisters who had been taken along on the big exodus to the New World. But it was just part of the saga, unquestioned like everything else in our fable. The official explanation was that Grandpa couldn't afford to buy Papa's ticket and figured on sending the money as soon as he had made some in America, a matter of a few months at the most. Meanwhile, the little left-behind boy was stashed with an uncle who would soon die. The child was then passed from family to family, allowed to sleep with the aged grandmothers and the feebleminded, who soiled their beds and howled half the night and didn't mind who they slept with. Poor Izzie, after many months of this, must have felt effectively orphaned, something I have only lately come to surmise, after over sixty years of knowing the story. Indeed, his orphanhood may well have contributed to the special warmth my second wife, Marilyn Monroe, never ceased to feel toward him; she was able to walk into a crowded room and spot anyone there who had lost parents as a child or had spent time in orphanages, and I acquired this instinct of hers, but not as unerringly. There is a "Do you like me?" in an orphan's eyes, an appeal out of bottomless loneliness that no parented person can really know.

My father's ticket arrived at last, and he was put on a train for the port of Hamburg with a tag around his neck asking that he be delivered, if the stranger would be so kind, to a certain ship sailing for New York on a certain date. Europe was apparently still civilized enough for such an arrangement, and after three weeks in steerage – the bottom deck where the light of day never

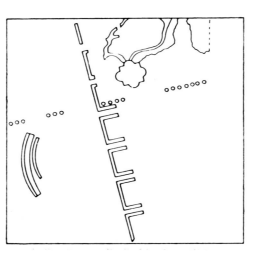

FEW CLUES AT SCENE

Police, Galvanized Into Action at Midnight. Found Little on Which to Base Search.

CRIME STARTLED WORLD

News Spread Quickly and the Largest Detective Force in History Was Mobilized.

shone, an area near the chains that operated the steering gear, where twice a day a barrel of salt herring was opened for the scores of emigrant families, from which, naturally, a child traveling alone got no more than the leavings – he arrived in New York with his teeth loose and a scab on his head the size, they used to say, of a silver dollar. His parents were too busy to pick him up at Castle Garden and sent his next-eldest brother, Abe, going on ten, to find him, get him through Immigration, and bring him home to Stanton Street and the tenement where, in two rooms, the eight of them lived and worked sewing the great long many-buttoned

cloaks that were the fashion then. Abe, a scamp, walked my father uptown pointing out building after building that their father, he said, already owned. Izzie was put into school for several months and then removed to take his place at one of the sewing machines in the apartment, never to see the inside of a school again. By the time he was twelve he himself was employing two other boys to sew sleeves on coats alongside him in some basement workshop, and at sixteen he was sent off as salesman by his father, Samuel, with two big steamer trunks filled with a line of coats for the Midwest stores. But, as he explained on my back porch more

than half a century later, "I got to the train station, but I come back home – I was still too lonesome for my mother. So I started out again the next year, and then I could do it." He told me this in his seventies and still, even then, felt somehow embarrassed by his dependency on his mother, a woman to whom, until he married at the age of thirty-two, he handed over his sizable weekly pay in return for an allowance. His three brothers had done the same.   *Arthur Miller*

Helmut Jahn, South Ferry Plaza, Project

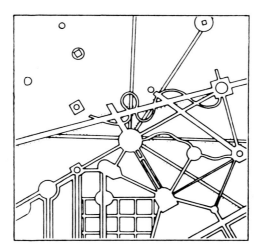

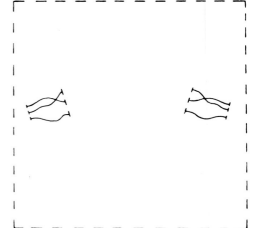

"Zoning"
Drawings by H. Ferris

33-433 (continued)

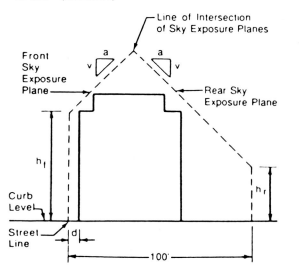

hf is the height at which the *front sky exposure plane* begins at the street line

hr is the height at which the *rear sky exposure plane* begins at the 100-foot line

d is the maximum *street wall* setback distance

v is the vertical distance

a is the horizontal distance

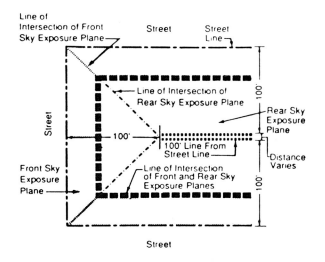

ILLUSTRATIONS OF SKY EXPOSURE PLANES

However, in accordance with the provisions of Section 32-42 (Location within Buildings), in C1, C2, or C3 Districts no *commercial building* or portion thereof occupied by non-*residential uses* listed in Use Group 6A, 6B, 6C, 6F, 7, 8, 9, or 14 shall exceed in height 30 feet or two *stories*, whichever is less.

In C4-1 or C8-1 Districts, for *community facility buildings* or *buildings* used for both *community facility use* and *commercial use*, the maximum height above *street line* shall be 35 feet or three *stories*, whichever is less.

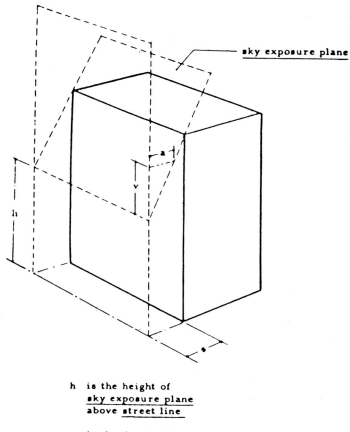

h is the height of **sky exposure plane** above **street line**

s is the depth of the optional front open area

v is the vertical distance

a is the horizontal distance

ILLUSTRATION OF ALTERNATE SKY EXPOSURE PLANE
SECTION 33-442

From the Zoning Map
The New York Planning Commission

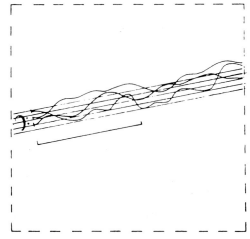

The World Financial Center

The key to the emergence of a round-the-clock global financial market and the establishment of the World Trade Center as its headquarters lies in the political, economic, and technological events of 1979 to 1981. It was at this point that the computer industry crossed the threshold into the era of the supermini and the PC. Networking made immense amounts of real-time computing and problem-solving capacity available on individual desktop terminals. Using the resources offered by artificial intelligence and expert systems, software companies began to devise high-powered systems of diagnosis and data management of the kind which are indispensable in share-trading and other areas of the financial market, and which are also essential to the running of the great temples of capitalism. The manufacturers of telecommunications equipment came up with new improvements in satellite technology, extended the information-carrying potential of coaxial and optic fiber cable, and optimized the automatic circuits which make the digitally integrated flow of data and images possible. These innovations created the conditions for the extension of financial trading from local and national levels to the global market.

At the same time as these developments were in train, finance capital was taking the reins of political power. The Carter administration, which had been committed to preserving at least a minimum of social justice, was succeeded by the regime of Ronald Reagan, who wholeheartedly rejected the very notion of social responsibility. Assisted by Caspar Weinberger and Donald Regan, the hard men from the world of high finance and the armaments industry, the "Great Communicator" used his inimitably cornball promotional style to persuade the increasingly lethargic electorate that the return to laisser faire economic policies would bring increasing prosperity to anyone who was not afraid of hard work. The main elements in these policies were a massive budget deficit; the pouring by the Pentagon of several hundred billion dollars into research in computers, software, telecommunications, and weapons systems; a major reform of the tax laws; and the deregulation of the money markets. All these four elements strongly favored the concentration and centralization of capital.

It was only at the beginning of the 1980s that computer and telecommunications technology reached a stage of development which made it feasible to computerize, partly or wholly automate, and integrate the functions of the money market. It has become possible to network these functions, not only on a company and national level, but on a global scale. The availability of information from all over the world on desktop terminals has given rise to computer or program trading, which offers the dealer a whole range of new financial instruments and strategies.

Many of the existing palaces of high finance on Wall Street or in the eastern part of midtown Manhattan are unsuitable for conversion into high-tech financial centers. Seeking a way out of this dilemma, two of the main players in the money markets – Merrill Lynch and Shearson/American Express – hit upon a project which had first been initiated in the 1960s, more by accident than design: Battery Park City, a narrow strip of reclaimed land on the Lower West Side of Manhattan.

Fortunately, the original building plan had been dropped. At the time when it was drawn up, the city of New York was broke, and few investors were prepared to finance new buildings. However, even if the economic climate had been more favorable, the plan would have failed: the scale of its conception was too gigantic, it called for huge investments, and the strategic distribution of the individual elements was wrong. When the economy began to boom again in 1978, the body responsible for the project, the Battery Park City Authority, decided to rethink the whole development. The following year, the urban planner Alexander Cooper presented a new plan which met with universal approval. On the basis of this realistic plan, which was conceived on a smaller, more human scale and included parks and promenades, the Authority began to cast about for well-heeled investors who would be able to finance the centerpiece of the development: the administration complex.

The complex is L-shaped; the connection between the long and short sections is supplied by a winter garden which opens out onto the piazza and the harbor. Traffic enters from the east, passing between two miniature towers which form a kind of gate. All the buildings are connected by a raised and covered walkway; two further walkways make for ease of access from the World Trade Center and the subway.

Olympia & York, owned by the Reichmann brothers and based in Toronto, is generally held to be the most successful real estate company of the postwar period. With assets of some twenty billion dollars, it is certainly the wealthiest company in the business. It owns and manages nearly one hundred high rise office blocks and administration complexes, in addition to significant chunks of other real estate in Canada and the USA. It also has a number of holdings in transport companies and in the oil, wood, food, and tobacco industries. The Battery Park City Authority could scarcely have chosen a more suitable partner for the building of the 1.5-billion-dollar World Financial Center. Everything went exactly according to plan. Construction work on the World Financial Center began in 1981, and in 1984 the towers, whose height varies between thirty-three and fifty stories, were let. The financial information company Dow Jones, the Oppenheimer merchant bank, and the Battery Park City Authority moved into the south tower A; the fifty-story tower C at the north end of the building was occupied by American Express and its subsidiary Shearson Lehman Hutton. The tenant of towers B and D, which differ in size, is Merrill Lynch.

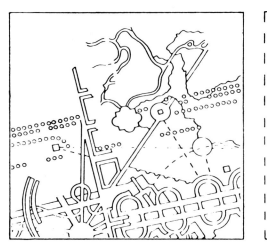

The business philosophy of Olympia & York is that it makes sound commercial sense to hire imaginative architects for new projects and to equip the buildings with the latest technology, which makes it possible to attract affluent tenants and reduce running costs. The company held a competition with the aim of finding an architect who could do more than design slick postmodern facades. The commission went to the Argentinian Cesar Pelli, Dean of the Faculty of Architecture at Yale University, whose design won on three counts. In the first place, it was perfectly adapted to the surroundings and complied exactly with the exceptionally detailed requirements laid down by the Authority; sec-

ondly, it was a coherent, unified whole, rather than a mere conglomeration of buildings; and thirdly, Pelli had brilliantly succeeded in designing the ensemble from the inside outward, taking the highly complex infrastructure as his point of departure. The infrastructure is unique: nothing like it has ever been seen before. Moshe Wertheim, an engineer with Olympia & York, points out that, during the planning phase, "technological explosion" took place, the maturest products of which were used in the World Financial Center: "The telephone was in the process of computerization; building systems which until then had been pneumatically controlled were being replaced by electronic

systems; security systems were also being computerized. In the World Financial Center we have three computer systems: for building management, security, and fire protection."

The building management computer controls the elevators and escalators, the heating and air conditioning, and the lighting in the public areas. This technology, which is used here for the first time on a major scale, has earned the World Financial Center the reputation of being the world's first "smart" building complex. However, all the visitor notices is that the elevators "speak" and that the lights automatically come on when he or she enters an empty room.   *Hans G. Helms*

Battery Park City, New York
Architect: Cesar Pelli. Photo Kenneth Champlin

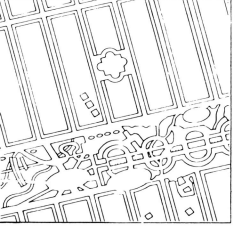

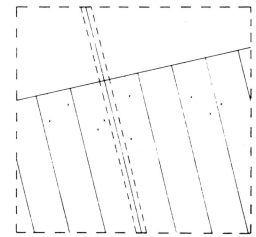

Gentrification

Once New York was the most rapidly growing city in the western world. In the mid-1970's, it appeared to have entered on a long-term decline. And today, a new phase in its history seems to be taking place. New York City seems to be entering a new growth phase. The trend, apparently, is "back to the city."

This process is often called "gentrification" – the movement into a neighborhood of higher income groups. It can be observed in New York as well as in other older cities in the U.S.A., e.g. Philadelphia, Boston, Cincinnati, Washington, D.C., Atlanta and San Francisco.

I want to argue, however, that in fact in New York City today much greater changes are taking place, that have consequences very different from those highlighted by the media reports. They do not constitute a "revitalization" of the city as a whole, but rather a redistribution of activities and population *within* the city. They lead to a much greater separation of groups from each other and a polarization of the city in general. No political leadership in the city has yet been able to deal effectively with these changes.

The key changes can be traced back to changes in the economic processes and relations of production in the 1970's, and to the political consequences that followed those changes, in particular the protest movements and the ghetto rebellions in the cities.

These economic changes had clear spatial consequences. The loss of jobs in manufacturing affected particularly the outer ring of the city, as well as the area between the financial center in lower Manhattan and the Midtown central business district. The neighborhoods where factory workers had lived declined, not in the sense that they lost major population, but more in the quality of the housing being provided and the support of public services and facilities. The decline affected particularly immigrants and unskilled workers, and particularly blacks and Hispanics. For them, racism reduced their possibilities even more than for others, and made their upward mobility and escape from deteriorating areas much more difficult than for earlier arrivals to the city. The situation in the ghettos, resulting from a combination of racism and economic change, grew steadily worse.

The expansion of the tertiary sector and in office employment, including the public sector, took place in other parts of the city, primarily in Manhattan and within Manhattan in the southern part of the island, below 96th Street. Here, and particularly in the area between the financial district and the commercial central business district and at their edges (and in areas easily accessible to them), were neighborhoods where the number of manufacturing establishments and the residences of their workers had diminished significantly. New business activities and new housing for those engaged in them moved into these "declining" areas. The conversion of old factory and warehouse buildings in Soho to luxury housing is one of the best known manifestations of this process.

So there actually is a significant movement of population in New York City, but it is a movement that is more a reshuffling of groups within the city (or a change in the numbers normally moving in and moving out), and it is concentrated very heavily in certain limited neighborhoods. It is less a movement back to the city from the suburbs (or from other parts of the country) than a reorientation of groups *within* the city, part of a reshaping of the city, a restructuring of form and uses within the city.

The results can be seen if one looks at the city in terms of its residential neighborhoods. The pattern becomes clear if one looks at specific parts of the city in conjunction with each other. In the South Bronx, for instance, there is an outward movement of higher-income households and an in-migration of poorer people, leading to devaluation and abandonment. In the West Side of Manhattan, or the Lower East Side, there is an in-migration of higher income households at the expense of poorer groups, leading to displacement and increases in prices and values of housing for the newcomers.

Thus the changes in the city have very different consequences in different parts of the city. Poorer households are increasingly segregated in neighborhoods with high rates of abandonment. Higher income households are both pushed and drawn increasingly to more central neighborhoods; from the outside that looks like a "return to the city." But what happens to those who formerly lived in these neighborhoods to which higher income households are moving? That leads to the problem of displacement, one of the most controversial housing and planning problems in New York today. A recent City Planning Department study offers some figures: in an area on the Upper West Side of Manhattan, where younger professional households with higher incomes are increasingly moving, the proportion of elderly households declined 19.9%, the proportion of blacks 24.6%, and of Spanish-speaking 21.3%. Rental units, earlier occupied by poorer households and singles, are converted to, or replaced by, luxury cooperatives or condominiums, and the number of units available to poorer residents is drastically reduced. The sales prices of buildings in the area increased over just four years by 227%.

The city administration and the political leadership is of course aware of these problems. A variety of new programs is being proposed to deal with the growing shortage of affordable housing: on the one hand, the number of vacant units, which normally in a healthy market should be around 5%, is less than 3% today, and on the other hand, stagnant or declining real incomes for many do not permit them to pay for even routine maintenance and repairs, not to speak of rehabilitation of abandoned buildings or new construction. In the absence of any tradition of municipal housing production, New York City must, whether it wishes to or not, find new ways to deal with its housing crisis.

Peter Marcuse

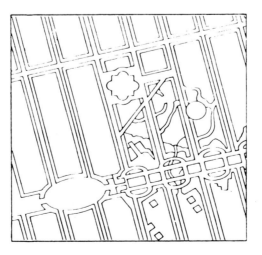

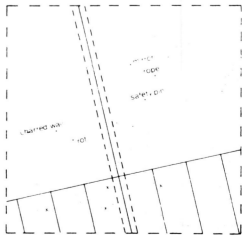

Photo: Camilo J. Vergara

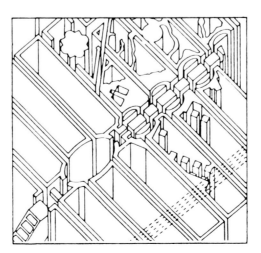
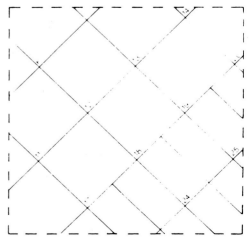

Charlotte Street 1981, South Bronx
Photo: Camilo J. Vergara

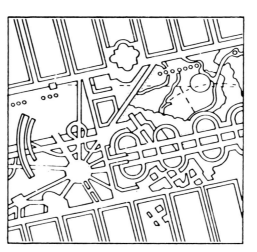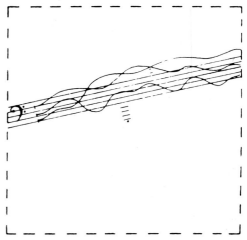

Charlotte Street 1987, South Bronx
Photo: Camilo J. Vergara

Charlotte Gardens, South Bronx
Photo: Camilo J. Vergara

Charlotte Street
Photo: Camilo J. Vergara

The Blind City

The view of Manhattan from the 110th floor of the World Trade Center: in the mist brewed up by the winds, the urban island – a sea within the sea – erects the Wall Street skyscrapers, dips low at Greenwich, rises up again to form the Midtown slopes, subsides at Central Park, and finally ebbs away on the other side of Harlem. For a brief moment, the eye freezes the image of the vertical swell, and the gigantic mass of the city comes to a standstill. It metamorphoses into a texture which brings together the extremes of struggle and misery, the tension between races and styles, the contrasts between, on the one hand, the buildings of what is now dismissed as the past – New York, the anti-Rome, has never learned to grow old gracefully – and on the other, the new intruders, which close off the space: paroxysms in monumental reliefs. The viewer can even "read" this seething urban universe, in which the architectural forms of a coincidence of opposites are set out; forms which were once designed on the smallest of scales, as mystical textures. In this scene of concrete, steel, and glass, which carves out a cold expanse of water between the Atlantic and American oceans, the excess of display and productivity finds a gigantic expression in the world's tallest scriptural signs.

What, I asked myself, is the nature of the erotics of knowing involved in the ecstasy, the emphatic enjoyment, which attends the deciphering of such a cosmos? What is the origin of the pleasure which we take in seeing a world – the product of hubris – as a whole, in surveying the most extreme of all human texts from above, in deciphering and condensing it?

To be transported up to the top of the World Trade Center is to be captivated by the power of New York. One's own body is no longer swallowed up by the streets, which direct it hither and thither, according to an unknowable law; down there, the body – as player or toy – is overwhelmed by the incoherent noise of sheer diversity and the nervousness of the New York traffic. With the city at one's feet, one rises above the mass, which drowns and blurs any clear awareness of self on the part of those who watch and listen. Rising above these waters, Icarus can forget the baseness of Daedalus in the endless teeming labyrinths. His elevation makes him a spectator. It establishes a sense of distance and transforms an intoxicating world into a text, which can be read with the eyes of the sun, of a god. He senses the ecstasy of a visual, a gnostic vibration. To be nothing but this point, looking and surveying – the fiction of knowledge. Afterward, one will fall back down into the dark space of the bustling mass, which one sees, but which itself is blind. A poster on the 110th floor confronts the pedestrian, who for a fleeting moment has become a seer, with the riddle of the Sphinx: "It's hard to be down when you're up."

The urge to see the city as a whole preceded the possibility of doing so. Medieval and Renaissance painting depicted the city in terms of perspective, seen from a point of view which was unreal. It invented the flight over the city and at the same time the representation which this made possible. The panorama transformed the spectator into a divine eye. It created gods. Has anything changed since the point when technology made an all-seeing eye possible? The fiction invented by the Old Masters has been translated into reality. Both the pictorial and the architectural creations that today are the concrete manifestation of Utopia are obsessed by the same extension of the human eye. The tower, 420 meters high, which forms the prow of Manhattan, is a continuation of this fiction; the fiction which creates "readers," which renders the complexity of the city legible and transforms its opaque mobility into a clear text. This vast tissue down there, laid out before one's eyes – is it anything other than a representation, a visual artifact, analogous to the facsimile made by the town planner or the mapmaker, who views the city from a distance? The city as panorama is a "theoretical" (that is, a visual) mirage. It is an image which can only emerge when real events are forgotten and distorted. The god as spectator who creates this fiction and who, like the god of Schreber, knows only corpses, has to distance himself from the obscure complications of everyday life.

However, the normal users of the city live down there, beyond the limit, where visibility comes to an end. Their life is an elementary form of this experience; they are the walkers, the wanderers, whose bodies yield to the pressure, the fine lines of an urban text which they write but cannot read. They play with invisible spaces: they have a blind familiarity with these places, like the familiarity between the bodies of lovers. The paths which meet in this tangle of interwoven lines – making unconscious connections, in which each body forms an element that is characterized among and by many others – defy all attempts to decipher them. Everything to do with the organization of the city takes place in a seemingly random fashion. The traces of these moving, intersecting "inscriptions" come together to form a complex story which has no author and no observer; a story composed of fragments of flight paths and transformations of spaces. In a banal and uncertain way, the inhabited city differs from the representation of the city.

There is a quality of strangeness in everyday life which defies the imaginary summarizings of the eye; which lies below the surface, or whose surface is merely a boundary which has been moved forward, a borderline which stands out against the visible. In this context, I would emphasize the visual panoptical or theoretical practices which stand in opposition to "geometrical" or "geographical" space. This manner of dealing with space leads back to a particular type of process, to a different (anthropological, poetic, or mythical) experience of space, to an opaque and blind mobility of the inhabited city, to a city of wanderers, which secretly inscribes itself in the clear text of the planned legible city.

Michel de Certeau

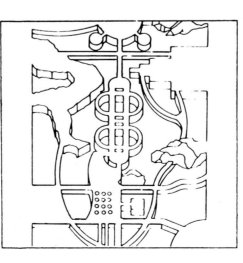

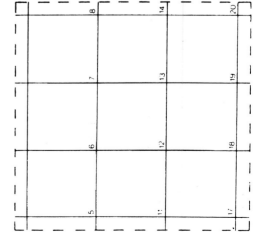

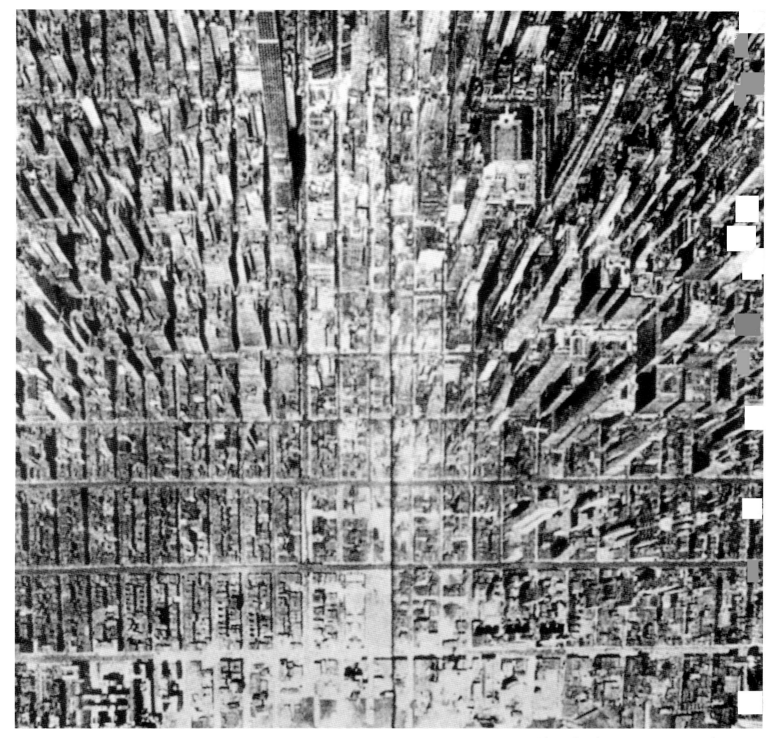

Aerial view of Manhattan

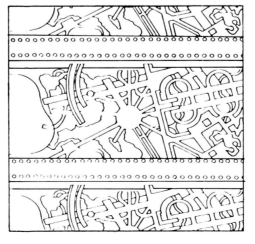
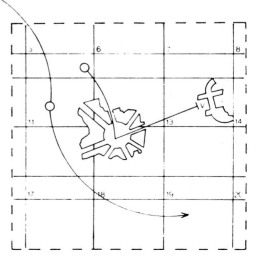

The airship "Hindenburg" over Manhattan

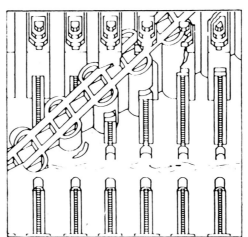
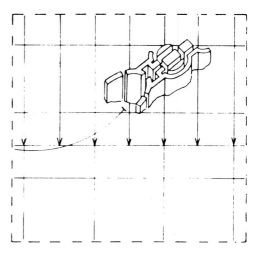

Frankfurt in ruins (1946)
Photo: Fred Kochmann

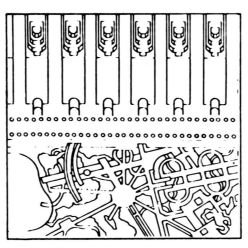

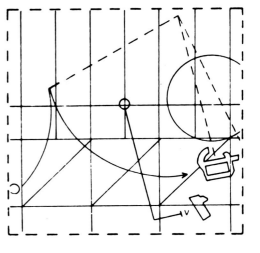

"Manhattan Landing"
Video picture, Saatchi & Saatchi

 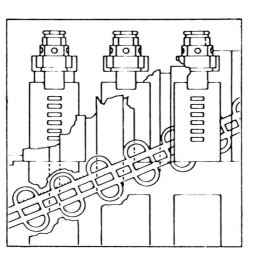 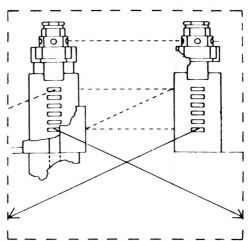

Bibliography

Certeau, Michel de, 'Umgang mit Raum. Die Stadt als Metapher.' In: *"Panik Stadt,"* *Stadtbauwelt 60/Bauwelt 48*, December 1978, p. 292 f.

Friedmann, John, 'The World City Hypothesis.' In: *Development and Change*, London 1986, vol. 17, p. 74

Helms, Hans G., 'Manhattans neue Kapitalfabriken. Das World Financial Center – technologische Ursachen und bauliche Folgen.' In: *Merkur* 477, November 1988, p. 928 ff.

Koolhaas, Rem, *Delirious New York. A retroactive manifesto for Manhattan*, New York 1980.

Marcuse, Peter, 'Die Bewegung "Zurück in die Stadt" (New York) – gibt es sie überhaupt?' In: *Die Zukunft der Metropolen: Paris, London, New York, Berlin*, ed. Karl Schwarz, exhibition catalogue Technische Universität Berlin, 1984, vol. 1, p. 215 ff.

Miller, Arthur, *Timebends. A Life*, New York (Grove Press) 1987.

Tschumi, Bernard, *The Manhattan Transcripts*, New York 1981 (The Park, p. 14 ff.)

Zoning Map. The New York City Planning Commission. The City of New York 1988

Buildings and
Projects
in New York

Numbers after the project titles
refer to the plan at the end of the book.

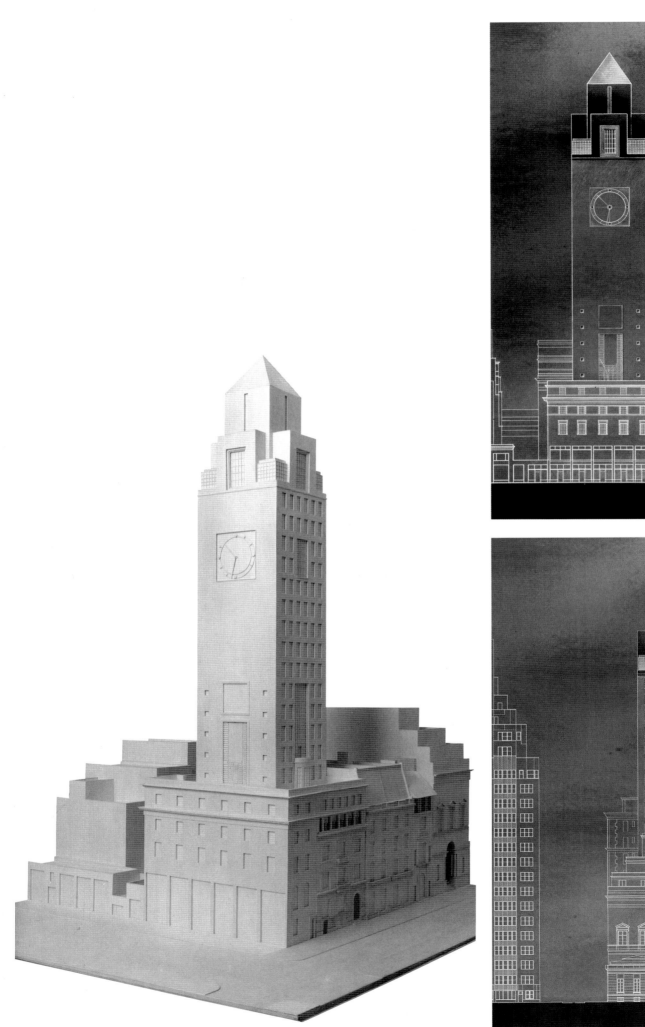

Agrest & Gandelsonas

APARTMENT BUILDING IN MANHATTAN   [53]

20 East 71st Street, New York, NY, Project, 1980

This project consists of the renovation of an existent 20,000 square foot limestone building and the addition of a new 36,000 square foot structure.

The building, located in Manhattan's Upper East Side, has attempted to establish itself as an example of urban architecture. It manifests a concern for the city and its history, while it responds to specific contextual requirements, such as type, scale and materials.

The project is conceived as an architectural reading of the meanings implied in the tower as a building type, such as a tripartite formal organization (base, shaft and top) and its symbolic role as a vertical mark in the townscape.

The east side elevation facing the avenue is treated as a clocktower, thus transforming the meaning of the building and recalling the referential origin of New York City towers: the tower in Italian towns.

The existent building has been transformed into the base of the new building. It has been partially modified to better relate and integrate both the adjacent corner building and the new tower on top. The facade and the most notable rooms and elements of the existing building have been preserved and restored.

The new building, as shaft of the tower, is responsive to the character of the neighborhood both in its fenestration – double hung windows – and its material – 3-inch Indian limestone facing on four sides. These features at the same time contribute to an efficient energy performance of the building. All rooms in every apartment have natural light, views, and cross ventilation, while retaining a simple plan that may be adapted by the user in the future. The facades address the specific conditions of each street.

The design emphasizes the top of the building as an element of urban architecture attempting to revive a major feature of New York's skyline long forgotten by modern architects.

Agrest & Gandelsonas

TOWNHOUSE [50]

110 East 64th Street, New York, NY, 1984

Description: A six-story, one-family townhouse that replaces an existing brownstone, built at the turn of the century.

This building with its limestone bowed facade acts like a hinge between its neighbors, a neo-Gothic church and a 1960s curtain wall building.

Agrest & Gandelsonas

250 WEST STREET

250 West Street, New York, NY, Project, 1988

Description: The design consists of a new "skin," new lobby, new vertical core, and complete interior renovation and conversion to offices of an existing eleven-story loft building facing the Hudson River.

A horizontal steel "belt" divides the building into two halves, articulated with a clock celebrating the vistas to and from the New Jersey shore and Liberty Island.

The bottom half of the facade is faced with flamed black granite, while the top uses the same motif in aluminum.

Emilio Ambasz

MUSEUM OF AMERICAN FOLK ART TOWER   [30]

West 53rd Street, New York, NY
Project, 1980–1981

Through private individuals and foundation support, the museum has been able to obtain a plot of land, 128 feet (front) by 100 feet (depth), on West 53rd Street, close to Sixth Avenue.

General Description of the Project: In the first period of the high-rise building in the mid-nineteenth century, such structures were built in the "column" typology: base, shaft, and capital. In the twenties, New York zoning regulations gave birth to the "setback". In the late forties, the prism marked its presence with Le Corbusier's original designs for the U.N. building. The design for the Museum of American Folk Art seeks to integrate these three typologies into a harmonious whole.

This building has been designed within a geometric envelope in order to better reconcile its presence with that of its prismatic neighbor to the west – the ABC tower – and in anticipation of the shape of a yet to be erected building on its east side.

The office floors have been broken up into three blocks and held in "suspension" within the prismatic envelope or frame in order to articulate its size, break its scale, and to better relate it to the different height of the medium-rise buildings behind. This visual organization allows a "reading" of the building in terms of

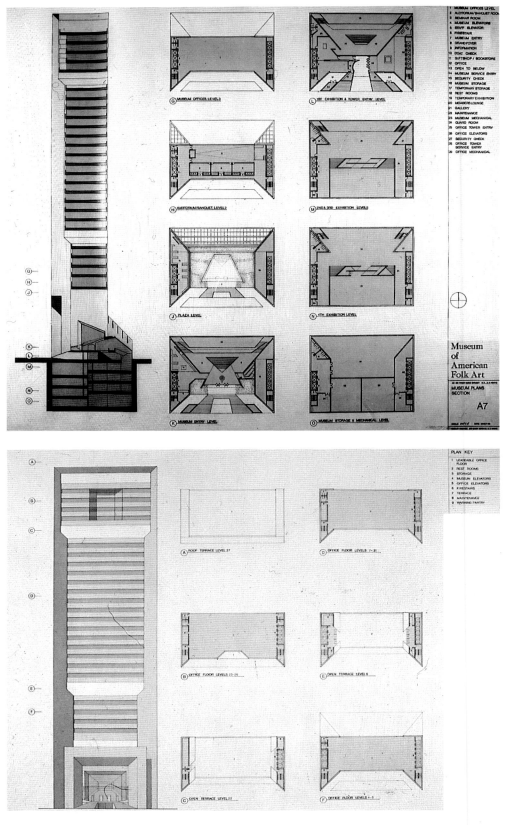

"base," "shaft," and "capital." At the same time, by setting these blocks forward as they ascend, and by expanding their horizontal span as the supporting piers grow taller and thinner, the architect has wished to dovetail this design with the folklore of New York's setback building tradition. By projecting these three blocks forward, the architect has also sought to emphasize an effect of masses overhanging the main entrance portal, thus directing all views toward it.

The free-standing entrance portal, designed as a proscenium frame, serves the museum as well as the office building. The portal's height has been set at 80 feet in order to respect the same horizontal height line as that of the Museum of Modern Art. Two symmetrical stairways, deliberately monumental in feeling, lead to the museum's entrance and foyer, while the entrance to the office tower is axial, directly on street level.

The building addresses the necessity of mitigating large urban scale by dividing itself into smaller building blocks, thus reducing the impression of overbearing mass, allowing light

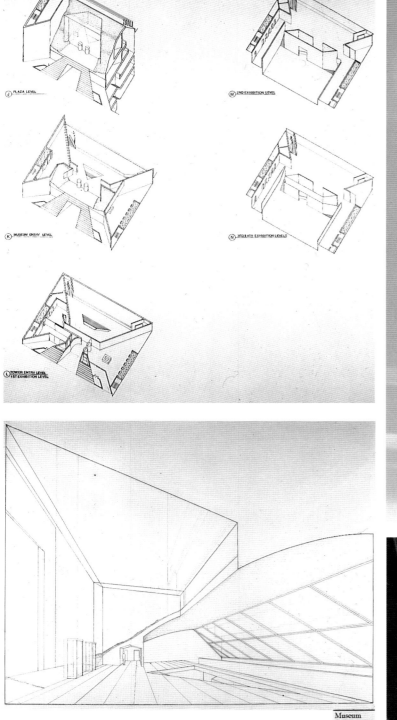

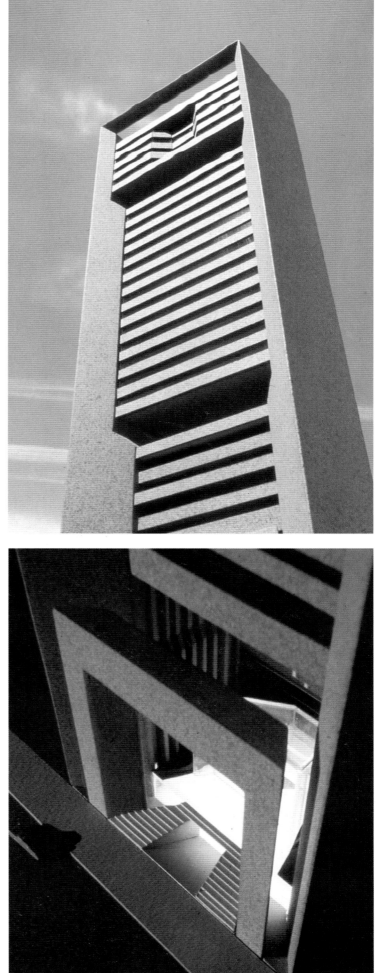

Museum
of
American
Folk Art

SECTION
PERSPECTIVE
MUSEUM
ENTRY

A3

to penetrate through, and clearly expressing the different interior functions without sacrificing a unified face to the street. Its various sections are held in place by the surrounding and defining framework of lateral piers.

Furthermore, this high building is not oblivious to its specific surroundings, reconciling its base's height to that of the old Museum of Modern Art's roof line, and relating its intermediate shaft heights to that of the twelve- and twenty-story buildings behind. Kept intentionally lower than the legally permitted maximum building height, this building acknowledges the urban respect due to 6th Avenue's visual primacy.

The elements of the design for this prototypical newsstand are based on an abstraction of a printing press. The form and profile is bold and simple. The back and roof form a continuous "newspaper" skin of graffiti-resistant, porcelainized aluminum. The newspaper skin runs over a brushed stainless steel "press roller" that houses a pull-down security gate. The newsstand features a large, convenient, printer's "drawer" that maximizes display and increases storage at night. The drawer is supported on casters that roll on tracks in the slab floor; it is pulled out in the morning and pushed in at night. It includes space for the display and storage of newspapers, magazines and candy.

The sides are porcelainized metal panels fastened to a steel frame with carriage bolts. The side panels are colored "big apple green" and the drawer is colored "big apple red." The newsstand sits on a slab-heated concrete base for winter warmth and is entered through a side door. Based on our conversations with numerous operators, the inside contains both specific and flexible storage for magazine, candy, cigarettes, sunglasses, and other items. The prototype conforms to the guidelines established by the Department of City Planning. A preliminary cost estimate indicates that based on the production of multiple units the cost of construction is approximately $12,000.00.

Anderson/Schwartz Architects

NEWSSTAND

New York, NY, Competition, 1988
Design Team: Calori & Vanden-Eyden Ltd., Louis Scrima

The elements of the design for this prototypical newsstand are based on an abstraction of a printing press. The form and profile are bold and simple. The back and roof form a continuous "newspaper" skin of graffiti-resistant, porcelainized aluminum. The newspaper skin runs over a brushed stainless steel "press roller" that houses a pull-down security gate. The newsstand features a large, convenient, printer's "drawer" that maximizes display space and increases storage at night. The drawer is supported on casters that roll on tracks in the floor; it is pulled out in the morning and pushed in when closing at night. It includes space for the display and storage of newspapers, magazines, and candy. The sides are porcelainized metal panels fastened to a steel frame with carriage bolts. The side panels are colored "big apple green" and the drawer is colored "big apple red." The newsstand sits on a slab-heated concrete base for winter warmth and is entered from one side. Following conversations with numerous operators, the inside was designed with specific and flexible storage for magazines, candy, cigarettes, sunglasses, batteries, and other items. The prototype conforms to the guidelines established by the Department of City Planning.

New York Newsstand

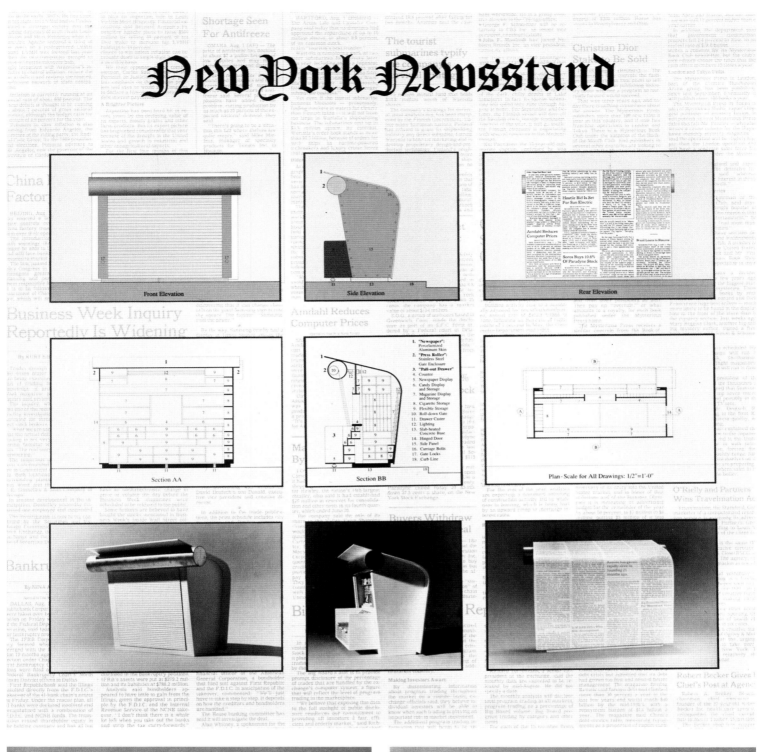

Front Elevation

Side Elevation

Rear Elevation

Section AA

Section BB

Plan · Scale for All Drawings: 1/2" = 1'-0"

1. "Newspaper": Porcelainized Aluminum Skin
2. "Press Roller": Stainless Steel Gate Enclosure
3. "Pull-out Drawer"
4. Counter
5. Newspaper Display
6. Candy Display and Storage
7. Magazine Display and Storage
8. Cigarette Storage
9. Flexible Storage
10. Roll-down Gate
11. Drawer Caster
12. Lighting
13. Slab-heated Concrete Base
14. Hinged Door
15. Side Panel
16. Carriage Bolts
17. Gate Locks
18. Curb Line

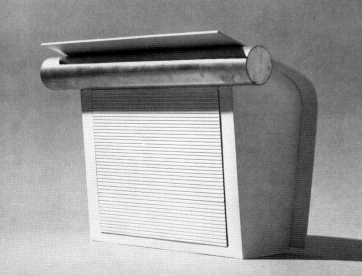

97

Arquitectonica

SOUTH FERRY PLAZA [1]

South Ferry Plaza, New York, NY,
Competition, 1984

South Ferry Plaza is a proposed mixed-use development to be located at the end of Whitehall Street on the southernmost point of Manhattan. The project includes the construction of a new ferry terminal as well as a seventy-story tower containing 850,000 square feet of office space atop a 456-room Meridien Hotel, plus health club, conference center, restaurants, and an observation deck. The project also includes the renovation of the historic Battery Maritime Building for use as the Seaman's Institute. Respect for the existing terminals and the city fabric resulted in the creation of the building as an island. This also makes the building a landmark at the southern tip of Manhattan to add to the tradition of several other landmarks on the river.

The tower is built on piles over the river and rises from the water on a rock base. This base rapidly dematerializes to reveal a futuristic glass tower. The lower levels within the base contain hotel delivery and service areas. The hotel and office arrival lobbies occur above these service areas and are connected back to the city by a glass block enclosed moving walkway and an automobile ramp that ends in a copper-clad drop-off rotary. A truck access drive is concealed under the walkway structure. A large pedestrian ramp links the lobby to a plaza created between the terminal and the museum. The levels above the arrival lobbies contain hotel services and conference and meeting rooms. A core of express elevators connects the arrival lobby with the main hotel lobby above. The typical hotel floors form a U-shape around a twenty-story atrium. All the hotel rooms face the water, while the atrium faces back to a view of Wall Street in the foreground and the rest of Manhattan in the background. Glass elevators take guests to their rooms while exposing them to this view through the atrium glass window to the north. The elevator enclosure rises from a pool of water restating the concept of the building itself.

The office building rises atop the hotel. It appears as a smoked glass tower rising from the main reflecting glass structure. The floor plate grows as the volume ascends to obtain up to approximately 30,000 square feet of floor area in the upper levels. The floor plates vary by the addition and subtraction of volumes at their perimeter, creating corner windows, bay windows, and terraces. The office building is accessed by express elevators to a skylobby connecting to local elevators. A health club with indoor pool and track is strategically located between the hotel and the office building to serve both. An observation deck and restaurant tops the building, cantilevering over Manhattan and the ferry departure lanes. A gold colored transmission tower and other sculptural forms complete the futuristic image of this tower.

Adjacent to the main tower is the new Whitehall Ferry Terminal for the Staten Island Ferry. The ferry terminal is designed as four expressionistic towers connected by a horizontal, rational, tinted glass structure which houses the waiting rooms. Leading to the main waiting rooms is a retail concourse. The terminal is entered through an elliptical glass block lobby with escalators and stairs. The complex is connected to bus systems as well as existing subway stations through a newly created landscaped plaza. A second plaza is situated at the waterfront, providing the required view corridor as well as outdoor dining and public access to the riverside.

Owing to immediate demand for ferry services, the station was designed as a structure independent of the tower. In response to the need for open space and to the zoning requirement for a view corridor at the end of Whitehall Street, the tower as originally planned was moved toward the water. It was thus possible to leave the existing Battery Maritime Building, a historic landmark, as a free-standing building that retained its integrity. A bridge connects the old and new terminals to provide for emergency use of the old slips and to provide continuity of the Esplanade from the East River to Battery Park.

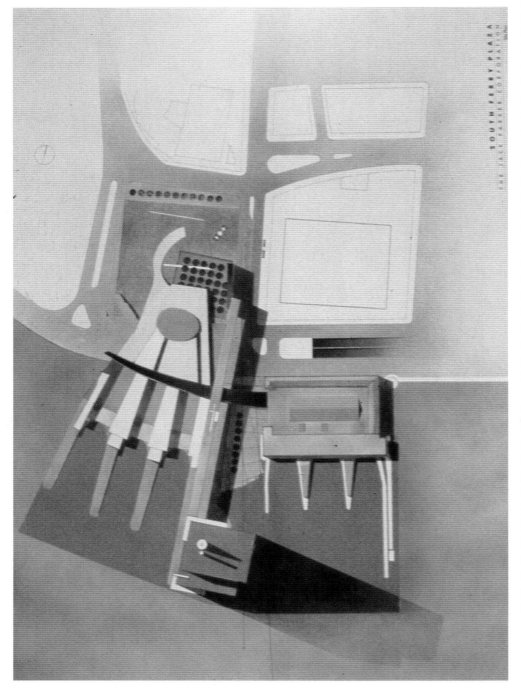

Vladimir Arsene
for Gruzen Sampton Steinglass Architects

BATTERY PARK CITY APARTMENTS [6]

Battery Park City Site 10, New York, NY, 1986 – 88
Design Team: Vladimir Arsene, Peter Samton,
Tim Schmidere, Carol Shu, Yu-hwa Hung,
Isabel Kraut

Battery Park City, situated on a landfill area at
the southern tip of Manhattan, is the result of
one of the most ambitious urban developments
of the 1980s in the United States. In its attempt
to stop the uncontrolled growth of the city, and
in its desire to check the proliferation of different styles, Battery Park City Authority mandated
a master plan and a set of design guidelines
modeled on the early twentieth-century apartments in New York's Upper East and West Sides.
Thus, not only an urban structure was laid
down, but also a unified style: masonry-clad
buildings with punched windows, stone bases,
and, most importantly, unarticulated and uniform facades.

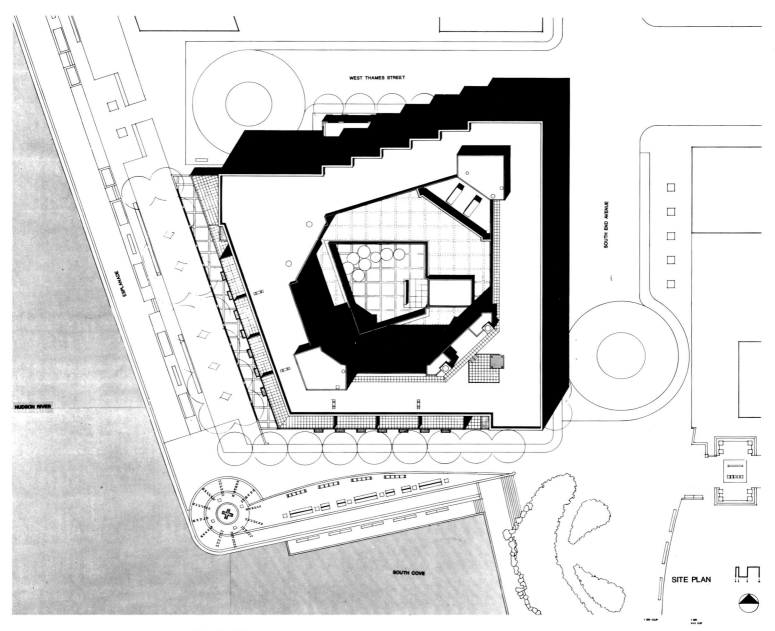

WEST THAMES STREET

SOUTH END AVENUE

ESPLANADE

HUDSON RIVER

SOUTH COVE

SITE PLAN

The 178-unit apartment building, which was completed by October 1988, was conceived under these guidelines. The building successfully modifies the massing originally imposed on it, and avoids becoming monotonous, while striving to reflect the complexity of the larger urban context and the proximity of water.

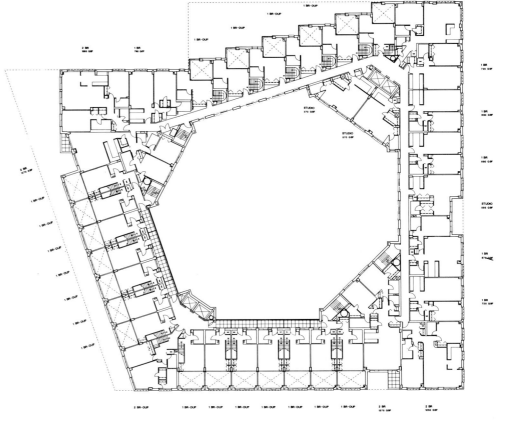

FLOOR 3,5,7

Edward Larrabee Barnes/ John M. Y. Lee, Architects

IBM TOWER (47)

590 Madison Avenue, New York, NY, 1983
Design Team: Edward L. Barnes, John M. Y. Lee,
Armand Avakian, Richard Klibschon

The IBM tower, forty-three stories high, is a five-sided sheer prismatic form with gray-green glass and gray-green polished granite detailed in sleek flush planes. The appearance of the building changes when viewed from different angles – sometimes it is a slab-like wall, sometimes a slender shaft, sometimes a tower cantilevering over the street corner.

The tower covers 40% of the lot, and it is built close to the existing sidewalk line. There is retail and exhibition space facing the street, and at the corner of 57th Street and Madison Avenue the building steps back under the granite cantilever to create an entrance to the main lobby and an open area for pedestrians at this vital New York City corner.

At the back of the building is a bamboo filled plaza garden as well as a pedestrian arcade leading from 57th to 56th Street along the back of the garden. A sculpture by Michael Heizer provides a focus in the open space at the corner of 56th Street and Madison Avenue. Thus it becomes an inviting meeting place, open all year round, a quiet haven from the noise and bustle of the street.

Groundfloor

Cafeteria Level

Typical Floor

102

Mario Botta

ICF EXHIBITION ROOM

New York, NY 19
Design Team: Mario Botta, Ugo Früh,
Stephen Lepp Associates, NY

The ICF showroom in the International Design Center New York has a purely representative, not a sales, function: furniture is intended to be exhibited there to its best possible advantage.

The entrance to the exhibition room is opposite the lifts. In order to get to the entrance, the visitor has to walk along the glass front surrounding the exhibition room – that is, around the whole courtyard of the IDCNY. Intended to prevent visitors from getting a glimpse of the showroom from the outside, a semicircular wall with a diameter of some sixty feet has been erected inside. The visitor thus having been made curious, he then enters the room and discovers the exhibits one after another.

A similar solution was found for the entrance area. Instead of the expected glass door, there is a small triangular exhibition area acting as a focal point outside the showroom. There are two side entrances in the concrete wall. Inside, a wall separates the reception area, the conference room, and the offices from the exhibition area. The semicircular, walled exhibition niches

are arranged in such a way that the exhibits are discovered only gradually. It is only when the visitor leaves the passage toward the office area that he gets an overall view of them.

On the north side, the exhibition room ends with a large square area in which wall and cupboard systems are exhibited. It also houses a cooking niche and storage space.

The inner side of the large central curved wall, which provides exhibition space for larger objects (in this case desk systems for offices), can be divided up by perforated metal plates. The sliding doors of the conference room and the elements in front of the window are also made of perforated metal to filter the light.

A further filter or transparent effect is created by the suspended ceiling, which permits the original concrete ceiling to be seen while allowing easy accommodation of the light and ventilation installations.

The intermediate walls of concrete bricks are left unplastered; equally, the support pillars and the concrete roof of the old industrial building have been left as they were, creating a sharp contrast to the exhibited furniture. Dex-o-tex, a dark gray wash usually used as the base for other floor coatings, was used for the floor and harmonizes well with the other materials utilized.

Excerpt from the dissertation of Ugo Früh, ETH Zurich, 1988.

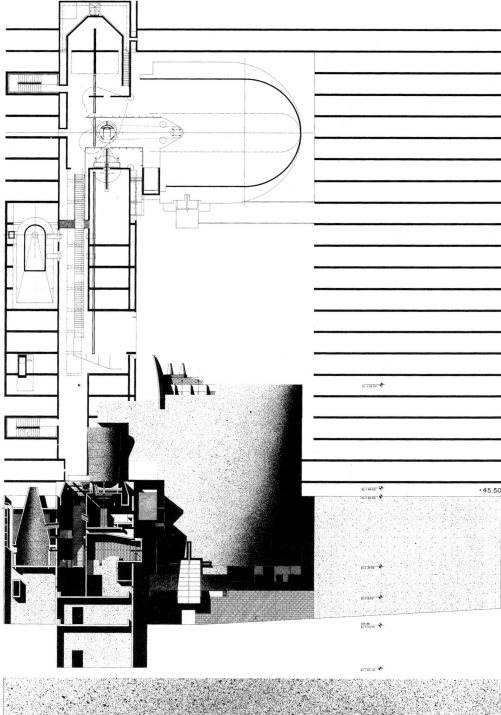

Neil M. Denari

MONASTERY   (15)

Eighth Avenue, Chelsea, New York, NY
Project, 1985

Location: A 210 foot square site fronting 8th Avenue between 21st and 22nd streets in the Chelsea section of New York.

Program: The monastery is a place of refuge from the insanities of the city. It is a building of questions, intended to generate a re-definition of existing modalities of spiritual expression.

Individual cells, a spherical confessional chamber, small chapels, the vestment machines, labyrinthine cloisters, and a main space of collective spirit (within the geometrically distorted cone) provide a highly potent mixture of traditional and contemporary readings of the monastery program.

Materials: The main structure of the building is reinforced concrete tinted green. The large cone is a thin shell concrete structure. Both parts are sheathed by pre-fabricated light-gauge COR-TEN steel panels.

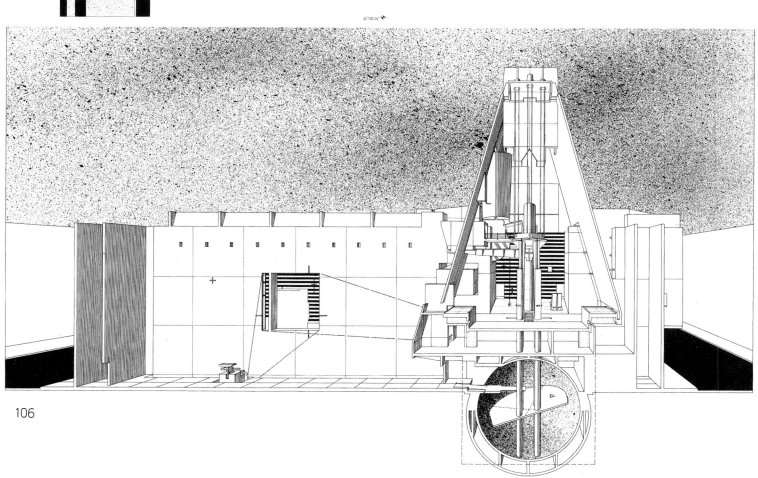

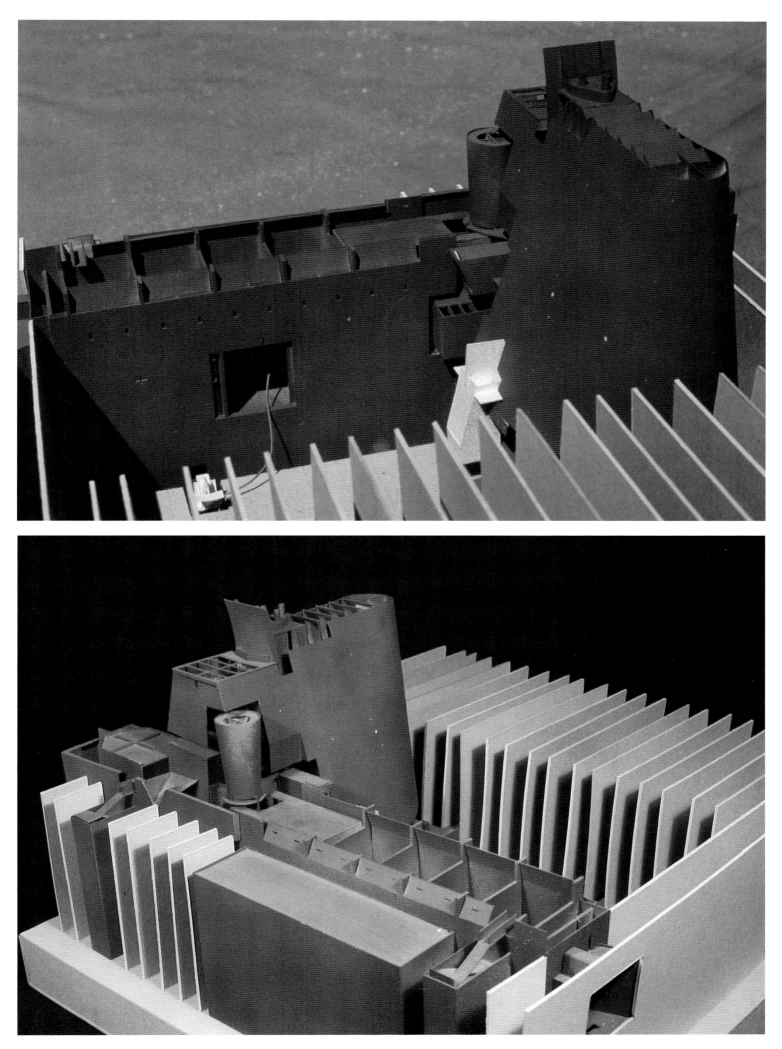

Diller + Scofidio

THE COLUMBUS CIRCLE PROJECT/TRAFFIC
ROTARY [25]

Columbus Circle, New York, NY
Installation, 1981

The architects have deliberately forgone providing a description in the conviction that the
installation speaks for itself.

Diller + Scofidio

SENTINEL, Art on the Beach [7]

Battery Park City Landfill, New York, NY
Installation, 1983

Inspired by the work of John Hejduk, the Sentinel is both building and costume for one
occupant. The structure has two scales, alter-
nates in gender, and operates as a timekeeper.
Black sand, sifting through the suspended
cone, acts as a diminishing counterpoise that
mechanically activates an arm to signal the
passage of specific time intervals.
 Material: stressed skin plywood panels,
structural lumber, sandbox foundation, steel
fittings and mask, plywood roof funnel.

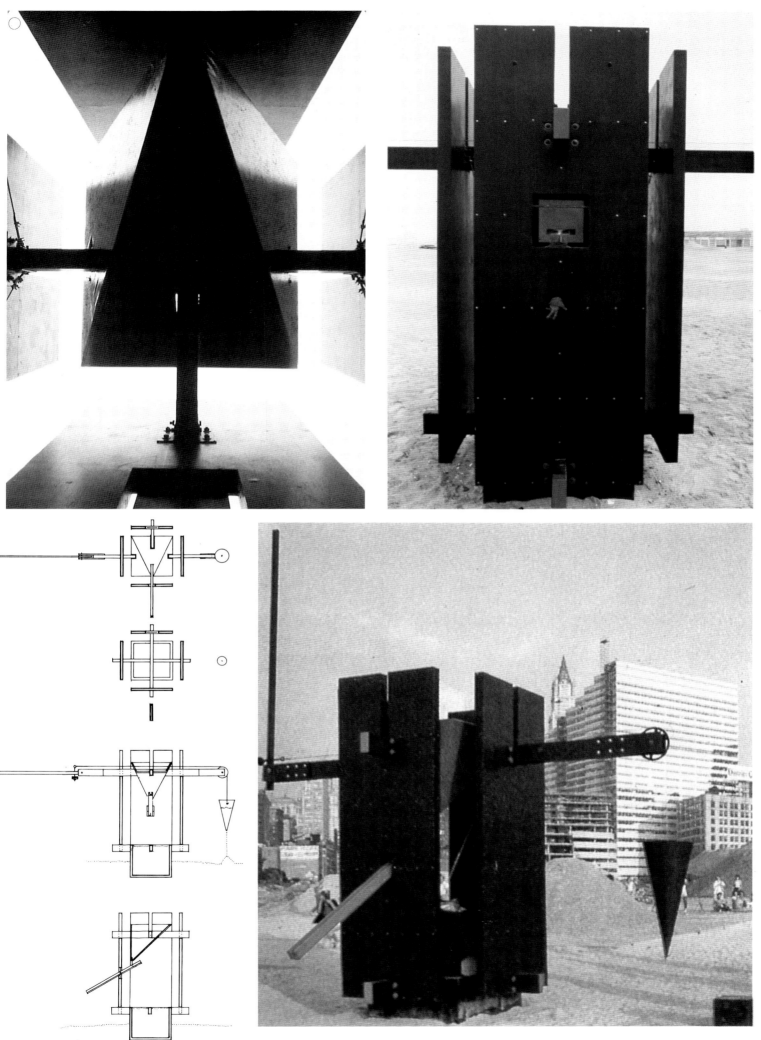

Eisenman Architects

FIREHOUSE FOR ENGINE CO.
233, LADDER CO. [78]

Rockaway Avenue, Brooklyn, New York, NY, 1985
Design Team: Peter Eisenman, Arthur Baker,
Ross Woolley, Mark Wamble, David Winslow

This fire station, designed for a run-down area
of Brooklyn, houses both a battalion chief and a
ladder company. It is intended as a public
marker, a literal "beacon" of unity on a site
which is roughly divided by two different grid
contexts and a major elevated mass transit line
marking the east/west division of the two grids.
Rather than the present-day trend to nostalgic
imagery when dealing with the context and history of a location, the building develops an
urban iconography within its own form. Here,
the imagery of the building does not refer to

super graphics or classical pastiche, but is in
itself the meaning of the site. It creates a union
of the two grids by superimposing the geometry
of the northern grid (recalling the imagery of the
elevated tracks) over the geometry of the southern grid (recalling the masonry scale of the
existing context). The roof members of the
superimposed grid contain red laser lights and
the beam ends contain a beam of light, so that
at night the structure is symbolically illuminated
and can be seen from passing trains as well as
from the street. When the engines are out at a
fire, the beam ends send out a beacon of red
light to complete the imagery.

Art Commission Award for Excellence in
Design, 1985.

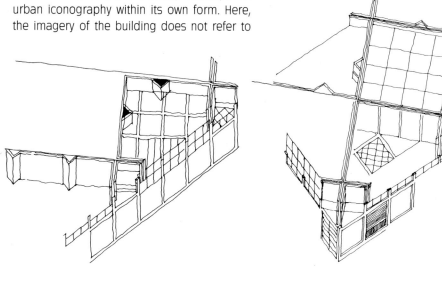

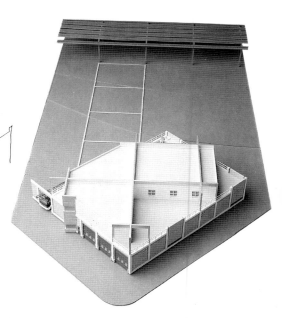

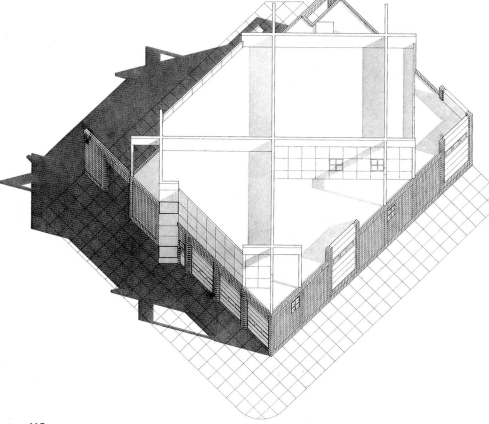

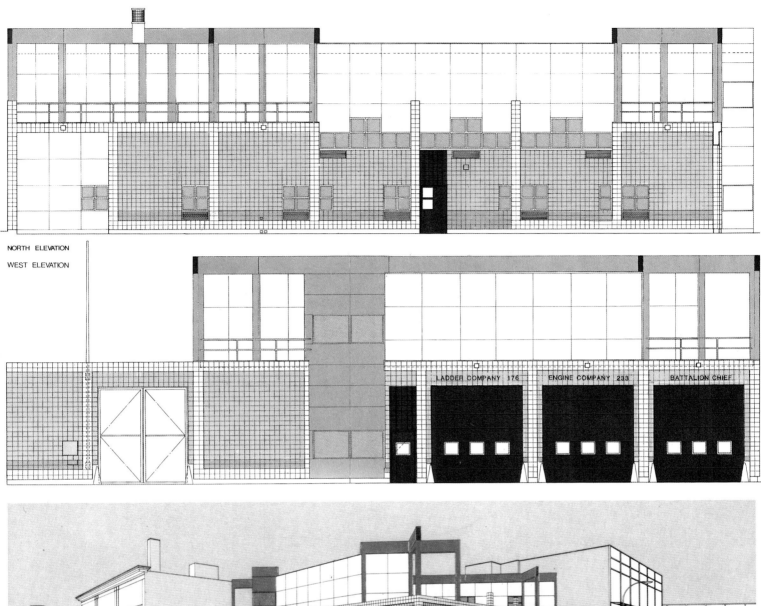

NORTH ELEVATION

WEST ELEVATION

LADDER COMPANY 176   ENGINE COMPANY 233   BATTALION CHIEF

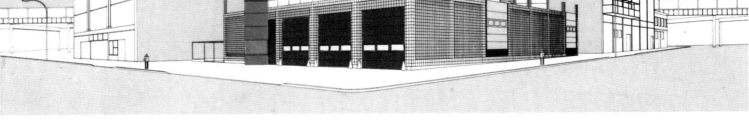

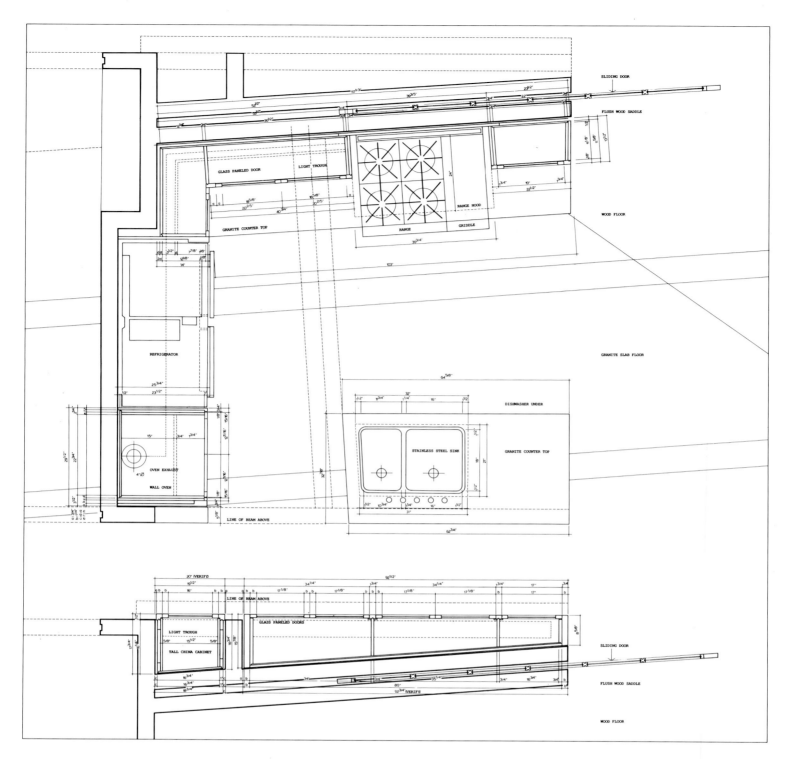

Peter Eisenman/
Faruk Yorgancioglu

FULLER/TOMS LOFT Residence and Studio

Cast Iron District in Lower Manhattan, New York, NY, 1986–1988

Design Team: Peter Eisenman, Faruk Yorgancioglu, Ragip Erdem, David Hohman, James Brown, Simon Hubacher, Haydee Graud, Osman Ataman

The idea for this project is similar to the same team's idea for the Wexner Center for the Visual Arts at Ohio State University in Columbus, Ohio. The important differences are twofold: the first is a question of scale; the second is the idea of an internal insertion which ultimately both disrupts and unifies. The site for this project is a 4,000 square foot loft in Lower Manhattan. The space is essentially a rectangular parallelepiped in the proportions of 100 to 40. The short side faces Broadway, which causes the two sides to be joined at something other than a right angle. As at Ohio State, the idea was to insert a foreign body into the existing context in such a way as to produce a disorienting relationship between old and new. And, as in the Ohio State project, the context provides a non-right angle geometry. The intersection of the two geometries was used to produce a condition where neither geometry was dominant in either the vertical or horizontal dimension. This produced the effect of displacing and destabilizing conventional devices for orientation. Here one can be in a room, yet because of its complex relationship with other rooms, find it difficult to orient oneself with respect to the context of the city, or to the simple coordinates of north and south. While there appears to be a dominant vertebrate system or order, as in Ohio State, this is fractured by the introduction of a seemingly different system. Traces of these counterposing systems can be read on the floor, the walls, and the ceilings. Now, in a sense, there is an order within an order and a scale within a scale. The structure of the loft space is understood piece by piece as one glimpses fragments of the integrating texts. The entire space has the effect of being a rare glimpse of some larger, usually invisible context of vectors, currents, and coded messages.

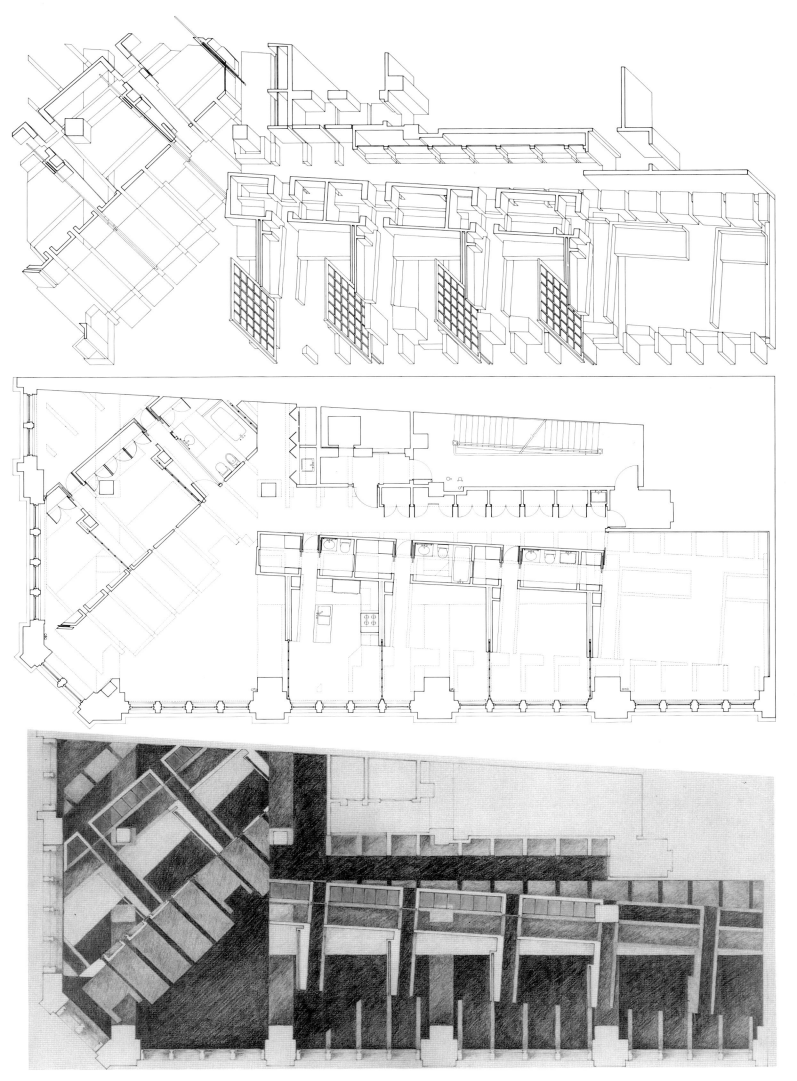

1100 Architect

RESIDENCE, WEST VILLAGE

West Village, Manhattan, New York, NY, 1988
Design Team: David Piscuskas, Juergen Riehm,
Ines Elskop

The project is the conversion of a 9,000 square foot steel warehouse originally built in 1912 into a residence and studio. As such, it is indicative of a proto-industrial typology in which man's workplace and domicile were united within, and completely occupied, one building. This required substantial reconstruction of the structure of the building, including the unification of two distinct systems of columns at ground level. The replacement of many columns with fewer, but stronger, columns permitted the free plan required in the workplace. Additions to the second story, which were completed in 1947, resulted in structural elements that had to be removed, as well as other alterations that were each dealt with independently in the design. For example, a double-height space at the building entrance had been created as part of an earlier renovation. A portion of this space adjacent to the entrance was maintained at its full height of twenty-six feet, while the remainder was enclosed beneath a new floor area, thereby lending a more human scale to the entry foyer.

Previous additions to the original brick, east exterior wall of the second story had been carried out in a haphazard, nondescript manner. As a result, what was once a distinct masonry wall which supported the vaulted roof structure of the building was obscured within a confluence of materials and methods from different eras. It was decided to restore integrity to this central, but simple feature of the building, so the openings through the brick were treated as true arches and, together with cast-iron pilasters, detailed as such. To this end, the openings were confined to four: one new window in that portion of the wall not supporting an addition, two openings through the wall to the two pre-existent additions from the 1940s, and one archway providing access to a stairway to a new addition one story higher, supported in part by the original brick, east exterior wall of the building.

The new addition is composed of two L-shaped walls: one, atop the roof, is of relatively ligthweight stud frame construction, while the other, above the old brick bearing walls, is of masonry construction matching the original work and essential to the support of the new addition. The cylindrical form of the stair and its enclosure is derived from the surrounding landscape of watertowers on rooftops that is particular to this area of Manhattan.

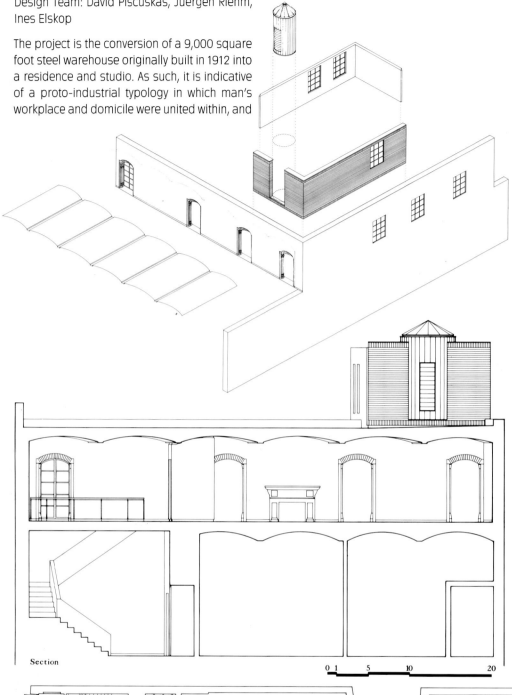

Section

0 1   5   10   20

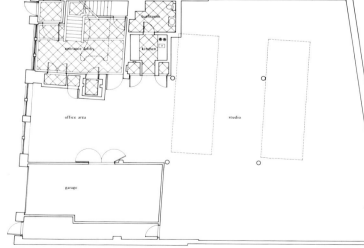

First Floor Plan

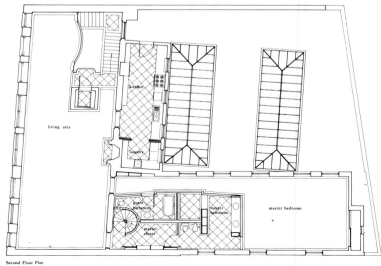

Second Floor Plan

114

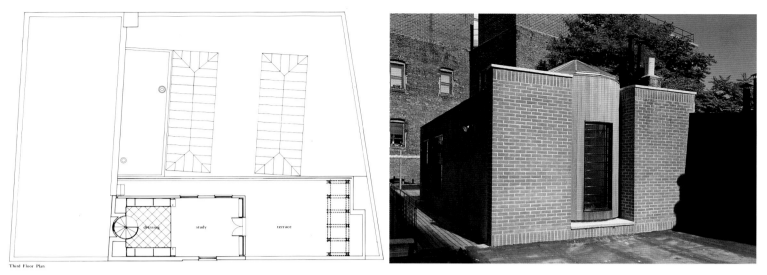

Third Floor Plan

dressing study terrace

115

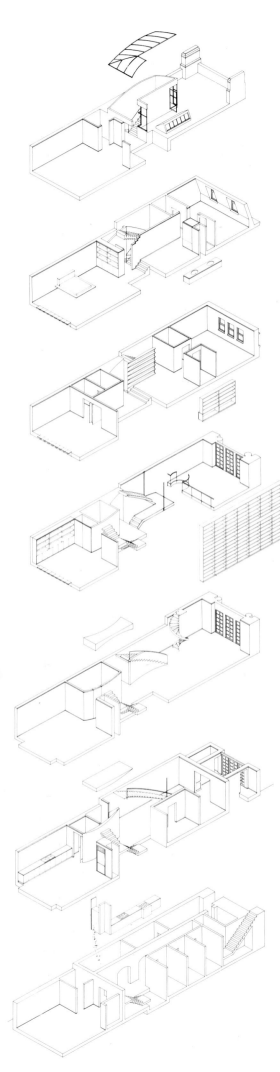

1100 Architect

TOWNHOUSE, UPPER EASTSIDE

Upper Eastside, New York, NY
Project, 1988
Design Team: David Piscuskas, Juergen Riehm,
Ines Elskop

This 9,500 square foot house for a family on a typically long (100 feet) and narrow (20 feet) parcel in Manhattan was designed in accordance with an exact and comprehensive program. The overall condition of an existing structure on the site warranted its removal, save for the street-front facade of the building which was to be retained and restored. Floor levels within the proposed new building, were determined by the location of existing windows within this facade, and by the sloping grade between the front and rear. In this way, split-level floors were created which lessened the perceived length of the floor relative to its width and permitted the construction of the additional floor area necessary to satisfy the requirements of the project.

The proportions of the site prescribed a pronounced verticality for the building. In certain cases, functional links between floors were more important than those along a single floor level. The most public places of the house are disposed on the first three levels, with the large kitchen located at the rear of the first floor, and the main dining room directly above. Also on the second level is the grand double-height salon and library. The arced staircase dominates the central portion of the house, ceremoniously joining these public levels. In addition, the staircase and elevator were designed to share their respective landings at each floor, and so become paired in a manner unusual to the Manhattan townhouse.

The rear garden elevation celebrates the inherent slenderness of the building in its composition and construction. Precast concrete panels articulate two piers (at each side of the portion projected into the garden) which perceptually support the rise of the main rear wall of the building. However, local regulations mandated a setback, so this wall is conceived as a skin, attached in a parallel plane to the structure, and, in its central portion, is in fact a curtain wall of tinted glass and steel. This assemblage suggests a building of taller size and larger scale than is actually the case, and avoids the truncated abbreviation of the ordinary three-window configuration of the adjacent buildings. Finally, the uppermost floor houses the quiet studio retreat.

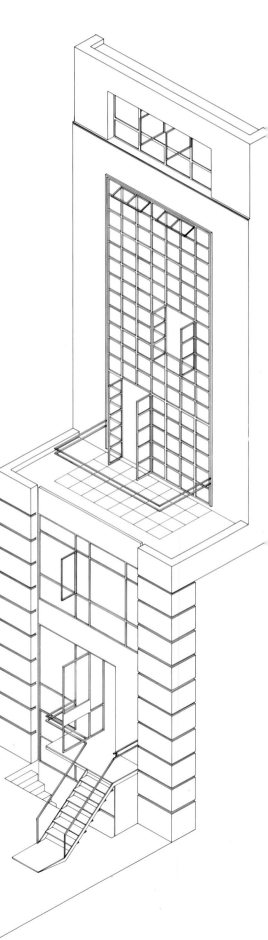

Michael Fieldman & Partners

AMBULATORY CARE BUILDING   [71]
The Staten Island Hospital

Staten Island, New York, NY, 1988
(under construction)
Design Team: Michael Fieldman, Miles Cigolle,
Rodney Crumrine, Stan Pearson, Clinton Diener

In recent years, health care institutions have been developing satellite buildings for ambulatory care services. The focus here has been to remove ambulatory patients from the intensity of a hospital setting, at the same time providing an environment which strengthens the patient amenity side by developing clinical clusters that bear more resemblance to a private office setting than to one of an institutional setting.

The architectural design reflects this approach in the development of an unusual circulation system whereby the main feeder corridor is at the exterior face of the building allowing a full sense of orientation to the users at any point. In addition, all waiting areas, reception and registration areas are adjacent to this spine so that the continuous window wall provides natural light to those areas, and contributes to the transitions and interplay between public and private spaces inserting a literal range of experiences from generic to specific - spine/waiting/registration to private examination room. Patients tend to spend the longest time waiting for their appointment and this attribute to exterior space and light, while gen-

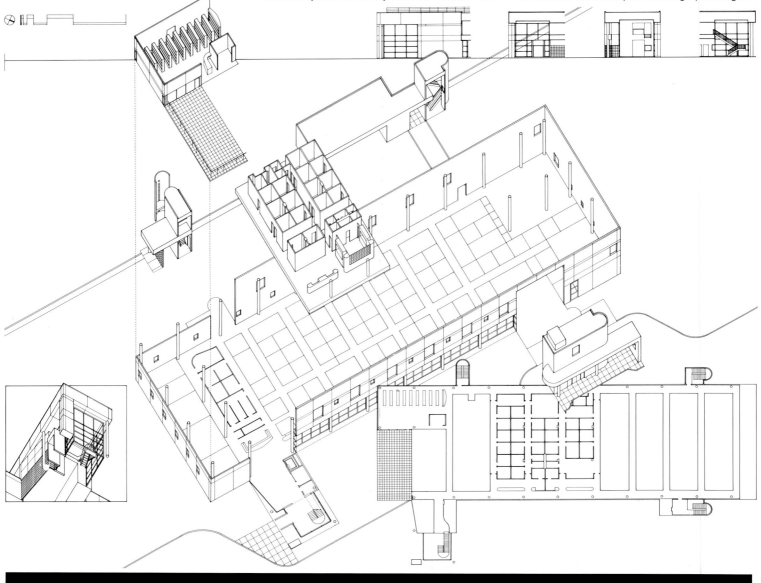

erally not found in healthcare institutions, is also considered a health benefit. From the circulation systems and adjacent waiting areas, patients can see the twin towers of the Verrazano Bridge which links Staten Island to Manhattan.

The building is externally direct in its geometry and is kept simple so as to enhance the reading of each clinical sense of place, in its strictest definition. The full program comprises 9 clinics with support administrative areas and pharmacy in 55,000 sq. ft. (5,100 sq.m.)

Vertical movement is physically and visually expressed through an open stair well. No level, therefore, is considered as secondary or internal space. All waiting spaces are clinic-specific. This new approach allows for the development of bright, open and commodious "rooms" which benefit from direct natural light, all the while broken down into discrete, intimate spaces that speak more to a private physician-type clinic. It is this approach to building, materials and circulation systems which provides for clarity in reading by the user, and contributes to the building's presence as a community resource rather than as a bulk mass with mysterious corridor systems leading to ill-defined spaces that are usually tension-producing. Here the building is alive, contributing to its everyday activities yet reinforcing the quiet and a calm that is so fundamental to patient care.

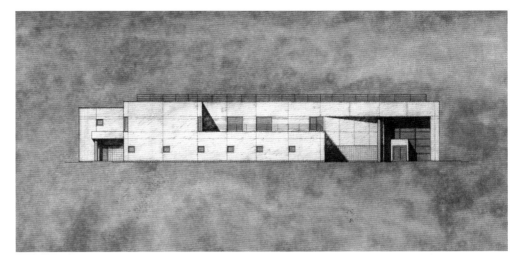

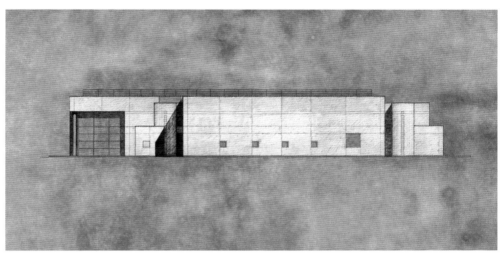

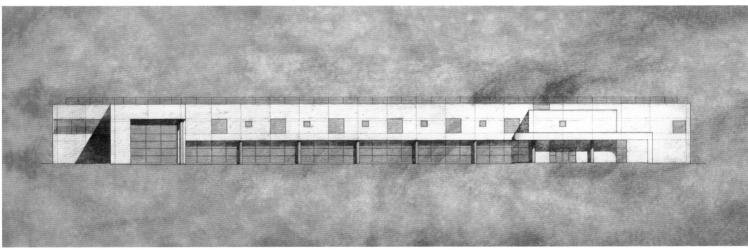

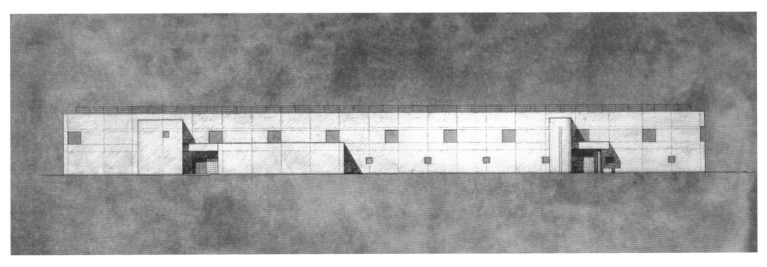

Michael Fieldman & Partners with Harry Wolf and Ove Arup & Partners

WILLIAMSBURG BRIDGE COMPETITION [10]

New York, NY, Competition, 1988
Design Team: Philippe Barriere, Miles Cigolle, Rodney Crumrine, Clinton Diener, Stephen Hennebery, John Jordan, Diane Lasko, Reini Martin, Ed Rawlings, Harry Wolf

The Williamsburg Bridge spans the East River in New York City, linking Brooklyn with Manhattan. When completed in 1903, it was the longest suspension bridge in the world. On April 12, 1988, the bridge was closed because extensive corrosion to the cables had dangerously diminished their strength. An international competition was held to explore options for bridge repairs and/or construction of a new bridge. Twenty submissions were made representing professional interest from the U.S., Great Britain, Canada, Belgium, West Germany, Spain, and Switzerland.

The submission was the result of collaboration between Ove Arup and Michael Fieldman & Partners, whereby Arup was responsible for the bridge design and Fieldman undertook the design and integration of the bridge ramps and approaches within the existing urban fabric, including development and conceptual design of new urban uses, housing, parks, and support recreation facilities.

The proposal called for a completely new crossing, as close as possible to the existing one so as to have the least possible adverse effect on the environment. The crossing is made by two double-decked cable-stayed bridges which carry road traffic on the upper decks, and subway trains and pedestrian walkways on the lower decks. To accomplish the work without disruption to vehicular or train traffic, the first of the new bridges will be constructed on the

south side of the existing one, together with approaches and ramps. The existing one will then be demolished and replaced with the second bridge so that the overall final capacity will have six lanes for automobiles (three per bridge), three subway tracks on the south bridge, and pedestrian walkways on the lower deck of the north bridge. The overall bridge length will be 3,400 feet with a main span of 1,765 feet. Each deck is 51 feet in width and the trusses carrying the main deck are steel boxes in 48-foot bays, 20 feet deep. The towers are 500 feet high, cables consist of 7-millimeter galvanized steel wires in parallel, protected with a sheathing of titanium grade stainless coated carbon steel.

On the Manhattan side, a new axis and structure begins a procession of green medians that re-establish Delancey Street as a significant avenue. The ramp onto the bridge will be a composite of public enclosed space, housing, and open park space. The new construction and parks will revitalize the housing on either side of the bridge by introducing recreation spaces, enclosed studio and rehearsal spaces, a green market, and 600 new housing units.

Williamsburg (a section of Brooklyn adjacent to the bridge) is an area of great diversity with mixed residential, industrial and commercial land uses, and an active working waterfront. Two new buildings, a ball court and new park dedicated to the "Art and Science of Bridge Con-

struction" will occupy the spaces under the bridge and along the waterfront. An amphitheater creates one of the most dramatic backdrops for open-air theater in the world. Views of the Brooklyn Navy Yard, the Con Edison buildings, the New York skyline, and the industrial activities of the waterfront north of the bridge make this park a place where the fascinating complexity of the city can be appreciated.

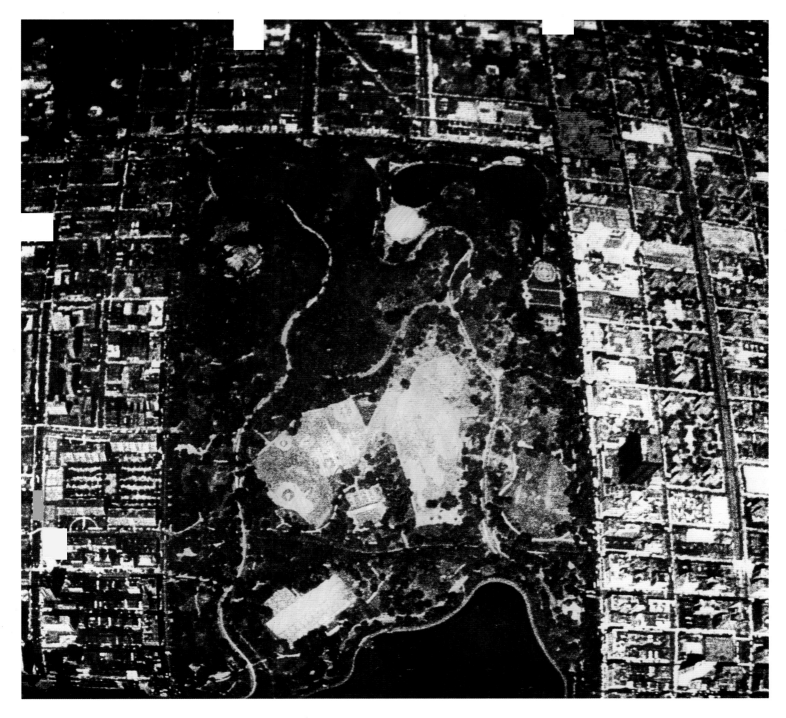

Giuliano Fiorenzoli

CENTRAL PARK, NORTHEAST CORNER   [59]

Central Park, Northeast Corner, Harlem,
New York, NY, 1978

The open space of Central Park in New York gives us an idea of the magnitude of the City itself. This void of vast proportions speaks of one of the highest urban densities man has ever conceived and built. And yet the park, with its rolling landscaped grounds, needs to fight for its survival, to resist the attacks of a City that is expanding irrationally in all directions, wherever physically possible.

In an attempt to stop the dramatic erosion of the park's edges, we propose to build a tower in the particularly significant corner adjacent to the Harlem district. Such a tower stands directly on the grounds of the park. It reaffirms through its location the rectangular geometry of the park while giving architectural definition to its north-east corner. The structural armature and the flexibility of a crane are metaphors for any activity that might be conceived and organized in its interiors or at its base, at the ground level.

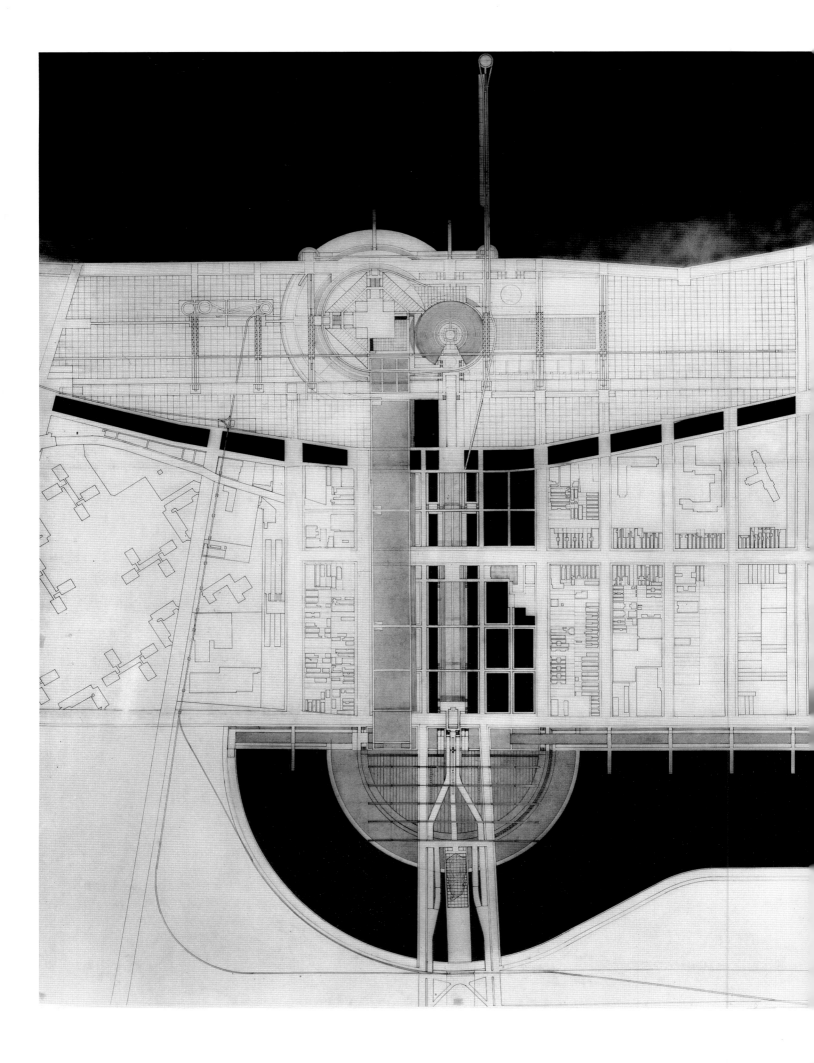

Giuliano Fiorenzoli

OCEAN FRONT HOTEL

Coney Island, New York, NY, 1983

The project for an ocean-front multi-purpose hotel is the result of a larger scale study that focuses on the future use of the well-known site of Coney Island amusement park. This study has produced a master plan which sets out the main guidelines effecting the entire reorganization of the park and its surroundings. A new urban corridor has been conceived with parks, squares, canals, pools, marinas, a new ocean front, and a more efficient transportation system to be connected to various metropolitan areas. Two large structures celebrate the terminal point of the corridor in what is the most critical part of the site. One structure is dedicated to the waterfront, with one of the most spectacular direct views of the ocean. A square, fronted by three casino buildings, receives the pedestrians approaching from the park, while a second square, partially contained by the large

hotel, provides direct access to the open public boardwalk a few feet above the sands of the beach. The hotel presents two very distinctive and separate views to the onlooker: one that relates to the view of Manhattan, the other that celebrates the myriad lights of sea and sky and those of the private terraces. In the 800-foot-tall tower, there are features, such as the large courtyard, suggestive of the more private use of the upper part of the building. An observation level represents an additional internal articulation of the hotel. Special elevators depart from this level following a route that takes the passengers outside the main volume of the building and back to it after an exciting ride in space. The building is crowned by a weather station and a communications center.

James Ingo Freed
for I. M. Pei & Partners

JACOB K. JAVITS CONVENTION CENTER
OF NEW YORK   [18]

655 West 34th Street, New York, NY, 1979–1986
Design Team: James I. Freed, Charles T. Young II,
Thomas Baker

A state-of-the-art exposition and convention center, planned as the largest under one roof in America.

The variously graded site, 21.9 acres in an under-utilized area along the western riverbank of midtown Manhattan, stretches five city blocks from 34th Street to 39th Street. It is bordered on the west by Twelfth Avenue and the Hudson River, and rises from eighteen to thirty-two feet to the Eleventh Avenue viaduct in the east.

Among the many challenges involved, the most exacting focused on structure, integration, and circulation. The first of these, structure, was resolved with a modified space frame and truss system: a lightweight double layer structure in which steel tubes are connected to spherical nodes. The system was selected for flexibility as well as texture and optical effect; at times it seems to lose its volumetric character and appears instead like a lacey linear web. The space frame combines architecture and structure inseparably; the skeleton itself becomes a visual attraction while providing a coherent frame for the building's diverse functions.

Integration and Urban Instrumentality: How could an urban setting assimilate a building which stretches continuously across four city blocks and which accommodates over 85,000 people (more than three times the tenant population of the Empire State Building)? In this respect, the space frame's small rhythmic patterns help to reduce the building's apparent scale. The interior terrazzo pavement, animated by shifting daylight, has the same reductive effect. And so does the building's reflective glass skin dividing the 1,000-foot facade into more easily comprehensible 90-foot bays. (The 90-foot module is repeated throughout the building; it was determined by the aisle and booth requirements of standard trade show practice). Even more important for integration is the play of solidity and transparency in which the vast interior, flooded with natural light, combines indoor and outdoor views.

The grandest of the public spaces consists of a series of stepped entry bays, or pavilions, which rise like a pile of hollow glass cubes to the height of a fifteen-story building. This monumental lobby is officially known as the "Crystal Palace."

The second major public space is the "Galleria": a block-long commercial street lined with cafes and shops, and bridging the upper exhibition hall. It terminates in the west with the River Pavilion, a stepped, double-story restaurant overlooking the river. The "Concourse" completes the Center's indoor public spaces with a 75-foot-high glass vestibule stretched along the entire front elevation. Pierced by multiple entrances, the Concourse was designed for registration, exhibition overflow, and flexibility of circulation. The Center's public spaces are completed by a one-acre outdoor plaza, animated by kiosks and a fountain, and located opposite the main entrance to the Crystal Palace at 35th-36th Streets.

Installed along the inner west wall of the Concourse is the Javits Center's concrete "Core," a freestanding "building within a building" over whose low roof natural light filters into the exhibition halls. The Core houses glazed suites from which managers can observe the show floors. It also contains rest rooms, meeting rooms, and, importantly, twenty-four escalators that provide equal access to the upper and lower exhibition halls.

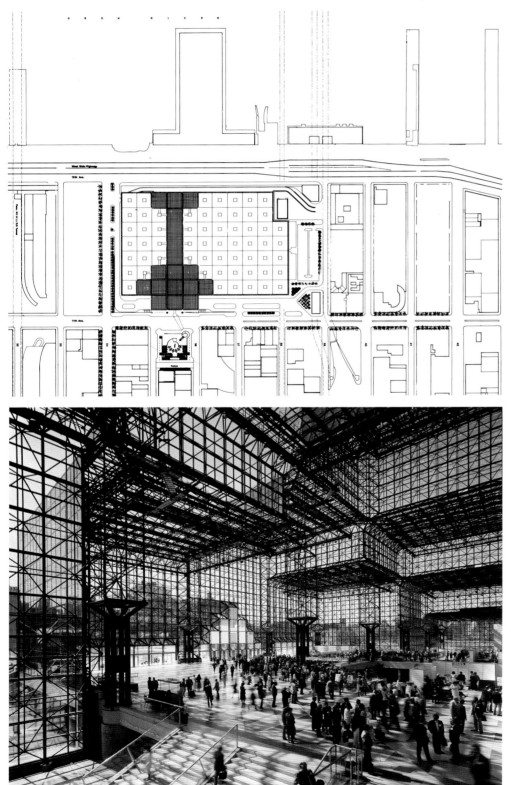

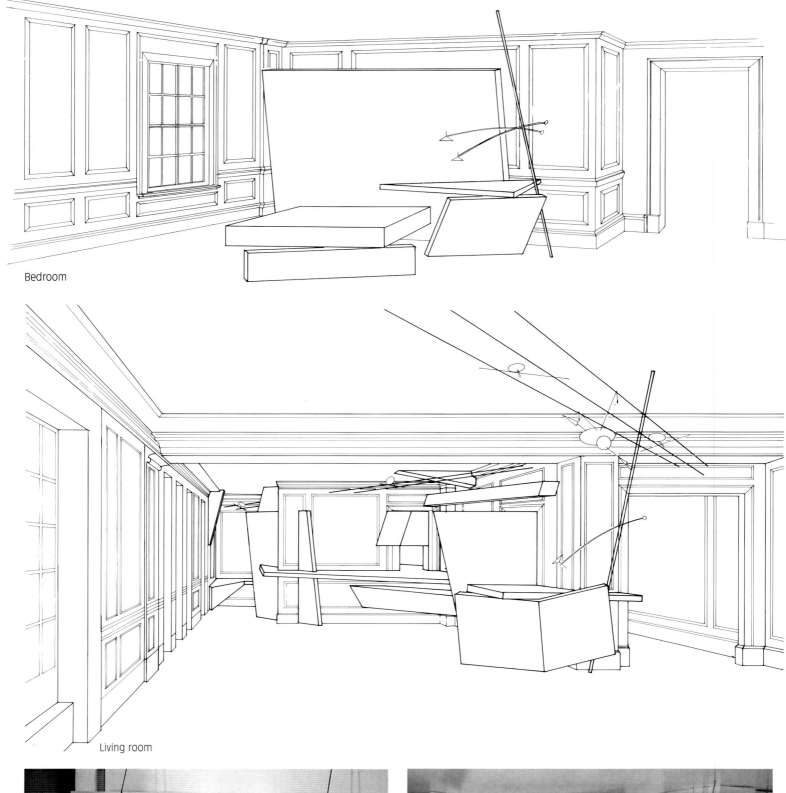

Bedroom

Living room

Giovannini & Associates

DUPLEX PENTHOUSE   [12]

Gramercy, New York, NY, 1989

A four-member family with contemporary tastes and an active lifestyle purchased a duplex apartment that perpetuated, through its floorplan, the mentality inherent in its 1910 origin and 1931 remodeling. The task was to reorganize the plan to reflect new, informal living-patterns, while retaining the moldings and other historic details and removing as few walls as possible.

The design called for the removal of a 1931 upstairs bath and a 1931 living/dining room wall to re-establish the original openness in the apartment's main rooms. It also called for a reorganization of the functional service spaces downstairs, and of the rear bedrooms upstairs. The issue of recasting the character of the spaces without removing many walls or historic details was approached by drawing up "Fields of Desire" with the new occupants.

Upstairs, space needs for the master bathroom and closets pressured the surrounding new master bedroom suite and adjoining bedroom spaces. Downstairs, the fireplace, the south-facing front windows, and a new "media column" combined to open up the floor, bringing these features deeply into the space. A new fabric of parts – architectural furniture – was invented to modify walls like adjectives. The pieces appear to penetrate the walls and floors, establishing an independent spatial field that dissolves the old apartment's sense of compartmentalization. At the same time, the molding on the old walls has been extended and disciplined in order to affirm its classical character and give it greater consistency.

EXISTING FLOOR PLANS

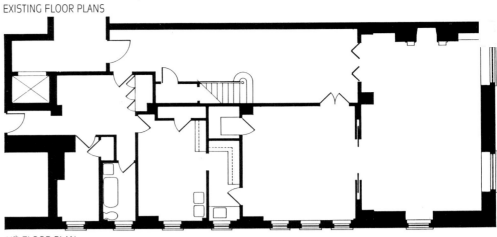

11th FLOOR PLAN

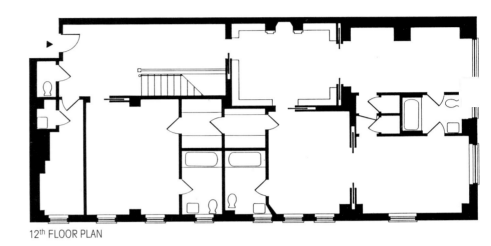

12th FLOOR PLAN

NEW FLOOR PLANS

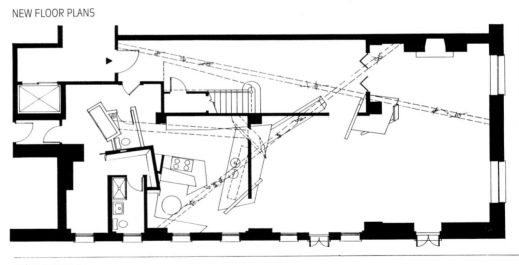

11th FLOOR PLAN

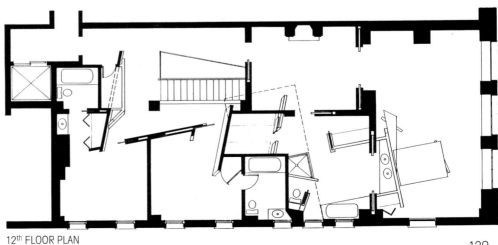

12th FLOOR PLAN

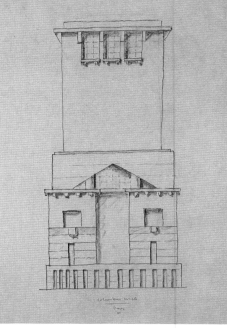

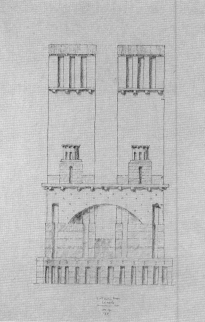

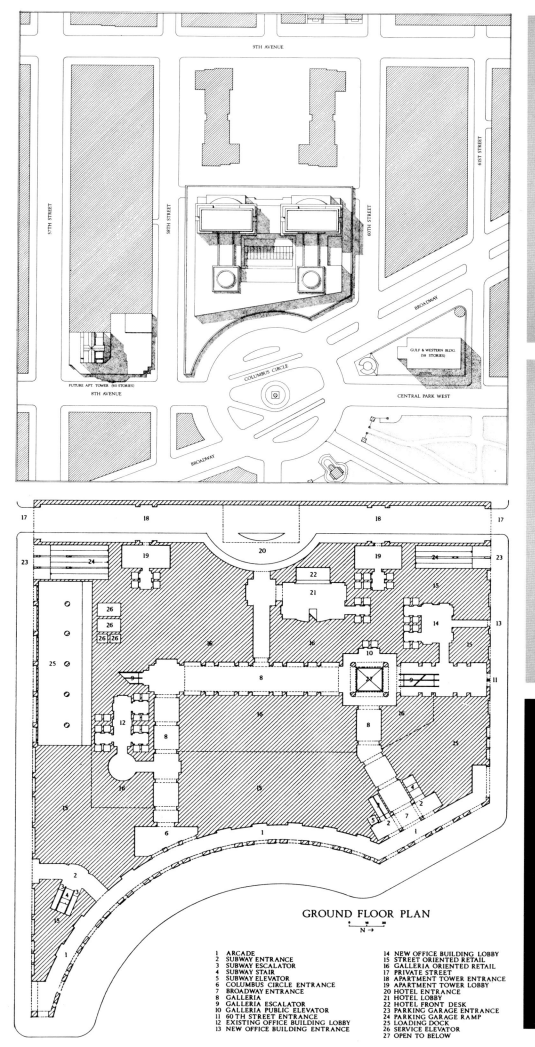

GROUND FLOOR PLAN

N →

1 ARCADE
2 SUBWAY ENTRANCE
3 SUBWAY ESCALATOR
4 SUBWAY STAIR
5 SUBWAY ELEVATOR
6 COLUMBUS CIRCLE ENTRANCE
7 BROADWAY ENTRANCE
8 GALLERIA
9 GALLERIA ESCALATOR
10 GALLERIA PUBLIC ELEVATOR
11 60 TH STREET ENTRANCE
12 EXISTING OFFICE BUILDING LOBBY
13 NEW OFFICE BUILDING ENTRANCE

14 NEW OFFICE BUILDING LOBBY
15 STREET ORIENTED RETAIL
16 GALLERIA ORIENTED RETAIL
17 PRIVATE STREET
18 APARTMENT TOWER ENTRANCE
19 APARTMENT TOWER LOBBY
20 HOTEL ENTRANCE
21 HOTEL LOBBY
22 HOTEL FRONT DESK
23 PARKING GARAGE ENTRANCE
24 PARKING GARAGE RAMP
25 LOADING DOCK
26 SERVICE ELEVATOR
27 OPEN TO BELOW

Michael Graves
with the Gruzen Partnership

THE COLUMBUS CIRCLE PROJECT   [22]

Columbus Circle, New York, NY
Competition, 1985

In 1985, as a result of the imminent completion of a major convention center in New York, the City offered the site of the existing Coliseum for sale to developers. Interested developers were asked to submit not only their bids and programs of use but also architectural designs. The Graves scheme, designed in conjunction with the Gruzen Partnership, proposes a large mixed-use development of the site, including major retail space at the base, offices and a hotel at the middle level, and apartments in the two high-rise towers. Total area is approximately 2,300,000 square feet.

The tripartite division of the building both articulates its various uses and helps integrate the building into the surrounding urban context. The building's base reinforces the curve of Columbus Circle and is similar in height to neighboring structures. The twin apartment towers, though larger in size, make symbolic reference to many of the West Side residential buildings facing Central Park. Major retail outlets, restaurants, places of entertainment, and related activities are located in the base of the building to bring new life to this neighborhood and to continue the urban pattern already established in the nearby Lincoln Center district.

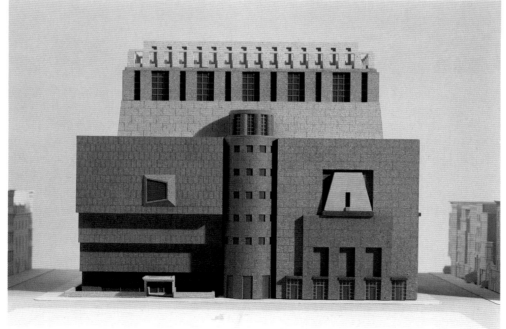

Michael Graves

WHITNEY MUSEUM OF AMERICAN ART [56]

Madison Avenue/East 75th Street, New York, NY
Project, 1985–1988

The Whitney Museum of American Art, located at the corner of Madison Avenue and East 75th Street, occupies a building designed by Marcel Breuer. The museum is planning to expand its building southward along Madison Avenue to East 74th Street. The site is located within the Upper East Side Historic District and the Special Madison Avenue Preservation District and is therefore subject to special zoning requirements and design guidelines.

Stylistically, the Breuer building, a modern monument finished in dark gray unpolished granite, is in distinct contrast to its context of smaller scale and more elaborate facades. The particular design challenge of this project is therefore to accommodate the apparent contradictions of a modern aesthetic and figurative, traditional architecture. Further, in order to make the old and new sections legible as one museum, as required by the program, it is necessary to bind together the two halves of the building in plan and in elevation. The proposed designs unify the existing building and the addition by means of a central vertical cylinder ("hinge") between them and an upper level structure connecting them.

The program for the addition includes 31,600 square feet of new exhibition space for the permanent collection; a 250-seat theater for the museum's public education programs; an orientation gallery; a Works on Paper Study Center; an expanded library; and additional space for offices and services. As required by zoning guidelines, the expanded museum will also include commercial retail space on the ground floor along Madison Avenue. The theater will be located at the lower levels of the addition. Exhibition space will begin at the second floor level and continue through to the sixth floor. Offices will occupy the top two floors, and mechanical equipment will be located in a penthouse on the roof.

For the major planes of the exterior walls, Graves chose a gray red agate granite whose tonality and veining are similar to the gray granite of the existing building. Stone of this color harmonizes with Breuer's material and yet remains distinct so as not to diminish either the proportions or the object quality of the existing building. The new color also harmonizes with the brownstone and brick colorations of other buildings in the neighborhood. The same gray red agate is used throughout the facade in different cuts and finishes which allow distinctions among the different elements of the composition.

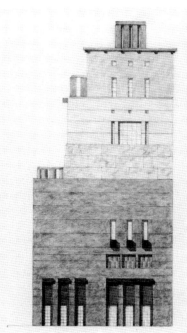

985

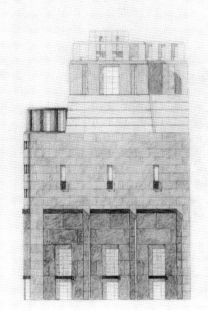

987

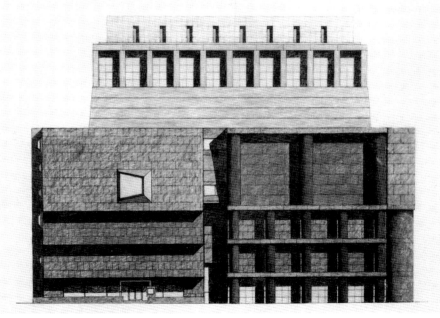

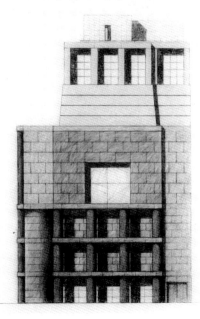

988

Gwathmey Siegel
& Associates Architects

INTERNATIONAL DESIGN CENTER [67]
Thomson Avenue, Queens, New York, NY
1984 (Center II) and 1985 (Center I)
Design Team: Bruce Donnally, Stephen Lepp
Associates, P. C. Architects

The IDC NY complex is located in Long Island City. It consists of four adjacent buildings, all built during World War I, which lie near the foot of the Queensboro Bridge exit roadway. Together, these buildings provide 2,000,000 square feet of space for the interior furnishings industry in the form of new showrooms, design studios, and restaurants, as well as three major spaces for multi-use audio-visual exhibitions and productions. Centers I and II have been completely converted; Centers III and IV await conversion.

Centers I, II, and III originally had their main entrances on Thomson Avenue at the north side of the complex. These entrances have been retained, but the buildings' main entrances have been relocated and oriented to the plaza south of Center II. This plaza is the focus for IDC NY, and will later become a landscaped park.

Since the site of the plaza was once intended to receive an addition to the Center II building, the south facade was never finished with the brick and terra-cotta veneer that the three street facades received. In the conversion this facade was resurfaced in stucco and, with the

addition of a new catwalk beam for lighting and banner display, designed as the ceremonial gateway to the complex.

Center II was the first completed conversion. Like the other two buildings, it is constructed wholly of cast-in-place concrete floors and columns. Its eight typical floors and roof-top penthouse wrap in a U-shaped configuration around an open court. A trussed bridge spans the two long sides and creates the two major spaces of the building: A 50 × 125 × 120-foot-high interior atrium, and a 50 × 75 × 120-foot-high open court behind the south facade.

Extending from this open court through the "gateway" is a glass barrel-vaulted skylight which serves as an entrance canopy and a transparent ceiling for the new south lobby. A new ten-story elevator tower, attached to the trussed bridge, catches the skylight and rises from the lobby floor up through the open court.

The interior atrium is the focal space of Center II. Though originally open to the sky, it has been covered with a series of ridged translucent plastic skylights and its rough concrete piers and spandrels replaced in gypsum board. On each floor a nine-foot-wide balcony/corridor circles the atrium and provides access to all the showrooms.

The translucent plastic panel system used in the atrium skylights has also been used to replace the original single-glazed steel frame windows in the exterior walls.

Center I was completed shortly after Center II. Its basic organization is the same – a skylit central atrium surrounded by showrooms – but its dimensional configuration and orientation to the plaza required different solutions.

The atrium in Center I is lower and much longer than the one in Center II. The conversion takes advantage of the space's great length by floating the elevator core in its center and running a cascading steel staircase down the west side of each half. These stairs and elevators connect the perimeter balcony/corridor system which rings the atrium. A barrel-vaulted skylight built of the same materials as the skylight in Center II runs along the entire length of the space.

A new arcade has been recessed into the west facade of the building corresponding to the length of the plaza across the street. The new main entrance is located in this arcade.

As far as possible the existing materials of these buildings have been restored so that the original industrial character can be preserved. New building colors were deliberately chosen in light, neutral tones to accentuate the drama of the showrooms and building signage.

The pedestrian bridge over 30th Place links the third, fourth, and fifth floors of Center I and Center II. Its trapezoidal shape is determined by the different floor elevations which the three ramps connect. It is sheathed in corrugated aluminum siding painted in the bridge red-orange used throughout the IDC graphics. Two large gridded circular windows centered over the street visually anchor the dynamic composition between the two buildings.

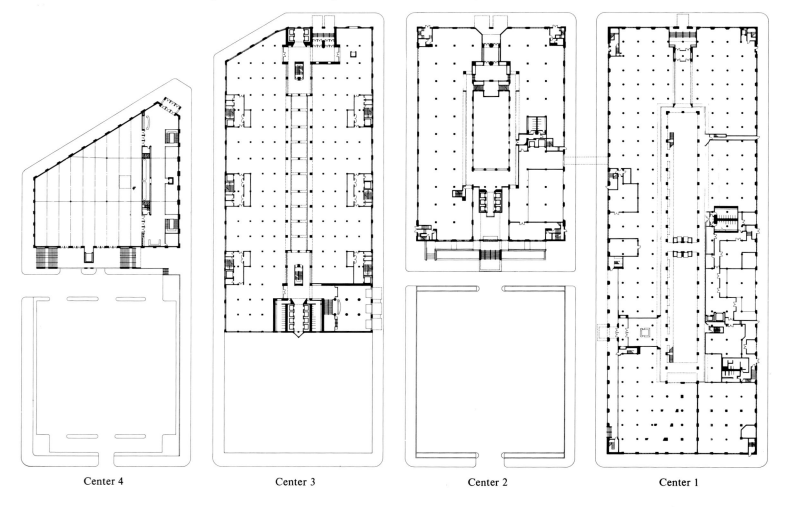

Center 4   Center 3   Center 2   Center 1

Gwathmey Siegel
& Associates Architects

SOLOMON EQUITIES, INC.   [35]

1585 Broadway, New York, NY, 1989
Design Team: Gerald Gendreau, Bruce Donnally,
Emery Roth & Sons, P.C.

This new 1,400,000-square-foot, forty-two-story office building occupies the entire westerly blockfront of Broadway between 47th and 48th Streets.

The curtain wall is an assemblage of blue-green glass, etched glass, mirror glass, silver-gray aluminum panels, and polished stainless steel.

The design presents a modulated stepped base, which relates to both the pedestrian scale at the street and a representative "public building" image; a transitional middle; and an extended articulated top – all within the ethic of a modern skyscraper that has a compelling silhouette, a dynamic graphic, and a multiple scale presence.

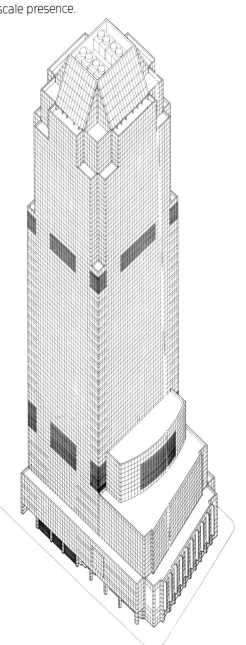

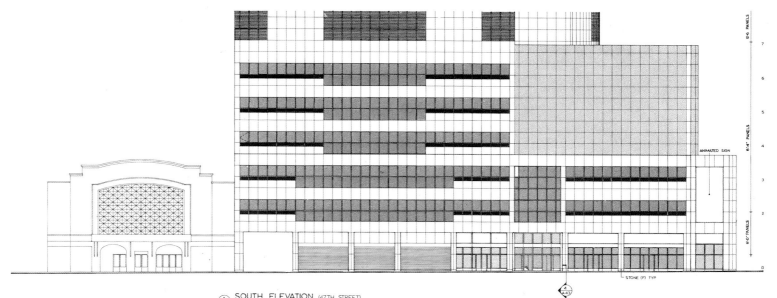

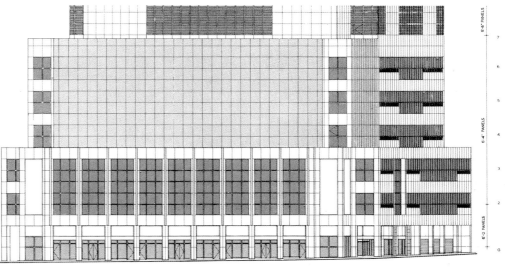

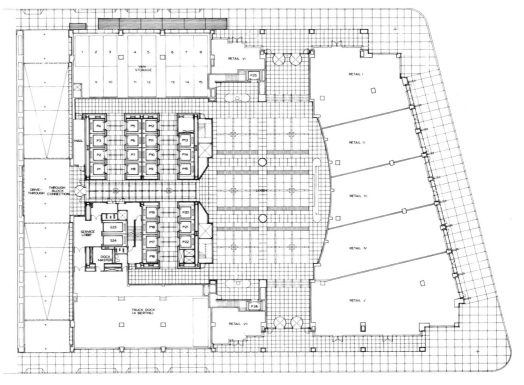

1 SOUTH ELEVATION (47TH STREET)
A-24 1/16"=1'-0"

2 EAST ELEVATION (BROADWAY)
A-24 1/16"=1'-0"

GROUND LEVEL
1/16"=1'-0"

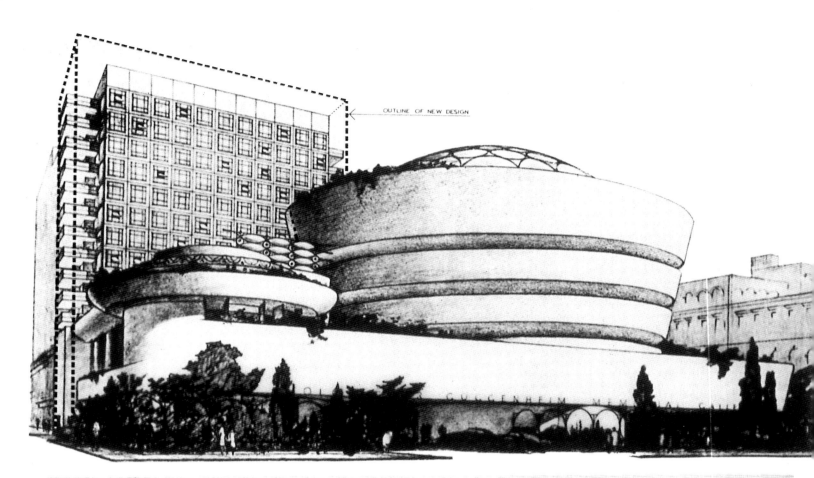

OUTLINE OF NEW DESIGN

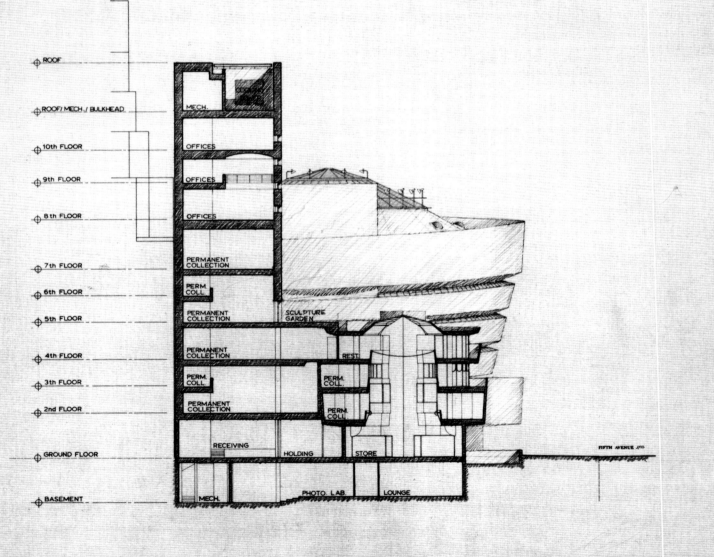

ROOF

ROOF/MECH./BULKHEAD

10th FLOOR

9th FLOOR

8th FLOOR

7th FLOOR

6th FLOOR

5th FLOOR

4th FLOOR

3th FLOOR

2nd FLOOR

GROUND FLOOR

BASEMENT

MECH.

OFFICES

OFFICES

OFFICES

PERMANENT COLLECTION

PERM. COLL.

PERMANENT COLLECTION

PERMANENT COLLECTION

PERM. COLL.

PERMANENT COLLECTION

SCULPTURE GARDEN

PERM. COLL.

PERM. COLL.

REST

RECEIVING

HOLDING

STORE

FIFTH AVENUE

MECH.

PHOTO. LAB

LOUNGE

SECTION THRU SMALL ROTONDA LOOKING SOUTH

Gwathmey Siegel
& Associates Architects

THE GUGGENHEIM MUSEUM ADDITION   [58]

Fifth Avenue/East 89th Street, New York, NY
Project, 1988
Design Team: Jacob Alspector, Pierre
Cantacuzene

The addition to The Guggenheim Museum refers directly to both Frank Lloyd Wright's proposed annex of 1949–1952 and William Wesley Peters' existing annex, which was orginally designed as a ten-story structure. History and precedents were regarded as primary factors in the proposed design.

The Wright design for the annex (see illustration top left) was intended to present a background facade, thus integrating the objectness of the original structure into the context of the Manhattan grid. The abstract, orthogonally gridded concrete and glass curtain wall was rendered as a referential plane in counterpoint to the dynamic, curvilinear forms of the original museum.

The entire original structure through the fourth floor of the small rotunda, the existing annex, and the proposed fifth and seventh floor double-height galleries will be devoted to new exhibition space. At the fifth floor, the existing annex columns will be extended vertically to accommodate the addition, which is primarily solid. The major exterior material is limestone, chosen for its immediate and historical contextual references to Fifth Avenue and adjacent

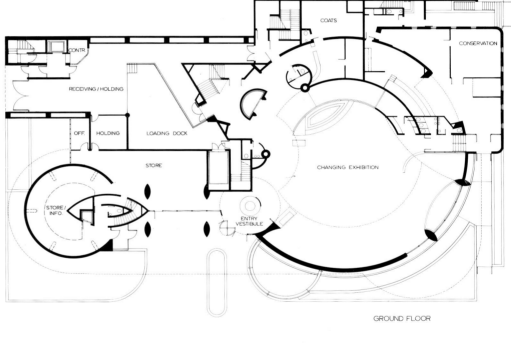

GROUND FLOOR

Fifth Avenue

neighborhood buildings as well as for its sympathetic neutrality and color in relation to the original structure.

The expanded exhibition space, which would include the heretofore inaccessible seventh level ramp of the large rotunda, would make it possible, for the first time, to offer a continuously integrated and accessible series of exhibition spaces within the original structure, the existing annex, and the new addition. The public would experience the entire interior of the Frank Lloyd Wright building as well as new revealing exterior views of both the building and the park

from the proposed new sculpture roof terrace at the fifth floor.

The proposed addition addresses the context of 89th Street and the general neighborhood fabric, in both scale and materiality, while allowing a positive yet subtle mediation and transition to the original structure. The west facade, articulated as an edge on 89th Street, becomes the neutral gridded plane on Fifth Avenue, presenting the original building as an object in space, while also giving it for the first time a background of intentional and contextual response.

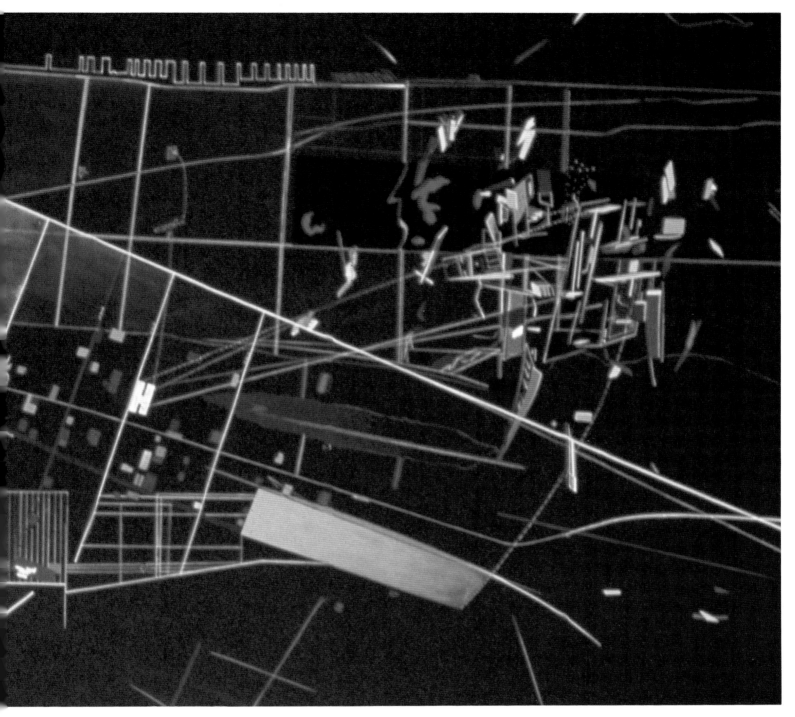

Zaha Hadid

A NEW CALLIGRAPHY OF THE PLAN

New York, NY, Project, 1988

An architectural response to the works, or rather, to one particular work of Le Corbusier, and an attempt to do something that related to it posed certain difficulties. The works of Le Corbusier have had a relatively small direct and conscious influence.

We would rather say that the works of Oscar Niemeyer, as being indirectly influenced by the Corbusian Principles, were more relevant. Subsequently, the direct effect has to do with a new calligraphy of the plan with the fundamental difference being the approach to, or reaction to, modern urban principles.

The sketch chosen for this project was a Christmas card of New York City made by Le Corbusier. His Ville Radieuse for Manhattan illustrates what is fundamentally a misjudgment of the urban conditions of New York. Corbusier erodes the existing Manhattan fabric only to replace it with a carpet of bland modernism.

Manhattan relies on the cultural layering of the city, which is further intensified by its congestion. The new Manhattan injections must be specific, condensed explosions.

The present sketch relates to a recent project proposal for the reconstruction of a hotel in New York City. The polemic is of a series of explosions occuring within the confined space, but with an intensity that implies a new way of living; a re-definition of the "hotel" and "metropolitan living".

This particular intervention outlines floor-by-floor proposals and variations to the hotel as it could exist in New York. Conceptually, the random pattern of activities is intended to intensify further the explosions or actions as they occur throughout the urban grid.

Through this very specific series of explosions, there exists the possibility of continuing the metropolitan urban intensity without eroding the existing fabric. This is the theory which we propose and which we present as a new calligraphy for the plan.

Hardy Holzman Pfeiffer Associates

FIREMEN'S TRAINING CENTER   [65]
Ward's Island, New York, NY, 1975

Program: Master Plan for a training complex to include education/administration building and eight training/service facilities with supplementary site development on landfill acres on Ward's Island, New York.

The Firemen's Training Center serves as academic and physical training facility for all New York City firemen. Three specific activity areas accommodate the Center's varied programs: Physical Training, Service, and Education/Administration. Physical Training facilities include Fire Tower, Basic Training Building, and Advanced Training Group. The Advanced Training Group is a row of "practice" buildings – replicas of a loft building, a tenement, and a frame dwelling – designed to be repeatedly burned. Service facilities include Mask Service Unit, combined Firehouse-Marina Facility, and

Garage. Because of their function and requirement for low maintenance, Training and Service Buildings are simple concrete structures faced with brick. All are patterned with horizontal stripes. The buildings are set within a hard-surfaced training strip along a common spine. This spine is defined by a major access road and 12-foot-high earth berm which isolates the Education/Administration Building from the noisy activities of Physical Training and Service Facilities.

The Education/Administration Building is metal clad, 365 feet long with a steeply sloped roof which merges into a landscaped earth berm on the south side. It rises to a height of several stories on the north. The north wall has two contrasting fenestration patterns which animate its large northern expanse. Trainees enter the building through five corrugated steel culverts which diagonally intersect the earth berm. Public entry is through a vestibule adapted from a water storage tank.

Inside the Education/Administration Building classrooms are windowless rectilinear boxes (requested by the client to limit distraction and ensure concentration), organized along diagonal corridors. This placement of rotated volumes within the sloped enclosure defines a variegated open space the length of the building. An open mezzanine housing administration areas opens into this space, partially enclosing areas below. Along the length of this large volume are arranged a library, lunchroom, firemen's store, orientation and exhibition areas. (It can also accommodate training functions during inclement weather.) The bright colors and exposed mechanical equipment complement this lively and varied interior.

Hardy Holzman Pfeiffer Associates

BROOKLYN CHILDREN'S MUSEUM   [68]

Brooklyn, New York, NY, 1977

Program: A new facility, set in an urban park, for the nation's oldest children's museum, using an open-plan participatory learning environment.

The Brooklyn Children's Museum is buried forty feet below grade (with one exposed corner) so that the adjoining Brower Park extends across its roof. A playground and open-air theater, together with an assemblage of elements from industry, transportation, and agriculture, are also part of its exterior. An interstate highway sign announces the building's location; a highway pedestrian bridge spans the courtyard and links the rooftop play area with Brower Park; a grain silo serves as fire exit; both traditional park benches and I-beam sections provide seating; and a 1907 Queensboro Bridge train kiosk becomes its entry pavilion.

Inside, the museum is bisected diagonally by the main circulation route, a 180-foot-long series of corrugated steel culverts, which descends from the entry kiosk to an enclosed courtyard on the lowest level. This "People Tube," glowing with a spiral neon rainbow, has a stream flowing down one side and is broken into sections so that each segment opens onto one of four exhibition levels.

Emphasis throughout the museum concerns a "hands-on" learning process, and exhibits are designed so that children can participate in scientific experiments involving 500 of the 20,000 objects in the museum's collection. Workshops, resource library, dance studio, photography studio and darkroom, and a marketplace provide additional learning opportunities. A former gasoline storage tank encloses a semicircular auditorium on the lowest level. Perhaps the most unusual exhibit is a giant clear plastic model of a protein molecule which children can climb through in a variety of ways.

Hardy Holzman Pfeiffer Associates

BRYANT PARK RESTAURANTS   [41]

Bryant Park, Avenue of the Americas between
42nd and 41st Street, New York, NY, 1988–1991
Design Team: Hugh Hardy, Malcolm Holzman,
Norman Pfeiffer, Victor Gorg, Rafael Peli, Evan
Carzis.

Bryant Park is one of the few true public squares in New York City. To preserve and revitalize this Beaux-Arts Square, the comprehensive program combines construction of two restaurant pavilions and four kiosks with basic landscape alterations to increase public access to the Park and, simultaneously, to preserve its best features. With the project's completion, the park's potential as a first-rate urban amenity, a source of rest and inspiration, and a hub of cultural and educational activity should be fully realized.

Project Description: The overall design character of the restaurant pavilions takes its inspiration from the decorative tradition of Parisian parks. Based upon layers of enclosure which integrate these buildings with the park, the two 5,250-square-foot structures flank the monument to William Cullen Bryant on the west terrace of the New York Public Library. Each pavilion has an inner layer of glass and steel surrounded by an outer layer of wood trellis-work covered with vines, which will change seasonally in their color and mass. Ground level planting and the weathered wood of the trellis both soften and enliven the pavilions, integrating them with the surrounding landscape. The trellis is composed of patterned columns, set on cast stone bases which support a paneled frieze of lattices. The pavilions are eighteen feet high and seat approximately 175 people each. Identical on the outside, each restaurant will have a different character on the inside, and each will serve different types of food. Operable French doors and windows on both structures are adjustable and create opportunities for open-air dining in warm weather or enclosed dining in cooler months.

Steven Holl Architects

SHOWROOM FOR THE PACE COLLECTION   [54]

888 Madison Avenue, New York, NY, 1986

The site for the Pace Collection showroom is an existing two-story limestone structure with the corner of the building sliced back. A new foundation at the edge of the urban grid was set for the new showroom, completing the corner with a steel-mullioned window affording the maximum showroom glass.

An idea of counterpoint characterizes the essentially linear architecture. Small sandblasted amber glass panels are set against the horizontal steel bars of the main mullions. Along 72nd Street the bars are predominantly horizontal, while along Madison they are predominantly vertical. The sandblasted glass drawings carry the contrapuntal idea to the detail scale. Along Madison Avenue these drawings are in lines, while the 72nd Street facade shows the same drawings extruded into planes. It is as if the shop itself were a block of wood with end grain and edge grain differentiation. The awning is a curve against the straight lines of the mullions. Inside, the idea is carried further in the guardrailing, where a curve fuses against simple horizontal bars, dislocating them vertically to miss connecting along the curve. The ceiling is a free arrangement of rectangular voids (containing lighting and A. C.) set against the flat horizontal plane.

The main interior wall is integral color green plaster of a fresco-like quality with blued steel shelves (exhibiting scale models of the furniture) which carry out the dialogue of planes set perpendicular to the wall surface.

Steven Holl Architects

GIADA [55]
(Shop selling ladies' fashion)

904 Madison Avenue, New York, NY, 1987

The site is on a very busy section of Madison Avenue, midblock betwen 72nd and 73rd Street. The 14 × 30-foot shop is both compressed and oppressed by the large building above.

Concept: To express this compression on the exterior with slightly bulging elements in glass: a pushed-out corner transferring to the shop front, a dense cast-glass bulge, a bulging awning, and so on. The interior concept is to relieve this compression.

Exterior materials express the "densification" of the idea in a rough-finished cast-glass window joint alongside a two-inch-round glass bar joint which sits on a three-inch slab of glass. The brass plates which contain and define the front are acid-etched to a dull red with flathead and roundheaded screws spaced according to conceptual pressure. Brass plates are doubled in the area containing a large vertical glass bulge. Everything is organized according to a logarithmic spiral of proportional relations from exterior to interior.

Interior materials include terrazzo in a cloud-like hand-sprinkled form to enhance the "floating" floor, brass and bronze wire screen for tiny light fixtures in light frames which protrude and recede into ceiling openings, and light ash doors to the changing rooms. Not recognizable as conventional "doors," there are L-shaped sections and an "interfingering" door. The toilet area contains light-weight spun-aluminum cones as sinks.

An eight-inch void below the floating floor was utilized, with pockets and trap doors opening up for various exhibiting devices and occasional customer's seats.

Steven Holl Architects

FIFTH AVENUE APARTMENT [52]

Fifth Avenue/East 69th Street, New York, NY,
1983 –1984

Design Team: Steven Holl with Mark Janson and
Joseph Fenton

The renovation of an L-shaped apartment is an investigation of elemental architectural composition in three modes: the linear, the planar, and the volumetric.

The dining area is in a linear mode: a linear chandolier is made of three types of lines; a linear table with four linear chairs sits on a carpet patterned with all types of lines.

The living area is in a volumetric mode with stuffed cylindrical sofa cushions, a volumetric coffee table, and a volumetric carpet.

The studio and bedroom are in the planar mode with a planar drawing board, planes of walls that unfold to become doors, and a carpet with woven planar elements. An L-shaped wall dividing the apartment from the entrance foyer records this investigation in a progression of sandblasted glass drawings that repeat these modes.

Steven Holl Architects

MOMA TOWER APARTMENT　[31]

11 West 53rd Street, New York, NY, 1987–1988

The interior renovation and design of fixtures and furniture began with a simple concept arrived at during the first encounter with the Manhattan site. The apartment tower rises directly up from its lot line, intensifying the experience of the Manhattan grid. Standing in the front corner window, the N-S and E-W geometry ("X" and "Y" directions) of the urban perspectives outside are particularly emphasized by the vanishing point in the vertical "Z" dimension. (From here the tower appears to be leaning out over 53rd Street.)

This experience inspired the organization of all the elements in the apartment according to a lyrical illumination of the X, Y, and Z directions.

Plaster walls in the X direction are charcoal black integral color, while plaster walls in the Y direction are yellow. The Z dimension is emphasized in a long narrow corner lamp at the entrance, in an intersected pole lamp near the main corner window, and in linear verticals in the furniture. Three wool carpets were fabricated for the apartment, one based on the X, one on the Y, and one on the Z dimension. Furniture especially designed for the apartment includes a dining table in which the X Y Z dimension is emphasized at its steel center, while its edges are vaguely free form.

The elements present the original idea in a variety of ways – literal, poetic, systematic, intuitive. Seen together, they do not become a collection of more or less equivalent examples; the differences in means prevent this. Their association is less didactic and more mysterious; the elements serve to form a ground for each other. Only in this indirect way does the original X Y Z idea prepare a relation between the parts.

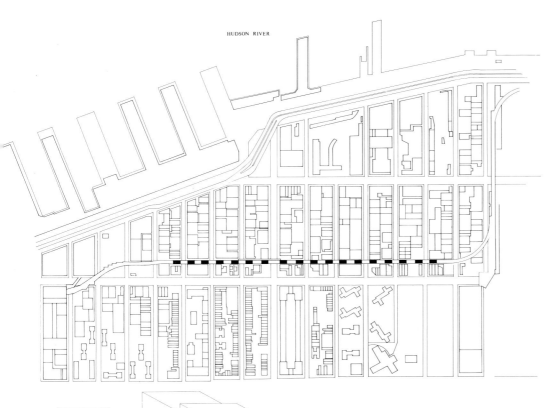

HUDSON RIVER

Steven Holl Architects

BRIDGE OF HOUSES [17]

West 19th – West 29th Street, New York, NY
Project, 1981
Design Team: Steven Holl, Mark Janson, James
Rosen, Joseph Fenton, Susan Powadiuk

The site and structural foundation of the Bridge
of Houses is the existing superstructure of an
abandoned elevated rail link in the Chelsea area
of New York City. This steel structure is utilized in
its straight leg from West 19th Street to West
29th Street parallel to the Hudson River.

With the decline of shipping activity on the
west pierfront, the vacant warehouse buildings
are now being converted to residential lofts.

This project offers a variety of housing types
for the Chelsea area, as well as an elevated
public promenade connecting with the new
Jacob Javits Convention Center (see page 126)
on its north end. Height and width of the houses
is determined by the structural capacity and
width of the existing bridge.

Four houses have been developed in detail,
emphasizing the intention to provide a collection of housing blocks offering the widest possible range of social-economic coexistence. On
one extreme there would be houses of single
room occupancy type (SRO), offered for the
city's homeless. Each of these blocks would
contain twenty studio rooms. On the other
extreme, some of the houses would be luxury
apartments. Each one of these blocks would
contain three or four flats. Shops line the public
promenade below the houses.

The new houses would be built in an alternating pattern with a series of 2 000-square-foot
courtyards – 50% open space. All new houses

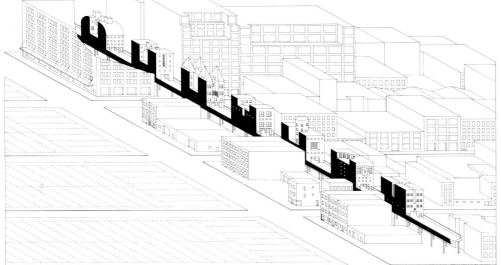

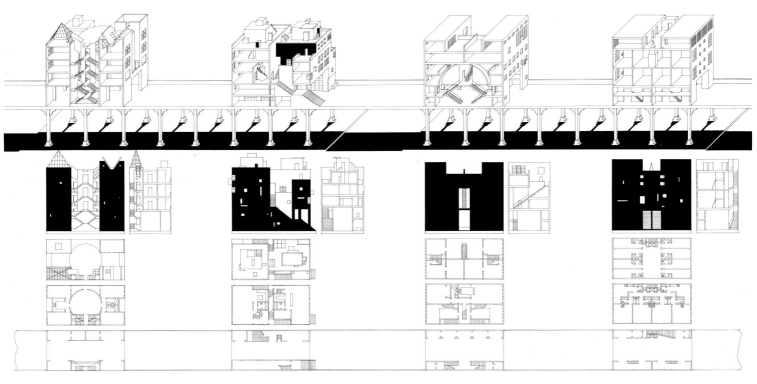

would be built to align with the existing block front at the street walls, reinforcing the street pattern. The ornamental portions of the rail bridge over the streets remain open.

Construction Statistics:

Floor area: 18 houses of 146,500 square feet, built in an alternating pattern with 172,000 square feet of exterior courtyards.

Structure: lightweight metal frame construction, sheet metal stud wall partitions, six-inch blanket fiberglass insulated walls.

Floors: lightweight concrete on metal decking. Fiberglass blanket sound insulation.

Windows: insulated glass, aluminum frames, baked enamel finish.

Roofs: built-up roofing, wire glass skylights.

Exterior: reinforced exterior rendering on wire lath. Acid stained metal panels.

Doors: solid core wood, sandblasted glass drawings at entrance doors, brass lever handles.

Arata Isozaki & Associates with James Stewart Polshek and Partners

BROOKLYN MUSEUM [73]
Master Plan and Renovation

188 Eastern Parkway, Brooklyn. New York, NY
Competition, 1988 –1990
Design Team: Arata Isozaki, James Stewart Polshek

The master plan for the addition of 320,000 square feet to the Brooklyn Museum and the renovation of the existing builcing was selected in an international competition. A new plaza, around which the new galleries, auditorium, education wing, and restaurant facilities are organized, contains outdoor performance spaces and exhibition areas overlooking the Brooklyn Botanic Gardens. A fundamental ingredient of the scheme is the rationalization of circulation, which separates services, scholars, individual visitors, and educational groups. Further, the design solution re-establishes pedestrian connections to the adjacent, but at present inaccessible, Brooklyn Botanic Gardens. The unfinished rear facade of the existing building will be unified by a modern architectural vocabulary defined by a flush limestone grid and sandblasted stainless steel infill panels. Parking for 1,000 cars and all loading and art storage facilities are located under the new addition.

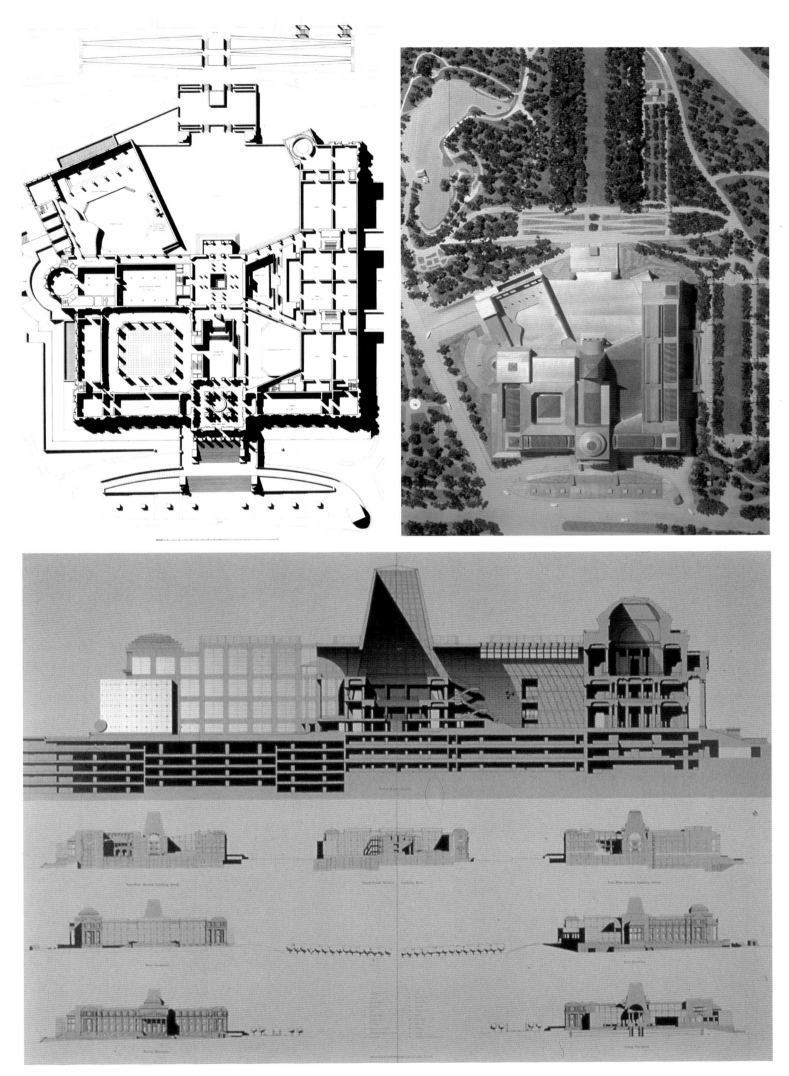

155

Helmuth Jahn
Murphy/Jahn

THE COLUMBUS CIRCLE PROJECT [23]

10 Columbus Circle, New York, NY
Competition, 1985

Ten Columbus Circle occupies a 150,000-square-foot site at Columbus Circle between 58th and 60th Streets, which is currently occupied by the New York Coliseum. The project is envisaged as a multi-use complex of office, hotel, and residential spaces totalling approximately 2.64 million square feet of new construction. Typologically, the complex is composed of two elements: (I) the base structure, which will reinforce the Columbus Circle geometry and establish the inner plaza, (II) the tower structure, which at 1,275 feet in height will be a recognizable image on the Manhattan skyline.

The tower is conceived of as a segmented hollow octagonal tube raised 100 feet above grade. A 230-foot-high slot is provided to reinforce the 59th Street view corridor that was previously vacated at this site. The first fifteen floors, with a width of 105 feet, provide approximately 1,156,675 square feet of office space with floor sizes of approximately 29,700 square feet and 23,700 square feet. The upper floors of this segment are bridged together to provide approximately 58,500-square-foot floors. The tower then sets back thirty feet at the skylobby level, 300 feet above grade. This level houses the main residential and hotel lobbies. The remainder of the tower will be comprised of approximately 550,000 square feet of hotel space and approximately 938,000 square feet of residential space. This portion of the tower terraces up in a spiralling configuration from the north-east to the south-east providing commanding views of Central Park and the Hudson River. The residential character of the tower is further enhanced by the use of balconies at the building's perimeter.

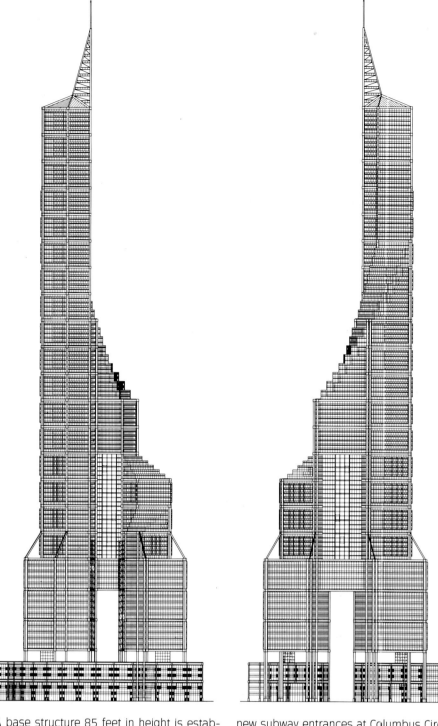

A base structure 85 feet in height is established at grade and contains retail space and new subway entrances at Columbus Circle and Broadway. Office and residential entries are located at 58th Street with additional office and hotel entries at 60th Street. Five floors of loft type office space are also provided.

The building is modulated into six-story increments by expressing the structure at these points. The glass skin of the office tower is treated in an abstract way by using a simple grid, thereby relating to the nature of office space as bulk space. Individual balconies are used for the hotel to create the next level of texture which expresses the individuality of the hotel's rooms. The residential portion utilizes full-length balconies in order to express the larger nature of the units. The base structure is treated as a highly ornamented building in itself, utilizing stone and glass as infill materials within a structural expression on a scale smaller than that of the tower.

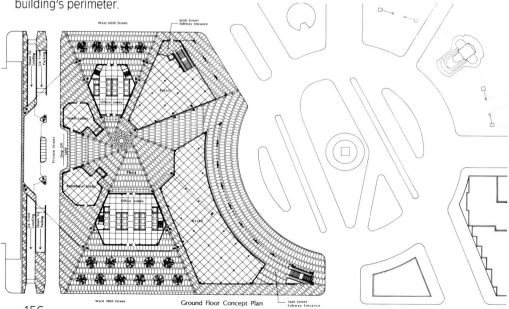

Ground Floor Concept Plan

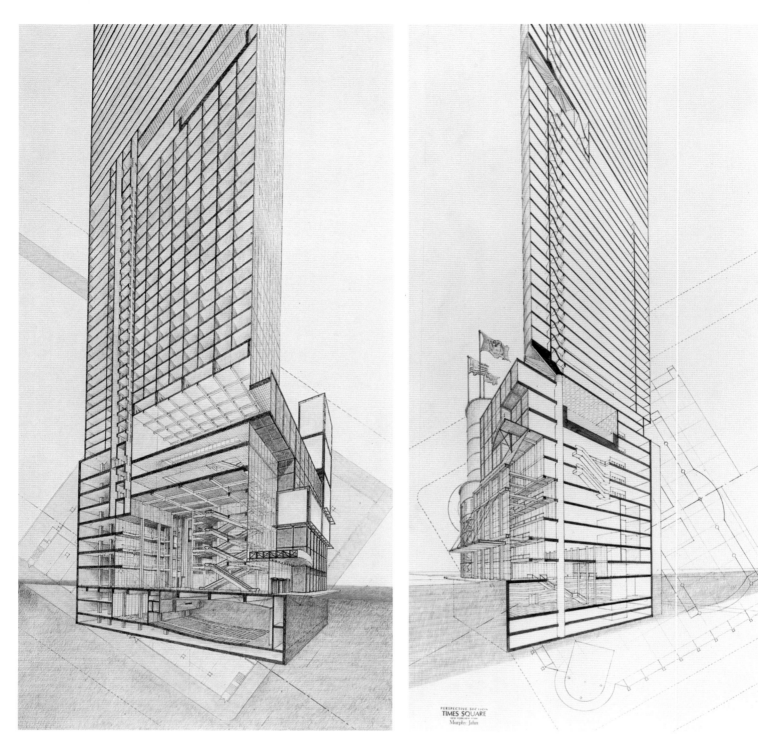

PERSPECTIVE SECTION
TIMES SQUARE
NEW YORK CITY
Murphy/Jahn

Helmut Jahn
Murphy/Jahn

TIMES SQUARE [37]

Times Square, New York, NY
Project, 1985

The Times Square Project is seen as a building embodying the essential vitality of America's premiere urban space. The building's base acts contextually to maintain the uniform street wall height of existing buildings on the square. The tower, asymmetrical and setback, penetrates the base retail and hotel function floors to form the major Broadway retail entry. Abundant, con-

trolled exterior signage serves to decorate and animate both the building and the square in keeping with a major tradition of the neon glitz of Times Square.

The mixed-use nature of this building further serves to enhance and enliven the square. Theaters, retail space, hotel, and residential functions maintain the presence of people and activities consistent with the nature of Times Square.

This building contains a total of 900,000 square feet on 58 floors. Four, 600-seat theaters occupy the first level below grade. Entry to the theaters is via the atrium which serves as the focal space for five floors, 125,000 square feet, of retail space. The galleria connects 45th Street, 46th Street, and Broadway Avenue. 437,000 square feet of hotel space is entered

from 45th Street off Broadway. The two-story ground floor lobby acts as a transition space to the three-story, 7,000-square-foot skylobby located on the 6th floor. Four hotel function floors, containing restaurants, meeting rooms, and ballrooms, occur at and above the lobby level. The asymmetrical tower placement allows for a long span ballroom and meeting spaces. Twenty floors with thirty rooms per floor provide 600 hotel bedrooms. The shared health club at the 32nd floor separates the 287,000 square-foot residential portion of the project from the hotel below.

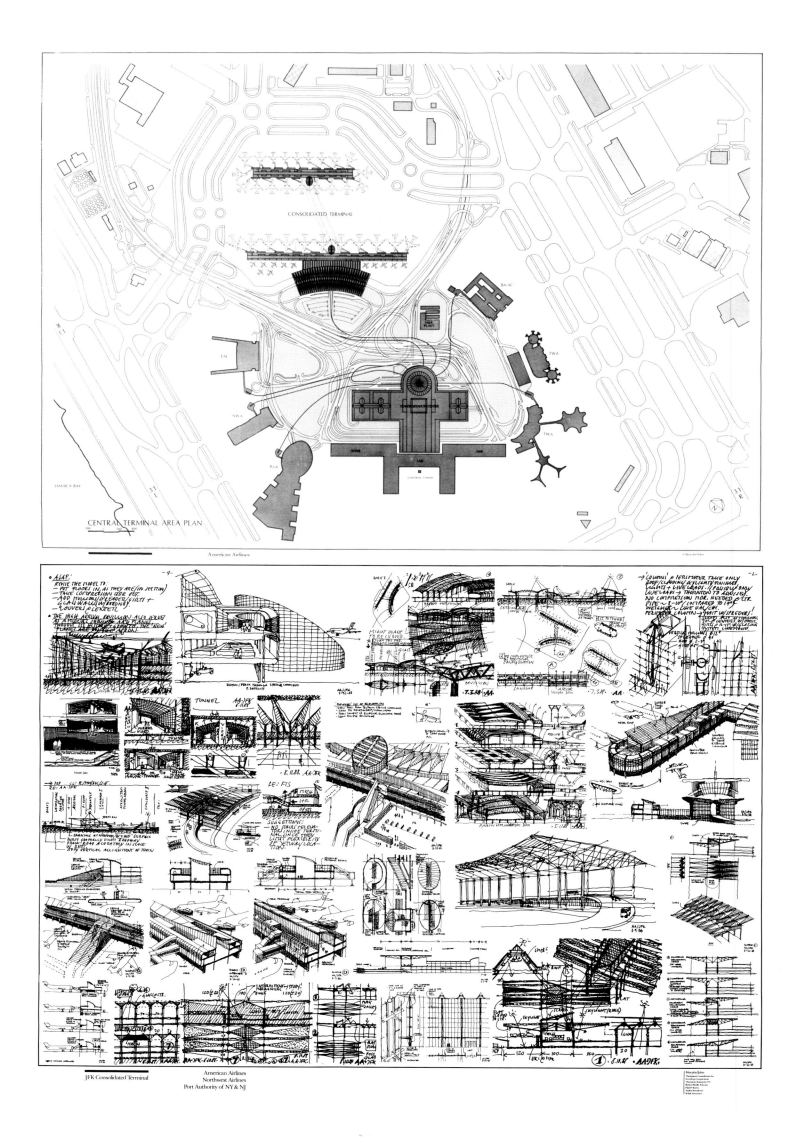

CENTRAL TERMINAL AREA PLAN

American Airlines

JFK Consolidated Terminal

American Airlines
Northwest Airlines
Port Authority of NY & NJ

Helmut Jahn
Murphy/Jahn

CONSOLIDATED TERMINAL FOR AMERICAN AIR-
LINES AND NORTHWEST AIRLINES   [76]

JFK Airport, New York, NY
Competition, 1988

The terminal is a four-level structure with (1) the lower level containing all Federal inspection services areas, domestic claim areas, mechanical/electrical space and a large meeters/greeters lobby for the arriving passengers; (2) the grade level containing both inbound and outbound baggage systems, the PDS station, and mechanical space and ramp operations; (3) the upper level containing ticketing, gate facilities, VIP lounges, and the enplaning curbfront; (4) the penthouse level containing the FIS arrivals corridor and mechanical fan rooms.

The satellite concourse is configured as a three-level structure with (1) the grade level containing ramp operations and mechanical/electrical rooms, (2) the upper level containing gate facilities and concessions, and (3) the penthouse level with FIS arrival corridors and mechanical fan rooms. All passengers will reach the aircraft by a system of shallow (1:12) ramps which connect the loading bridges to the upper-level boarding areas and the penthouse level FIS arrivals corridor.

Boarding passengers will arrive at the ticket lobby either by the PDS system, the pedestrian bridge from the parking structure, or the enplaning curbfront. The ticket lobby consists of two sides, both of which contain 425 feet of ticket counter. From the ticket counters passengers proceed through security to the adjacent terminal gates or down the escalators to the connector passageway to the satellite gates.

International arrivals at the satellite or terminal gates will proceed through the loading bridges and ramps to the penthouse level FIS corridor. This corridor will lead them to a central collecting atrium and down escalators to the lower level where they will enter the FIS processing area. Satellite arrivals will cross under the apron via moving walkways to reach the FIS.

Domestic arrivals will proceed down the ramp to the upper-level gate area and then proceed to the central atrium area to escalators taking them to the lower-level domestic baggage claim. Satellite arrivals will cross under the apron via moving walkways to the terminal lower level before arriving at domestic claim. After claiming baggage, passengers will proceed directly to the deplaning curb or go up one level to the pedestrian bridge to the parking structure. Passengers will also proceed up one level to the PDS station for transport to the central terminal complex to reach buses and limousines or to transfer to another terminal.

Helmut Jahn
Murphy/Jahn

425 Lexington Avenue, New York, NY, 1983–1988

The project site occupies the full block frontage between 43rd and 44th Streets along the eastern side of Lexington Avenue in midtown Manhattan. The site context consists of ten- to twenty-story, high density, institutional, commercial, and office developments. Their architectural character can be described as rectangular, setback, all-masonry or all-glass structures. A distinguished celebrity within this context is the Chrysler Building, situated directly across 43rd Street south of the project site. The formal, material, and symbolic features of this significant architectural presence had a decisive influence on the building's design concept.

The building contains 565,000 square feet in thirty office rental floors above one level of ground-floor commercial space. These floors range in size from 27,750 square feet in the base floors to 15,950 square feet in the twenty-three floors of the tower. Special tenant floors located at the 30th and 31st floors share a two-story atrium and contain 17,000 square feet and 13,900 square feet respectively. Two levels are below grade: Level C-1 provides valet parking for 100 cars and Level C-2 contains an additional 35,179 square feet of rental area.

This new development is subject to the recently mandated provisions of the Midtown Zoning Code, a crucial determinant of architectural form. Three interrelated sets of criteria governed the following design areas: building height and setbacks, retail and street wall continuity, and "bonusable" urban amenities such as plazas.

The overall building typology is an innovative variation on the theme of an "architectural column." Conceived as a refined symmetrical architectonic mass, the base creates a suitable foundation for the "column image." The height of its street facades is dictated by the provisions above, while the recessed chamfered corners reflect precisely the dimensions required for street wall continuity.

The plan of the tower is a 119 × 139-foot rectangle having strongly chamfered corners. Rising from the stepped and similarly chamfered base, the shaft leaves a street wall reinforcing context to emerge gradually as a freestanding, omni-directional form. Vertical accentuation of the skin emphasizes its twenty-three stories, a height which relates compatibly with the base of the Chrysler building.

The tower form does not attempt to compete with the pyramidal spire of the Chrysler Building. The top, like the capital of a column, hovers over the shaft and base and, in a contrasting gesture, flares outward at the height at which the Chrysler tower steps inward.

A manneristic palette of reflective and textured glass types, half-round and triangular projecting mullions, and accent surfaces of granite, marble, and limestone is used for the exterior architectural design. In detail, textured glass bands divide the elevations horizontally and vertically into tripartite areas.

Vertical triangular mullions frame the main facades and create a grand portal or arched pattern on these elevations. The chamfered and flush silicone glazed corners slice through this form with a horizontal expression. Single-story bands of textured glass at the top and bottom of the tower begin and end these scaled movements up the facade.

Dark green granite and marble with buff colored limestone paneling serve to transform the "glassy" image of the building at the retail wall, main entrances, and plaza. They are designed to introduce a higher quality of material finish at these focal locations and relate the building to its masonry surroundings.

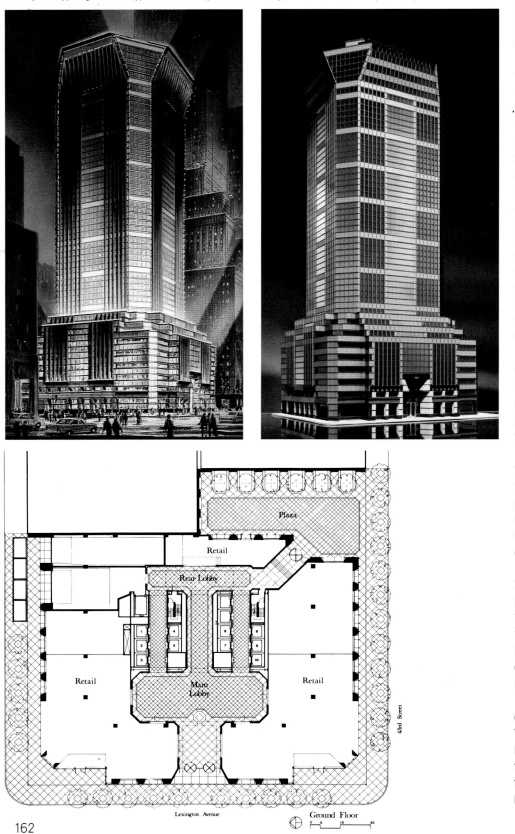

R. M. Kliment & Frances Halsband

COMPUTER SCIENCE BUILDING [60]

Columbia University, New York, NY, 1981–1983
Design Team: R. M. Kliment, Frances Halsband,
Jack Esterson, Alejandro Diez, Lynn Hewitt, Leo
Blackman, Elaine Felhandler, Terrance Goode,
Charles Rudolf, Mark Wright

The building houses the Department of Computer Sciences, a new department formed within the School of Engineering. The facilities of the department include administrative offices, faculty and graduate student offices, a departmental lounge, a conference room, computer laboratories, a terminal room, and a machine room. Also included in the project are a new entrance and a new student lounge for the School of Engineering.

The site is at the northeast corner of the 1894 McKim Mead and White campus plan for Columbia University. The building is constructed on top of the four-story podium of the Engineering Terrace building of 1960, south of and adjoining the Mudd School of Engineering of 1958, both by Voorhees Walker Smith Smith and Haines; north of the Schermerhorn Building of 1897 and the Schermerhorn Extension of 1926, both by McKim Mead and White, and under the Fairchild Life Sciences building of 1974 by Mitchell/Giurgola.

The building organizes the disparate elements of the context into a coherent whole, and the building is in turn completed by them. The materials and general proportions are drawn from the adjoining buildings: limestone, granite, and brick. The primary, elaborated elevations on the east, west, and in the courtyard are of limestone with polished granite pilasters that mark the rhythm of the structure, and with bluestone panels that simulate windows or openings to establish the appropriate relationship between solid and void. The secondary, plain walls at the courtyard setback and at the service court are of brick.

The building contains 38,000 square feet, of which 18,000 are renovated space used primarily for the computer labs and for mechanical equipment. It is constructed of steel frame and is sheathed in stone and in brick. Windows are clear anodized aluminum.

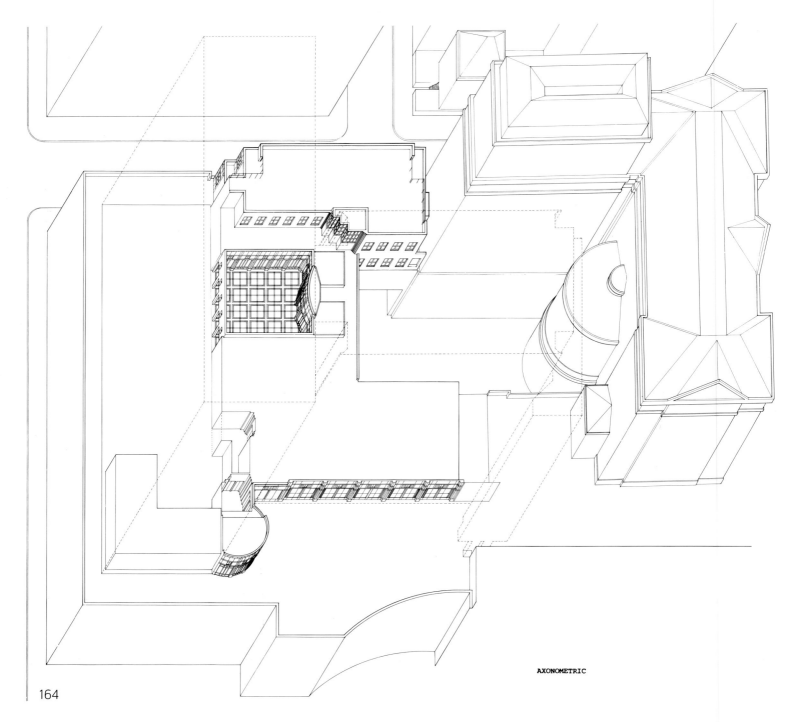

AXONOMETRIC

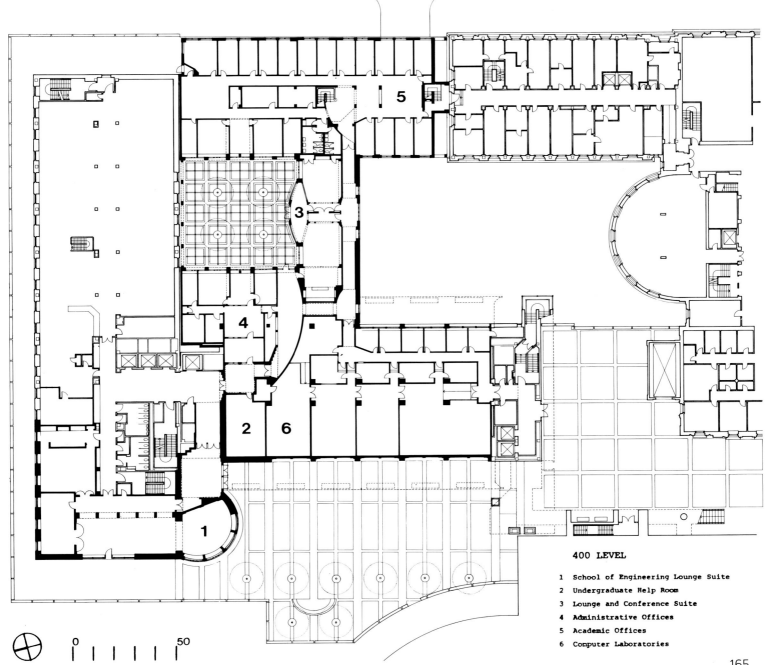

400 LEVEL

1 School of Engineering Lounge Suite
2 Undergraduate Help Room
3 Lounge and Conference Suite
4 Administrative Offices
5 Academic Offices
6 Computer Laboratories

0 | | | | | | | 50

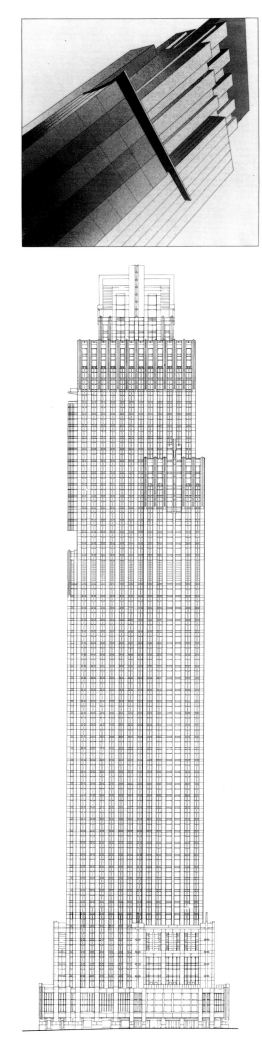

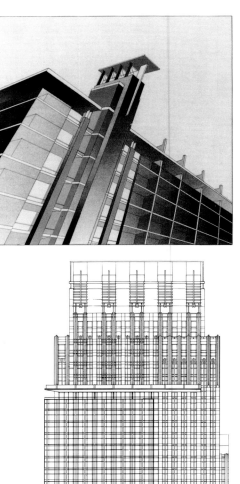

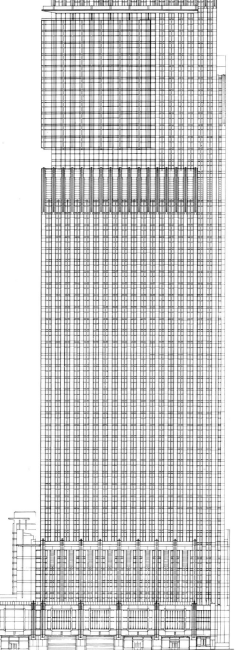

EAST ELEVATION

49TH STREET (WEST) ELEVATION

Kohn Pedersen Fox Associates

ROCKEFELLER PLAZA WEST   [36]

Seventh Avenue, New York, NY
Project, 1988

The management of Rockefeller Center intends to build the last element of the Rockefeller Center complex, its western-facing entrance, on a site on Seventh Avenue, between 49th and 50th Streets and adjacent to Exxon Plaza in Manhattan. The building will house offices, an educational-technical center for the performing arts, and will link into the underground concourse network.

The contrasting models of modernism, Rockefeller Center and Times Square, form the context for the project, and inform its design. The lessons offered by these fantasies of the city have allowed for a consideration of the building as an assemblage, the pieces of which resolve the various site conditions, while the whole is both monumental and dynamic, embodying the energy of the modern city.

Four major elements compose the building. A central core pins the building to the site and defines it on the skyline, acting with the RCA Building as a "bookend" to the Exxon Building. Around this core variously sized elements are placed, creating a condition of rotation which terminates the east-west axis of the complex and creates a new relationship to the Times Square valley to the south. The variety of scales described by these elements, as well as their irregular composition, allows the building to graft itself onto the existing cityscape. The building is clad in limestone and clear glass, with stainless steel ornamentation placed on the surface of the stone to articulate setbacks and to shimmer in the sunlight.

A two-tiered podium, slid toward the west, defines the Seventh Avenue street wall. This surface is covered by electronic signage, and a building entrance is indicated by a tower of light. An irregular configuration is created at the Plaza to the east, resolving site conditions and providing the main entrance to the building.

A portion of the building element facing Times Square is disengaged and transformed into a sign-like object made of glass and metal, specially lit at night, hovering over the Square and acting as an agent in its definition.

Construction is scheduled to begin in October 1989.

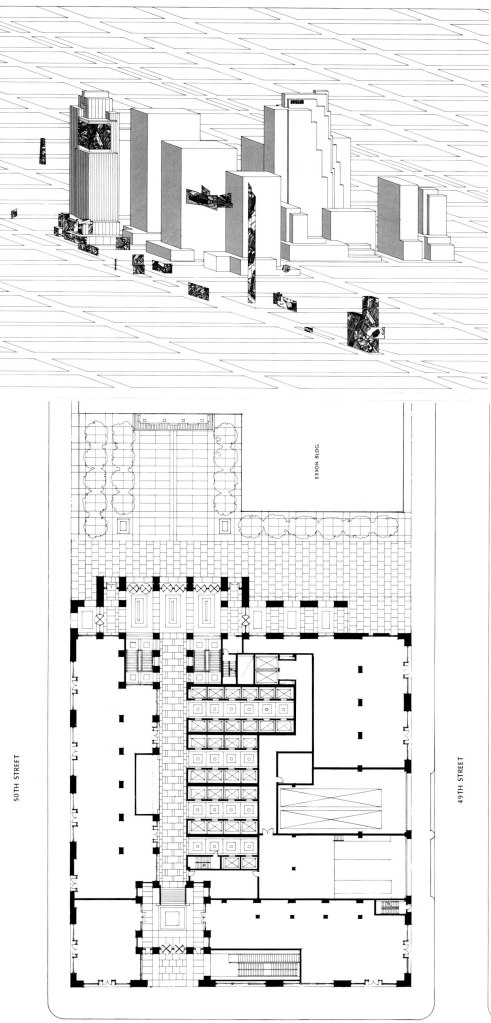

Kohn Pedersen Fox Associates

HERON TOWER [46]

70 East 55th Street, New York, NY, 1987

70 East 55th Street is an office building planned on a Manhattan sidestreet between Park and Madison Avenues. It is a smaller building, twenty-six stories with floor plates of only 5,000 square feet.

This project is a clear example of the attention given to the issues of the street wall, specifically, the establishment of a human scale along the street and the creation of an exterior public space, a "street room," by the street walls. The solution here involves giving the building a distinct base, middle, and top from all points of view. Thus, as one approaches the building along 55th Street, the first seven stories, forming the effective street wall, and rising to a setback at eighty feet above street level, have a complete composition of base, middle, and top. This then forms the base for the next view of the building, so that the building has again, from the ground to the 21st floor, a complete composition of base, middle, and top. Finally, the 55th Street facade as a whole forms a complete composition, the first seven stories serving as the base, the next fourteen as middle, or shaft, and the top five stories, including the two-towered crown, as top.

70 East 55th Street stands with the adjacent older buildings at the sidewalk, creating a consistent street wall. Its entry and lobby take advantage of the street room provided by the plaza in front of the new building across the

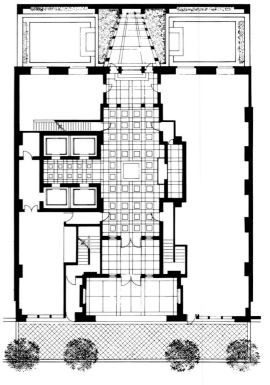

GROUND FLOOR

street to the north. The lobby is of gray, black, and pink marble with stainless steel trim. In order to create the impression of spaciousness on a constrained site, the garden behind the lobby makes use of the age-old device of forced perspective.

Rather than the two-dimensional "skin" that covers most modern buildings, the architects have tried to achieve the impression of depth without resorting to the actual methods of older buildings which would be unreasonably expensive today. The front facade combines dark and light gray granite; light gray granite quoining wraps around to the side facades, which are differentiated by brick cladding (the side walls are party walls). Other elements, such as the lighted spheres and the painted stainless-steel panels at the 7th and 21st floor setbacks, provide actual depth. But perhaps the most important factor in the achievement of depth is the use of the tripartite window. This window sets two side panels to the back of the mullion while the center panel sits flush with the stone. The effect is that of a thicker, more expensive facade, providing the rhythm and texture that allow this building to relate to its older neighbors.

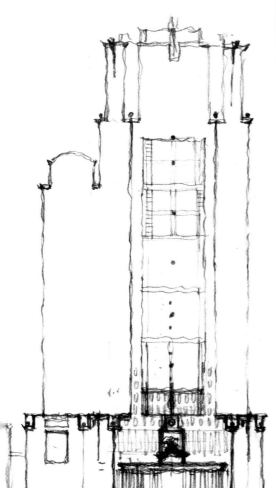

Kohn Pedersen Fox Associates

135 EAST 57th STREET [48]

135 East 57th Street, New York, 1987

This building is located at the intersection of two streets of very different characters, 57th Street and Lexington Avenue in New York City. This condition is reinforced by a zoning district division that runs down the middle of the site. The district at the corner mandates a plaza; the portion which runs along 57th Street is required to maintain the street wall. Compositionally, then, the building is divided into two distinct building masses, each conforming to its own proper zoning code.

This division accomplishes two things: it creates two slender towers of a size and scale appropriate to 57th Street, and it provides separate entrances for the two principal programmatic components of the building: one for the office tower, on the plaza, and one for the retail complex on 57th Street. The section of the building along 57th Street is twenty-eight

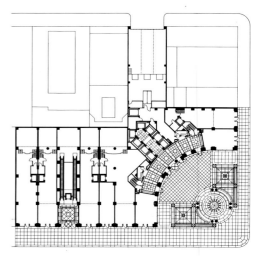

stories high. The six-story base of the building is designed to complement the brownstone townhouses that line 57th Street, one of New York's great retail streets. Street level townhouse shops with their own entries function as independent units. The wall at the base has been heavily rusticated in order to give a sense of solidarity and strength to the facade. The entrance to each store is surrounded by an area richly profiled in a combination of bronze and stainless steel.

The entry in the center of the 57th Street facade leads into a three-story retail complex which is a major component of the project. This area will be devoted to the international antiques trade and will be the center of this activity in New York. Small shops are organized around two major spaces on two concourse levels of the project. Materials will include marble columns, stone and teak floors, plaster ceilings, and glass storefronts. An exhibition room, lecture hall, bookstore, and refinishing facilities will contribute toward making this more like a museum than like a conventional retail mall.

On the corner, the portion of the building that wraps around the quarter-circle plaza on the intersection rises to thirty-one stories. A thirty-foot-high tempietto on the plaza marks the street wall. The office lobby is entered from the plaza. The two-story space is modeled roughly on the Villa Papa Giulio in Rome, and is detailed in a rich palette of materials, including Verde Antique and Belgian Black marble, gray granite, stainless steel, and bronze.

Careful consideration has been given to the way the building will appear at night. The numerous setbacks and the light gray granite facades will make this project as dramatic by night as by day.

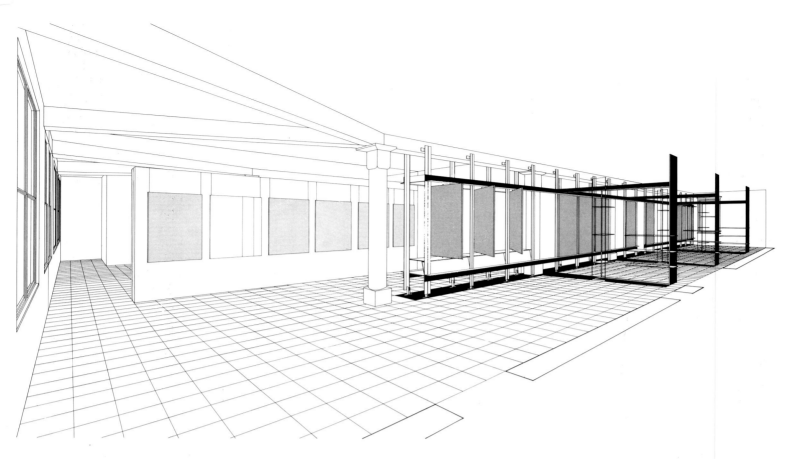

Kolatan/Mac Donald Studio

THE "M" LOFT
Chelsea, New York, NY, 1988

The loft was to provide a family of three with a place to live and work, as well as exhibition space for their extensive art collection. It was important that the design take into consideration the process of change over time by allowing for flexibility of reprogramming space in future.

The family's collection can be divided into three parts:
– abstract paintings
– surrealist photography
– American Indian pottery.

The design of the loft is an attempt to challenge the boundaries of reality. The aluminum wall which runs almost the entire length of the space is at first sight predictably a separator/divider, but at second sight it serves another, rather pragmatic purpose, that of containing storage, and it fulfills a further function of acting as a display background for the surrealist photography.

The particular use of mirror and glass introduces a sense of ambiguity between transparency and reflection. A large mirror is placed against the wall, seemingly in between the (actual) space and the (virtual) space, implying transparency and creating a second axis perpendicular to the actual direction of the space. Glass planes set within the space create frame within frame, as a false perspective implying reflection similar to that which occurs in mirrors placed opposite each other. Glass shelves are suspended by steel cables, seemingly floating in space, defying gravity.

The existing space, the floor, walls, ceiling columns, and beams, are treated as an "object trouvé" onto which the constituent elements of the new design are superimposed. Though the interplay between the two transforms the reading of both and suggests a spatial collage, it is possible at any given point in the space to see both objects in their respective completeness.

The elements of the new design have bolted connections. The aluminum wall and glass planes can be demounted and reconfigured in a new place according to new needs.

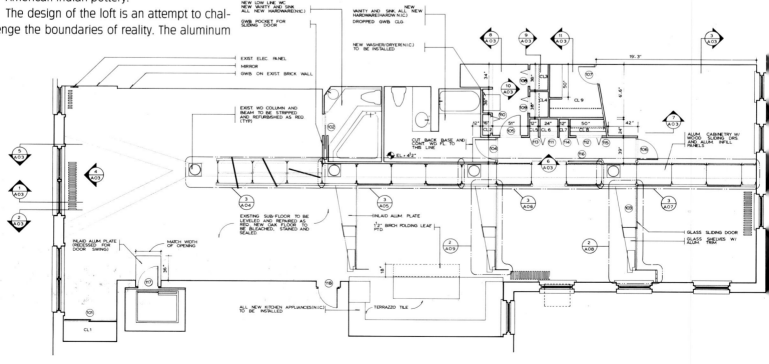

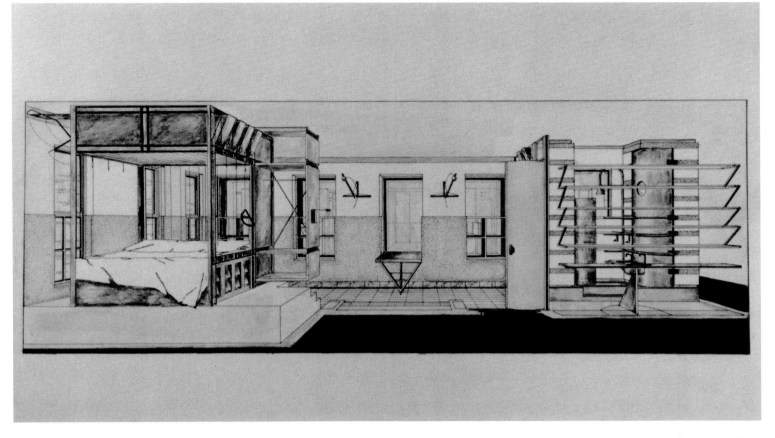

Kolatan/Mac Donald Studio

AN APARTMENT FOR AN ACTOR/DANCER

Soho, New York, NY, Project, 1988

The Actor's Apartment was designed to express its occupant's lifestyle, and responds to the modern human condition characterized by rapidly changing cultural demands/desires, and the increasing importance of individual space.

Our proposal thus centers around the possibility of using generic space for more than one specific function. The main focus of the project is the 12 × 24-foot central space which is analogous to a stage to be occupied by different "sets" or furniture at different moments in the daily routine. When not in use, the furniture retreats into walls or podiums or is transformed for other uses. This space contains cooking, dining, recreation, working, entertaining, and sleeping functions.

The two primary constituent elements of the space, the "window wall" and the "mirror wall," extend the space optically and metaphorically by providing a link to the exterior world, the city, and by suggesting another world beyond the mirrors. The ambiguity introduced by the mirrors operates also on another level: in the apartment the actual and virtual worlds which together determine the existence of the actor/dancer coincide.

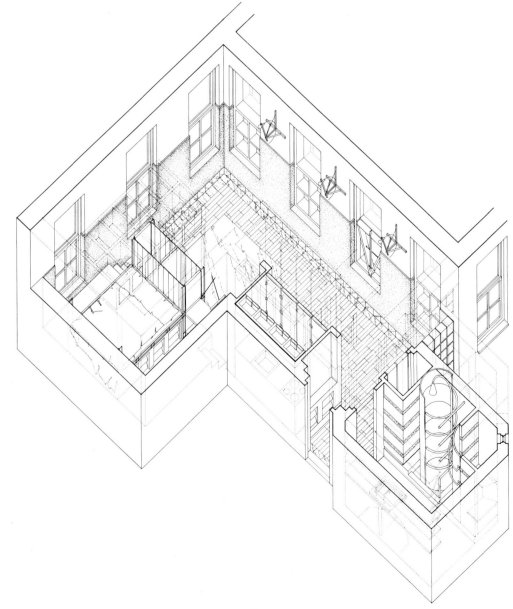

173

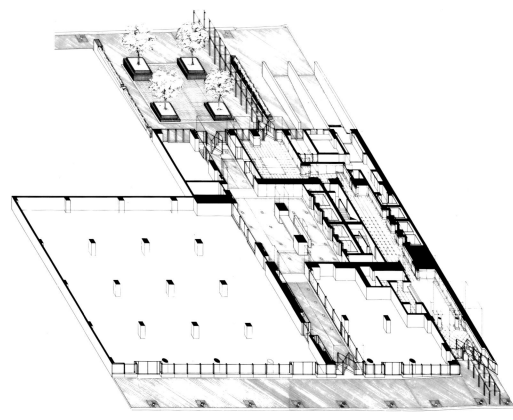

Lobby Axonometric

Harry Macklowe

METROPOLITAN TOWER [29]

140 West 57th Street, New York, NY, 1987
Design Team: Peter Claman/Schuman, Lichtenstein, Claman & Efron, Harry Macklowe, William Derman, Sheldon Werdiger

The restrictions of the through-block site required the residential tower to be planted on a dominant commercial base. The result is a unique 716-foot-tall triangular tower with a northeast orientation capitalizing on some of New York's most spectacular views.

Sheathed in an exquisite sleek monolithic glass skin, the tower's mass carves the sky with a pure "anonymous" face. One floor is indistinguishable from another as the facade reflects the sky, the clouds, and the lights of the city.

Site Axonometric

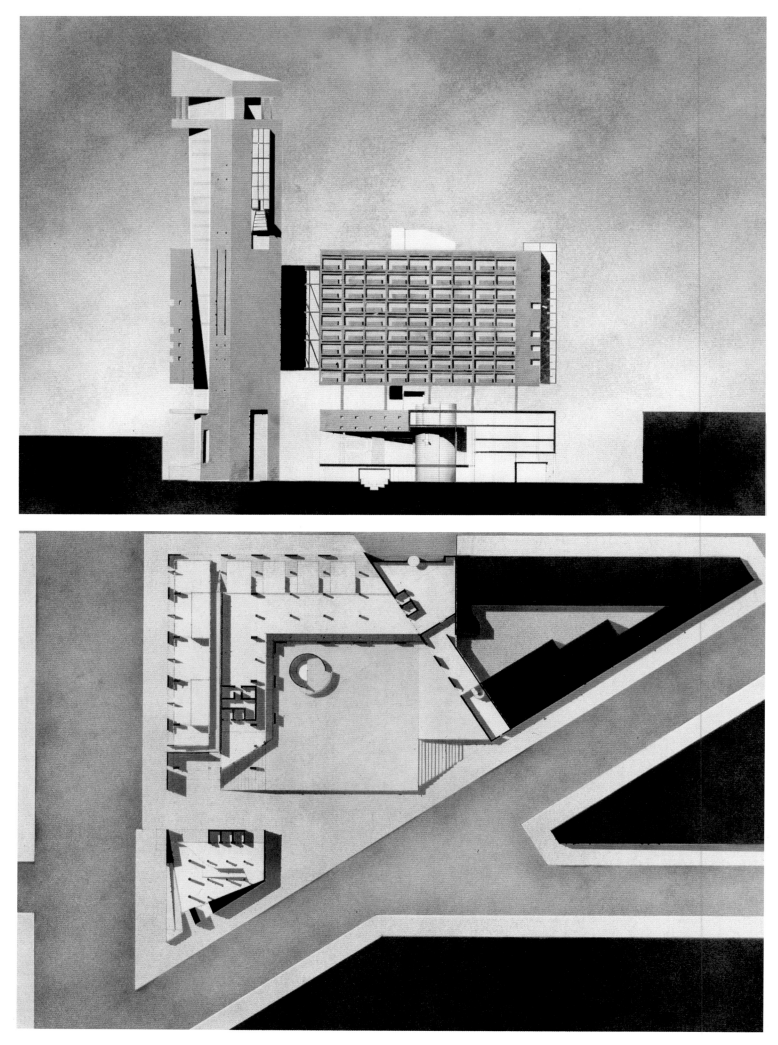

Masque

STUYVESANT PLAZA   [11]

Stuyvesant Street / Third Avenue / Tenth Street,
New York, NY, Project, 1985
Design Team: Douglas Frederick, Ann Cederna

This multi-use project includes commercial retail facilities and administrative offices, studio apartments and a roof garden. The tower is connected to the subway below grade, via a five-story entrance foyer/restaurant.

At the southern apex of the triangle, the tower forces re-routing of traffic with the intention of signalling the diagonal collision in the grid. The building edges on the normative grid street frontage, while carving out space on the interior for the diagonal site. This public space can be seen in plan to respect both geometries, normative and diagonal.

The straight grid presents the fabric while the deformed grid allows accent, that is, rhythm is enriched by counter rhythm. These, then, must be the functions of this site, to support the weave of the grid and accommodate the counter condition – the diagonal. This approach can be seen in massing and elevation; order depends on disorder, rhythm relies on counter rhythm, and logic can collaborate with the accidental.

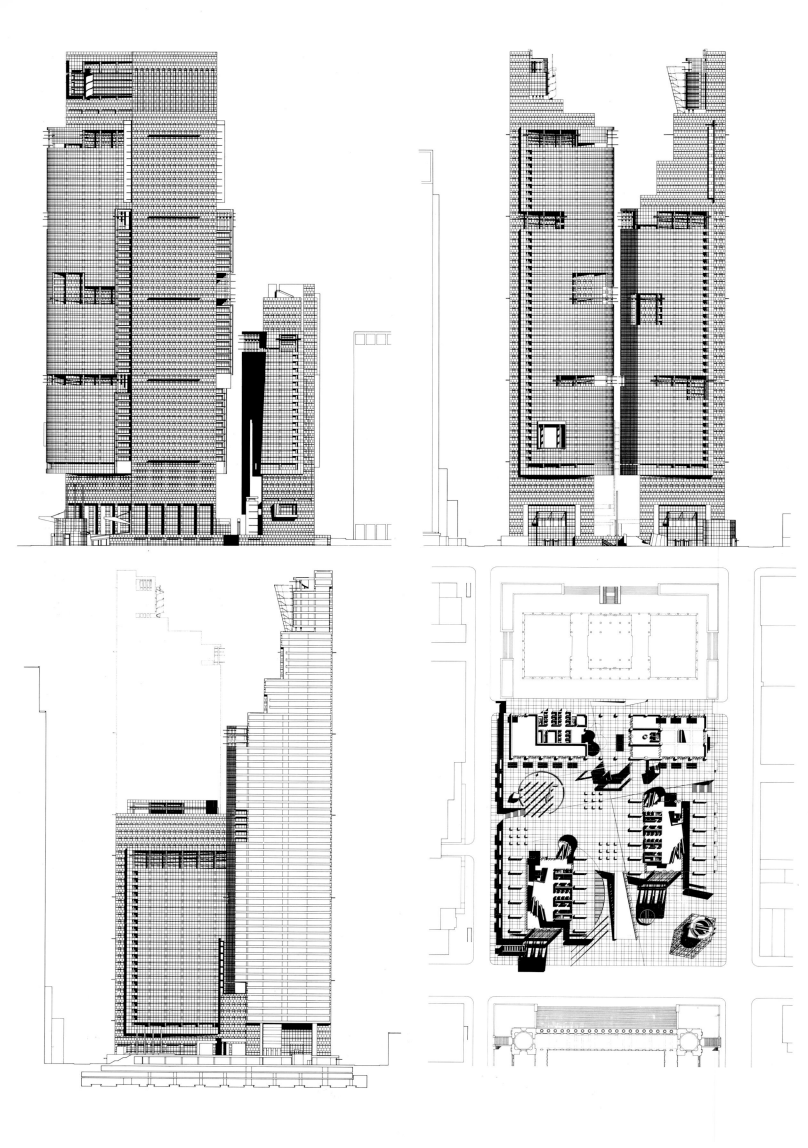

Richard Meier & Partners

MADISON SQUARE GARDEN
SITE REDEVELOPMENT   [19]

Madison Square Garden, New York, NY
Competition, 1987

The program calls for the redevelopment of the present Madison Square Garden site into 4.4 million square feet of office space including trading floors.

The influences on the site are the implied and real future growth of this part of the city, which will occur to the west, past the Post Office with its low height and full block dimension. The physical location of One Penn Plaza, the proximity of Two Penn Plaza, the way in which people move under and through that building to the site, and, finally, the grid pattern of Manhattan are all important factors in the siting of the project. The city's grid condition is reinforced by the form and placement of the towers on the edge of the site. The disposition of the South Tower, placed slightly in from Eighth Avenue, provides a preferred southern exposure for it as well as for the North Tower and the plaza. The East Tower relates in size to the somewhat random low-scale nature of the surrounding buildings.

The entire project is placed on a raised podium with the trading floors beneath. This raised plaza is lined along its perimeter with shops and restaurants. Access to the site is provided on all sides by a series of stairs and ramps; the major east-west access is accommodated with a sloping grade to Eighth Avenue.

Mitchell/Giurgola Architects

SHERMAN FAIRCHILD CENTER
FOR THE LIFE SCIENCES   [61]

Columbia University, New York, NY, 1977
Design Team: Romaldo Giurgola, G. Daniel Perry, Steven Goldberg, Dart Sageser, Jan Keane, Jack Cain

The Sherman Fairchild Center is designed to house members of the Department of Biology at Columbia University in a high quality working environment.

The site, on the northeast corner of the Columbia campus, terminates a major campus walkway which is flanked by several large-scale Georgian-style buildings. The Center is located on top of an existing one-story lounge set on four floors of research facilities which had to remain in operation throughout construction. Each new floor had to maintain a direct, ramped connection to the adjacent structure and several floors were renovated to provide matching quality laboratory space.

The new building provides flexible laboratory space as well as related administrative and conference areas. A six-story unit houses the laboratory service spaces and a seven-story unit houses the communal areas.

The smaller, non-lab unit is placed across the axis of the public walkway, where its siting and configuration define a new entry court to the existing engineering complex to the north. The exterior detailing and large-scale fenestration relates to, and continues, the progression of the Georgian buldings which flank Campus Walk. Seminar rooms and galleries provide places for formal as well as informal meeting. Interior finishes are deliberately muted and softened in contrast to the laboratory areas. Carpeting, lower ceiling heights, and warm finishes are used to provide a quiet atmosphere more conducive to casual interaction.

The larger laboratory unit is located on the more private part of the site. Its scale, fenestrated with more regularized openings, relates to the existing engineering building to which it connects. The plan was determined by arriving at an optimum area-relationship between laboratories and their required service spaces. The resultant configuration required a greater width than was provided by the existing column bays of the lounge below. The transition between the laboratories and the lounge is accomplished by one-story-high transfer trusses, which also serve to relate the new, higher floor-to-floor heights to the old engineering building levels.

Desk areas are placed at the windows of the building with wet lab services within; shared equipment and circulation areas are located in a central core. Mechanical work is run exposed from above this core to the laboratories on a modular basis. Supply air is 100% exhausted to eliminate the spread of exhaust air. Shafts housing the fume hood exhaust ducts are located on the exterior walls of the building in order to lighten the structural loads and provide the framework for a double layered exterior wall system, which consists of an inner aluminum and glass curtain wall, and an outer sunscreen of precast concrete faced with red tile.

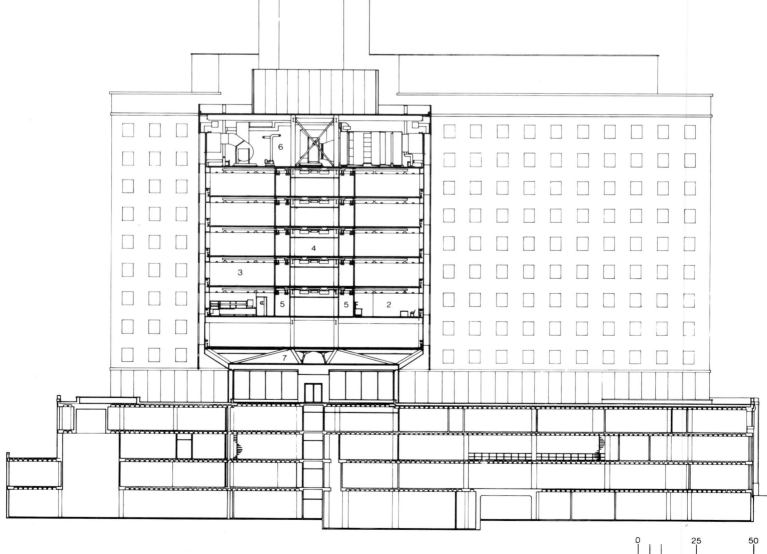

1 entry   3 laboratory   5 corridor   7 transfer truss
2 office   4 pause area   6 mechanical   8 seminar

Section East-West

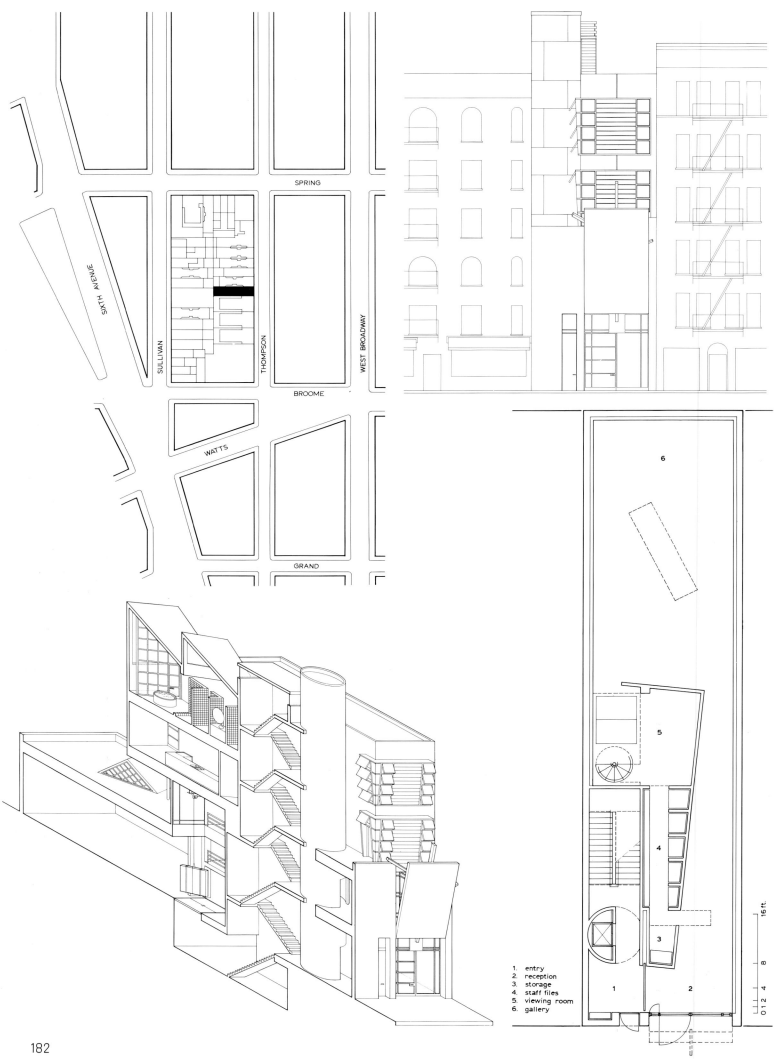

SPRING

SIXTH AVENUE

SULLIVAN

THOMPSON

WEST BROADWAY

BROOME

WATTS

GRAND

1. entry
2. reception
3. storage
4. staff files
5. viewing room
6. gallery

16 ft.

8

0 1 2 4

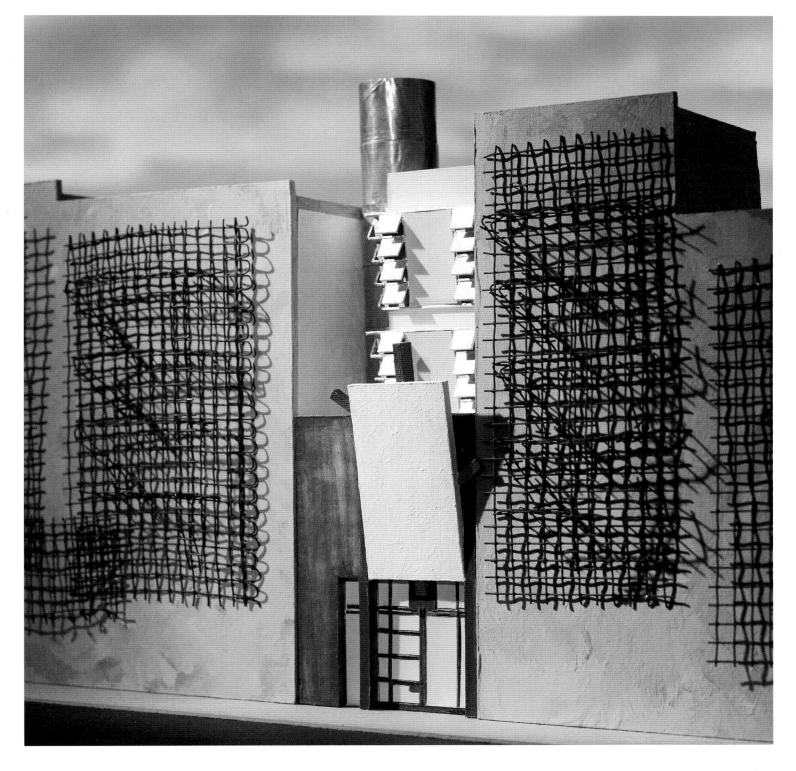

New York Architects

SOHO TOWNHOUSE   [81]

Thompson Street, New York, NY
Project, 1987
Design Team: Frank Lupo, Daniel Rowen

The site for this building is a 25 × 100-foot plot mid-block on Thompson Street in Soho. The program combines a public art gallery special-izing in large-scale twentieth-century painting and sculpture and a private residence for the gallery's owner.

The gallery occupies the basement, first floor, mezzanine, and second floor. Its program includes storage requirements, main and pri-vate viewing rooms, staff areas, and a director's office. Art work can be moved vertically from storage to viewing areas via a trolley beam. The spiral stair allows the staff to move independ-ently from visitors and clients.

The residence sits on top of the gallery and is set back from the street. Its program includes formal entertainment spaces, an exercise facil-ity, and the maximization of outdoor spaces and natural light.

The relationship of the residence to the gal-lery is an interpretation of the tradition of "the merchant's home over his shop" which is so typical of Thompson Street and the adjacent neighborhood. The active roofscapes and sculptural facades of the project are an expres-sion of the uniqueness of the program and allow the building to distinguish itself in scale from its surroundings.

The construction materials include load-bearing party walls, granite veneer and stucco panels over structural steel studs, steel joists, aluminum window systems, curved metal panels, and standing seam galvanized clere-story roofs.

Proposal: The current Times Tower would be stripped to its structural steel frame. This frame would be bead-blasted and sealed with a clear aircraft quality epoxy resin. The open frame would be outfitted with a pair of electronic video screens supported by two pivoting structural masts. These screens would be made of a matrix of high-intensity, micro-diameter light fibers that become transparent when not transmitting images. In their closed position, these screens would complete the geometry of the original frame. There would be a cantilevered observation deck at the base of the pivot screens that would be accessible by public elevators. The very top of the Tower would not be connected by any means of vertical circulation and would be reached only by the imagination.

Opinion: The history of Times Square has always been exciting and exuberant in its predilection for change. As an open steel frame, the proposed Tower symbolizes that quality and commemorates the very building that gave the square its identity. The original frame and the new electronic screens will act as a bridge between the past and the future. Just as the headlines were hung from the windows of the old Times Building, video news will flash across the screens, reestablishing the tradition of the Tower as a source of information. And as the surrounding walls of Times Square become less eccentric in the future, the proposed Tower will continue to embody those images and expectations always associated with 'the crossroads of the world'—big, bright, dramatic, large enough to be a vessel for the city's collective dreams. As the red ball has always fallen at New Year's, so too will the electronic pivot screens mark the passing of time, opening at sunset and closing at sunrise; they will display and record history at a scale suited to an urban space accustomed to grand and romantic gestures.

THE TOWER STRIPPED BARE BY TIME EVEN

New York Architects

TIMES SQUARE TOWER   [38]

Times Square, New York, NY
Competition, 1984
Design Team: Frank Lupo, Daniel Rowen

This project was designed as an entry in the Times Tower Competition held by the Municipal Arts Society (New York City) and the National Endowment for the Arts. It was one of the six winning projects.

Proposal: The current Times Tower would be stripped to its structural steel frame. This frame would be bead-blasted and sealed with a clear aircraft quality epoxy resin. The open frame would be fitted out with a pair of electronic video screens supported by two pivoting structural masts. These screens would complete the geometry of the original frame. There would be a cantilevered observation deck at the base of the pivot screens that would be accessible by public elevators. The very top of the tower would not be connected by any means of vertical circulation and would be reached only by the imagination.

Opinion: The history of Times Square has always been exciting and exuberant in its predilection for change. As an open steel frame, the proposed tower symbolizes that quality and commemorates the very building that gave the square its identity. The original frame and the new electronic screens will act as a bridge between the past and the future. Just as the headlines were hung from the windows of the old Times Building, video news will flash across the screens, reestablishing the tradition of the tower as a source of information. As the red ball has always fallen at New Year's, so too will the electronic pivot screens mark the passing of time, opening at sunset and closing at sunrise.

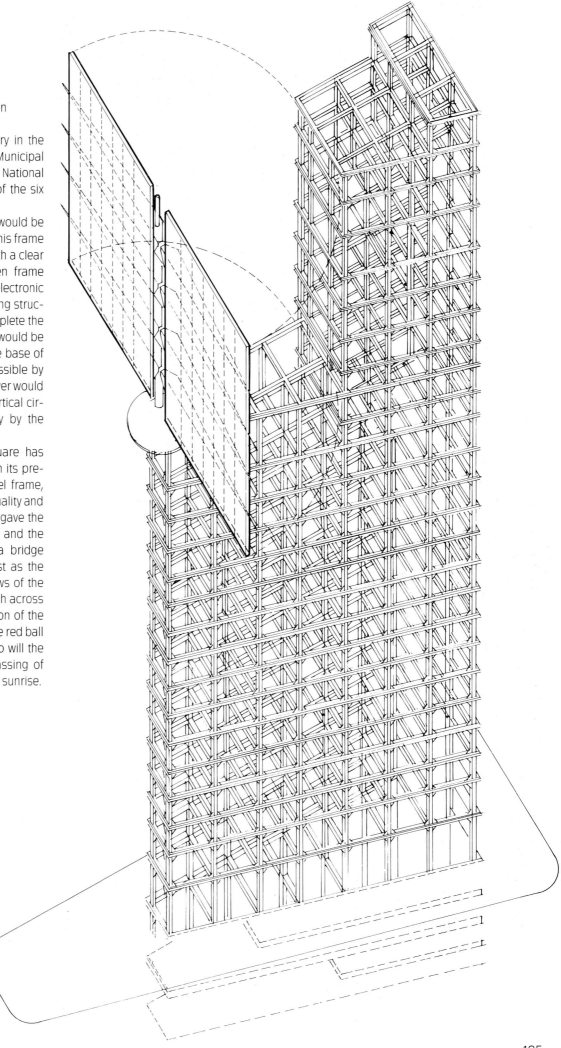

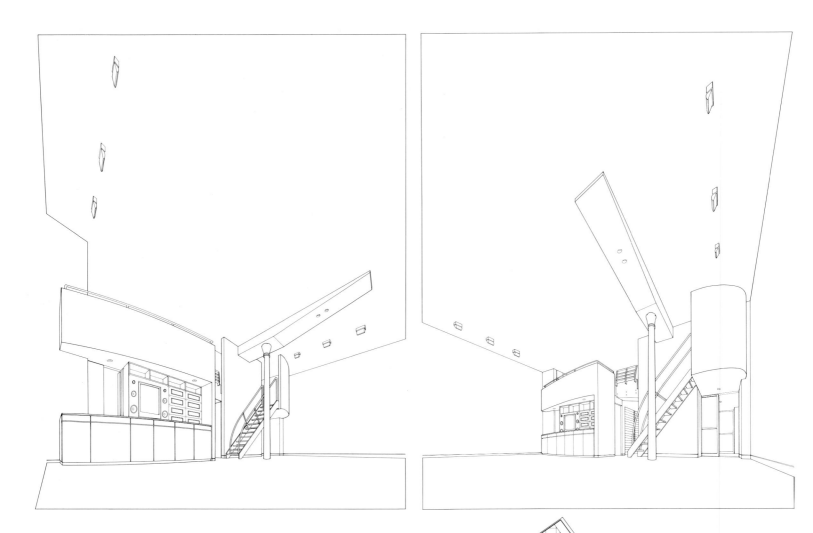

New York Architects

PRIVATE APARTMENT   [82]

77 Bleecker Street, New York, NY, 1986–1989
Design Team: Frank Lupo, Daniel Rowen

The design of this 1,500-square-foot apartment has elements similar to both a small house and a large cabinet. The program called for one open bedroom and one closed office that could double as a guest suite. Though the plan space was limited, the program required these two components to be as distant from one another as possible.

The strategy was to consolidate the entire program to the dark side of the plan creating a large double-height living/dining room along the exterior window wall and balcony. The mass of the remaining space was cleaved in two and separated, providing the desired distance for the bedrooms, yielding a tall and narrow library space that leads from the entry to the light.

Vertical circulation is gathered into a combination of a steel ladder, a curved landing, "the dipsy-doodle" (an up-and-down staircase mediating an existing beam), and "the bucket" (a steel cantilevered bridge spanning the library corridor to the bedroom loft).

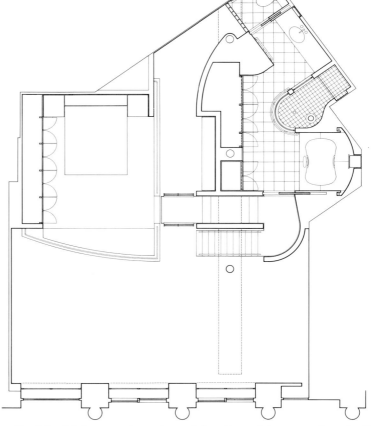

The living/dining room is a volume defined by the light and the city views from the tall windows on one side, and by the sculptural facade of the bedroom loft and stair/bridge combination on the other side. The scale and plan location of this room allow for the ambiguity of it being read as an outdoor space from which the facades of the "dwelling" can be viewed. The intention is to permit an understanding of the entire apartment from within its boundaries.

New York Architects

RESTAURANT/BAR   [14]

52 Eighth Avenue, New York, NY, 1986
Design Team: Frank Lupo, Daniel Rowen

The intention of the design of this restaurant in downtown Manhattan was that the architectural rendering established the decorative motif, but that the space was abstract enough for artists to display their work there on a rotating basis.

The facade of the restaurant was off limits, as it is part of a building protected by the Landmarks Preservation Commission. The rest of the interior is executed in pigmented plaster. This technique allowed for a maximum of decorative expression without compromising available wall space. The theatrical lighting fixtures can project images during or between exhibitions.

The long yellow brow crossing over the back bar is intersected by "Barface," a sculptural element intended to give the bar area its own identity.

OMA

Office for Metropolitan Architecture

THE CITY OF THE CAPTIVE GLOBE

New York, NY, Project, 1972

The City of the Captive Globe is devoted to the artificial conception and accelerated birth of theories, interpretations, mental constructions, proposals, and their infliction on the World. It is the capital of Ego, where science, art, poetry and forms of madness compete under ideal conditions to invent, destroy, and restore the world of phenomenal Reality.

Each Science or Mania has its own plot. On each plot stands an identical base, built from heavy polished stone. To facilitate and provoke speculative activity, these bases – ideological laboratories – are equipped to suspend unwelcome laws, undeniable truths, to create nonexistent, physical conditions. From these solid blocks of granite, each philosophy has the right to expand indefinitely toward heaven. Some of these blocks present limbs of complete certainty and serenity; others display soft structures of tentative conjecture and hypnotic suggestion.

The changes in this ideological skyline will be rapid and continuous: a rich spectacle of ethical joy, moral fever, or intellectual masturbation. The collapse of one of the towers can mean two things: failure, giving up, or a visual Eureka, a speculative ejaculation:

A theory that works.

A mania that sticks.

A lie that has become a truth.

A dream from which there is no waking up.

At these moments the purpose of the Captive Globe, suspended at the center of the City, becomes apparent: all these Institutes together form an enormous incubator of the World itself; they are breeding on the Globe.

Through our feverish thinking in the Towers the Globe gains weight. Its temperature rises slowly. In spite of the most humiliating setbacks, its ageless pregnancy survives.

The City of the Captive Globe (1972) was a first, intuitive exploration of Manhattan's architecture, drawn before research would substantiate its conjectures.

If the essence of metropolitan culture is change – a state of perpetual animation – and the essence of the concept "city" is a legible sequence of various permanences – then only the three fundamental axioms on which the City of the Captive Globe is based – Grid, lobotomy, and schism – can regain the terrain of the Metropolis for achitecture.

The Grid – or any other subdivision of the metropolitan territory into maximum increments of control – describes an archipelago of "Cities within Cities." The more each "island" celebrates different values, the more the unity of the archipelago as system is reinforced. Because "change" is contained on the component "islands," such a system will never have to be revised.

In the metropolitan archipelago each Skyscraper – in the absence of real history – develops its own instantaneous "folklore." Through the double disconnection of lobotomy and schism – by separating exterior and interior architecture, and developing the latter in small autonomous installments – such struc-

tures can devote their exteriors only to formalism and their interiors only to functionalism.

In this way, they not only resolve forever the conflict between form and function, but create a city where permanent monoliths celebrate metropolitan instability.

Alone in this century, the three axioms have allowed Manhattan's buildings to be both architecture and hyper-efficient machines, both modern and eternal.

The projects are interpretations and modifications of these axioms.

Excerpt from: Rem Koolhaas, *Delirious New York*, New York 1978.

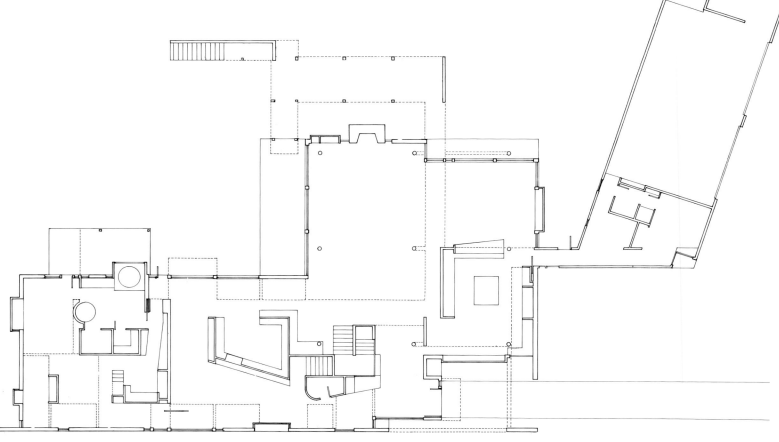

First Floor

Second Floor

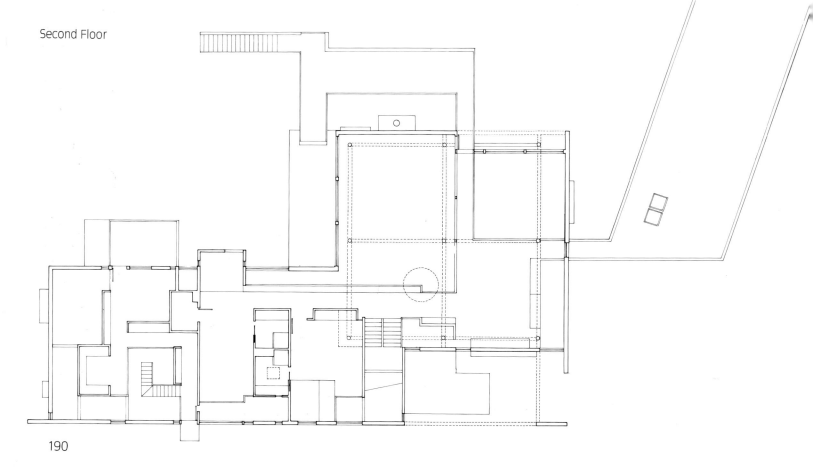

190

José Oubrerie

LONG ISLAND HOUSE

Long Island, NY, 1987

Built in 1987, containing 1,000 square feet, and
initially projected as a 45 × 45-foot extension
to an existing house, this mansion is built partially on the remaining basement of the house
and partially on the projected extension built for
a family.

N–S

E–W

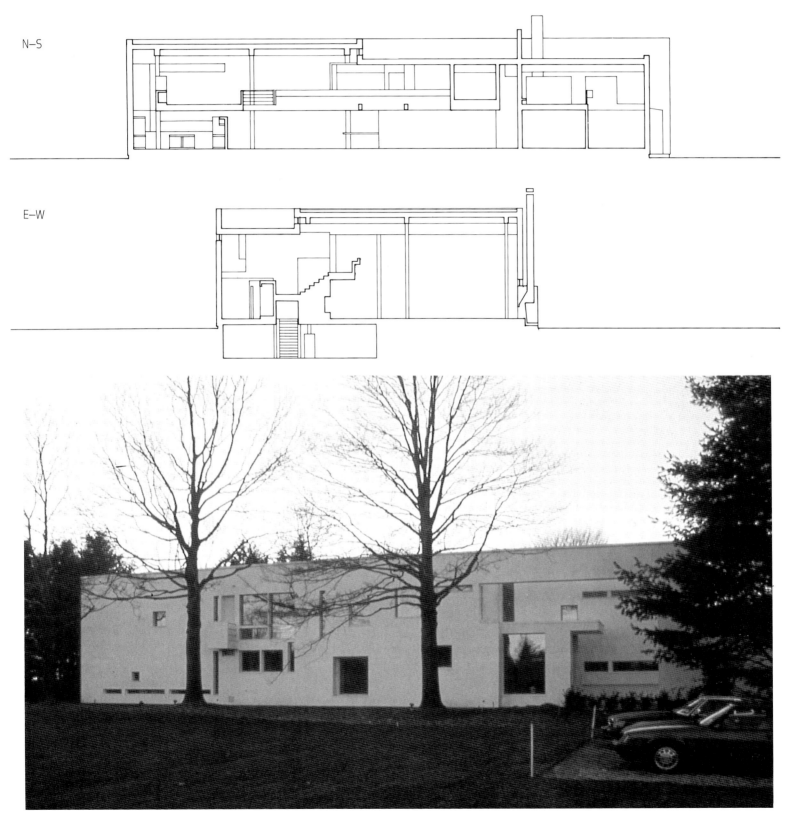

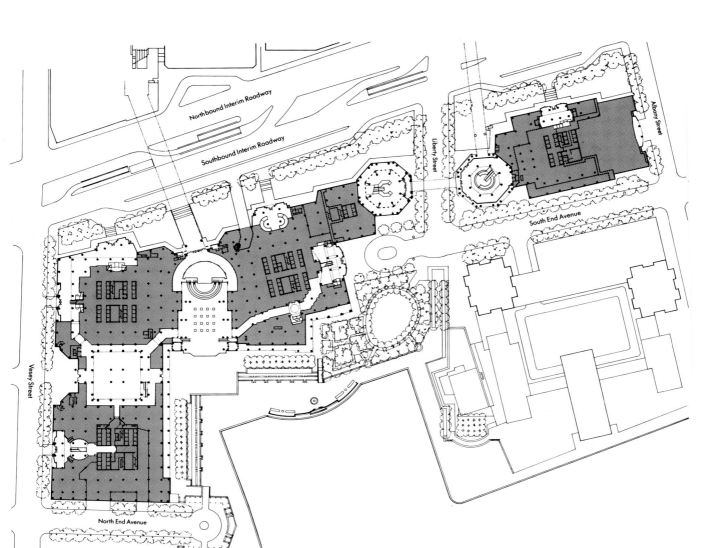

Cesar Pelli & Associates

WORLD FINANCIAL CENTER　[5]

Battery Park City, New York, NY
Competition, 1982–1988
Design Team: Cesar Pelli, F. W. Clarke III,
Tom Morton, Jon Pickard, Mark Shoemaker,
Jeff Paine and others

The World Financial Center is just west of the World Trade Center on a landfill site on the West Side of Lower Manhattan bordered by the Hudson River, West Side Highway, Vesey Street, and Liberty Street.

The project includes 6 million square feet of offices, 300,000 square feet of retail space, and 250,000 square feet of lobby and public spaces on 13.5 acres of landfill. There are four office towers ranging in height from 34 to 51 stories, a Winter Garden, an enclosed, skylit courtyard, and a 3.5 acre, landscaped public plaza.

The design for the World Financial Center creates major forms that both continue and celebrate the historic skyline of Manhattan. The four reflective glass and granite towers rise from a continuous granite-sheathed base. The proportion of granite to glass is greater at the base of each tower and gradually lightens into completely reflective glass skins. At various intervals corresponding to the heights of sur-

rounding buildings, the towers are set back and ascend visually toward distinctively shaped tops.

The skyscrapers surround and define a public plaza that is the heart of the waterfront edge of the Battery Park City development. Adjacent to the plaza, the Winter Garden creates a great open hall enclosed in a glass vault 125 feet in height, 120 feet in breadth, and 200 feet in length.

The two nine-story octagonal building wings on either side of Liberty Street have been designed to create a gateway from the city to the river.

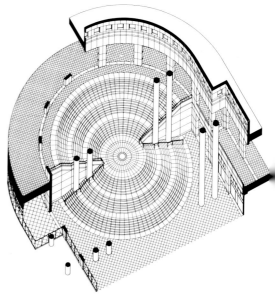

Cesar Pelli & Associates

CARNEGIE HALL TOWER [27]

152 West 57th Street, New York, NY, 1988–1990
Design Team: F. W. Clarke III, Kevin Hart,
Malcolm Roberts, Robert Bostwick, Mitchell
A. Hirsch and others

Program: 59-story tower (485,000 square feet
of leased office space; 25,000 square feet for
Carnegie Hall support).

The tower is a commercial venture using Carnegie Hall's development rights, but it is also an
expansion of the Music Hall and is designed to
be a harmonious addition to the landmark's
family of masses. Using modern construction
methods and modern means of architectural
expression, the new tower will extend the composition of the Music Hall and reinterpret its
system of ornamentation and massing.

The new tower recalls the shape of the building's studio additions and is formed of two
interlocking slabs of different sizes. The six-
story height of the tower's base is determined
by the major cornice line of the Music Hall.
Above this level, the tower is set back to respect

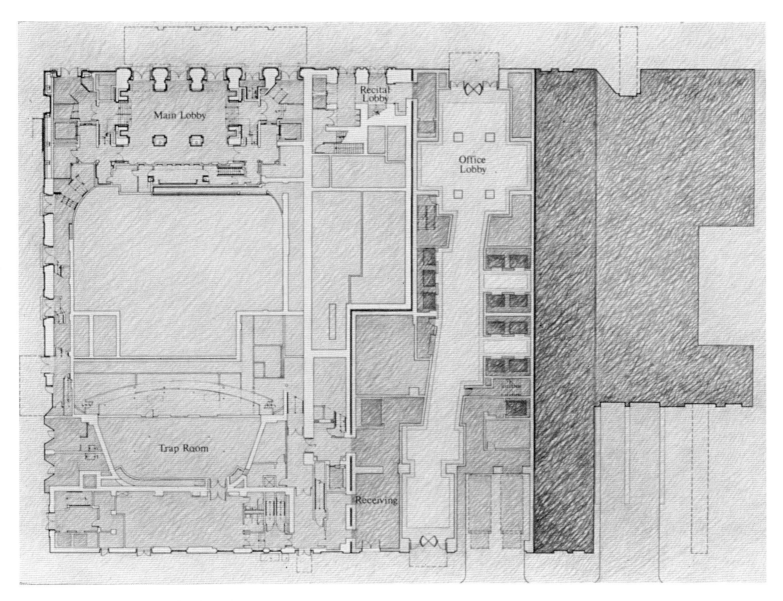

the Carnegie Hall campanile with its large overhanging cornice.

The tower's facades recall those of the Music Hall. Each side is divided into three parts: two corner "towers" and a central field. These elements, and the two components of the tower, are bound together by wide colored bands at six-story intervals, like the Music Hall cornice, which is also a colored horizontal element binding together different pieces of the original Hall.

The tower top is a dark frieze beneath an open metalwork cornice, analogous to the attic story of the Music Hall, expanded to be in proportion with the height of the tower. The shorter tower component has a small version of this top.

Over a cast-in-place, concrete structural tube, the exterior skin is, like Carnegie Hall, primarily brick. The basic color was chosen to complement the Music Hall; three compatible colors are used to create the pattern in the central fields. Window sills, lintels, and accents are pre-cast concrete, colored to recall the terracotta decoration of the Music Hall. The frieze at the top is dark green glazed brick.

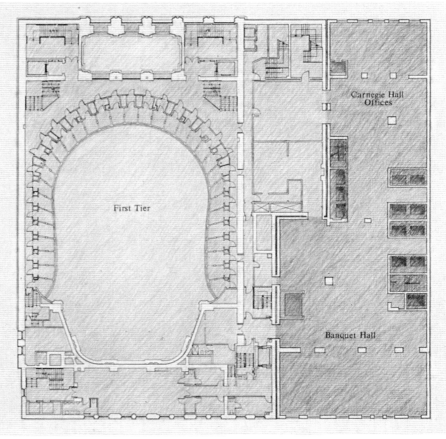

Cesar Pelli & Associates

THE MUSEUM OF MODERN ART   [32]
Gallery Expansion and Residential Tower

11 West 53rd Street, New York, NY, 1984
Design Team: Cesar Pelli, F. W. Clarke III, Diana
Balmori, Tom Morton, Malcolm Roberts

Program: Renovation of existing space and addition of new wing to provide a total of 384,000 square feet of museum space. Design control of the residential tower built on top of the new wing.

Doubling of the existing museum gallery space plus a new auditorium, two restaurants, a bookstore, and a 30% increase in office and service space.

Concrete frame with a multi-colored glass curtain wall.

The Museum sought to resolve its operating deficits by building a residential tower in the air rights directly over the new galleries. The skin of the new tower and museum building, through a complex patterning of mullions, tinted vision glass, and eleven shades of spandrel glass, offers a unique facade that is suited to the urban context in color, pattern, and scale. The public spaces in the new museum are larger than before and clearer in organization. Vertical movement is achieved primarily by means of a series of escalators enclosed in a glass hall, which opens new views of the museum garden, 54th Street, and parts of uptown Manhattan.

The facade on 53rd Street, designed by Philip Goodwin and Edward Durell Stone in the 1930s, continues to be the symbol of, and entrance to, the museum, and maintains its now historic relationship with the rest of the block. The new addition and glass hall have not sought to homogenize or transform the existing disparate elements of the museum; rather, these new pieces have been introduced to fulfill functional needs and to organize and rejoin the parts with respect to their identification with the museum's history.

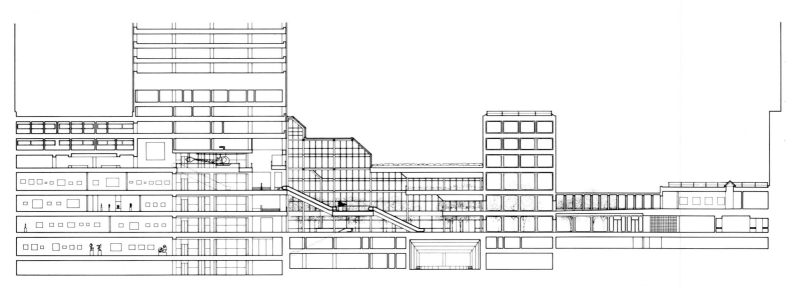

Section Looking North

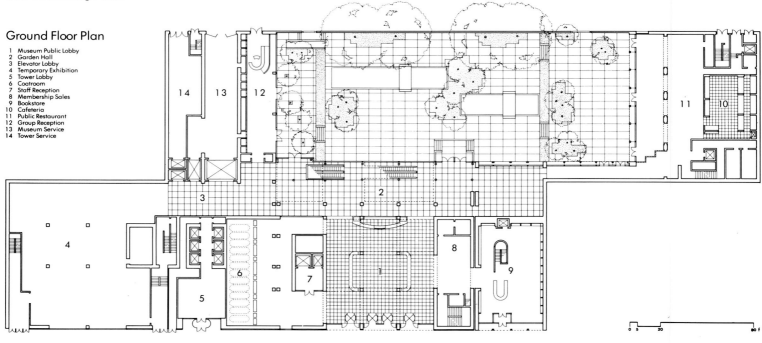

Ground Floor Plan

1 Museum Public Lobby
2 Garden Hall
3 Elevator Lobby
4 Temporary Exhibition
5 Tower Lobby
6 Coatroom
7 Staff Reception
8 Membership Sales
9 Bookstore
10 Cafeteria
11 Public Restaurant
12 Group Reception
13 Museum Service
14 Tower Service

James Stewart Polshek and Partners

500 PARK TOWER [49]

500 Park Avenue/59th Street, New York, NY, 1984
Design Team: James Stewart Polshek, James Garrison, Richard Olcott

This mixed-use development includes the restoration of one of New York's twentieth-century architectural landmarks – the former headquarters building of the Pepsi-Cola Corporation at Park Avenue and Fifty-ninth Street – and the addition of a new 250,000-square-foot, forty-story residential and commercial tower. The new structure has been designed to harmonize with the carefully restored existing building. The first eleven floors, which contain commercial office space, are sheathed in a flat, pale green glass and aluminum curtain wall that reflects the proportions and transparent elegance of the smaller, older structure. The condominium floors are faced with gray-green granite and punctuated by a pattern of deeply set windows that clearly express the residential nature of the space. The shifts of scale and texture visually de-emphasize the new construction, thereby reinforcing the presence of the original structure.

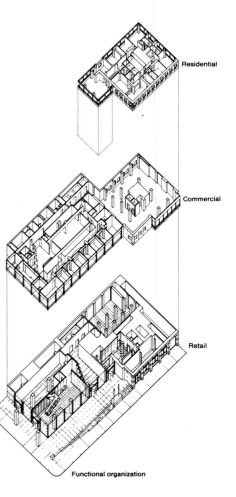

Residential

Commercial

Retail

Functional organization

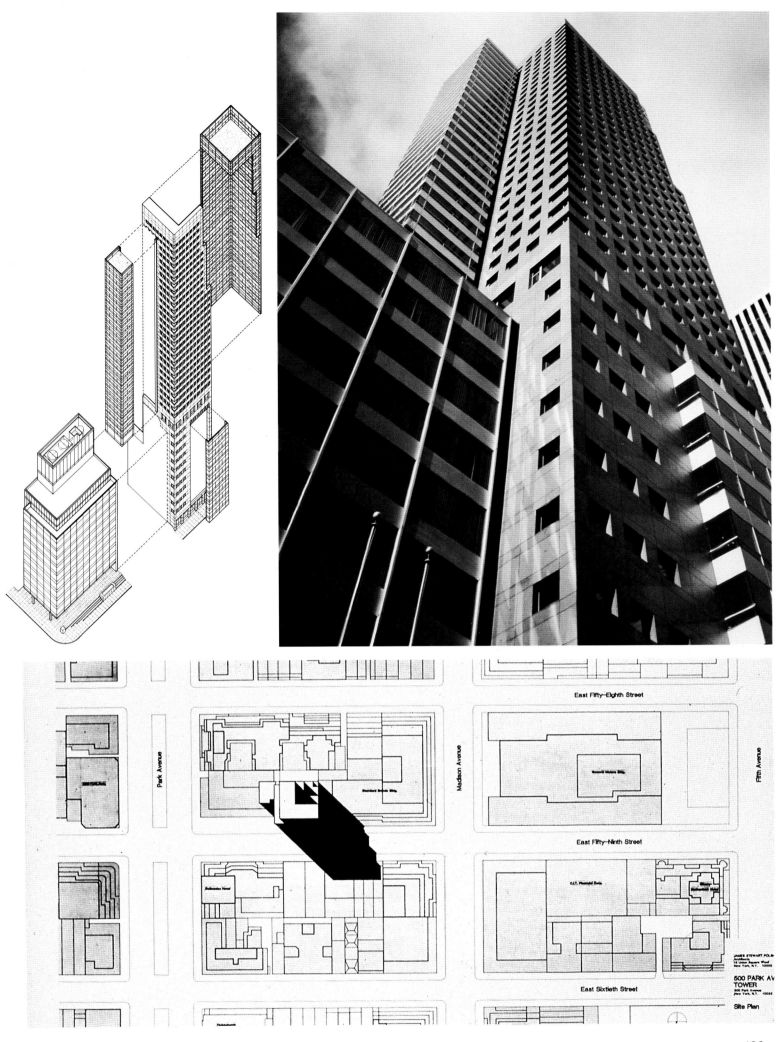

James Stewart Polshek and Partners

CARNEGIE HALL RESTORATION/RENOVATION [28]

156 West 57th Street, New York, NY, 1986
Design Team: James Stewart Polshek, Tyler H. Donaldson

Given the building's landmark status, the nearly impossible construction schedule, the budget, the necessity for working in and around occupied studios, and, perhaps most importantly, users' memories and expectations, the restoration and renovation of Carnegie Hall posed an especially exciting challenge. The new lobby, completely renovated main hall and Weill Recital Hall, and newly created Kaplan Rehearsal Space demonstrate both the importance of ceremony in spatial transitions and the social impact of carefully designed public spaces. The need to develop circulation systems to facilitate these transitions was identified in the extensive programming phase. The first of the systems separates audiences and visitors from performers and stagehands, while the second promotes social (and artistic) interaction among musicians, singers, and dancers by means of informal meeting places at nodes of vertical circulation. Design of new backstage shops, rehearsal spaces, and dressing rooms have transformed this late nineteenth-century hall into a twenty-first-century facility. The design of the new marquee, lighting fixtures, railings, and graphics announce the late twentieth-century changes without compromising the nineteenth-century landmark.

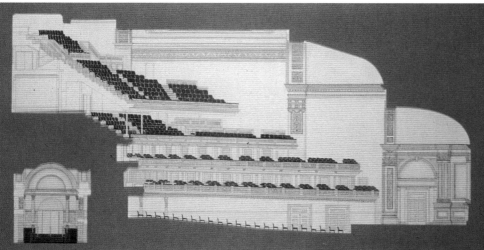

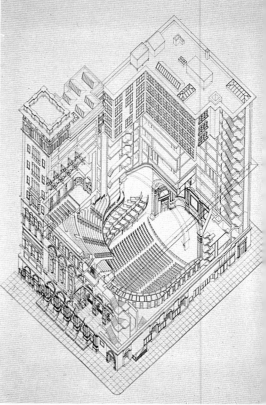

James Stewart Polshek and Partners

NEW YORK COLISEUM COMPETITION [24]

Columbus Circle, New York, NY
Competition, 1985

This proposal to build an eighty-story building above New York's Coliseum focuses on a 600,000-square-foot Health and Science Mart in the existing building. By starting its composition from the base provided by the Coliseum and the first vertical element provided by the old office tower, the design can then add the new hotel as a transitional linear north-south element to lead up to, and culminate in, the eighty-story residential tower on the north side of the site. The tower itself is capped with variegated forms associated with telecommunications devices. Dominating them is a giant globe, changing color with the seasons,

reflecting the phases of the moon, and housing New York's most unusual restaurant. The result is a unique, dynamic architectural composition which enfolds Columbus Circle and turns the corner from midtown to the West Side around the corner of Central Park, a composition which echoes the composition of the towers at the opposite corner of the Park. New and old building elements are clad in a mixture of stone and glass which expresses the mixture of residential, scientific, and commercial uses which occurs in the development and at this point in the City.

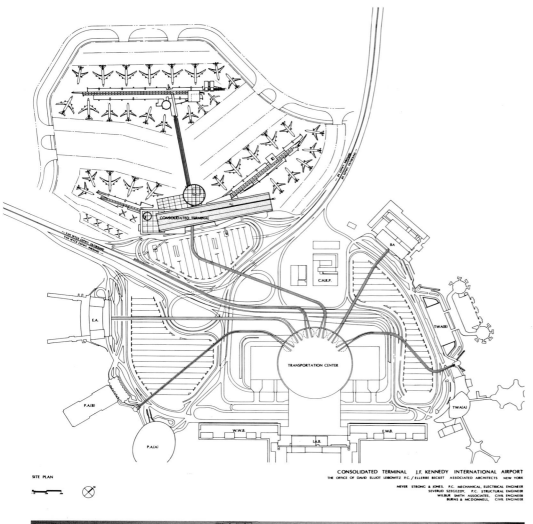

SITE PLAN

CONSOLIDATED TERMINAL J.F. KENNEDY INTERNATIONAL AIRPORT
THE OFFICE OF DAVID ELLIOT LEIBOWITZ P.C. / ELLERBE BECKET ASSOCIATED ARCHITECTS NEW YORK

MEYER STRONG & JONES, P.C. MECHANICAL, ELECTRICAL ENGINEER
SEVERUD SZEGEZDY, P.C. STRUCTURAL ENGINEER
WILBUR SMITH ASSOCIATES, CIVIL ENGINEER
BURNS & McDONNELL, CIVR ENGINEER

Peter Pran, Carlos Zapata, David Leibowitz, Gilbert Balog

for Ellerbe Becket

TERMINAL FOR AMERICAN AIRLINES AND NORTHWEST AIRLINES [77]

JFK Airport, New York, NY
Competition, 1988
Design Team: Peter Pran, Carlos Zapata, David Leibowitz, Gilbert Balog, Wayne Fishback, Vatche Aslanian, Maria Wilthew, Darius Sollo-hub, Curtis Wagner, Eduardo Calma, Frank Yu, Mohammed Reza Samii, James Robinson, Antonio Rodriguez, Keith Doble

Eighty percent of the traffic are international flights and 20% domestic flights.

One part of the new terminal will be a satellite. This allows a layout that accommodates the forty-four gates, and also allows for two 747 taxiways between the main terminal and the satellite.

In the first phase, the FIS, the central portion of arrivals and departures (with ticketing), and the satellite will be built, so as to allow the present AA Terminal and the present NA Terminal to continue to operate fully.

In the second phase, all AA and NA gates will be moved to the satellite, the old terminals will be torn down, and the entire new terminal will be completed.

The overall design has as its main statement and strength a long, curved, floating steel roof that rises up out of the ground and spans the entire arrival and departure area.

The glass cylinder, placed adjacent to the nearly all-encompassing steel roof, contains the arrival/departure station for the automatic trains/vehicles going to and from the Transportation Center, as well as the arrival/departure station for the automatic trains moving back and forth between the main terminal and the satellite. It also contains a bar and restaurant that cantilever out into the large, round, interior atrium; from the restaurant, people will have a panoramic view of all the airplanes arriving and departing.

In the main part of the terminal – that is covered and enclosed by the large floating steel roof – are the arrival and departure floors.

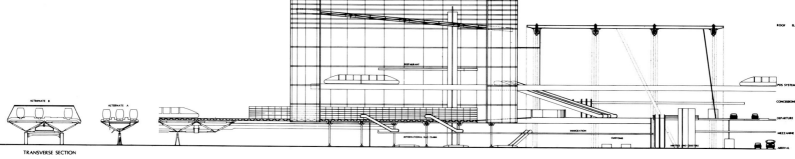

TRANSVERSE SECTION

0   25 FT.

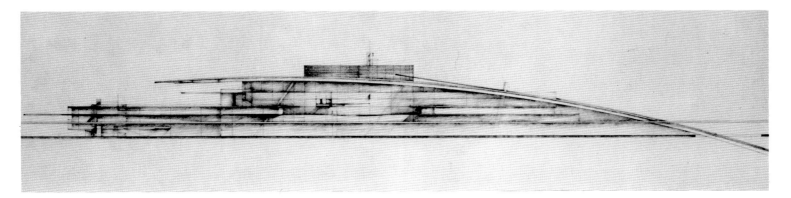

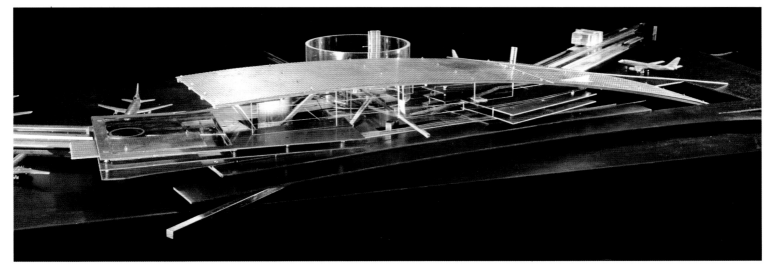

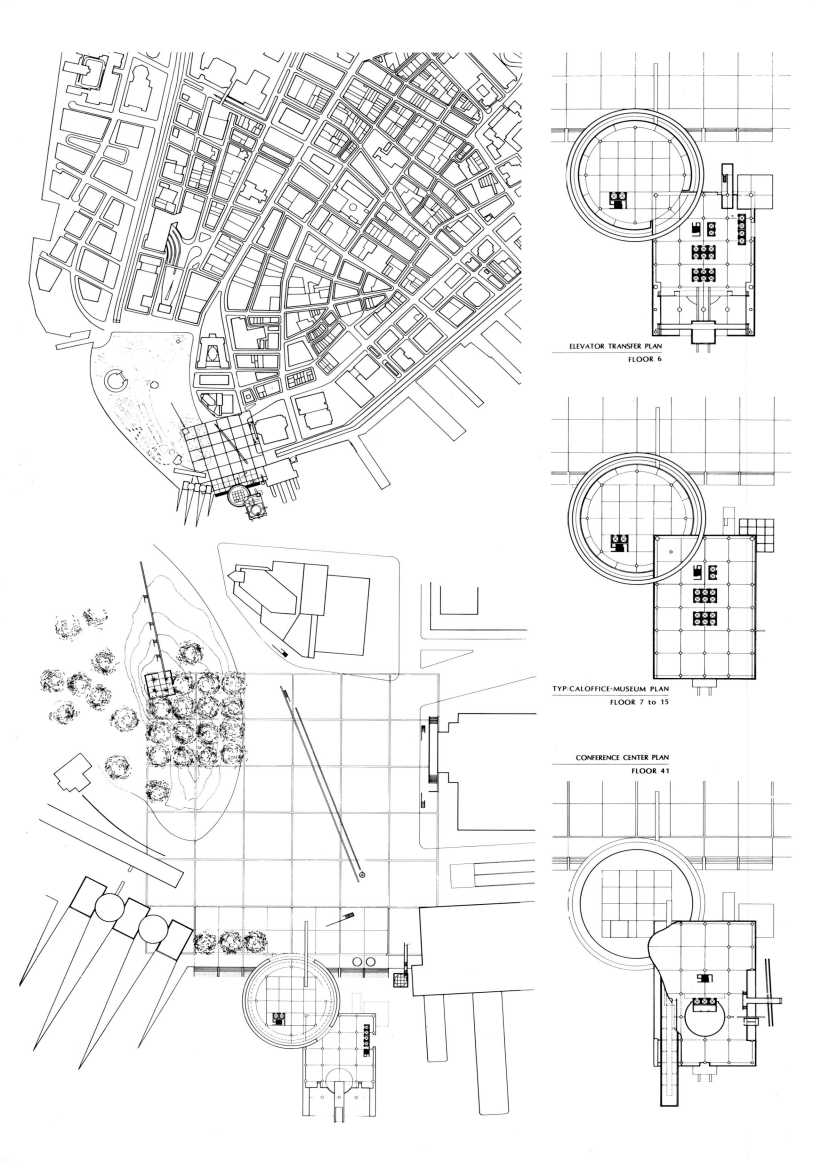

ELEVATOR TRANSFER PLAN
FLOOR 6

TYPICAL OFFICE-MUSEUM PLAN
FLOOR 7 to 15

CONFERENCE CENTER PLAN
FLOOR 41

Peter Pran, Carlos Zapata

for Ellerbe Becket

SOUTH FERRY PLAZA   [2]

South Ferry Plaza, New York, NY
Competition, 1986
Design Team: Peter Pran, Carlos Zapata, Maria
Wilthew

The specific urban setting for the South Ferry Plaza at the southern end of Manhattan must give the basic clues to the design approach. To develop a contextual design solution on this specific site, it is essential to respond to its asymmetrical condition. On the east side of Whitehall Street, there is a massive collection of forty- to seventy-story highrise buildings, and on the west side of this street there is Battery Park. Whitehall Street can be seen as the final extension of Broadway, and it acts as an axis perpendicular to the waterfront. The South Ferry Plaza site can be called the most challenging of the key sites presently available in New York City – and the one with the greatest potential; the building design must therefore make an authentic contemporary design statement of substance on behalf of New York City.

The South Ferry Plaza project presented here has responded to the unique urban setting, with a contextual and reconstructive architectural design in an asymmetrical formal balance. The building complex is placed partly on land and partly in the water, thereby defining the edge condition of this site; the cylinder that pierces/ intersects the orthogonal highrise coming out of the water is anchored to the land. This complex is further developed as an interior entity, with a series of varied functions and spirited spaces, placed at different floor levels throughout the height of the seventy-story building.

The building complex includes a museum in the cylindrical building block and offices, conference center, hotel, TV/radio station, and restaurant in the orthogonal highrise block. The main entrance, a grand public hall, and the museum entrance define the ground floor. A new ferry terminal is added to the west of the new highrise complex. The highrise building's differentiated functions and spaces are expressed in the exterior massing and articulation, creating an inside – outside architectural dialogue. The building design connects to the rich heritage of highrise design in New York City and is clearly contemporary in its architectural language.

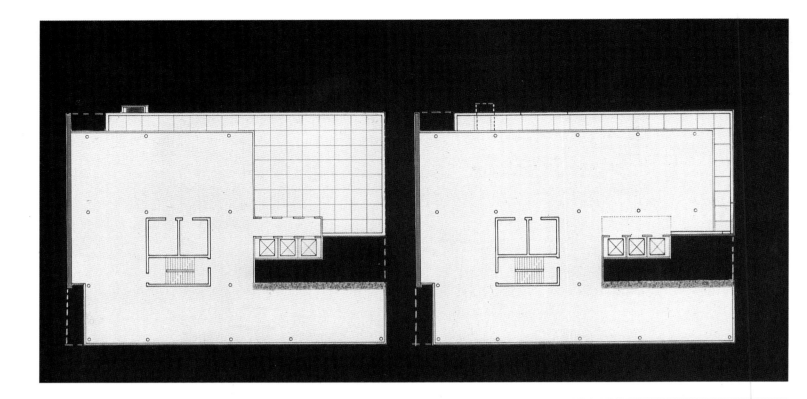

Pascal Quintard-Hofstein
PQH Projects

MID-RISE ON WEST 42nd STREET [20]

West 42nd Street, New York, NY
Project, 1986
Design Team: Pascal Quintard-Hofstein and
Veronique Berthon

Office building on West 42nd Street between
Seventh and Eighth Avenues.
- Answer to the zoning: a "mid-rise."
- A building grounded: the monolithic mate-
rials are lifted, the transluscent materials are
grounded.
- System of entrance: the space of the in-
between, the gap, entering between two vol-
umes.
- The elevator shaft is a vertical movement vis-
ible from the street.
- A void under the roof: a mid-sky lobby.
- A move toward the Hudson River.

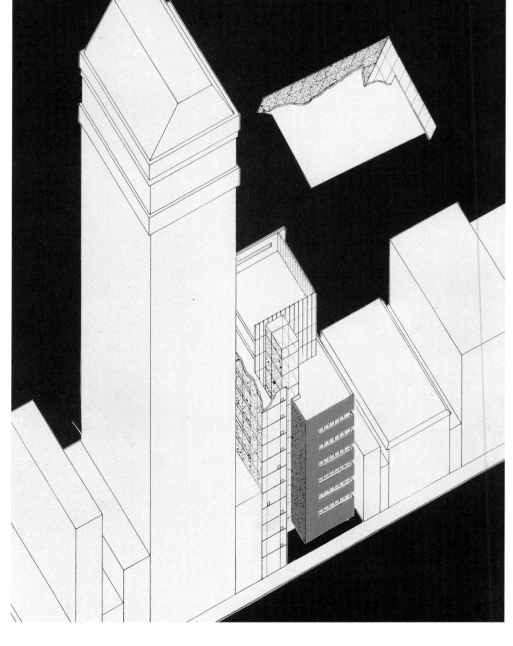

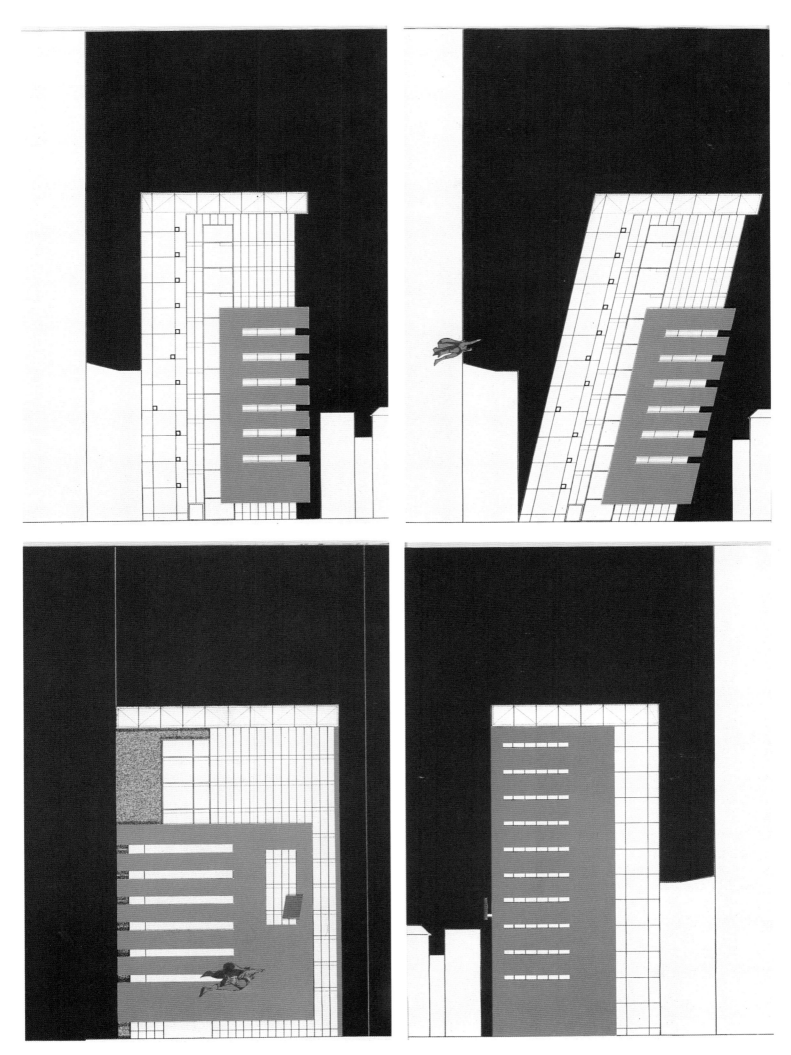

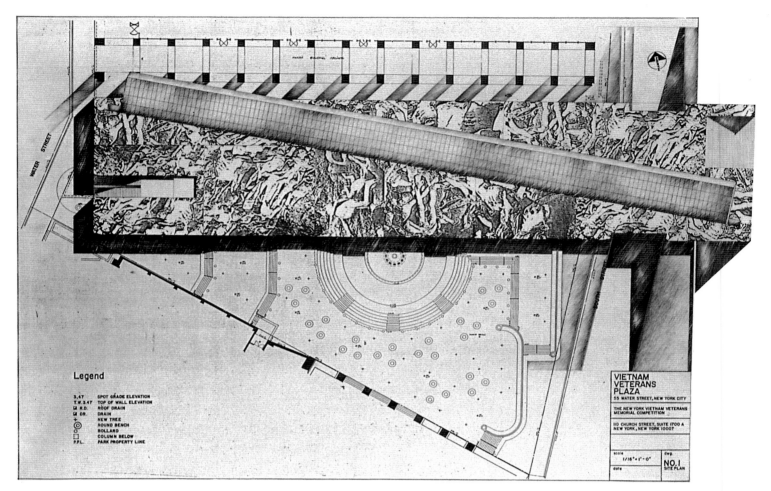

VIETNAM
VETERANS
PLAZA
55 WATER STREET, NEW YORK CITY

THE NEW YORK VIETNAM VETERANS
MEMORIAL COMPETITION

110 CHURCH STREET, SUITE 1700 A
NEW YORK, NEW YORK 10007

scale   dwg.
1/16" = 1'- 0"   NO. I
date   SITE PLAN

Legend

3.47   SPOT GRADE ELEVATION
T.W 3.47 TOP OF WALL ELEVATION
R.D.   ROOF DRAIN
DR.   DRAIN
+   NEW TREE
⊙   ROUND BENCH
□   BOLLARD
□   COLUMN BELOW
P.P.L.   PARK PROPERTY LINE

George Ranalli

VIETNAM VETERANS MEMORIAL   [3]

Vietnam Veterans Plaza, New York, NY, 1984

WAR OF DESPAIR: WAR OF ASSASSINS

The Vietnam War was the epitome of waste and destruction. It was not a just war in the sense of a heroic effort to deter an evil force in the world. Rather, Vietnam was born out of politics, economics, and a severe paranoia, hence despair. We have come to understand how senseless and unjust an action this was and the internal shame and disgrace it has brought us

as a people. The Vietnam War demoralized and divided our country to the point that we are still trying to rebuild and heal our emotional and physical wounds. Coming home from Vietnam was not the same as it had been in returning from Germany or Japan. World War II had a morality. Vietnam saw murder, assassination, and mutilation as a way of life. The veterans came back in anguish and confusion, to a society equally confused and anguished. Nobody knew what to do.

To build a monument is a strong, positive, and collective symbol. It is a support to the social-political system which created it. There is no way to build a negative, singular one, or a

monument which only symbolizes death, without reinforcing the politics essential to its fabrication. This continues the dilemma. Previous periods of monument-making in the US did not know this conflict and torment. Any monument built to this war or in memory of those killed in action will be co-opted by the government as a positive verification of its action. That is inevitable.

The project is a monument to friends and colleagues, as well as the others killed in Vietnam. It is to remain a drawn monument, more to symbolize the futility of their death. The drawing is both a memorial and a protest. It refuses to be used to promote further conflict where people are killed needlessly or in wars which begin with the illicit and nefarious activities of our government. It is to slain friends that this memorial is dedicated. Refusing to donate design ability to help continue this kind of aggression is the best memorial to their memory. True monuments can only exist when the hearts and souls of people are united in a common cause, in the search for truth and justice.

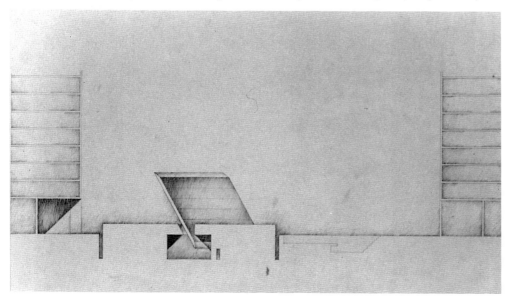

George Ranalli

RANALLI STUDIO [13]

100 West 15th Street, New York, NY, 1982–1983

A small residence and studio is the subject of this renovation in an old industrial building in New York. A new set of forms was introduced into the open existing space, opposite a large wood-framed window. Static and dynamic elements appear dense and solid but in fact they contain dressing rooms, closets, dining table, and bedroom. Strong volumetric manipulation allows the program to be accommodated and provides for light to be admitted to all spaces. The plastic quality of the material provokes form and space into emerging and makes their presence felt in the large light-filled room. Shadows which appear in the voids help to increase the depth of the spaces.

The smooth plaster form is the base from which, and upon which, more precious materials are used. The dining table is imbedded in a steel and brass holder set in a cut in the plaster form. A steel T-section suspended from the anchoring element is projected outward to a pedestal of raw steel shapes. Long and tense, the T is absorbed in the vertical plates of the pedestal. The structure supports a thin slab of polished green marble. Stairs are fabricated in veneer plywood with brass nosings. All of this contrasts the existing white room with its heavy masonry wall and wood floor.

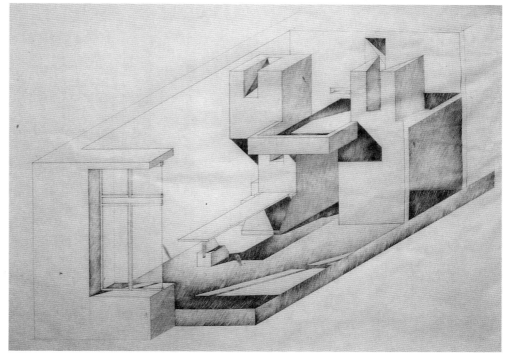

George Ranalli

FIRST OF AUGUST STORE   [51]

860 Lexington Avenue, New York, NY,
1975 –1976

First of August is the renovation of a women's dress shop on Lexington Avenue in New York City. It consists of a renovated second floor, with display space, dressing rooms, cashiers desk, a beauty care facility, and a new facade linking the second floor to the existing first floor. In an effort to create a facade unlike the adjacent commercial enterprises brash commercialism and signage was avoided.

The new facade extended the space of the interior, vertically joining the first and second floors of the shop and providing an entrance for the residential tenants. The steel grid structure allowed for a form which could provide maximum openness and density of construction. Welded steel sections were important in extending the dialogue of materiality. The frame was pre-fabricated in sections and erected at the site. The new facade, the old brownstone wall, and the new interior wall form a series of spaces that choreograph movement from the street into the interior. They also are about the making of a wall in all its material possibilities.

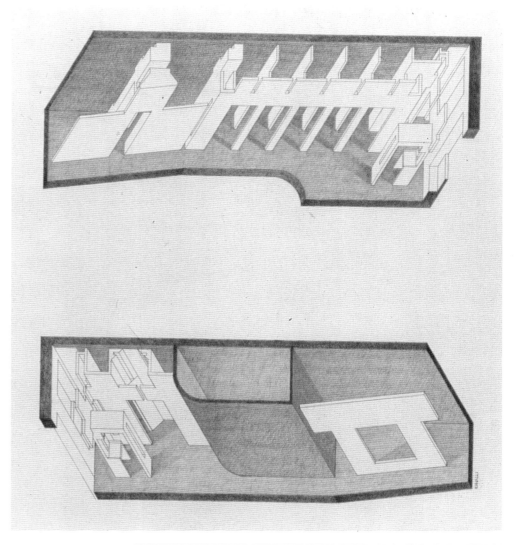

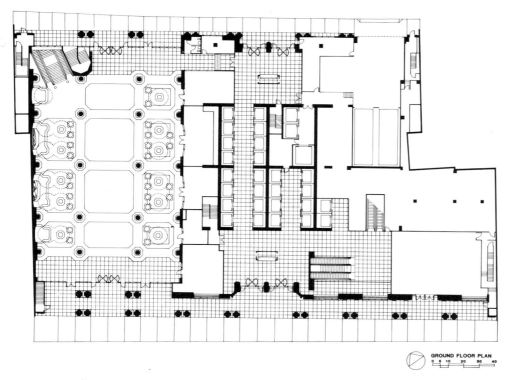

Kevin Roche, John Dinkeloo and Associates

J. P. MORGAN HEADQUARTERS   [4]

60 Wall Street, New York, NY, 1988

Following successive visits to Wall Street, the conclusion was reached that the narrow canyon quality of Wall Street was a unique attribute which should be preserved, so the design maintains the street wall and cornice line by means of an arcade. The idea of the column is used in a schematic way to articulate the form of the shaft of the building, and appears again at its top in an illusion created by a series of bay windows. The curtain wall materials are gray and green granite, bronze painted aluminum mullions, and antique silver reflecting glass; a ceramic backed glass is used instead of granite for the horizontal stripes in the tower's recessed planes. The mansard roof, which contains mechanical, microwave, and satellite communications equipment, seeks to relate to the other towers on Wall Street, some of which have characteristically pyramidal devices on top.

GROUND FLOOR PLAN

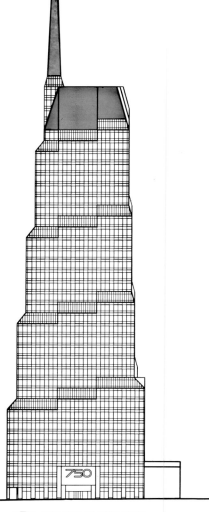

7TH AVENUE ELEVATION

Kevin Roche, John Dinkeloo and Associates

750 SEVENTH AVENUE [34]

750 Seventh Avenue, New York, NY, 1989

The building has a narrow island site at the northern edge of the special theater zoning district. Zoning requirements for setbacks limit the maximum area of floors to a progressively stepped building that was the basis for early massing studies. The form is a helical tower, which gives the building a dynamic feeling rather than the static one of stacked diminishing boxes. To accommodate a rental market looking for maximum floor size with maximum interior planning flexibility, the core is pulled to

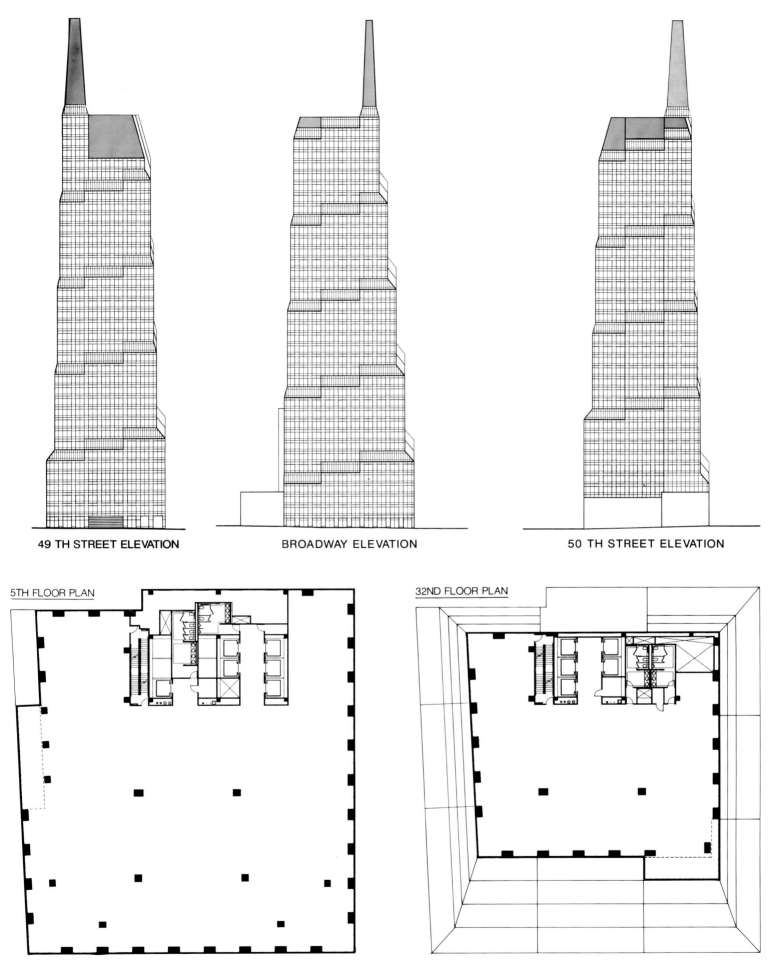

49 TH STREET ELEVATION

BROADWAY ELEVATION

50 TH STREET ELEVATION

5TH FLOOR PLAN

32ND FLOOR PLAN

the north and logically resolves zoning encroachment/recess regulations. The floor areas decrease from 22,000 square feet to just over 10,000 square feet. Mechanical and theater spaces are located above the street floor to provide blank areas without obstructing office views for the 17,664 square feet of special signs which are incorporated directly into the skin of the building. It is a completely glass clad building composed on a five- and ten-foot grid, where the structure is expressed by a ceramic coated glass for the horizontal and vertical grids, and the vision panel is expressed with a dark gray reflecting glass. The tapering building and its slightly erratic nature is influenced by the ziggurat which is an ascending spiral, an ancient form that derives originally from the ramp used for the construction of a building.

Kevin Roche, John Dinkeloo and Associates

UNITED NATIONS PLAZA I AND II   [44]

between 43rd – 45th Streets and First–Second Avenues, New York, NY, 1969 –1976

In response to several requests from the United Nations, the City and State of New York joined together to create a special public corporation as the development entity which would be supportive of the United Nations' presence in Manhattan. A program study was undertaken, which was for approximately five million square feet of office space, a 600-room hotel and a large complex of retail and commercial service space. The site selected was between 43rd and 45th Streets, and First and Second Avenues. The plan has three, forty-story towers connected by a 500-foot-high closed courtyard standing on the commercial retail parking base. It recognizes the existence on the site of a portion of Tudor City, an early and very successful residential development, and the U.S. Mission to the United Nations. It also contemplates a bridge

connection across First Avenue into the underground of the United Nations complex, permitting a secured passage from the hotel and some of the office buildings for the United Nations personnel. The intention for the enclosed space is to create at every ten-story height an additional sidewalk service area.

Issues of the local community and a general decline of the real estate market in the early seventies forced the Corporation to reduce the project to a single, first-phase tower which has office space on the lower twenty-six floors and a hotel on the upper levels. Later, a second tower of similar size and use was added to complete the project on the site.

It was decided to cover the entire exterior surface of the building with a blue/green glass which is divided into a small grid-like pattern emphasized by six-inch-deep horizontal aluminum bands and three-inch-wide vertical aluminum mullions. The shapes of the towers

were dictated by the zoning setback requirements, the variations in use from an office building to a hotel (which only needs to be sixty to sixty-five feet wide), and the opportunity to establish some relationship with the adjacent low-rise buildings, and, certain minimalist sculptural leanings.

The exterior of the second building is the same gridded glass as the first facade and its form derives primarily from a cutting manipulation of the south side; this 45° chamfer provides views of the river from the new building and avoids obstructing the views west from the original building. Both hotels have a new shared lobby and "porte cochere" on 44th Street. The design includes all of the public spaces for the hotel, the hotel rooms, furnishings and decorations. The entrance lobby uses a series of domes of different shapes to illuminate the check-in area, and the lounge area uses columns which are glass clad and take their form from the columns of the Central Park Zoo. There is also a small lounge which borrows its design from the Wisteria Garden in Central Park. The canopy over the sidewalk is permitted here, exceptionally, because the whole original site was a specially designated design district for the United Nations by the city.

Smith-Miller + Hawkinson

SOHO GALLERY [9]

141–145 Wooster Street, New York, NY,
1985–1988
Design Team: Henry Smith-Miller, Laurie
Hawkinson, Annette Fierro, Celia Scott, Craig
Konyk, Sam Anderson, John Conaty, Urs Egg,
Alice Weatherford, Ruri Yampolsky

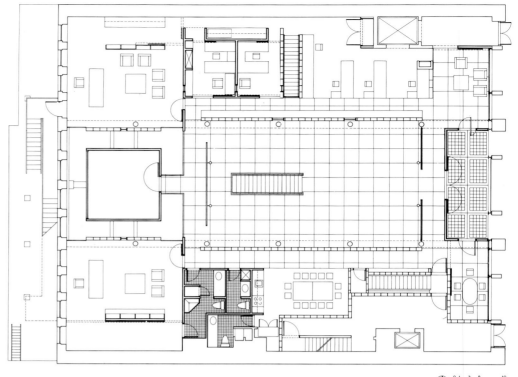

Once used as D.I.A. Art Foundation "Work-shops," this "loft" space of 10,000 square feet, located on Wooster Street in New York, was rehabilitated to serve as the headquarters and exhibition space for a private art gallery and art publishing house. The program required the development of controlled exhibition space(s), high security, and compliance with the New York City Department of Landmarks review.

On both entry (street) and cellar levels the organization of the existing loft building struc-ture, that is, perimeter bearing walls and interior open columnar space, is reinforced through the disposition and development of the program elements, their configuration and material detail.

The open exhibition space and central stair with risers made of glass lead from the entry area at the street to the showroom at the rear of the building in the cellar below. The architec-tural "promenade" from street to court traverses the plan and section of the floor and simultaneously depicts the organization of the gallery and its de-constructed and re-con-structed condition. The buildings' structural system of columns and beams is deliberately interrupted by the stair and revealed at the floating "ark" exhibition space and two-story void at the rear of the building. In the double-height space the original inside elevation of the building's perimeter wall is exposed and becomes the fourth wall of the space.

New opaque concrete block bearing walls, parallel to the building's own, are seen in opposition to layers of translucent sandblasted glass.

The double-height void and opaque solid "ark" space at the back of the building is also translated to the new streetfront apparatus. The streetfront device or apparatus both accom-modates the program and transmits the idea of security as well as restructuring the proportions of the building's facade. The implicit central "void" remains apparent at the street level, while a series of track mounted steel panelled "bi-fold" doors moderate the streetfront edge, from open to closed. The doors and panels are proportioned and detailed to incorporate and reinforce the building's existing ordering sys-tems, as well as accommodating the placement of a nonconforming pilaster.

The large spaces to either side of the central gallery are the offices of the principals.

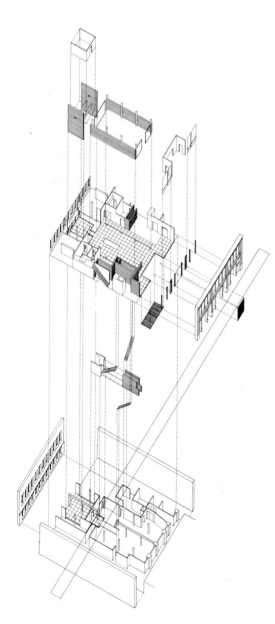

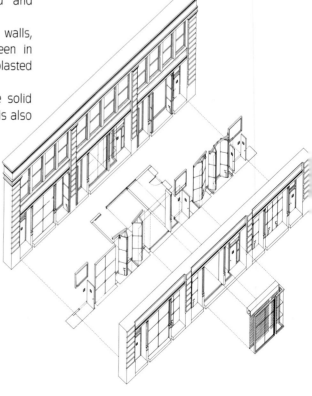

EAST ELEVATION   SECTION   SECTION   WEST ELEVATION

0 2 4 8   16 feet

Robert A. M. Stern Architects

RESIDENCE

Brooklyn, New York, NY, 1983–1986
Design Team: Alan Gerber, Anthony Cohn, David Eastman, William Georgis, Warren A. James, Kristin McMahon

This single-family detached house occupies a narrow lot in an established neighborhood. The design attempts to refine the architectural themes that typify the neighboring houses, and to establish a unique identity through the quality and character of its detailing and the rich mixture of its materials. The basement and first floor are rusticated with alternating bands of red brick and granite, while the second floor is faced with cream-colored stucco. The walls are punctured with painted steel casement windows and capped by a green-glazed tile hipped roof. The dormers serve as clerestories for the second floor bathrooms, providing additional light to the middle of the house.

Rooms are gathered about an entry hall that rises two floors through the house and culminates in a gilt dome. The constricted space requirements are perceptually aggrandized by generous twelve-foot ceilings and by the arrangement of the rooms along an axis that permits space to be visually borrowed from adjacent hallways and rooms.

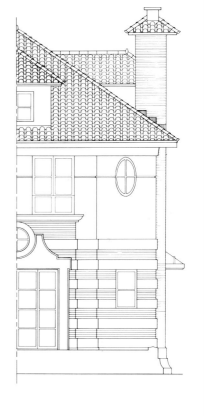

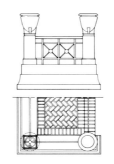

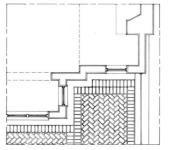

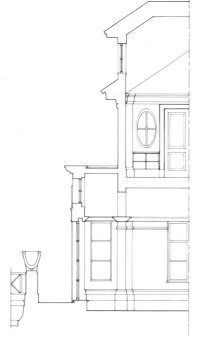

220

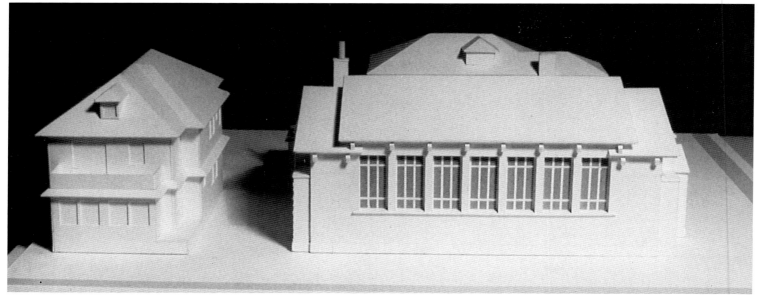

Robert A. M. Stern Architects

KOL ISRAEL CONGREGATION [75]

3211 Bedford Avenue, Brooklyn, New York,
NY, 1988
Design Team: Thomas A. Kligerman, Augusta
Barone, Victoria Casaseo, Peter Dick, Caryl
Kinsey, Timothy Lenahan

This synagogue for a growing congregation
occupies a corner site in an established residential neighborhood. The massing is arranged
to present a civic scale along the major avenue
and a more intimate entrance front on the residential cross street. The brick, stone, and tile
exterior adapts the Mediterranean vocabulary
of the surrounding houses to the public scale
and use of the new structure.

To accommodate an otherwise oversized
congregation and conform to stringent zoning
setback and height limitations, the entire site
has been excavated to allow for a large
sanctuary level below grade. The building is
entered at a half level; members of the congregation either walk up a level to the balconies or
walk down to the main sanctuary level.

SOUTH ELEVATION

INTERIOR EAST ELEVATION

The Stubbins Associates

CITICORP CENTER [45]

Lexington Avenue, New York, NY, 1973–1978

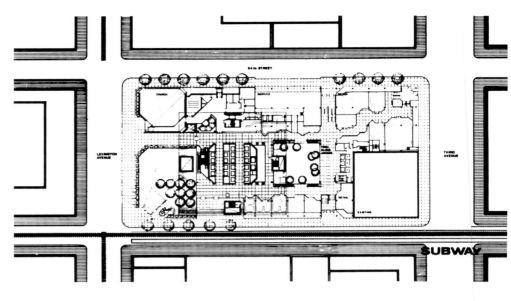

One of the most striking features of the project is the elevation of the tower 114 feet above the street, supported on four piers. The piers are located at the mid-point of each face of the tower, leaving the corners to cantilever into space. Several factors strongly influenced this particular design: zoning, the politics of real estate assemblage, economics, and aesthetics. The site afforded the opportunity to physically relate the project to the existing subway mezzanine under 53rd Street by including a lower level plaza and connecting this into the subway area. Control of the key real estate parcel was held by Saint Peter's Lutheran Church. Their turn-of-the century neo-Gothic structure and related buildings covered almost 30% of the site. By elevating the tower and opening the corner, it was possible to incorporate a new facility free in appearance, and in fact, from the bulk of the tower.

Another distinctive feature is the crown, or sloped top, of the tower. The original concept was to include 100 condominium apartments in the crown. Each unit would have an enclosed balcony, sloped and facing south. At the time, this was not politically possible, and the apartments were dropped from the program. The form of the crown was so significant, however, that it was retained. Cooling towers and mechanical equipment occupy the majority of its interior. On the sloping face of the crown solar collectors can be installed when they become economically justifiable.

Each floor has an area of 24,400 square feet. Within the forty-five feet from the core to each exterior wall there are no columns to interrupt the flexible office space. A 4' 9" building module is used throughout. Elevator service is by a double deck system utilizing twenty shafts (forty cabs) broken down into three vertical zones. Service is extremely efficient with a floor/car ratio approaching 1:1. Bright, reflective aluminum panels and reflective, double glazed insulating glass provide the exterior cladding of the entire project.

Within the low-rise portion of the complex is a seven-story skylit atrium or galleria. Surrounding the galleria on three levels is a retail shopping facility. The four upper levels around the galleria accommodate executive offices for the client. Access into the galleria is provided from 53rd and 54th Streets by means of a through-block arcade. Access is also provided from Third Avenue and Lexington Avenue.

Brick paving visually unifies all the public circulation areas, within the galleria, around the block on the sidewalks, and within the plaza area.

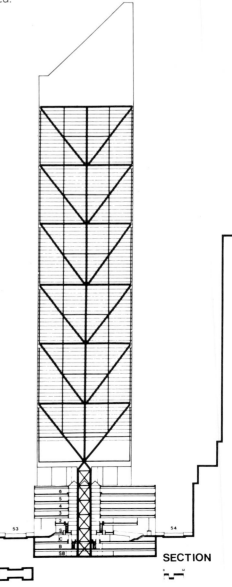

SECTION

Swanke Hayden Connell

STATUE OF LIBERTY [69]

Liberty Island, New York, NY, 1986

The responsibilities entrusted to the firm by the National Park Service were threefold: to restore the Statue as a sculpture, as a structure, and as a symbol; to create a new visitor transportation system within the pedestal; and to provide for a new museum within the fort at the Statue's base.

The diagnosis of the Statue's problem took more than a year of work. Drawings had been lost or destroyed. Research was conducted in Paris, at the Bartholdi Museum in Alsace, and at all available sources in New York City and Washington, D.C., in an attempt to understand how the Statue worked. The route of discovery took the architects to the use of models, computer analysis, chemical testing, and photogrammetry. Through these techniques, the architects were able to define the problem areas and to recommend proper solutions.

One of the mandates in the restoration effort was to design a museum in the base and to supply plans for a fitting and impressive entrance to it. To accomplish this, an entrance structure, built in the 1960s, was removed. With this structure gone, the Centennial entrance could now be centered on a monumental paved promenade. The Centennial doors for this entrance are of cast bronze with bas-relief sculptures in ten panels which tell the story of the present restoration. The pair of doors, each twenty-one feet high and four-and-a-half feet wide, is a dignified entrance to this important monument.

Research and experiment proved that the architects were right in their assumption that within the base there was a hidden tunnel which had been blocked up. The old torch and flame, which was removed in 1984, has been placed in the center of the Grand Hall. Visitors may view the exhibits on either side and in the balconies or can climb a staircase to enter the imposing space of the pedestal, and ascend by elevator to the cavity of the Statue. From there, they can view the vastness of the Statue's cavity and can climb the helical stairs to the crown.

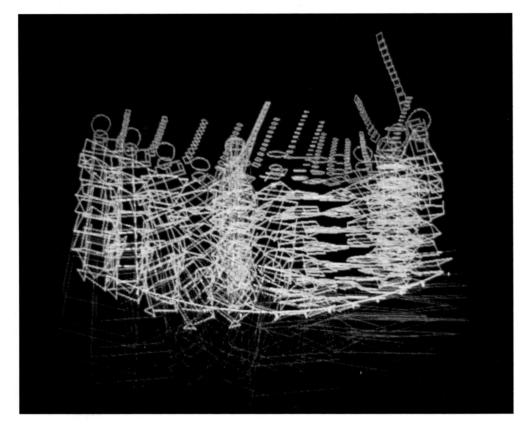

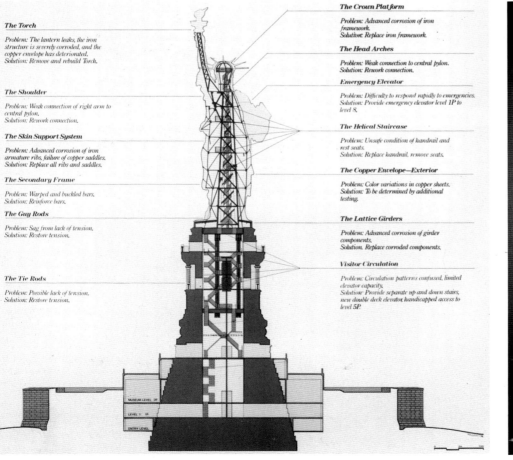

The Torch

Problem: The lantern leaks, the iron structure is severely corroded, and the copper envelope has deteriorated.
Solution: Remove and rebuild Torch.

The Shoulder

Problem: Weak connection of right arm to central pylon.
Solution: Rework connection.

The Skin Support System

Problem: Advanced corrosion of iron armature ribs, failure of copper saddles.
Solution: Replace all ribs and saddles.

The Secondary Frame

Problem: Warped and buckled bars.
Solution: Reinforce bars.

The Guy Rods

Problem: Sag from lack of tension.
Solution: Restore tension.

The Tie Rods

Problem: Possible lack of tension.
Solution: Restore tension.

The Crown Platform

Problem: Advanced corrosion of iron framework.
Solution: Replace iron framework.

The Head Arches

Problem: Weak connection to central pylon.
Solution: Rework connection.

Emergency Elevator

Problem: Difficulty to respond rapidly to emergencies.
Solution: Provide emergency elevator level 1P to level 8.

The Helical Staircase

Problem: Unsafe condition of handrail and rest seats.
Solution: Replace handrail, remove seats.

The Copper Envelope—Exterior

Problem: Color variations in copper sheets.
Solution: To be determined by additional testing.

The Lattice Girders

Problem: Advanced corrosion of girder components.
Solution: Replace corroded components.

Visitor Circulation

Problem: Circulation patterns confused, limited elevator capacity.
Solution: Provide separate up and down stairs, new double deck elevator, handicapped access to level 5P.

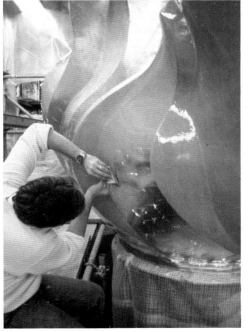

Swanke Hayden Connell

FELDMAN TOWER 45   [40]

120 West 45th Street, New York, NY, 1987–1988

Program: 400,000 square feet of office and retail space.

Site: The 28,000-square-foot mid-block site is in New York City's theater district. An existing three-story landmark theater must be preserved at the south portion of the site. An existing easement agreement with an adjacent property owner dictates a 35-foot wide, 90-foot deep, and 175-foot high open space at the development's east boundary.

Solution: The most important element of the project is the large entrance space mandated by the easement agreement. This fourteen-story outdoor space will provide views and daylight to adjacent office spaces and add to the building's identity along the street. A prominent American artist's contribution, the concept of twenty live trees growing directly on the courtyard structural braces, will filter south sunlight and buffer the effects of northern winds at the courtyard. The trees will also provide much needed natural imagery to the highly structured space.

The tower portion of the project is intentionally very simple, consisting of L-shaped floors clad in the iron spot brick and limestone tradition of the theater district. The limestone base establishes a human scale in the streetscape consistent with the neighborhood. Similarly, limestone accents in the tower serve to soften the scale and describe the organization of the tower form.

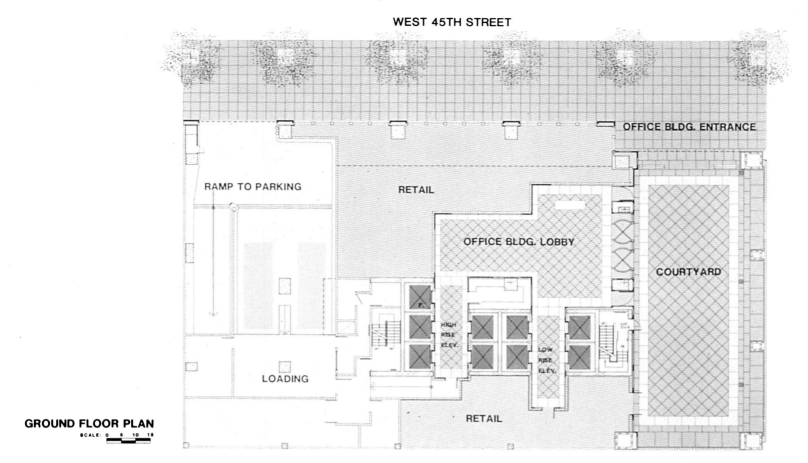

WEST 45TH STREET

OFFICE BLDG. ENTRANCE

RAMP TO PARKING

RETAIL

OFFICE BLDG. LOBBY

COURTYARD

HIGH RISE ELEV.

LOW RISE ELEV.

LOADING

RETAIL

GROUND FLOOR PLAN
SCALE: 0   5   10   15

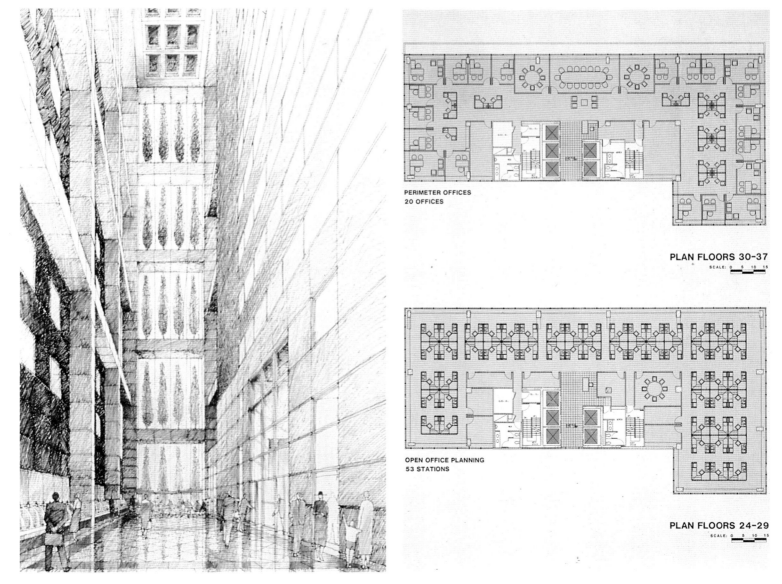

PERIMETER OFFICES
20 OFFICES

PLAN FLOORS 30-37
SCALE: 0   5   10   15

OPEN OFFICE PLANNING
53 STATIONS

PLAN FLOORS 24-29
SCALE: 0   5   10   15

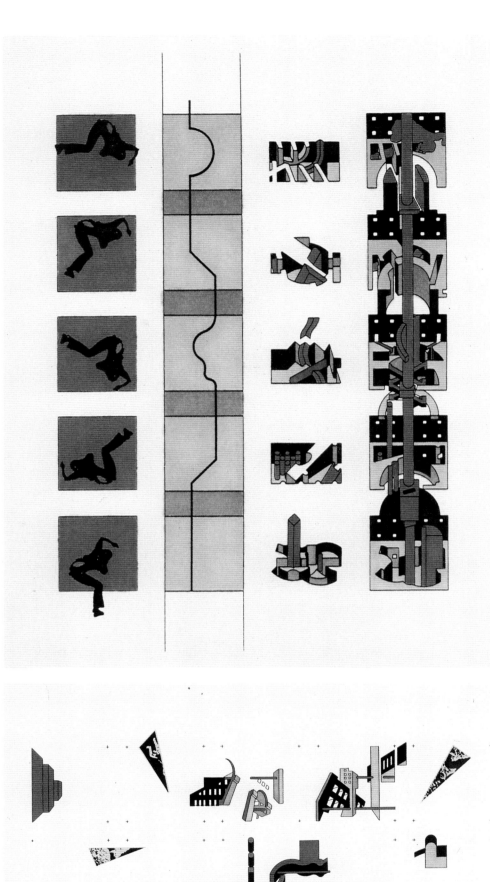

Bernard Tschumi Architects

THE MANHATTAN TRANSCRIPTS

New York, NY, 1981–1982

"The Manhattan Transcripts" differ from most architectural drawings insofar as they are neither real projects nor mere fantasies. They propose to transcribe an architectural interpretation of reality. To this aim, they use a particular structure indicated by photographs that either direct or "witness" events (some would say "functions," others would call them "programs"). At the same time, plans, sections, and diagrams outline spaces and indicate the movements of the different protagonists – those people intruding into the architectural "stage set." The effect is not unlike an Eisenstein film script or some Moholy-Nagy stage directions. Even if the "Transcripts" become a self-contained set of drawings, with its own internal coherence, they are first a device. Their explicit purpose is to transcribe things normally removed from conventional architectural representation, namely, the complex relationship between spaces and their use; between the set and the script; between "type" and "program;" between objects and events. Their implicit purpose has to do with the twentieth-century city.

The "Transcripts" are about a set of disjunctions among use, form, and social values. The non-coincidence between meaning and being, movement and space, man and object is the starting condition of the work. Yet the inevitable confrontation of these terms produces effects of far-ranging consequence. Ultimately, the "Transcripts" try to offer a different reading of architecture in which space, movement, and events are independent, yet stand in a new relation to one another, so that the conventional components of architecture are broken down and rebuilt along different axes.

While the programs used for "The Manhattan Transcripts" are of the most extreme nature, they also parallel the most common formula plot: the archetype of murder. Other phantasms are occasionally used to underline the fact that perhaps all architecture, rather than being about functional standards, is about love and death. By going beyond the conventional definition of use, the "Transcripts" use their tentative format to explore unlikely confrontations.

The Manhattan Transcripts
1977

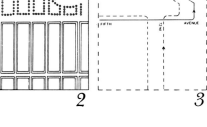
1   *2*   *3*

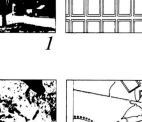
1   *2*   *3*

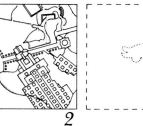
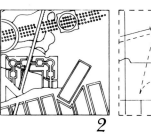
1   *2*   *3*

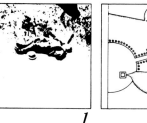
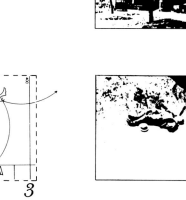
1   *2*   *3*

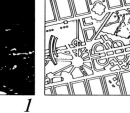
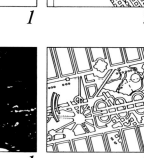
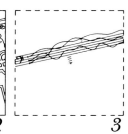
1   *2*   *3*

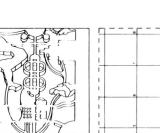
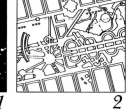
1   *2*   *3*

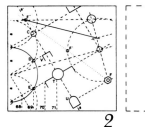
1   *2*   *3*

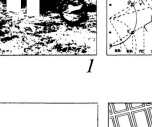
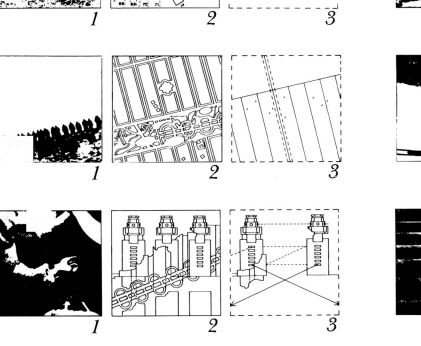

1   *2*   *3*

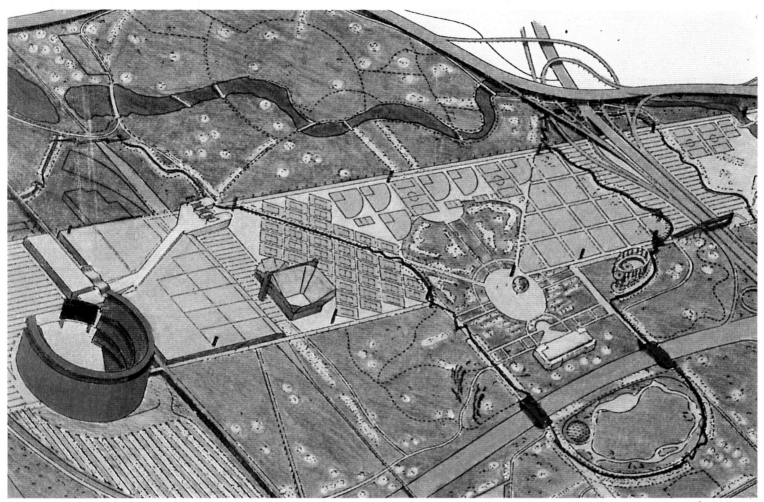

Bernard Tschumi Architects/ FMCP Task Force

FLUSHING MEADOWS CORONA PARK   [79]
Overall Plan

Flushing Meadows Corona Park, New York, NY
Project, 1988–1989
Design Team: FMCP Task Force. A collaborative
effort by Bernard Tschumi, Karen B. Alschuler,
William R. Alschuler, Nicholas Quennell, Alan
Plattus

Flushing Meadows Corona Park, New York, is
a 1,250 acre (4 miles by 1 mile) strip of land near
La Guardia Airport that includes marinas, Shea
Stadium, USTA Tennis Championship Grounds,
the site of the 1939/1964 World Fairs, and two
large lakes. Design strategy includes new site
plan, with active sports and recreation areas,
and reconsideration of major cultural facilities,
including Queens Museum, the Hall of Science,
Ederle Theater, New York Pavilion, etc.

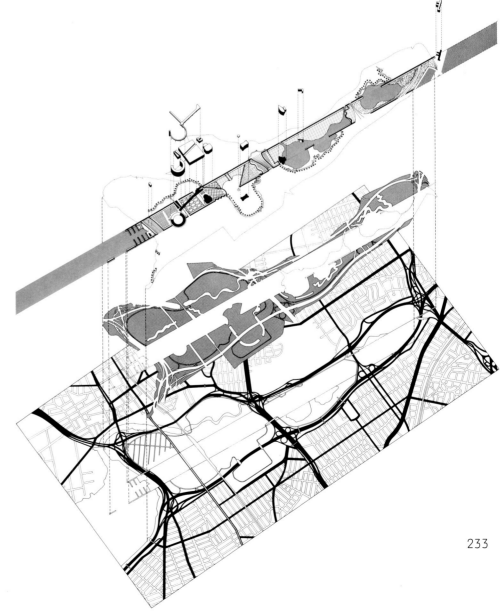

233

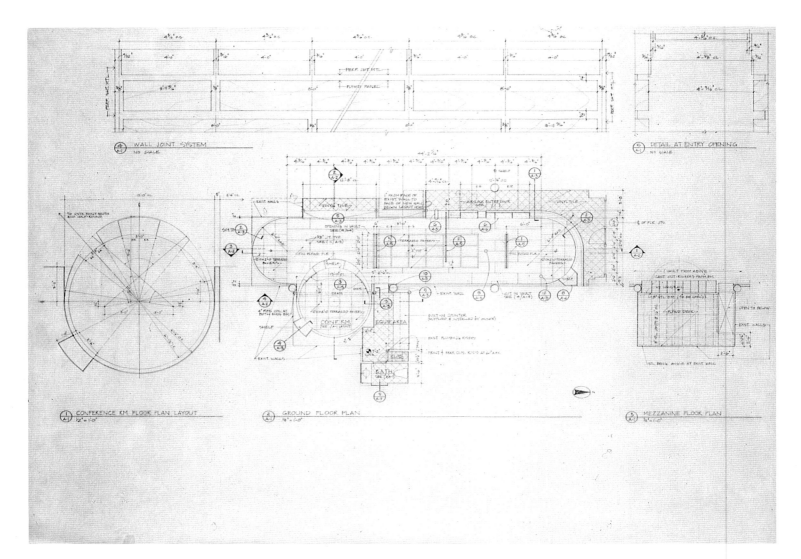

UKZ Design, Inc.
Kiss, Zwigard

GLOBUS GROWTH GROUP   [80]

44 West 24th Street, New York, NY, 1988

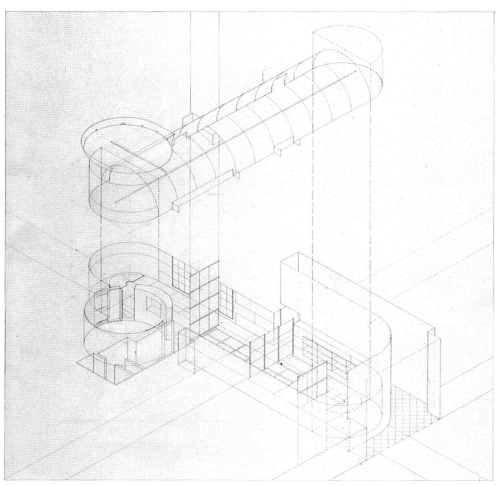

Program: Corporate headquarters for a small investment group, consisting of general office space for two partners, an accountant, and a receptionist, conference room for eight people, mailroom/office equipment area, and storage. Space of approximately 1,300 square feet with storefront and a 1:5 width to length proportion.

This project deals with the plastic manipulation inherent in dynamic architecture. The main focus is on the definition of space through the manipulation of descriptive edges. The main space contains all the work areas with the two partners located at opposite ends. An egg-shaped conference room partially intersects the main room. The mailroom/office equipment area is located off to the side of the main room adjacent to the conference room. The entry is relocated to coincide with the center of the main room. The main space has a perforated sheet metal vaulted ceiling and curved end wall surfaces, cabinet grade plywood walls, and floors with terrazzo paved insets. The conference room has a suspended steel and Lexan lighting structure with sheet metal walls and terrazzo floor. The dividing screens are stainless steel frames with Lexan thermoclear infill.

UKZ Design, Inc.
Ungers, Kiss, Zwigard

PAN AM BUILDING ROOFTOP DEVELOPMENT   [42]

Vanderbilt Avenue/East 45th Street, New York, NY, Project, 1980

Program: A major space for varied public functions, such as a nightclub, casino, bars, restaurant, a skyline-promenade, and space for live broadcasting of small shows.

Site: On top of the Pan Am Building in Midtown Manhattan. Almost half of the existing roof is taken up with the building's air conditioning exhaust.

Solution: The new structure is independent of, but in harmony with, the existing building. Independent, so it may be perceived as an addition rather than an extension which creates an ensemble integrating the Helmsley Building. Harmonious, in the sense that it follows the already established symmetry. The result is a completely glass enclosed spherical structure supported by a four-column steel frame; in essence a concept that assumes the iconic qualities of the existing one. However, in contrast it seems to "float" above the Heliport to accent the very tentative connection to the existing building. The intent is not to divert the focus of the Pan Am Building itself but to create a sense of completeness by combining two structures of universal architectonic language which are at once integrated and independent of each other.

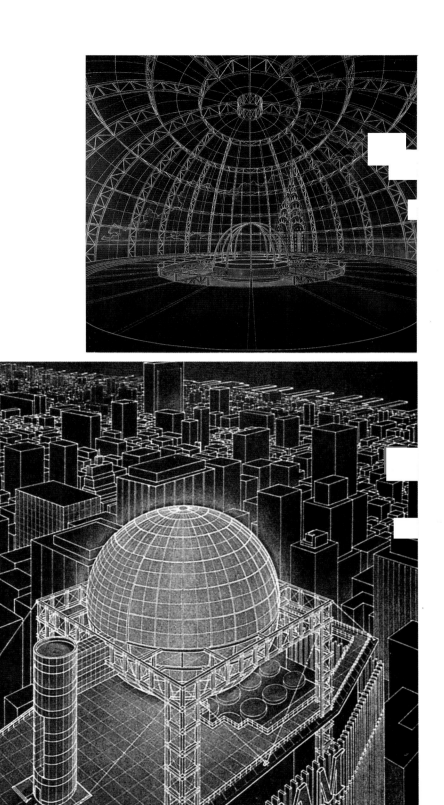

235

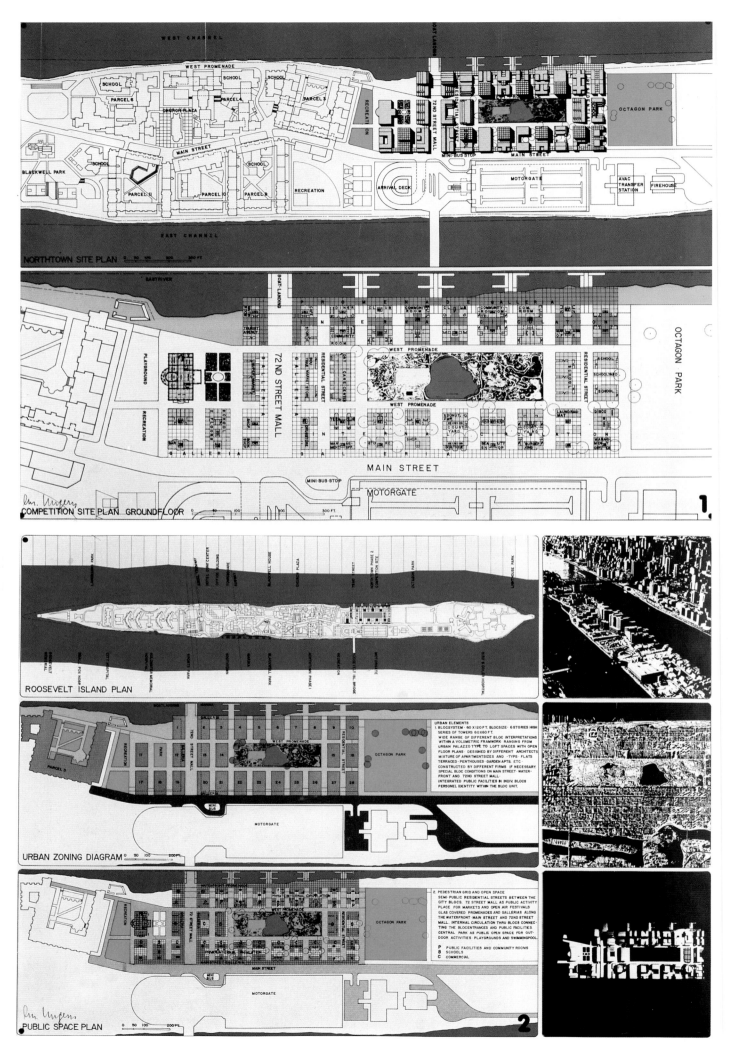

NORTHTOWN SITE PLAN

COMPETITION SITE PLAN GROUNDFLOOR

ROOSEVELT ISLAND PLAN

URBAN ZONING DIAGRAM

URBAN ELEMENTS

1. BLOCSYSTEM · 60 X 120 FT. · BLOCSIZE · 6 STORIES HIGH SERIES OF TOWERS 60X60 FT.
WIDE RANGE OF DIFFERENT BLOC INTERPRETATIONS WITHIN A VOLUMETRIC FRAMEWORK RANGING FROM URBAN PALAZZO TYPE TO LOFT SPACES WITH OPEN FLOOR PLANS · DESIGNED BY DIFFERENT ARCHITECTS · MIXTURE OF APARTMENTSIZES AND -TYPS · FLATS TERRACED · PENTHOUSES · GARDEN APTS. ETC · CONSTRUCTED BY DIFFERENT FIRMS IF NECESSARY · SPECIAL BLOC CONDITIONS ON MAIN STREET · WATERFRONT AND 72ND STREET MALL
INTEGRATED PUBLIC FACILITIES IN INDIV. BLOCS · PERSONEL IDENTITY WITHIN THE BLOC UNIT.

2. PEDESTRIAN GRID AND OPEN SPACE
SEMI PUBLIC RESIDENTIAL STREETS BETWEEN THE CITY BLOCS. 72 STREET MALL AS PUBLIC ACTIVITY PLACE FOR MARKETS AND OPEN AIR FESTIVALS · GLAS COVERED PROMENADES AND GALLERIAS ALONG THE WATERFRONT · MAIN STREET AND 72ND STREET MALL. INTERNAL CIRCULATION THRU BLOCS CONNECTING THE BLOCENTRANCES AND PUBLIC FACILITIES · CENTRAL PARK AS PUBLIC OPEN SPACE FOR OUTDOOR ACTIVITIES · PLAYGROUNDS AND SWIMMINGPOOL.

P   PUBLIC FACILITIES AND COMMUNITY ROOMS
S   SCHOOLS
C   COMMERCIAL

PUBLIC SPACE PLAN

Oswald Mathias Ungers

ROOSEVELT ISLAND COMPETITION [83]

Roosevelt Island, New York, NY
Competition, 1974

The design refers to images directly related to the particular location. It is based on an urban three-block system defining urban elements like a mall, called 72nd Street Mall, residential streets, and a central park.

All the elements are stated as a direct reference to the Island of Manhattan and are meant to intensify the "genius loci." The blocks are 60 × 120 feet, six stories high, and contain 20 – 30 apartments of different sizes, orientation, and plans. A diagrammatic plan establishes a basic building envelope for 28 equal urban blocks. Within that envelope the architectural interpretation can vary from the loft space, the standard urban block to the urban palazzo or villa type interpretation. The blocks will be differentiated first by functions, such as small, medium, or large size apartments; second by types, such as terraced houses, courtyard blocks, and corridor types; third by units, such as garden apartments, penthouses, flats, or duplex arrangements; fourth by plans, such as flexible open floor plans, fixed arrangements, and special plan types; and fifth by location, such as proximity to the park, waterfront, or regular street locations. The design proposal only provides a number of alternatives as possible interpretations. As the plan reaches its final stage the variations could be expanded. Consideration of different construction methods, issues determined by a number of different developers, or realizations in stages over a longer period of time could be accommodated.

The plan also allows not only for the participation of tenant groups who could participate in determining the final design of their urban block, but also a number of different architects could be involved in the design of the block units and make their individual urban-villa interpretation.

The intention of the scheme is to enforce a wide range of design interpretations within a general framework. Traditional blocks could be sitting next to a more sophisticated modern design or technologically more advanced scheme. To demonstrate the concept of variation the White House metaphor is used as an example. It stands for the most elaborate and specific apartment type block.

Each block contains some sort of public facility on the ground floor. Most of the shopping facilities are located along Main Street and 72nd Street Mall, while the community rooms, cafés, and bars are on the waterfront. All the facilities are connected by a glass-covered galleria on the outside of the development.

A more informal, semi-private circulation runs through the center of the blocks connecting the facilities on the ground floor. The location of the two schools and the day care center is such that it relates directly to a larger open space. The public open space is designed as a common central park which contains playgrounds, places for outdoor activities, and a public swimming pool. The park space is conceived as an analogy to Central Park in Manhattan.

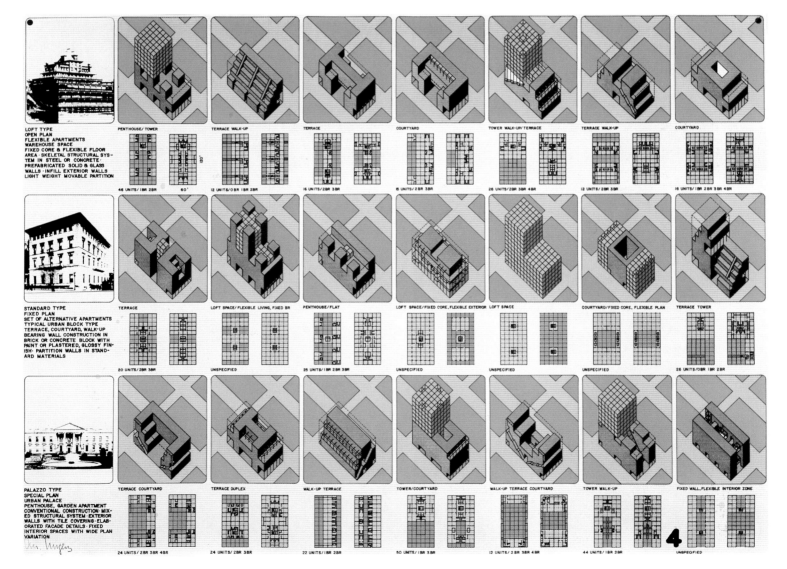

Simon Ungers

NEW YORK CITY WATERFRONT COMPETITION   [16]

Battery Park City to 54th Street, New York, NY
Competition, 1987

The New York City Waterfront Competition was sponsored by the Municipal Art Society of New York. The site extends along the Westside from Battery Park City to 54th Street. In the words of the competition brief, "this is an idea competition aimed at encouraging imagination and thought about the form, activities, and character of the edge of Manhattan on the Hudson River." Although the intent of the competition is commendable, it is difficult to imagine that a truly purposeful and public urban strategy could be implemented in a city controlled by private interests. This entry is about the futility of a realistic proposition. Instead it envisions a "drying-up" of the Hudson River to expose an abstracted geological formation based upon diagrams of subterranean granite formations. The project is an allegory.

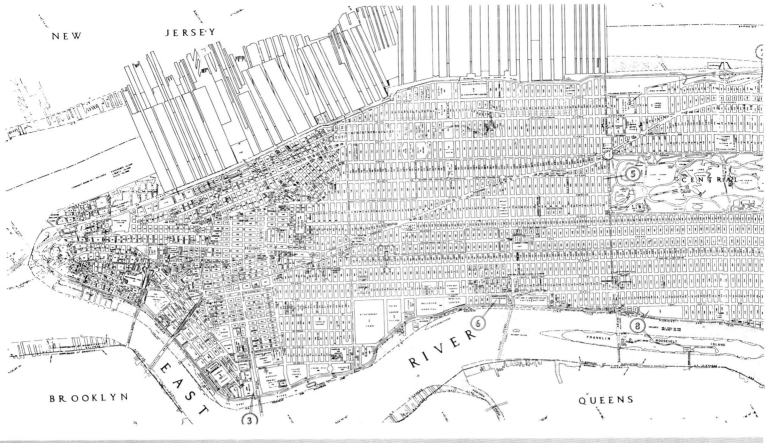

Venturi, Rauch and Scott Brown

TIMES SQUARE PLAZA DESIGN [39]

Times Square, New York, NY
Competition, 1984

A design was required that would retain references to the popular, glittering, commercial-sign architecture associated with Times Square and that would contain at the same time qualities consistent with the proposed new high-rise buildings to surround it.

This design proposes a Big Apple: a piece of representational sculpture which is bold in form yet rich in symbolism, realism with a diversity of associations. It is popular and esoteric – a Big Apple symbolizing New York City and a surrealistic object evoking René Magritte or a Pop Art monument in the manner of Claes Oldenburg. It is stark in its simplicity and monumental in scale; but it is also ambiguous in scale because of its very simplicity.

Contrasts and ambiguities in scale along with unusual juxtapositions are traditional means of creating surprise, tension, and richness in urban architecture. Some New York examples are the Statue of Liberty, the Little Church around the Corner, and Trinity Church on Wall Street.

The round form of the Big Apple provides an appropriate counterpoint to the bulk and angularity of the surrounding buildings. Despite its size, it promotes also a sense of openness and airiness in the space through its shape and "floating" quality. This apple, 90-foot-plus in diameter, is the modern equivalent of the Baroque obelisk identifying the center of a plaza.

The base for the round sculptural apple would be angular and architectural, a replication in elevation and material of the bases of the surrounding buildings to promote the architectural unity of the complex. It will include the traditional element of nighttime and daytime glitter characteristic of the buildings along the sidewalks. A moving news sign that forms the architrave of the base structure will be reminiscent of the former New York Times sign. The interior uses of the base are open to future consideration but could be used for many purposes, for example, tourist information facilities, an international book store, the TKTS ticket outlet, or a panoramic museum of Manhattan.

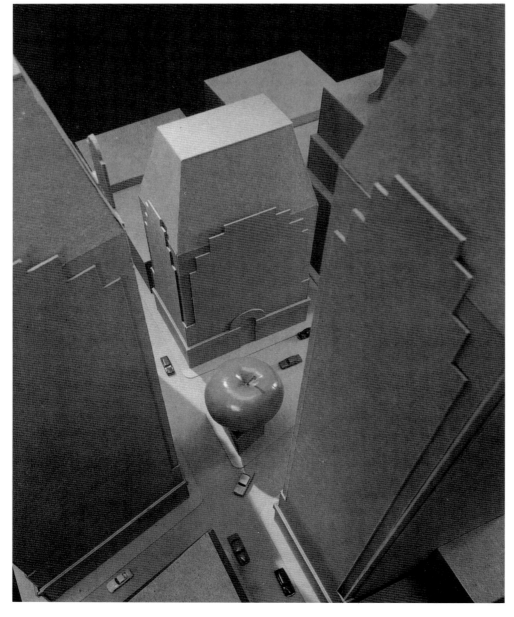

241

Venturi, Rauch and Scott Brown

WESTWAY [8]

New York, NY, Project, 1985

This continuous 97-acre riverfront park was designed as part of the $ 2 billion transportation project which was stopped in late 1985 by Congressional action. Its intent was to reopen the waterfront to the people of Manhattan, create new vitality along the river, and enhance the rich public environment of the individual neighborhoods as they interconnect with the Hudson River.

Venturi, Rauch and Scott Brown, in association with landscape architects Clarke & Rapuano Inc., were responsible for design and programming of the park system, development of a new street system and such other highway-related architectural elements as ventilation buildings, tunnel portals, signage, lighting, and finishes. The project also involved complex client and public design review processes and the coordination of community participation in those reviews.

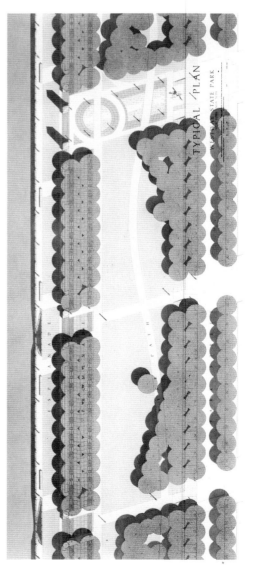

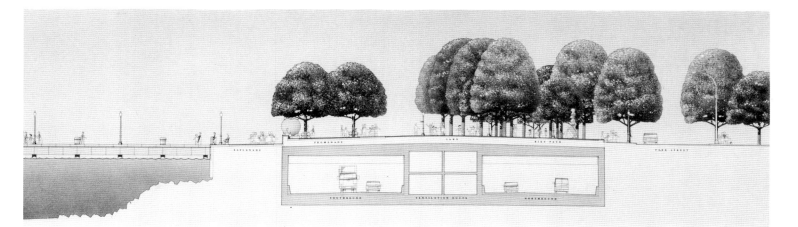

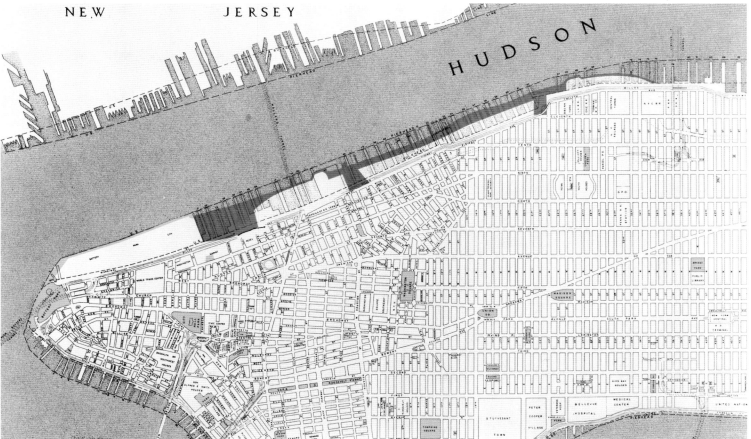

Vignelli Associates

OFFICES OF VIGNELLI ASSOCIATES [84]

475 10th Avenue, New York, NY, 1987
Design Team: Lella and Massimo Vignelli, David
Law, Michele Kolb, Lev Zeitlin, Robert Skolnik,
Robert Traboscia, Briggs MacDonald

The objective of this project was to design an office for a firm involved in two- and three-dimensional design, and to express visually the firm's philosophy and character regarding design. This project is a testing ground for new ideas in order to experience their tangible and intangible qualities in time.

Much of the exploration concerns ordinary materials that are applied in extraordinary ways. Furniture is made of crude steel sheets and tubes as they come from the foundry. Walls and doors are covered with square sheets of hand-waxed lead. Gold leaf is applied to industrial steel tubing and used as a base for a steel-topped table. Aluminum grids are finished with a random brushed pattern contrasting with sandblasted squares of glass. Particle board, stained white and lacquered, is used like fine wood to panel office walls, to encase the library in shelving, and to construct work stations in the studio. Corrugated galvanized steel forms a wall dividing the design studio from the service areas. All furniture and materials were developed especially for this project.

Rafael Viñoly Architects

THE MANHATTAN CONDOMINIUM   [33]

135 West 52nd Street, New York, NY, 1986

The project is located between the Avenue of the Americas and Seventh Avenue, and extends through-block from 52nd Street to 53rd Street. Toward the Avenue of the Americas, the site is bounded by the J. C. Penney Tower, and toward Seventh Avenue by the Sheraton Center. The "slab" portion of the building completes the wall of the block suggested by the corresponding plane of the main shafts of the Sheraton and the J. C. Penney buildings. A glass volume projects in front of this wall creating a midblock center-piece. Its gridded curtain wall attempts to be an overlap of the Sheraton's horizontal and J. C. Penney's vertical facade patterns. This positions the building as both an integral part of its context as well as a seemingly free-standing tower. A public galleria at the ground level is one link in a chain of through-block connections starting with the Equitable Life Building to the south and extending to a proposed tower to the north. A monumental wall transverses the Manhattan galleria, aligning with the eastern edge of the larger Equitable galleria in an effort to mediate the change in scale from one galleria to the next.

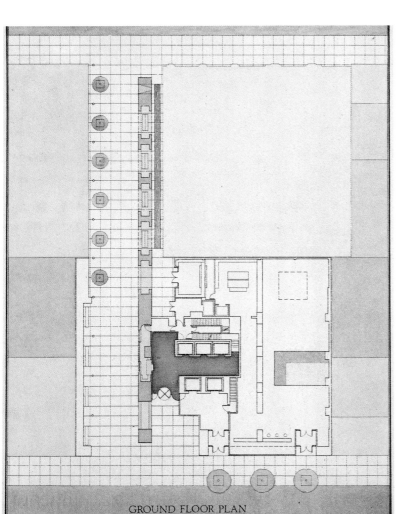

GROUND FLOOR PLAN

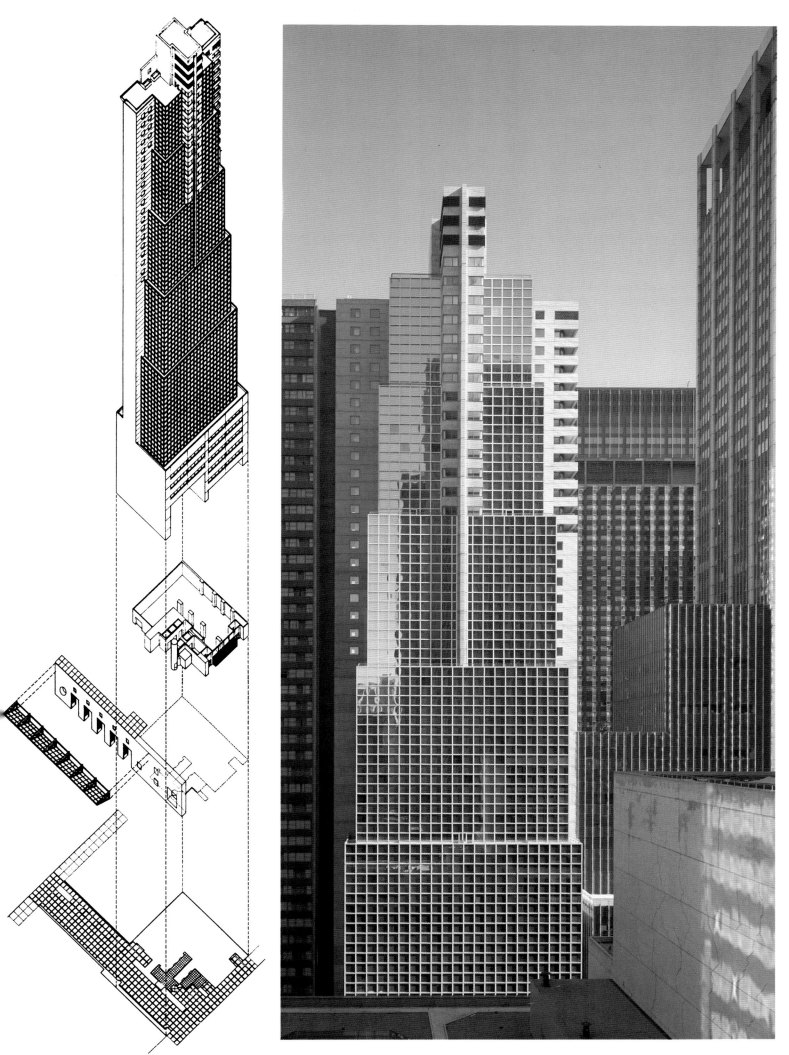

Rafael Viñoly Architects

JOHN JAY COLLEGE OF CRIMINAL JUSTICE   [21]

899 Tenth Avenue, New York, NY, 1988

A complex program for a 52,000-square-foot library, 750-seat theater, classrooms, administration space, a variety of common areas, and physical education facilities including a 25-meter pool and NCAA-sized gymnasium is distributed so that the components requiring the larger, long-span spaces are located in the annex, while library, classroom, and administrative functions are within the existing structure. The design for the annex and the sixth floor contrasts with the Flemish-Renaissance style of the existing building. The main common space for the school is an interior court along the entry axis that will be surrounded by the two-story library. Varying types of common areas are located throughout the facility, including an outdoor cloister at the classroom level and a running track and terrace on the roof.

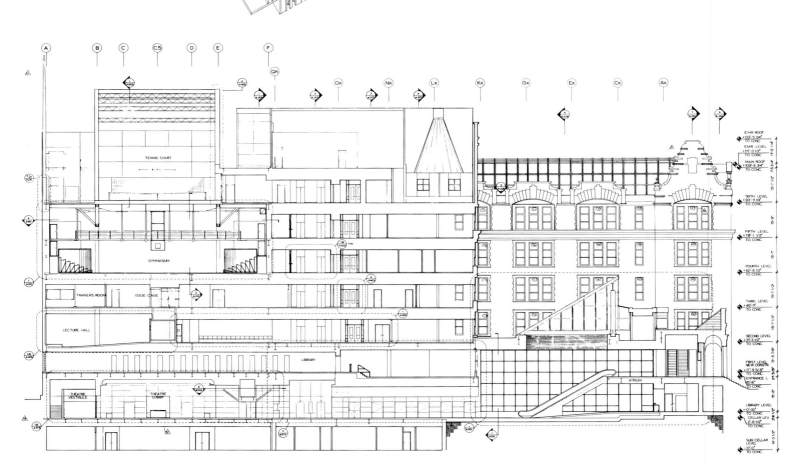

VIEW FROM NORTH EAST

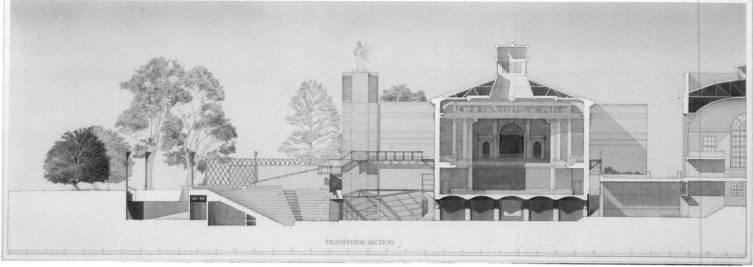

TRANSVERSE SECTION

Rafael Viñoly Architects

SNUG HARBOR MUSIC HALL   [72]

Staten Island, New York, NY
Competition, 1988

Snug Harbor comprises an orderly disposition of Greek Revival buildings, set in a bucolic, overgrown landscape. The temple form is the prototype for the complex and, throughout the building and expansion of Snug Harbor, has been adapted for many different functions. In the site's new incarnation as a cultural center, this model should continue to be respected.

The curved driveway that leads to the front of the Music Hall is realigned and regraded to connect with the path between the two rows of buildings. The front stair is extended to meet this new level, creating a "porte cochere" for a new ground level entry. Also, an amphitheater echoing the curve of the drive is introduced to the east of the existing structure.

The formal pairing of the Music Hall and the now demolished Randall Memorial Church was originally acknowledged by the placement of the Neptune Fountain on an axis that bisected the two and now culminates in a tower that will serve as a base for a sculpture which will be a marker for the performing arts complex.

Snug Harbor's performing arts complex will ultimately include three buildings: Veterans Memorial Hall (the former chapel), the Music Hall, and the Recreation Hall to the west. An

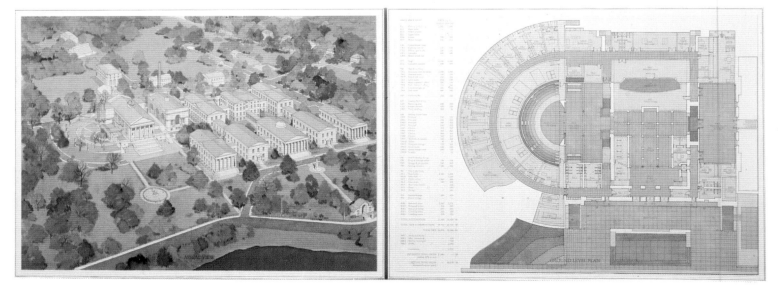

VIEW FROM NORTH EAST (CUT-AWAY)

EAST ELEVATION

elevated garden terrace links these three buildings.

The south facade of the Music Hall is relocated to accommodate a deeper stage. Viewed from the east, the composition of the tower, sculpture, fire stair, pergola, and the lantern and east facade of the Music Hall serves as a stage set for the outdoor performances.

The foyer is entered under a glass canopy which passes through the "porte cochere." Immediately past the glass entry doors are two ticket booths to either side. To the right is a new elevator and stair connecting to the existing lobby. To the left is a coat room and a corridor that leads to the public toilets, telephones, and the public access to the support areas.

Beyond the foyer is the passage which perpendicularly joins the hall, that, in turn, is the vestibule for the new lobby at the east end and the rehearsal room opposite. Two sets of stairs located at either end of the hall lead directly into the auditorium, through openings that were formerly fire exits and are now acoustically separated entrances.

The new lobby is a glass enclosure opening onto the amphitheater and the park. From outside, it reveals the original arched foundations of the Music Hall, and the new spaces within.

The rehearsal room is entered from the hall or from the outside. Neither means of entry requires going through the auditorium. The theater support functions are linked to this room by doors on the southern end of the east wall.

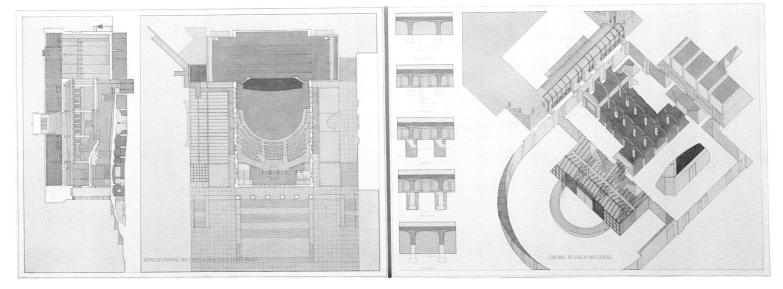

LONGITUDINAL SECTION & BALCONY LEVEL PLAN

CHOBY AT GROUND LEVEL

Voorsanger & Mills Associates

BROOKLYN MUSEUM [74]
Master Plan

Brooklyn, New York, NY
Competition, 1986

Three essential objectives in the Brooklyn Museum's building program governed the design of our master plan: first, the desire to expand the museum's facilities in phases rather than in one single addition; second, the desire to respect the original, landmarked, Beaux-Arts building; and third, the desire to connect to the adjacent Brooklyn Botanic Garden.

In our opinion, phased construction is the most important formal component of the museum's program which calls for the addition of approximately 500,000 square feet of galleries, offices, storage, and public support facilities – virtually doubling the size of the museum.

It was decided to make each of the five new construction phases a self-contained formal element hinged to a new spatial armature pinwheeling around the north-south axis of the museum. Each phase would comprise a memorable exterior image and coherent interior circulation as well as new galleries, offices, storage, and support spaces – with approximately one-fifth of the entire program allotted proportionally to each phase. The museum would then be functionally and formally independent at each stage, with or without the completion of the entire master plan.

The master plan is predicated on the notion of the building as connected fragments, in this case, the building as a cluster of fragments arranged in a taut pinwheel configuration with

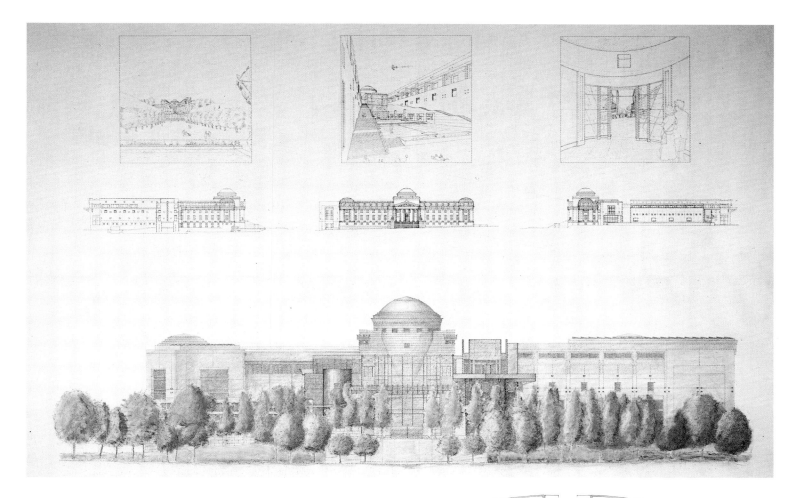

an underlying cruciform circulation armature organizing the structure and its spaces. The circulation routes are always on the periphery of the building, so that the visitor is oriented by definitive space and a clear view of the building and the surrounding gardens.

The order in which additions are made can be altered, and future additions can logically continue beyond the present program.

GUIDER PARK URBAN REDEVOPMENT

S_2

S_3

K

J

H

M

L

F

G

N

P

E

D

C

B

A

S_1

MASTER PLAN · PHASING DIAGRAM

253

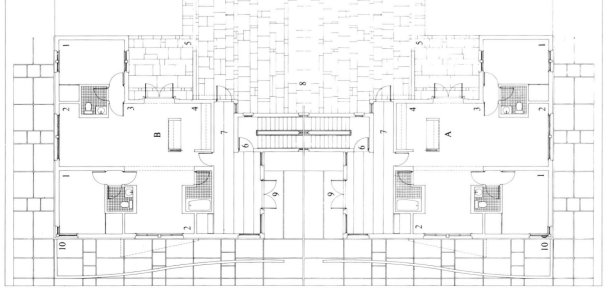

A	HANDICAPPED UNIT
B	HANDICAPPED UNIT
1	Bedroom
2	Living
3	Dining
4	Kitchen
5	Handicappped unit Terrace
	Entry Lobby
	Entry Lobby
6	Stair
7	Corridor/Hall
8	Public Garden
9	Entry Courtyard
10	Front Yard Gardens

Voorsanger & Mills Associates

"VACANT LOTS" HOUSING STUDY [64]

1000 Faile Street, South Bronx, New York, NY, 1987

Design Team: Bartholomew Voorsanger, Kevin Gordon, Randall Cude, Enrique Colmenares, Satoshi Ohashi, Anne Elizabeth Perl, Medea Eder

The project involves the development of eight cooperative apartments, with two to three dwelling units (bedroom/baths) for a total of twenty-two bedroom and bath combination units. Contextual and zoning constraints dictate the construction of a four-story building with a small basement to contain mechanical and ser-

vice systems, and a roof devoted to gardens for the units and a laundry facility.

Ground Floor: Two small entry lobbies serve the north and south wings of the building, and two handicapped persons' apartments. Each of these apartments has two bedrooms and opens to the rear garden with a precinct specifically allocated for handicapped seating. The ceiling height at this level will be 8 feet clear.

Second Floor: The second floor contains two apartments of three dwelling units (bedroom/ bath) per apartment. The ceiling height will be 11 feet clear and will offer each dwelling unit additional height of 4 feet for a loft above the bathroom/closet area. This additional height makes available dual uses such as a study area, studio or work area, or nursery.

The communal living area is shared by each unit holder, with a common kitchen and single lavatory with bath.

Third Floor: To the north, there will be a three dwelling unit simplex apartment with an 8-foot clear ceiling height. To the south is entry to two duplexes encompassing the third and fourth floors.

Fourth Floor: The north apartment is simplex with 11-foot clear ceiling height. The southern apartment is a duplex, having 11-foot ceiling heights in the upper level. The dwelling units at this level will have provisions for lofts.

Roof: There will be six areas owned and maintained as gardens by the six suites above the ground floor, to be used at their leisure.

Voorsanger & Mills Associates

HOSTOS COMMUNITY COLLEGE & ALLIED HEALTH COMPLEX [63]

475 – 500 Grand Concourse, Bronx, New York, NY, 1985 – 1990
Design Team: Bartholomew Voorsanger, Tom Brashares, Satoshi Ohashi, Shu Hashimoto, Paula Murphy, Daniel Alter, Noel Clarke in association with Hirsch/Danois Architects

The existing campus for the only Hispanic Community College within The City University system of New York straddles the entry to the Grand Concourse at 149th Street, consisting of a converted warehouse (475 Grand Concourse) and the 500 Grand Concourse classroom facility built in the mid-1970s. The enlarged campus will add three more phases of construction: Allied Health Complex: laboratories, school library, and classrooms (101,500 square feet, projected completion 1990); Theater, Gymnasium and Bridge Complex (designed by Gwathmey Siegel & Associates); renovation of 475 Grand Concourse and North Plaza (95,000 square feet, projected completion 1994).

The major public level of the campus is proposed at 23 feet above the street (3rd floor of the West Campus or bridge level). This floor becomes the circulation datum and entry to the major uses of the campus. A dialogue emerged between the architects as to the location of the pedestrian bridge, with the result that we responded to the bridge by locating a three-story cube – a porch overlooking the park and adjacent playgrounds – which becomes the departure point for the North/South spine and entry of the West Campus. The spine becomes a filter which has uses and circulation vertically and horizontally attached. The elements appended are the library, classrooms, laboratories, entry (at 149th Street and Grand Concourse) and the porch, and, at the roof, the major mechanical systems.

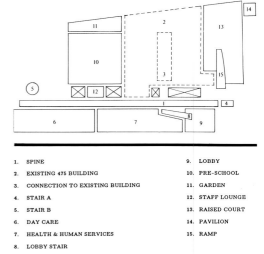

1. SPINE	9. LOBBY
2. EXISTING 475 BUILDING	10. PRE-SCHOOL
3. CONNECTION TO EXISTING BUILDING	11. GARDEN
4. STAIR A	12. STAFF LOUNGE
5. STAIR B	13. RAISED COURT
6. DAY CARE	14. PAVILION
7. HEALTH & HUMAN SERVICES	15. RAMP
8. LOBBY STAIR	

The existing 475 Grand Concourse will be renovated for laboratories and a major remedial learning center. The north plaza becomes an exterior reciprocal space to the interior atrium of the East Campus.

The ensemble of the West Campus responds to the existing Grand Concourse architecture by continuing the typical five-story elevational datum and by using contextual exterior materials: iron spot brick, the spine of a ribbed metal panel with a white reglet system, and white metallic mullions. The West Campus has emerged as an architectural dialogue with the Grand Concourse and the East Campus, and as an idea of an urban College.

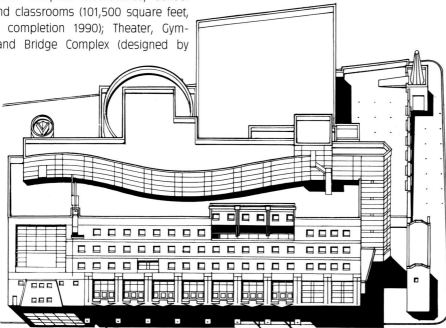

AXONOMETRIC AT GRAND CONCOURSE

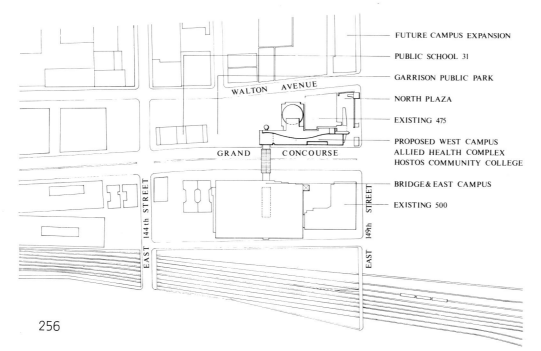

FUTURE CAMPUS EXPANSION
PUBLIC SCHOOL 31
GARRISON PUBLIC PARK
NORTH PLAZA
EXISTING 475
PROPOSED WEST CAMPUS
ALLIED HEALTH COMPLEX
HOSTOS COMMUNITY COLLEGE
BRIDGE & EAST CAMPUS
EXISTING 500

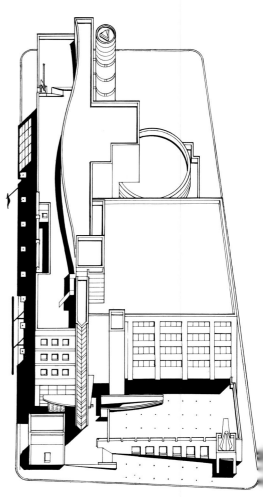

AXONOMETRIC AT 149TH STREET

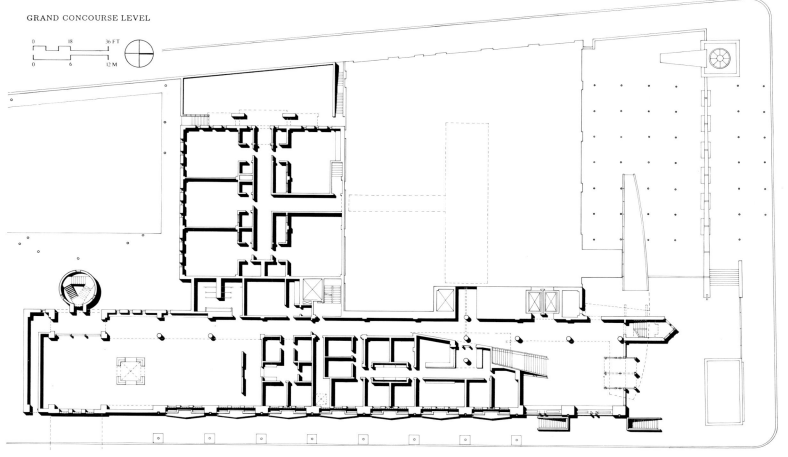

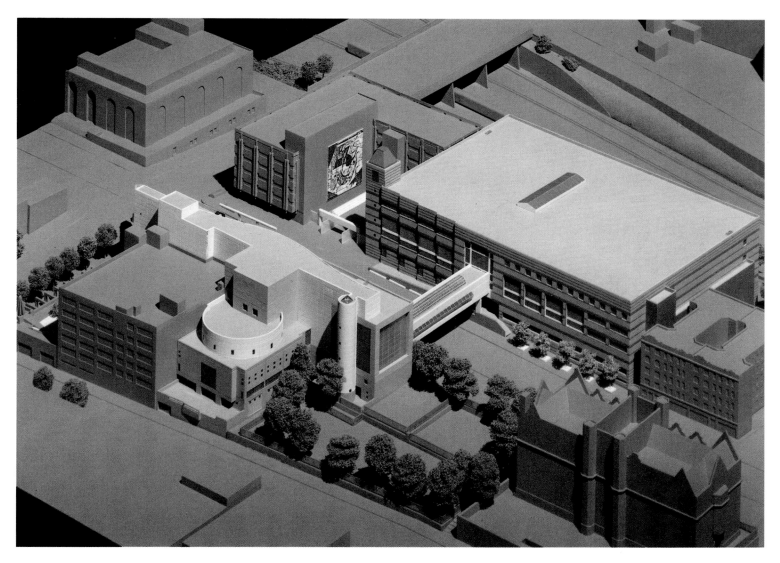

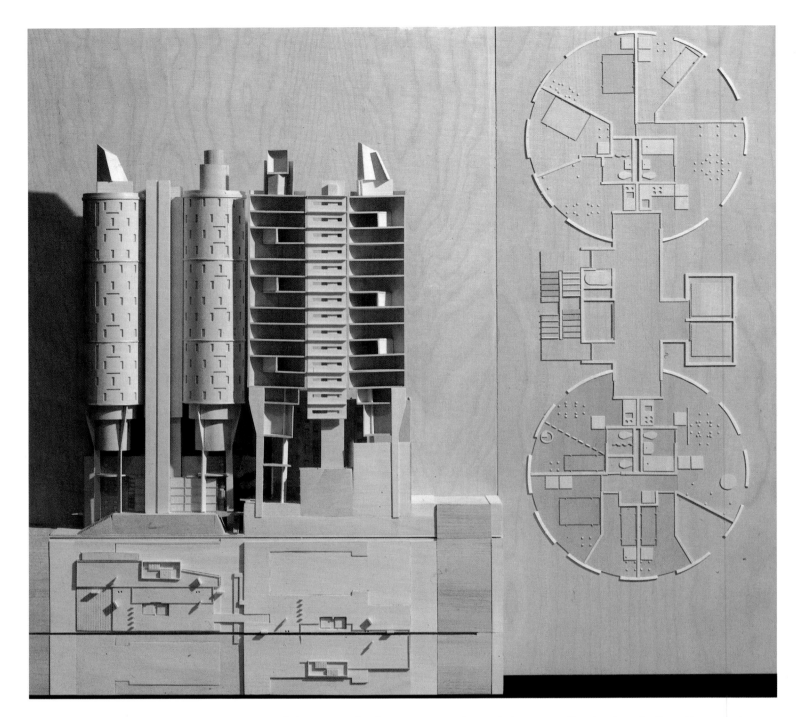

Tod Williams, Billie Tsien and Associates

"VACANT LOTS" PROPOSAL [62]

511 West 133rd Street, Harlem, Manhattan,
New York, NY, 1987
Design Team: Tod Williams, Billie Tsien, Rick
Gooding, Annie Chu, Marwan Al-Sayed, Tom Van
Den Bout, Thomas Gardner

This proposal accepts the open lot as a positive addition/subtraction to the dense Manhattan city block. It recognizes the importance of openings to the interior of the typical block. It does not, however, accept the vacancy of the open lot. It suggests that this exceptional condition of the open space implies a responsibility. This is a proposal for added density with neither diminution or destruction of available light, air, and urban resources. Instead, its intention is to provide an additional structure of housing alternatives.

The cylindrical towers, 35 feet in diameter, cast narrow shadows across the block. They are not walk ups, though stairways are used to communicate between several floors. The floor plans take their cues from lofts.

Communal accommodation, laundry, and children's play areas occur below the tower in private (for the community) indoor and outdoor space; commercial activity fronts on the street itself. For the apartments, open space with minimal plumbing and kitchen facilities is the starting point. Incentives would encourage individuals to create their own plans (including enlarged bathrooms and kitchens). Otherwise, more traditional apartment layouts are indicated. Within each cylinder, double-height spaces are proposed for additional floor area

as well as to give a feeling of increased space. As the exterior of each cylinder is structural, windows are both numerous and relatively small. A consistent window pattern is overlaid with additional openings that are view and site related. Although the general structural conditions of the cylinders are identical throughout, particulars of facade and especially of form and activity at street level would be determined case by case.

At 133rd Street, a broad stairway is used to enter the once vacant lot. Beneath the protective canopy of the structure, neighbors from the towers may gather and passersby cross through to 134th Street. The existing rubble stone retaining wall is revealed as an integral part of the street level garden. The lot is open but it is no longer empty.

Dig a hole to China

Tod Williams, Billie Tsien

THE COLUMBUS CIRCLE PROJECT   [26]

Columbus Circle, New York, NY, 1981

This is a speculative thought on the condition of Columbus Circle, New York City. Designated as a monument to Columbus, it has become a triangular island marooned in a sea of chaotic traffic.

The drawing suggests that the circle be made literally and that the excavation not only transform pedestrian and vehicular traffic but also expose to the air the archaeology of the city and of the earth below.

Tod Williams, Billie Tsien

STATUE OF LIBERTY   [70]

Liberty Island, New York, NY, Project, 1986

The Statue of Liberty sits upon a base designed by Richard Morris Hunt. This base is situated asymmetrically within the walls of an earlier star-shaped fortification. The fortification has an irregular relationship to the water's edge. The whole composite has an unsettled relationship to the island on which it rests. We proposed to site the statue within a square field of monumental columns. This assimilates the irregularity and captures the statue, the island, and water. Concrete columns rise to the height of Hunt's base. Atop each column is affixed a

free-wheeling copper rod. These rods whirl in the wind. During the day, they reflect glints of fiery light. They act as lightning rods during summer thunderstorms, and, at night, catch and reflect the movement of celestial and water-born phenomena.

Thus, while they provide an expanded sense of place and a celebratory atmosphere, they refer as well to the "rockets red glare." The dimension which they add not only enhances the character of the statue as a symbol of welcome but also poses alternate readings which touch upon aspects of power.

Buildings and
Projects
outside New York

Arquitectonica

THE RIVER CLUB

North Bergen, New Jersey, Project, 1987

This project attempts to provide a new image for condominium design along the Hudson River waterfront, while incorporating the functional and market requirements set forth by the developer.

This project is located on River Road, a heavily trafficked winding road linking the George Washington Bridge and the Hudson River west bank. The 69-unit apartment building is wedged into the hillside, and faces directly east to the spectacular Manhattan skyline. As in most suburban buildings, substantial parking requirements need to be accommodated. Because of the scope, the building needs to be raised to allow for ventilation at the rear. Accordingly the parking garage appears with the apartment slab resting above. The parking platform consists of a thick wall made out of large boulders very much like those seen in the Palisades behind. This wall is perforated by the entrance "porte cochere" and four elliptical openings into the garage. Supporting the large entrance opening is a row of square columns floating at an angle under the rocks.

The upper front, a dark green glass curtain wall, is interrupted by a series of angled balcony rows; a parody of the typical New York condominium towers, yet by itself a means of adding an aerodynamic quality to the facade design. These parallelogram balconies are clad in bright white marble, and extend six feet in front of the glass wall, appearing in different locations within the apartment units. The intermediate floor between the rock base and the "flag" above is curved and recessed with a shade of clear glass separating the two main bodies of the project.

The sides of the apartment building are extended to the ground.

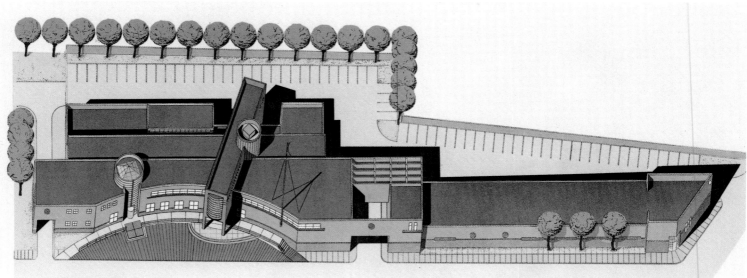

AXONOMETRIC

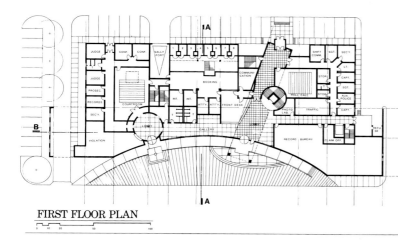

FIRST FLOOR PLAN

Vladimir Arsene
for Grad Partnership Architects

ELIZABETH POLICE HEADQUARTERS
AND MUNICIPAL COURT BUILDING

Elizabeth, New Jersey, 1985–1986
Design Team:
Vladimir Arsene, Marty Frauwirth, Ben Lee,
Dante Pedilla, Peter Pran

Part of Metropolitan New York, the City of Elizabeth lies across the Hudson River from Manhattan. Once a prosperous town and a major shipping port of New York, Elizabeth is now experiencing the beginning of an economic, social, and urban renaissance after many years of decline in the postwar period. Symbol of this renaissance, The Police Headquarters and Municipal Court Building is the largest single investment in the city in forty years and represents the municipality's search for the lost downtown urbanity and its prewar street walls.

The 575-foot-long, 96,878-square-foot complex is structured around a main and an annex building, housing together the municipal court, police headquarters, repair garage, electric bureau, and ambulance dispatcher.

Vladimir Arsene

for Grad Partnership Architects

UNIVERSITY SQUARE OFFICE BUILDING

Princeton, New Jersey, 1989
Design Team:
Vladimir Arsene, Vasant Kshirsagar, Robert McNamara, Kaushik Patel

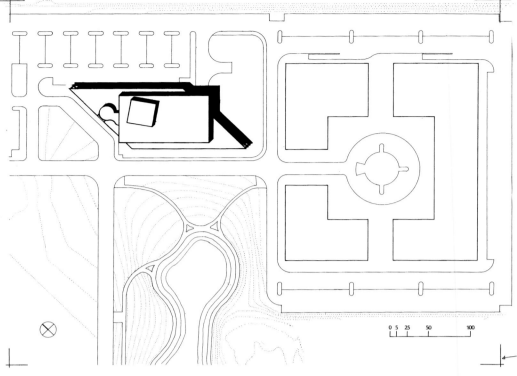

This is a speculative office building, a loft structure with a core for services and circulation, subdivided and rented to different tenants.

Accounting for 25% of all new construction in the United States, speculative office buildings represent a growing presence in the service-oriented American society.

Recently, as the competition for tenants has become extremely fierce, developers have been forced to abandon the box-like designs they once demanded for buildings which would serve as a sales tool by projecting an "attractive image."

Located in Princeton, New Jersey, the building presented here is also programmed to be a "sales tool" and at the same time must appease an increasingly anti-development oriented local community.

The building sets back above the third floor and actually generates itself from the articulation of lower and upper floors, while conforming to the zoning regulations and easing the concerns of the municipality about "an imposing building mass."

The second and third floors are shaped as a parallelogram to progressively bring more natural light as the sharp corners of the building are approached. The fourth and fifth floors reconstitute the box and balance the overall efficiency of the structure. Location of the entry is marked by the large, triangular canopy created by the second and third floors. A small atrium of large, clear glass block panels penetrates through the triangular canopy and hinges the articulation of the building.

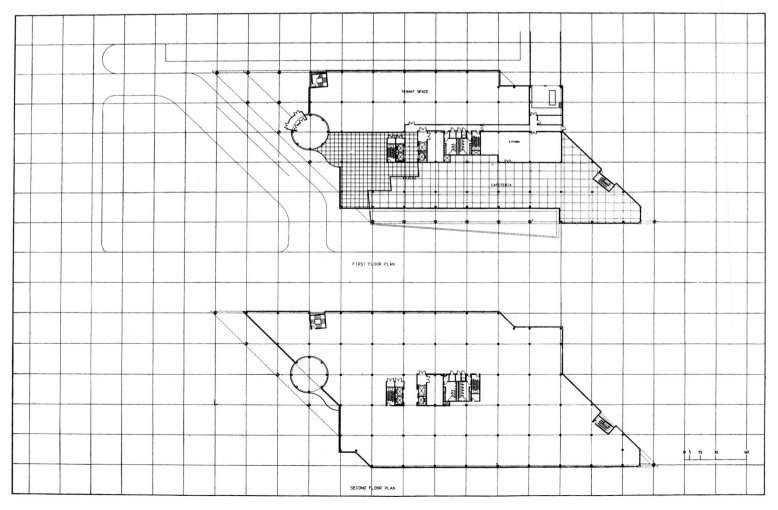

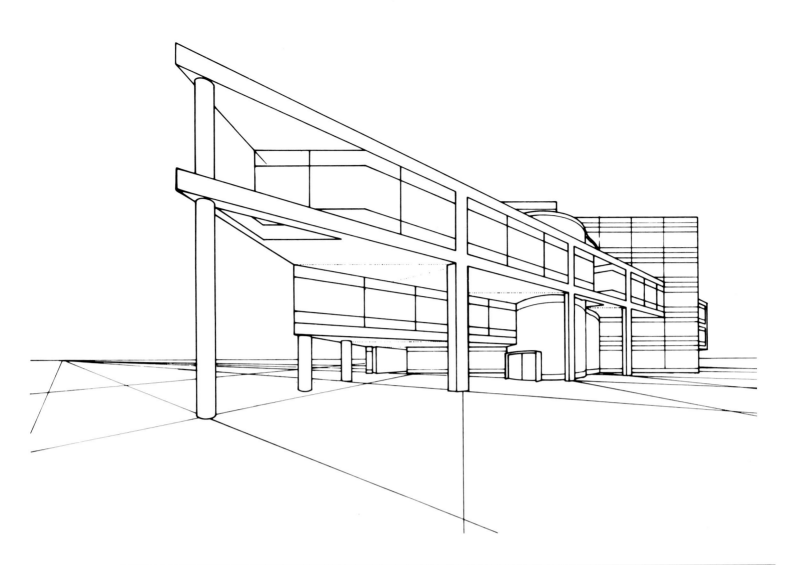

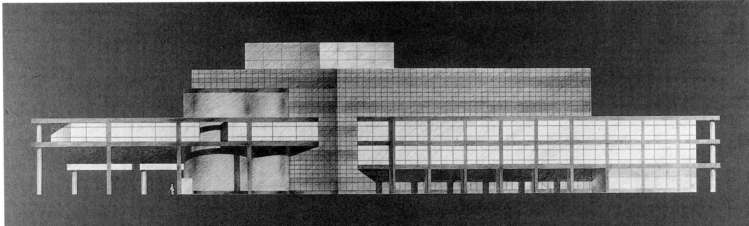

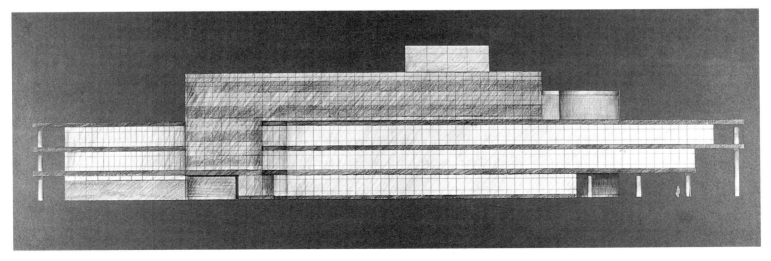

269

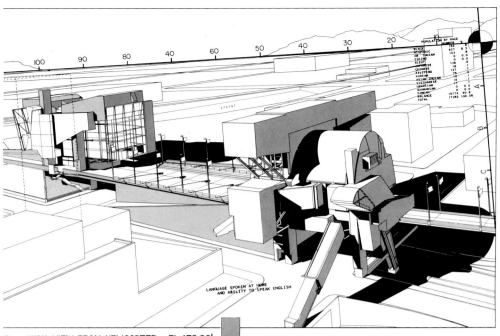

fig. no. WG11 VIEW FROM HELICOPTER   EL 478.00'

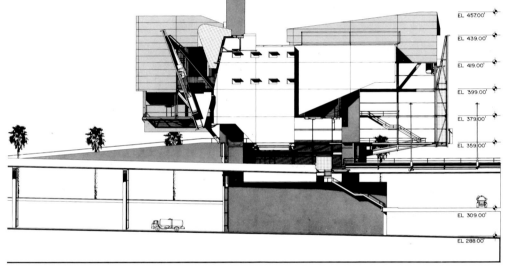

fig. no. WG13 SOUTH ELEVATION (B2)   ALISIO ST.

EL 457.00'
EL 439.00'
EL 419.00'
EL 399.00'
EL 379.00'
EL 359.00'
EL 309.00'
EL 288.00'

Neil M. Denari

WEST COAST GATEWAY

Los Angeles, California
Competition, 1988

Site: 35 feet above the Hollywood Freeway running between downtown Los Angeles and El Pueblo Park, the historical origin of the city.

Program: Design a structure which commemorates and celebrates the immigration of many diverse ethnic groups into Los Angeles over the past century. A ceremonial public space, landscaping, and structures incorporating various exposition-type functions are required.

Materials: Concrete foundations and vertical structural cores. Exposed steel framing in combination with steel and aluminum/glass curtain walls.

The project proposes two buildings to reflect the gap between the real and the simulated. Building One contains a small theater, traditional artists' exhibition spaces, an international restaurant, a library of cultural history, offices for administering local ethnic events, shops selling both imported goods and works by local immigrants.

Building Two proposes the realm of electronic communication as the continually moving, re-locating place. It is a vessel for contemporary uses and technologies, at once advocating the uses of simulation to close the distance between all people informationally. It bears the imprint of Los Angeles, the place of re-creation. Here one finds cinemas, exhibitions of contem-

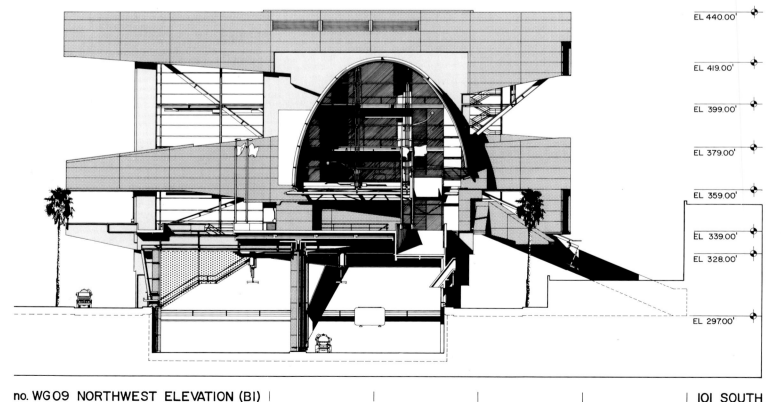

EL 440.00'
EL 419.00'
EL 399.00'
EL 379.00'
EL 359.00'
EL 339.00'
EL 328.00'
EL 297.00'

no. WG09 NORTHWEST ELEVATION (B1)   101 SOUTH

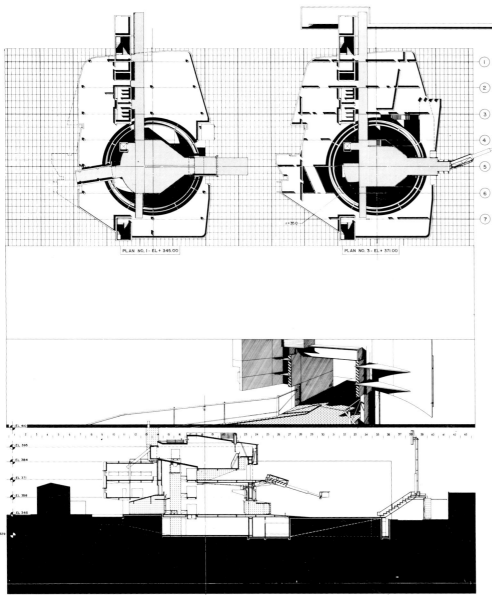

PLAN NO. 1 - EL + 345.00 PLAN NO. 3 - EL + 371.00

BUILDING SECTION N° I (NW-SE)

porary art and technology, and the environment of the "global village."

The outdoor plaza connects the two buildings over the freeway. It conceptually describes the movement from east to west and vice-versa. It is distorted to the diagonal to further bind Chinatown and El Pueblo Park to the central core of downtown. Finally, the project proposes an architecture of the present, one of transition and movement, which, at 30 feet above the freeway, is indelibly American.

Neil M. Denari

TOWN HALL

Leesburg, Virginia
Competition, 1987

Location: A block in the center of the historic district and commercial zone of Leesburg, Virginia, a town located 30 miles west of Washington, D. C.

Program: Typical town government requirements, including a Police Station and special council chambers. A 320-unit car park and public space development completed the program.

Materials: All columns, floor plates, and other vertical structures are painted, cast-in-place concrete. All other components are made of steel and aluminum fabrications.

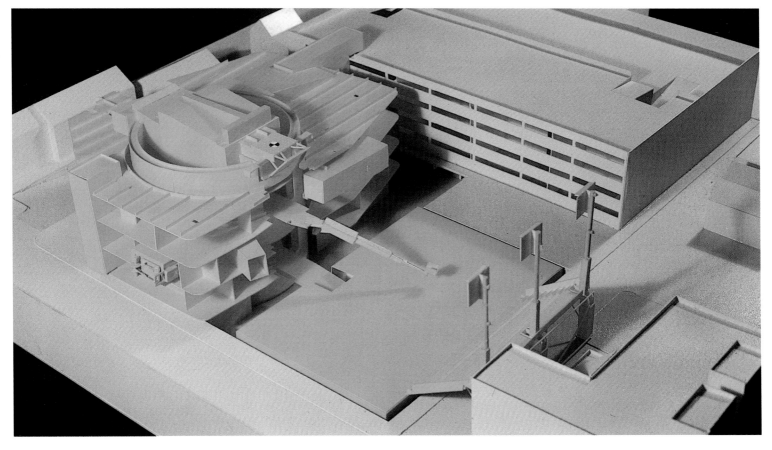

Diller + Scofidio

PLYWOOD HOUSE

Westchester, NY, 1980

The Plywood House, built on an existing foundation, replaces a house that burned to the ground.

The wood frame construction is sheathed with 4×8-foot stained plywood panels which are precut to receive stock windows. The facade is the result of the meeting between a non-specific serial strategy on its exterior surface and specific programmatic demands on its interior surface.

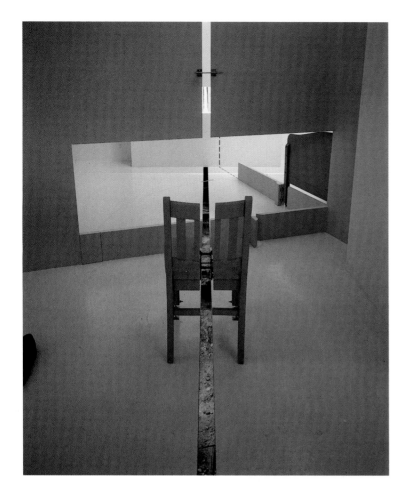

Diller + Scofidio

WITHDRAWING ROOM

Installation in a house by David Ireland, San Francisco. Sponsored by The Capp Street Project, San Francisco, 1987

The withDrawing Room: versions and subversions, a probe into the conventions of private rite.

The installation designates a "domestic field" in the interval between the skin of the house and the skin of the body. Within that field, the irreducible domestic unit, the resident, engages a series of architectural episodes, progressively private in nature. The first confronts the issue of the property line, of legal and moral limits. A second involves etiquette – a correct order. A third addresses the condition of intimacy, and the last examines the narcissistic impulse.

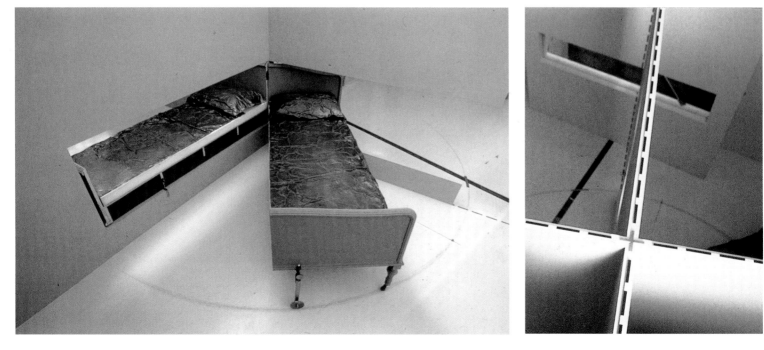

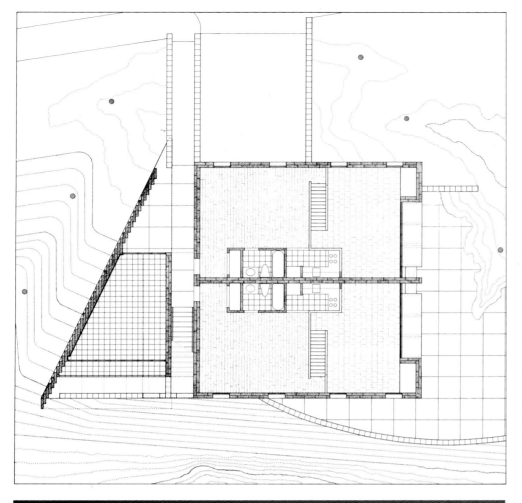

Livio G. Dimitriu
Urban Studies and Architecture Group

ARTISTS COLONY HOUSING PROJECT

Parker Street, Mission Hill, Boston, Mass., 1986
Design Team: Livio G. Dimitriu, Ali Adibsoltani,
Michel Gugliemi, Herbert Poole, Antonio Eraso

The project, because of programmatic, constructional, and budgetary constraints, consists of these entities working as an unbroken whole: the repetitive house/housing unit, the designed public space separating yet uniting the repetitive motif with a 2 + 2 residential unit, and the south end exceptional element containing the community meeting room/exhibit space.

Formally, the totality of the project proposes a wall effect between the community on Mission Hill, and the valley down below with other communities beyond.

The condition of "being in-between" suggests that the project acts as a fragment of a wall around a hill town, a reference which, while never part of the physical history of the area, has always characterized it psychologically. To design a project today in this location is an opportunity to articulate the "will" of the place to become precisely this: a "wall" and a "gate," separating yet uniting – the old concept of neighborhood in relation to the city itself. To be part of the greater whole also means to be able to preserve personal identity. This concept establishes the individuality of the row houses inside the project as a whole.

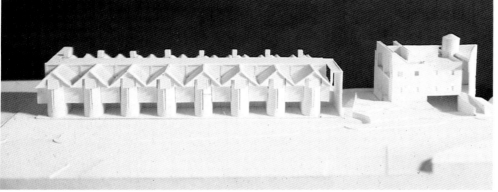

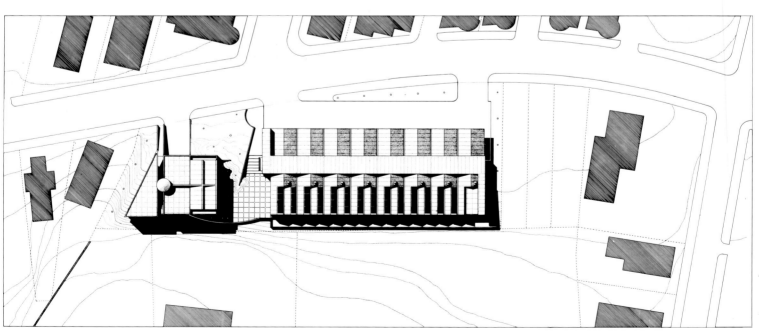

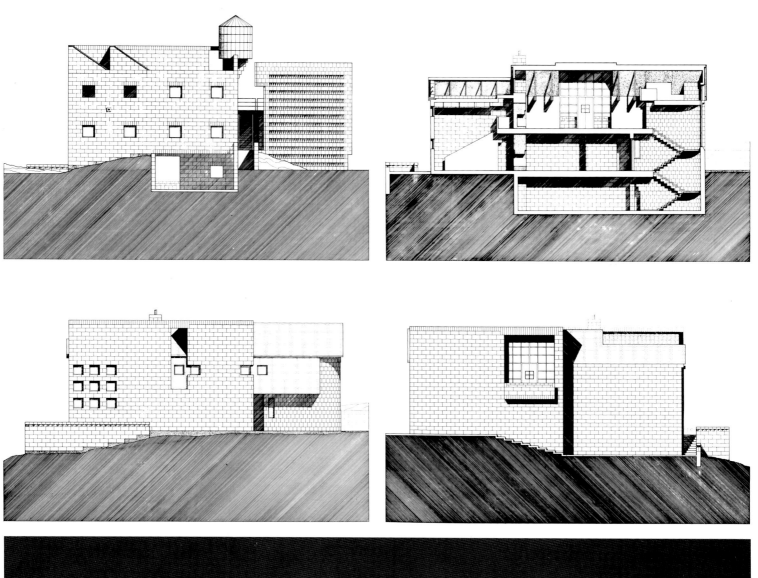

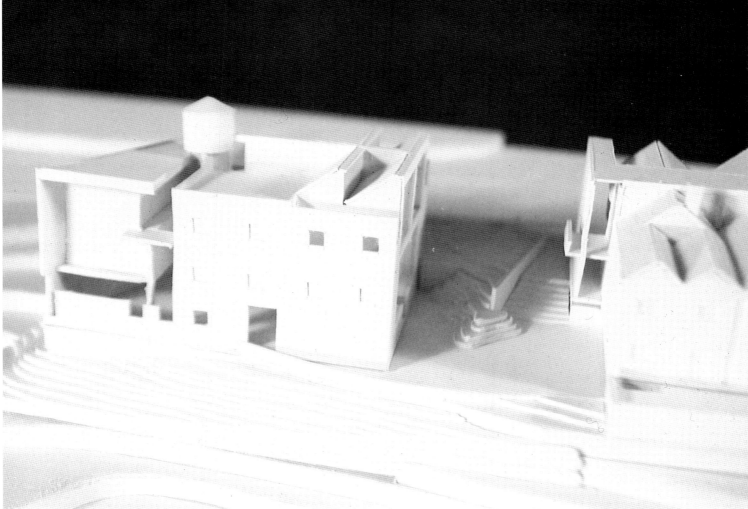

Livio G. Dimitriu

Urban Studies and Architecture Group

CASA MARABINI

Lugo di Romagna, Italy, 1987–1988
Design Team: Livio Dimitriu, Tzann Hour Fong,
Ali Adibsoltani, Connie Pfander, Herbert Poole,
Antonio Eraso

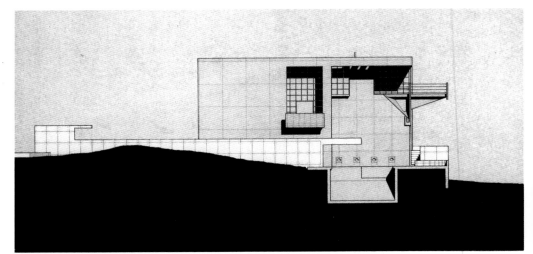

The house is located in the rather flat plain of
Romagna, Italy, between Ravenna and Bologna.

The plot of land is a trapezoid configuration
with a total surface of approximately 16,000
square feet. It slopes down thirteen feet from
the service road along the west boundary to the
east edge.

On the north edge of the site the boundary is
formed by an apple orchard, which has been
extended into the site as an expression of
ordered nature. On the southwest end of the
site, in order to ensure privacy for the pool area,
there is a proposed mound covered with a
rather dense planting of Mediterranean pine.

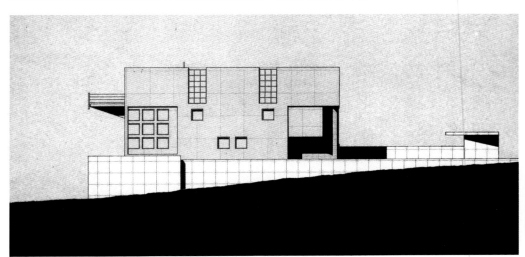

From the parking area one proceeds through
to an outside flight of stairs leading down
directly to the pool/outside entertainment area,
or enter the house through the main front stair
volume leading upstairs to the living room/
inside entertainment area. The same main stair
leads down to the basement storage and
mechanical equipment area. At the ground
level, it is possible to enter the downstairs
library/study and gallery space through a private entry off the parking area; there is also a
service entry directly to the gallery from the
breakfast and sunbathing terrace reached via
the north side of the building.

The ground level is divided by a through fireplace. This vertical element continues as a privacy wall through the house; at the living room
floor it separates the main space from the balcony overlooking the double-story space of the
gallery below; at the top master bedroom level
it separates it from the double-story space of
the living room below. The ground level gallery
is connected to the balcony by an internal stair.

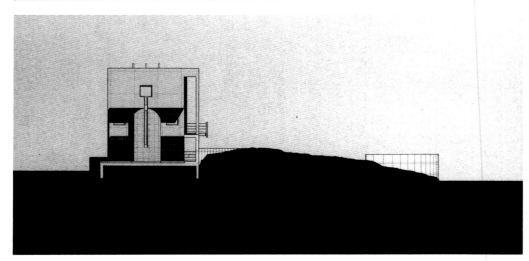

From the second floor living room area, serviced by a large open kitchen and a full bath,
there is a panoramic view.

The top floor master bedroom suite contains
a skylit master bath and a large walk-in closet,
as well as a sitting room. This set of functions is
connected to the actual bedroom by a bridge
overlooking the central two-story space of the
living room on one side, and the pool area on
the other side.

Compositionally, the house consists of
a rather solid volume, covered with sienna
colored stucco traditional to the area, inside
which the actual inhabited volume is stuccoed
with a peacock blue, borrowed from the traditional pottery of nearby Faenza.

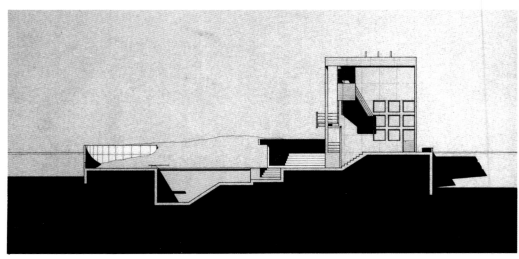

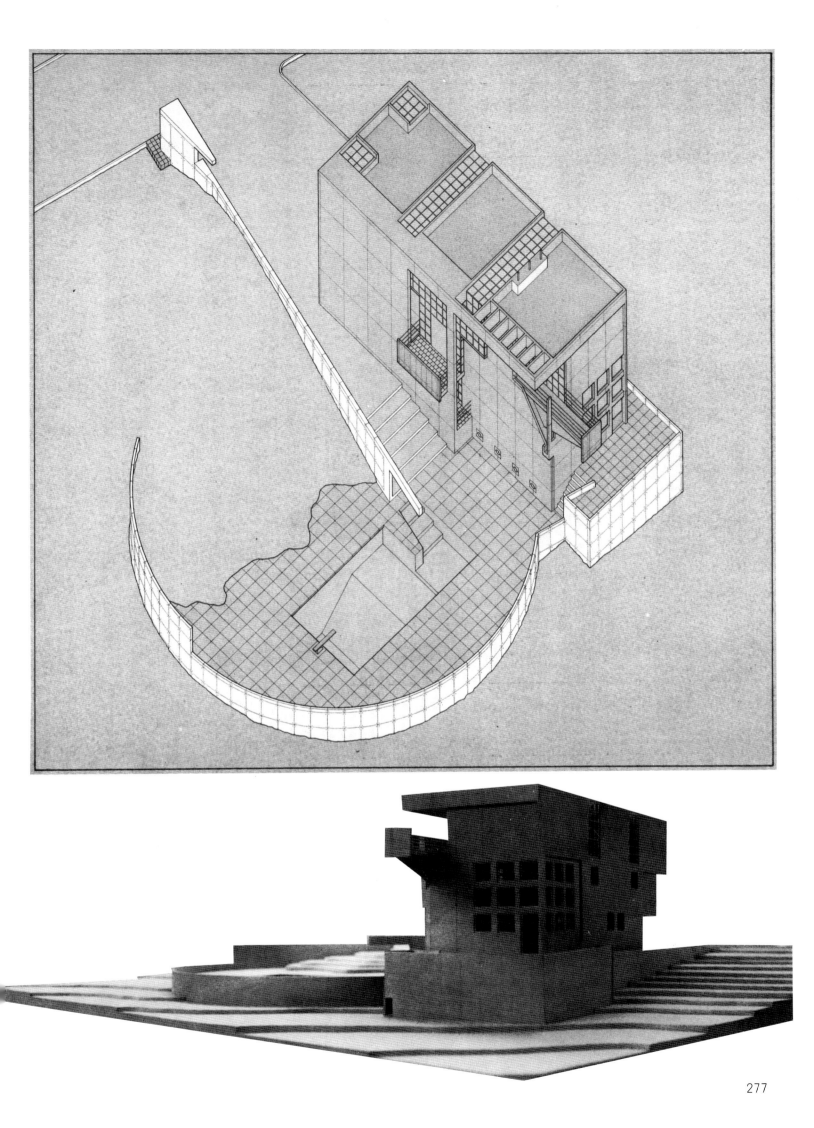

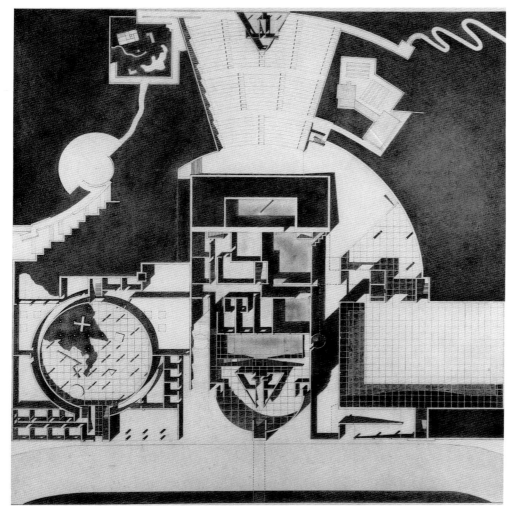

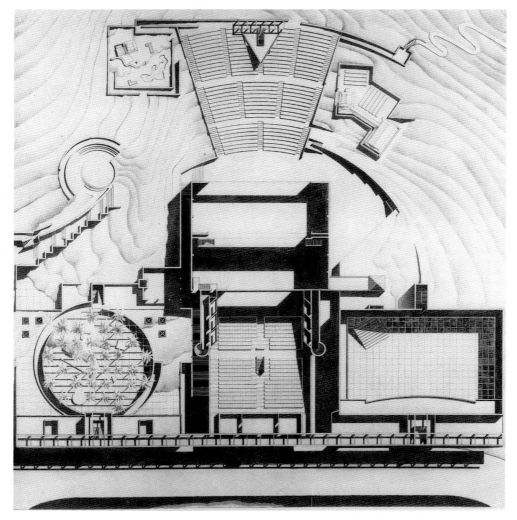

Livio G. Dimitriu
Urban Studies and Architecture Group

HAWAII LOA COLLEGE OF PERFORMING ARTS

Hawaii, 1985–1986
Design Team: Livio G. Dimitriu, Thomas Biao,
Ron Albinson, Carlos Zapata

Project Function: Learning Institution for Performing Arts, closed and open-air theaters, No theater, Tea Ceremony Garden, Polynesian open-air performance, landscaping, site planning.

The project respects the campus planning guidelines in the context of the landscape, orientation, and relationship to the view and the existing highway.

The proposal consists of three conceptual "bridges," an architectural element which connects and separates at the same time.

The Elevation: A unified and unifying facade providing an articulated wall effect parallel to the axis of the campus in contrasting juxtaposition to the mountainous landscape backdrop. Behind the facade the academic functions, the theaters, and the black box are layered from NW to SE. The gardens up the slope are the culmination of a SW-NE layering, blending with the drama of the Hawaiian landscape.

The Section: The SW-NE theaters axis produces a "bridge" connecting the NW-SE campus axis to the landscape backdrop uphill.

The Plan: The academic functions grouped around the sculpture garden connect through and under the theaters axis with the black box. The "bridge" in this case is a U-shape circulation which recognizes the land configuration. The U-shape orients the functioning of the project with respect to the valley below.

Theatre above Main Lobby
Truss Bridge

Masonry Screen Wall

Entry

— Sculpture Garden —

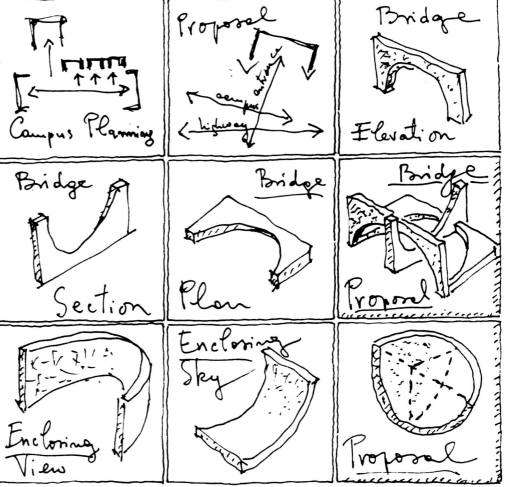

Campus Planning

Proposal

campus entrance

highway

Bridge

Elevation

Bridge

Section

Bridge

Plan

Bridge

Proposal

Enclosing View

Enclosing Sky

Proposal

Eisenman/Trott Architects

TRAVELERS FINANCIAL CENTER

Hempstead, New York, 1985
Design Team: Peter Eisenman, Arthur Baker,
Richard Trott, Michael Burkey, Richard Morris,
Faruk Yorgancioglu, Thomas Leeser, Peter
Thaler, Ross Woolley

A ten-story office building consisting of eight
floors of office space, a ground floor with retail
facilities, and a lower level of private dining
space and mechanical services.

The architectural concepts for the building
demonstrate a plasticity of from and surface
not ordinarily associated with a curtain-walled
office building. The "glass box" building is effectively broken into several different readings,
accomplished by a number of shifts in the plans
and elevations. The two geometries of the site
are encapsulated in the small-scale interplay of
wall, surface, and grid in the ceilings, floor, and
walls of the main lobby floor.

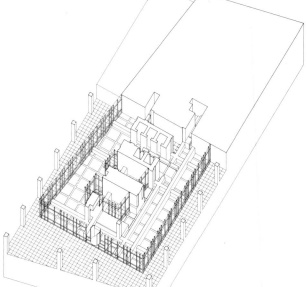

AXONOMETRIC OF LOBBY CEILING

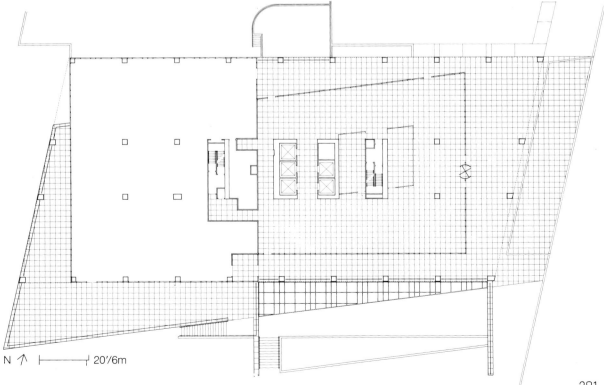

FIRST FLOOR PLAN   N ↑ ⊢————⊣ 20'/6m

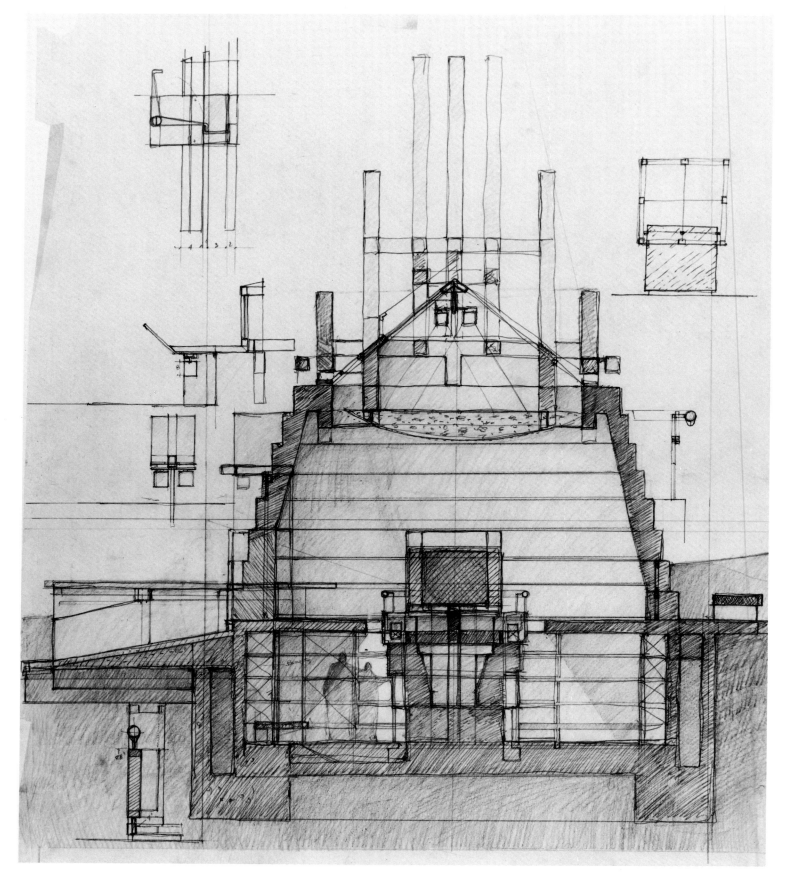

I had been asked by the members of a Middle Eastern family to conceive and study a structure to commemorate the loss of one of their most beloved and respected ones. The small one-room building stands in isolation on the green and well maintained grounds of a private estate, facing the still and silent waters of a pond.

To my surprise, I was never told of the man's identity. I only know him to be a writer. Indeed, a lower room in the building was required to store all his writings in the form of a private family library. These circumstances, and the way the subject was presented, made me think of a central plan for the structure. Above the body, suspended in the void of a room made of white concrete and with a copper ceiling, an abstract representation of the solar system is presented. Perfect metal spheres of various sizes and weights distance themselves from what appears to be the only center, the person to whom the building is dedicated. A space of physical gravity that wants you to connect to the complexity of events.

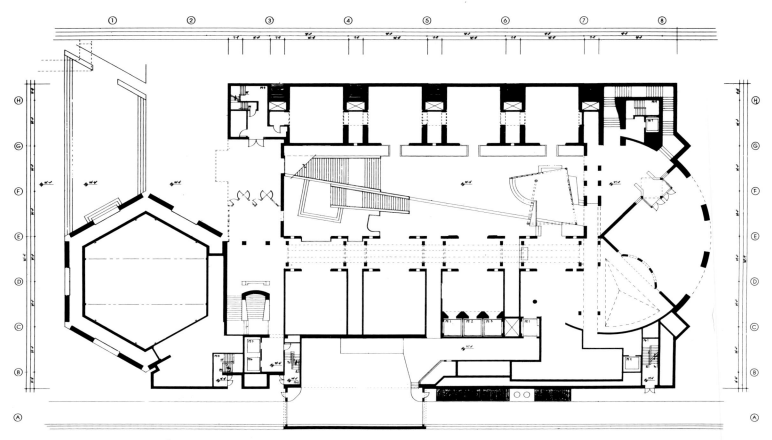

James Ingo Freed

for I. M. Pei & Partners

HOLOCAUST MUSEUM AND MEMORIAL

Raoul Wallenberg Place, Washington, D. C., 1986–1990

The Holocaust Museum and Memorial, proposed by Presidents Carter and Reagan and enacted into law by the Congress of the United States, is located between 14th and 15th Streets (Raoul Wallenberg Place) and the Mall in Washington, D. C.

What is a Holocaust Museum and Memorial – what does it mean – what can it be?

In my view, the Holocaust defines a fundamental, perhaps final, break with the optimistic conception of continuous social and political improvement underlying the material cultural development of the West. The depersonalization of both victim and victimizer (the latter by their actions, the former by arbitrary legislation) marks an event so terrible that perhaps nothing can encompass it fully, and nobody who has not lived it can understand it completely. Therefore, it is nearly impossible to deal with the subject matter; certainly it is impossible to aestheticize it. I also find it impossible to reconstruct the world as it was then in this museum/memorial, and I find it not desirable to attempt a scenographic approach with all its implications of "kitsch" and consequent devaluation and trivialization of that terrible and unprecedented event.

Therefore ... how does one start? In this case, I realized that the combination of the tectonics of the camp, the ghetto, and the style of the official buildings, along with a certain muted, somewhat abstract, symbolism, might serve as a starting point. With this, and the need to both "join" and "leave" Washington and enter another world, the Museum and Memorial were conceived. A discreet number of interior spaces (The Hall of Witnesses, The Hall of Remembrance, The Halls of Learning, to name a few) position the visitor and attempt to engage him not only intellectually but viscerally.

The museum's permanent exhibition will be located on the fourth, third, and part of the second floors; one circulates in a downward spiral.

The memorial is conceived of as an occupied space. The time of the specific monument – powerful, moving and speaking in a universal language is, in my view, gone. Now, a memorial space, humbled by usage, saved by disposition of space and light, contemplative by spareness of form and material, speaks through us and lets us mourn and perhaps be comforted.

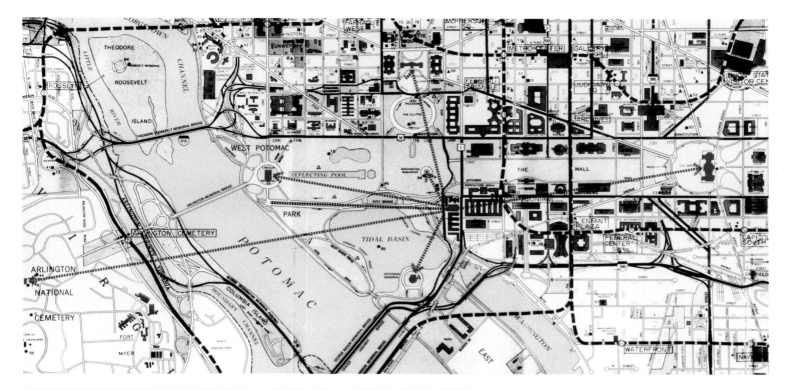

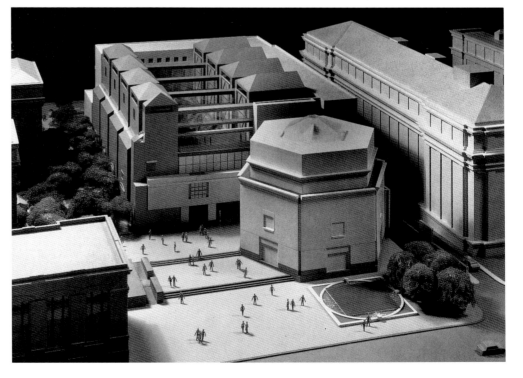

James Ingo Freed
for I. M. Pei & Partners

LOS ANGELES CONVENTION CENTER EXPANSION

Figueroa Street/Pico Boulevard,
Los Angeles, California, 1987–1992
Design Team: James Ingo Freed, Thomas Baker

The image of the Convention Center is of an evolving type particular to the later part of the nineteenth and to the twentieth century. The new exhibition hall expansion is to be south of Pico Boulevard and west of Figueroa Street, adjoining the Santa Monica Freeway and Harbor Freeway. This site's configuration shaped the solution of the new exhibition hall's proposed configuration, which is to include 350,000 square feet of new exhibition space with 60 meeting rooms, restaurants, and parking for 3,300 cars.

Two new public lobbies are proposed as entry to the new south exhibition hall and the existing West Yorty Exhibition Hall. These two public spaces are linked by the meeting room/special events/restaurant bridge that spans Pico Boulevard. This galleria/bridge is the principal organizing element facilitating movement from hall to hall for the entire complex.

Both lobbies are entered at grade level from either pedestrian/bus stops or from adjacent public parking and function as collective centers of information and orientation from which the public can proceed to their scheduled events.

The design problem was to set the new exhibition hall at the same level as the existing hall which enhances public circulation from exhibition to exhibition via the meeting room galleria. The exhibition halls themselves are flexible hangar-like envelopes, providing large amounts of undivided space for individual conventions, allowing up to three separate events to be presented simultaneously, or one major event.

The exhibition structure utilizes long-span steel trusses creating a virtually column-free space for booth layouts and conventions. The main exhibition hall is placed upon a poured-in-place concrete structure incorporating both the lower future exhibition hall as well as the parking levels.

The concept of meeting room clusters incorporates a 1,000 person general session room that is divisble into two rooms, contiguous pre-function space, storage space, a pantry serviced by a continuous service corridor, and breakout rooms providing assembly space for small group sessions. It is essential to the schematic concept that the meeting room clusters have direct access to the south and west lobbies yet have enough physical separation to function as a self-contained conference center.

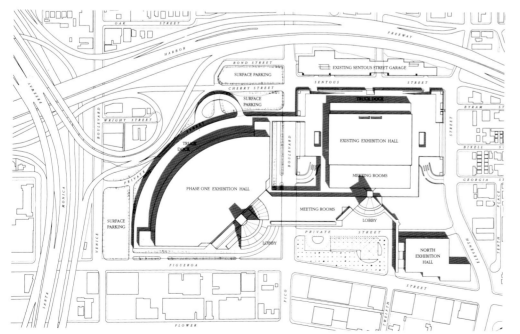

Giovannini & Associates

CARDIOLOGISTS' OFFICES

Washington, D. C., 1988

The program called for five doctors' offices, five examination rooms, staff offices, and spaces suitable for a collection of paintings.

The offices were placed along the window walls, and the examination and service rooms along the interior wall. All were configured so that the corridor would be wide enough to serve as a gallery. Doorways were recessed from the walls so that the frames, knobs, and doors themselves would not visually intrude on the space near the paintings.

The resulting corridor suggested the shape of a telescope, which introduced themes of perception and perspective. At the end of the telescoped corridor, on a transverse wall, a realistic mural was painted so that the corridor looks onto a "view" of the countryside. In the opposite direction, the corridor formed a collapsed telescope, without a view. In the waiting room at the entry, the perspective is "forced," with converging walls that focus on the receptionist's desk, which itself is built as a "forced" perspective of angled walls and sloping soffit and desk. Yet another illusion has been sandblasted on a wall of glass: a characteristic doorway has been "drawn" on the glass in Renaissance perspective, with the door left open.

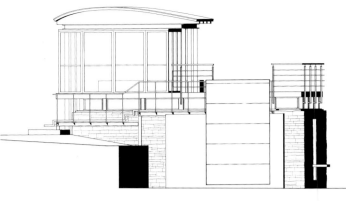

EAST

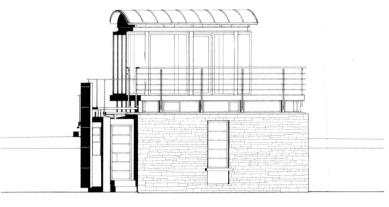

WEST
7° oblique

NORTH

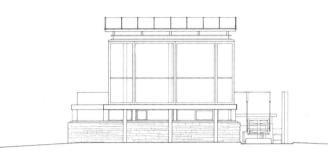

SOUTH
7° oblique

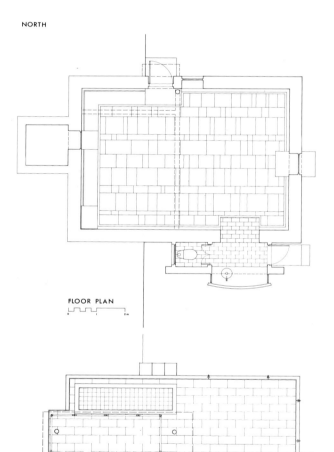

FLOOR PLAN

TERRACE PLAN

Keenen/Riley Architecture

MILL HOUSE PROJECT

Lambertville, New Jersey, 1989

The owners of a weekend country home, located about an hour's drive from New York City, wanted a place away from the main house where members of the family or guests could go to play pool, ping-pong, or cards, listen to music, dance, or read. They also wanted an outdoor room, screened-in, where they could go to sit on summer nights. Within this program we saw the elements of a building type largely forgotten in the twentieth century – the casino.

Off the drive leading into the property are the walls of an eighteenth-century mill house which will enclose the main space of the Casino. Measuring approximately 22 by 30 feet and made of two-foot-thick masonry walls, the ruin is partially burrowed into a steep slope beside the millstream.

Rather than making new openings into the structure, it was decided to preserve the existing stone walls and work with the few doors and windows present. Thus, to bring light into the Casino a clerestory was created which runs almost continuously around the building. A concrete slab becomes the roof of the Casino and the floor of the outdoor terrace above. On this terrace is the screened room, the roof of which is constructed of metal sheathing over a curved marine plywood sub-surface. From the outdoor room and the terrace one has a view of the property: a stream, a pond, an existing bridge and dam, a distant hill, and a swimming pool.

Inside, the Casino holds a small seating area, a pool table, which can be converted into a ping-pong table, bookshelves, and storage. A new construction is appended to the western edge of the mill house housing a WC and a kitchenette and supporting the bridge that leads to the upper terrace.

Much of this project refers to the dialectic established between the "heavy" and the "light;" "heavy" referring to the stone as material, to masonry as a method of construction, density, opacity, immobility, and the like, and "light" referring to the frame construction, lightweight materials such as metal and glass, transparency, spatial complexity, and so forth.

An attempt has been made to integrate the use of universally produced materials with more specific elements. As a model, we looked to Carlo Scarpa's bridge at Palazzo Querini Stampalia, where the hand-carved rail produced by Venetian gondola craftsmen is supported by industrially produced, welded steel sections. The contraposition of the universal and the specific is further articulated by the mill house walls. As historical remains, they lend a singular quality to the project.

R. M. Kliment & Frances Halsband

COMPUTER SCIENCE BUILDING

Princeton University, Princeton, New Jersey, 1986–1989
Design Team: R. M. Kliment, Frances Halsband, Alejandro Diez, Michael Nieminen, Karin Robinson, Martin Brandwein, Mark Caligiuri, Allan Jim

The building houses new facilities for the Department of Computer Science. It includes faculty and graduate student offices, seminar rooms, administrative areas, specialized classrooms, and a lecture hall.

The site was a parking lot at the eastern edge of the campus adjoining the School of Engineering of 1960, the Manuscript Library of 1975, the neo-Gothic Princeton University Press building and a street of small houses. Now relatively underdeveloped and isolated from the main body of the campus, the area was the subject of a planning study which recommended the formation of a new academic quadrangle and the strengthening of McCosh Walk as the primary east/west campus artery. In massing and in plan the new building engages its present context and establishes a language which subsequent buildings can use to form a new courtyard that extends the predominant spatial order of the campus.

The exterior of the building is composed about three entrance towers. The south entrance engages and concludes McCosh Walk. The west entrance links the building to, and defines the corner of, the future quadrangle. The northeast entrance links the building to the School of Engineering and to the secondary student circulation along the street. These entrance towers are of limestone and brick, in which limestone headers are introduced into the Flemish bond of the brick wall. Connecting the south and west entrances, and defining the eastern enclosure of the future quadrangle, is a glazed limestone arcade. The internal core of computer spaces, central to the offices that it serves, is projected to penthouse level to be visible from McCosh Walk. The seminar and social spaces within the curved south entrance tower overlook, and are clearly visible from, McCosh Walk.

The building contains 57,000 square feet of space. It is constructed of steel frame and is sheathed in Flemish bond red brick and limestone. Windows are aluminum painted gray.

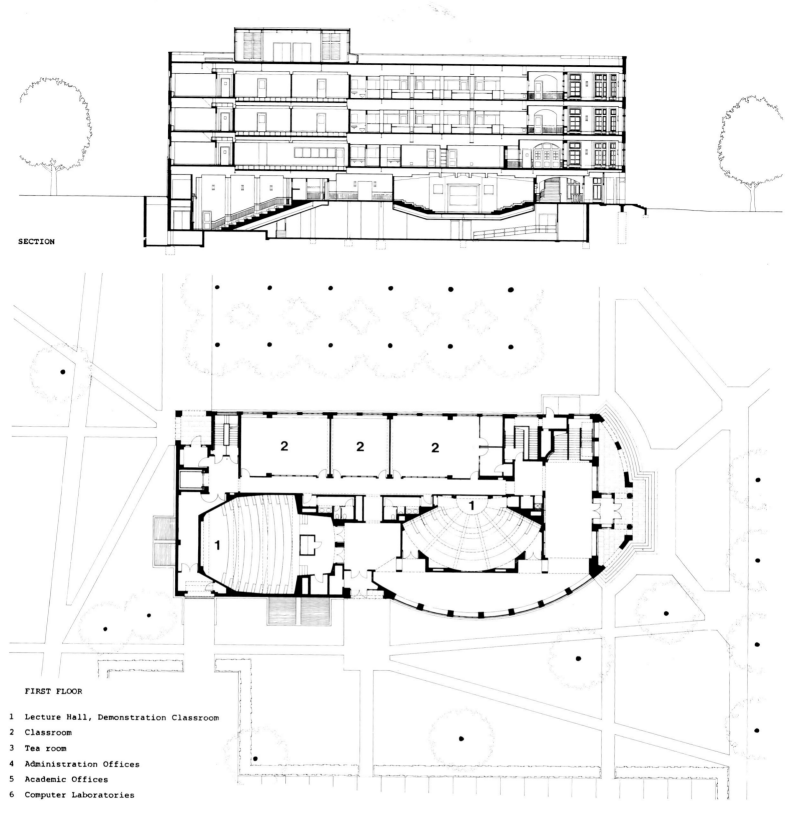

SECTION

FIRST FLOOR

1 Lecture Hall, Demonstration Classroom
2 Classroom
3 Tea room
4 Administration Offices
5 Academic Offices
6 Computer Laboratories

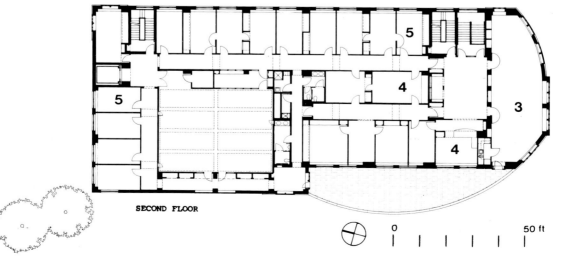

SECOND FLOOR

0   50 ft

291

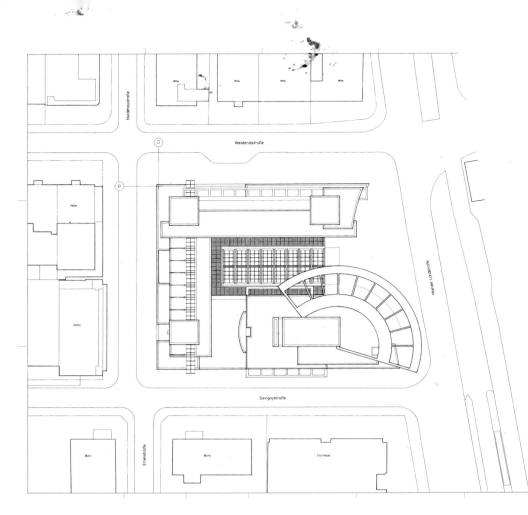

Kohn Pedersen Fox Associates

MAINZER LANDSTRASSE 58

Mainzer Landstrasse 58, Frankfurt am Main, Federal Republic of Germany, Project, 1988

This complex is located within the Westend of Frankfurt, along the Mainzer Landstrasse. It contains a 753, 494-square-foot commercial office tower and 20 apartments situated around a central winter garden. In order to minimize the office tower's impact on the residential neighborhood and to gesture toward Frankfurt Old City and the Main River, the tower has been placed on the westerly side of the site with the hotel and apartments arranged in an L-shape around it. The varying heights of the building elements relate to the lower residential community, the street wall, and the skyline formed by major commercial office towers. From a granite and marble base, the tower rises in reflective green glass and painted steel, terminating in a two-story loggia beneath a cantilevered crown. At the ground level is a large enclosed winter garden, intended to be a central focus of the community.

AXONOMETRIE TURM KRONE   1:50

AXONOMETRIE TURM LOGGIA   1:50

293

Krueck & Olsen Architects

HEWITT ASSOCIATES
EASTERN REGIONAL CENTER

Rowayton, Connecticut, 1986–1988
Design Team: Ronald A. Krueck, Keith Olsen,
Rob Falconer, Paul Dana

The project called for the expansion of office space, computer facilities, and support areas for the eastern regional center of an international consulting firm. The building is planned around the re-use of an existing 36,000-square-foot, turn-of-the-century manor house located on a fifteen-acre site overlooking the Long Island Sound. The existing structure is listed in the National Register of Historic Places and as an Architectural Landmark. A series of planning solutions was developed to investigate the problems and present alternative schematic designs. Each plan was intent on preserving and effectively using the meticulously restored mansion as a focal point for an expanded complex replicating, in contemporary architectural terms, the Tudoresque style of the mansion.

Floor Area: 100,000 square feet.

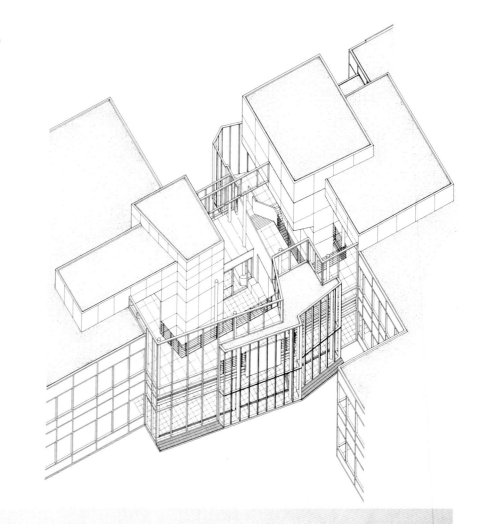

Masque

LE CANALOU

Bennett Point, Maryland, 1989
Design Team: Douglas Frederick, Ann Cederna

Located at Bennett Point, Maryland, the site for Le Canalou involves five acres with 450 feet of water front on the Chesapeake Bay.

Related to proportional systems of Malcontenta, this house plays upon objects and edge in the field, and on the territorial command capabilities of a linear bar. Set pieces in the garden then play against this backdrop, be they in green or in built forms. The building as a wall separates public approach territory from the waterside "res privata." The transition from public to private does occur, however, in that space pushes through the bar onto the terrace. As this area is then connected directly to the water, front meets back. Other bayside components situated in the garden are the dog run for the greyhounds, a screened gazebo, and a combination widows walk-storage shed to house the catamaran.

The building is designed on an eight-foot module, which is then the basis for a rationally progressive proportional system in vertical and plan dimensions. From end to end, inclusive of garage, the building suggests a symmetrical balance. We propose, however, that while architecture must establish the reigning order, so must it also accommodate the counter-condition: disorder. This approach can be seen in massing and elevation: symmetry is distorted, rhythm relies upon counter-rhythm, and logic can collaborate with the accidental.

Though the building can accommodate greater family occupation in the summer, during the winter months the owner may retire into the central body of the house while shutting down the remaining portion. Exterior building materials consist of stucco, glass block, and a standing seam metal roof. On grade, paving materials are primarily brick and stone.

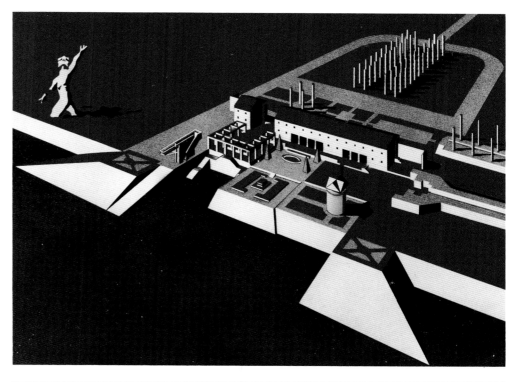

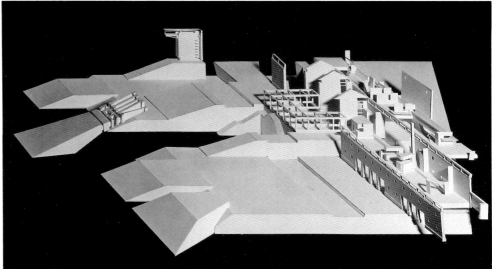

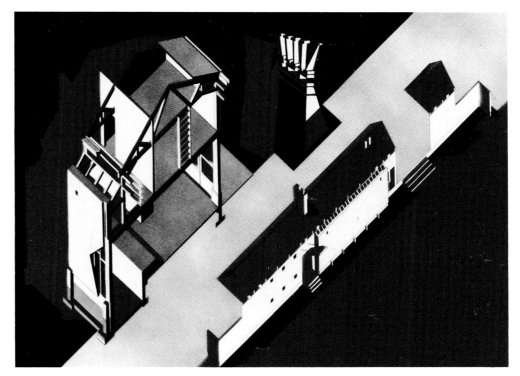

Richard Meier & Partners

BRIDGEPORT CENTER

Bridgeport, Connecticut, 1984 -1988

The design of Bridgeport Center offers a new direction for building in the urban environment. Rather than a single monolithic edifice, the Center is conceived as a composition of multiple buildings. It is the physical form of the City in microcosm: not an agglomeration of competing towers on separate blocks, but instead, the structure of a mixed, neutrally compatible complex of low and mid-rise buildings created with planned surroundings of human scale, embracing mixed uses, respecting existing open spaces while adding new ones.

This new complex on Main Street is responsive both to the prospect of the downtown area and to the established streetscape. The three-block center is the beginning of a strategic plan

for ordered change in the central core of downtown Bridgeport.

A five-story atrium is the focus of the building's internal organization. The east and west entries, as well as the parking garage, open directly to this space, which is the control and distribution point for the mid-rise office tower.

The existing onion-domed Barnum Museum is being restored as part of the project connected to the new building by the South Wing which will provide gallery space on the ground floor, a training center on the second floor, and an employee cafeteria on the third floor.

The exterior materials are porcelain steel panels in white and gray, granite and clear insulating glass. The granite will have a red tinge to reflect the coloring of the historic Barnum Museum.

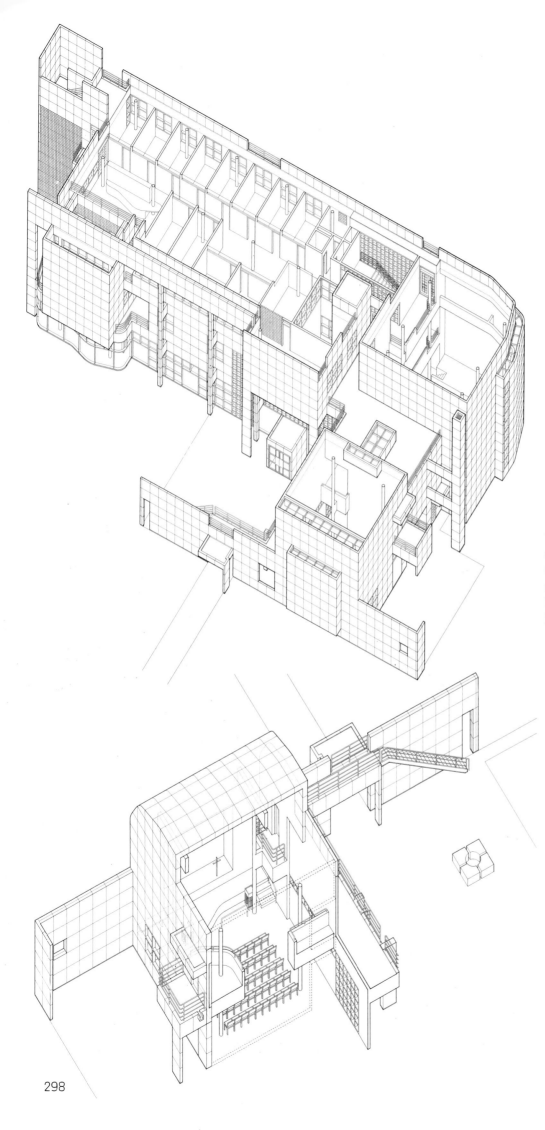

Richard Meier & Partners

THE HARTFORD SEMINARY

Hartford, Connecticut, 1978 -1981

This building in an urban setting was designed to serve an old theological institution's new role as an interdenominational center. The program for the 27,000-square-foot building called for a large meeting room, library, chapel, classrooms, and service, faculty, and administration areas. The building was designed to be a partly enclosed, inward looking organization of spaces and the center of a larger domain, reaching out and inviting the public, harmonizing with nearby residences and Gothic-style buildings while projecting a new image of scholarship, light and welcoming.

The character and spirit of the Seminary are defined and evoked by its architecture – light, space, form, and respect for the existing urban scale. A courtyard organizes spaces and, partly secluded by a wall, nevertheless invites passersby. Public spaces dominate private ones and, in keeping with the Seminary's democratic principles, no hierarchical distinctions are made among the private ones. A dynamic interpenetration of spaces projects clearly and legibly through the exterior. A composition of transparent glass and opaque white porcelain enameled steel panels, the exterior not only expresses the interior but reflects seasonal changes and, like the light-filled spaces, symbolizes the Seminary's role as a center of knowledge.

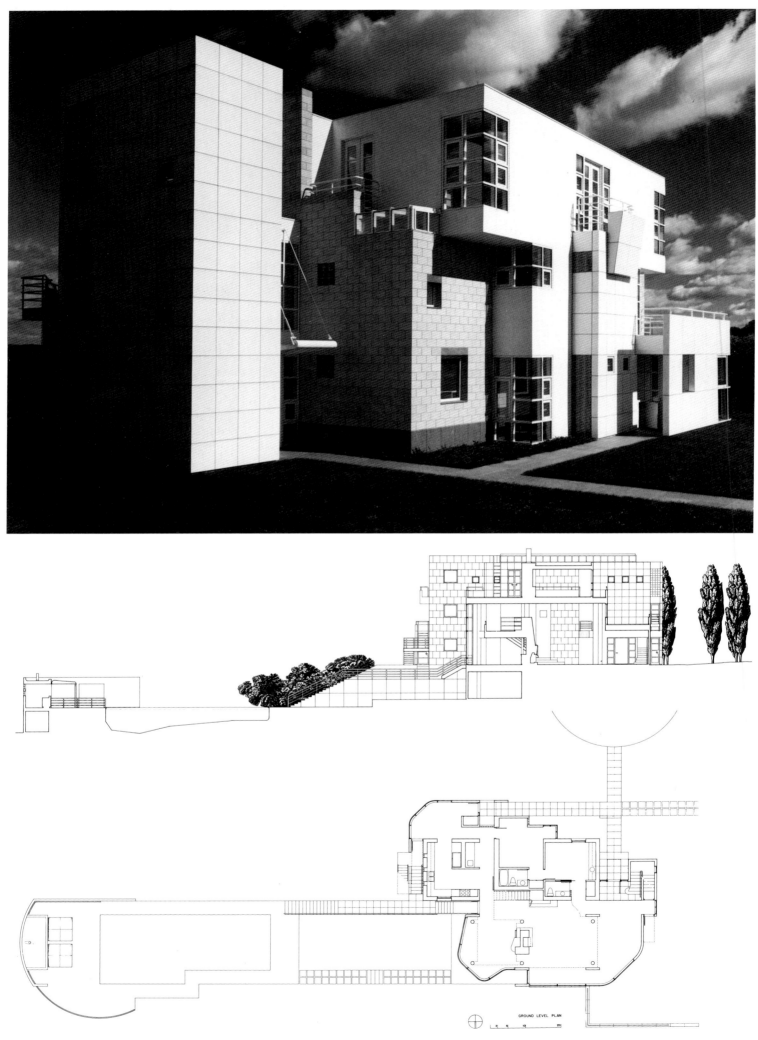

GROUND LEVEL PLAN

Richard Meier & Partners

WESTCHESTER HOUSE

Westchester County, NY, 1984 -1986

The rural, rolling hillside site for this house features a variety of views and a landscape inter-
laced with fieldstone walls. The house, garage,
and pool are sited near the highest elevation
and are ordered by an east/west axis that
bisects the house and extends into the landscape. A perpendicular site axis extends from
the approach area to the entry.

A thick-walled masonry volume contains the
intimately scaled private areas, and is the
center of gravity for the composition. The
masonry units relate in scale, color, and texture
to the existing fieldstone walls on the site and
form a defined three-level container for the
bedrooms, bathrooms, and kitchen.

In juxtaposition to the rectilinear private sector, a curvilinear metal panel and glass skin
forms the enclosure for the public areas. These
areas share a continuous space extending onto
terraces and into the landscape from each of
the three living levels.

301

Michael Mostoller and Fred Travisano

RENOVATION OF TRENTON TOWNHOUSES

Trenton, New Jersey, 1987 -1990
Design Team: Michael Mostoller, Fred Travisano, Randall Herko, Curtis W. Hoberman, Freda Lee, Lawrence Lindsey, Jeff McCue, Winifred Onyekonwu

Addressing the restoration of the urban fabric, the Trenton Townhouses project creates apartments in buildings that once housed working and merchant class families. The buildings were constructed in downtown Trenton from 1880 to 1920. The structures form a continuous street wall of brick with stone trim and wood doors, windows, and cornices. They have wooden floors and stone foundations. The restoration and transformation is based upon the translation of two-bedroom flat and three-

bedroom duplex prototypes into the individual conditions of each building. Use was made of standardized kitchens and bathrooms. Heating and cooling is by individual units.

These low-income accommodations use the traditional front–public/back–private organization of rooms. The front-room life of the family, as it eats and socializes, reinforces the strong street life of this part of the city. Back yards may be shared by two buildings using a passage from the front that can be locked with a gate.

Michael Mostoller and Fred Travisano

TRAVISANO RESIDENCE

5A Beacon Blvd., Sea Girt, New Jersey, 1987–1988
Design Team: Fred Travisano with Tony de Campos, Kyle Van Dyke, Pat Moran

The house for a family of six is used on weekends and in the summer. Activity during the day occurs outdoors on the boardwalk and the beach. The house comes alive at mealtimes and for entertaining. The complement to these activities is the vista of the sea. The major rooms are lifted off the ground and extended upward as far as possible in a double-height main salon for family and friends. The salon and parents' suite is capped by a barrel-vaulted roof which was built like an upside-down boat with large wooden ribs covered with planking. The unitary roof reflects the major purpose of this house as a "tower in the town" that, with its cascading terraces, "sees" the shore and the ocean.

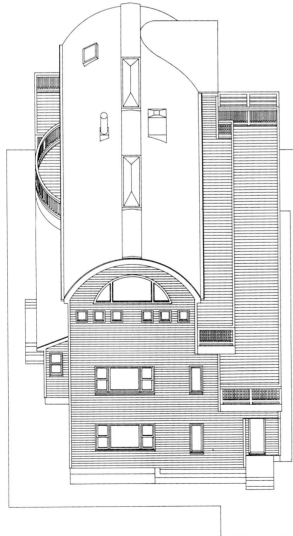

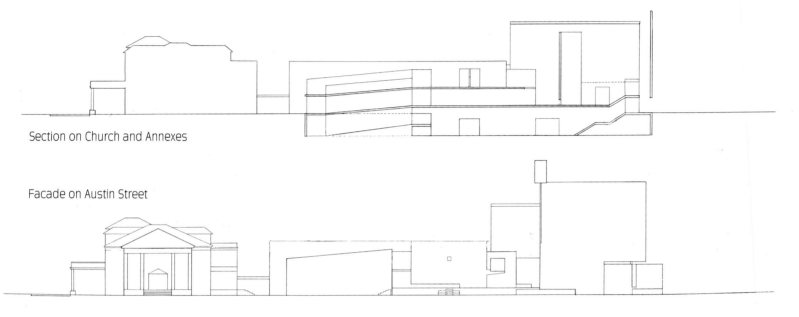

Section on Church and Annexes

Facade on Austin Street

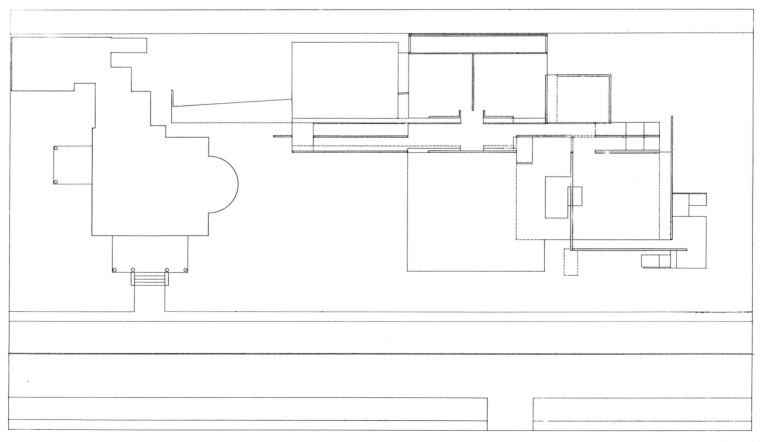

Ground Level

José Oubrerie

MAGNIFICAT

Houston, Texas, 1980 –1987

Complex community center. Initially a chapel over a shelter, the project was enlarged to be able to assume the different day-life functions of this Catholic community dedicated to the help of homeless, workless, and mentally ill people usually abandoned to the streets.

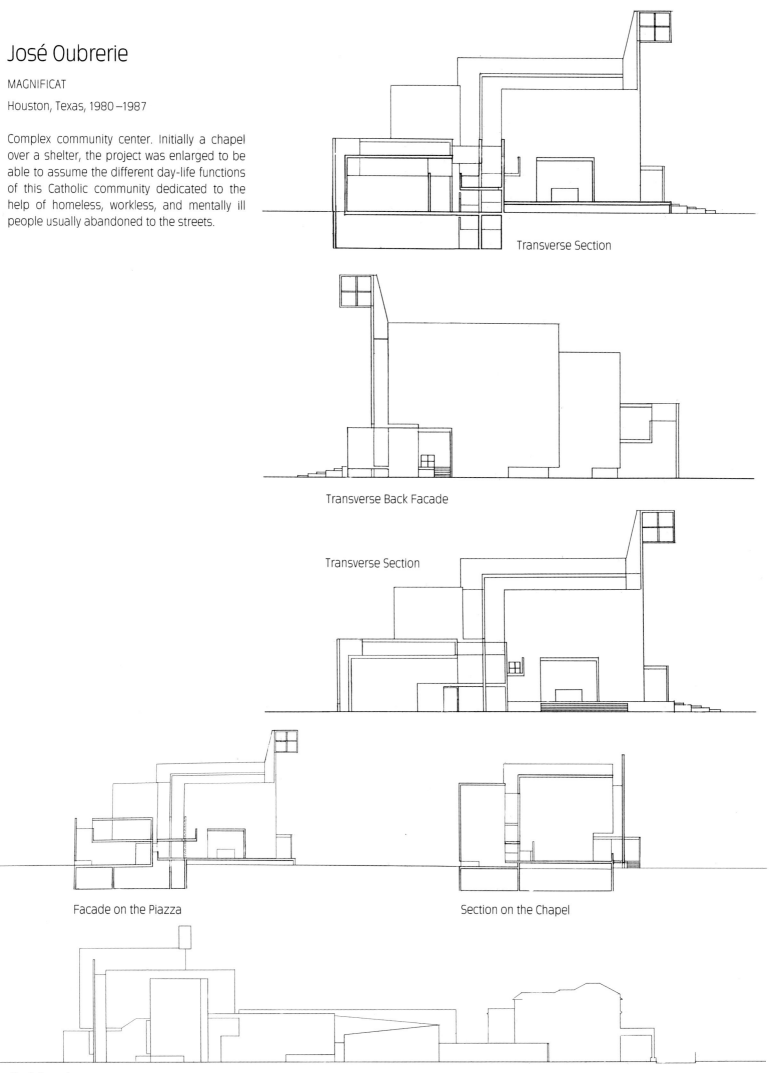

Transverse Section

Transverse Back Facade

Transverse Section

Facade on the Piazza

Section on the Chapel

Back Facade

Cesar Pelli & Associates

LEY STUDENT CENTER EXPANSION

Rice University, Houston, Texas, 1985–1986
Design Team: Cesar Pelli, Kevin Hart, Mark
Hesselgrave, Mitchell A. Hirsch, Rafael Pelli,
Diana Balmori

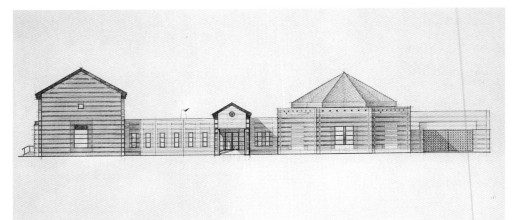

Program: Expansion of a 50,000-square-foot
student center to 75,000 square feet.

The Rice Memorial Center was constructed in
1958 for a student body of less than 2,000.
Enrollment at Rice has since more than
doubled, and student services and organiza-
tions have expanded with the increased numbers. The expansion fulfilled several crucial
campus needs, including the centralization of
all student services.

Referring to the original 1910 buildings and
campus plan by Cram, Goodhue, and Ferguson,
the addition's exterior is salmon-colored brick
detailed with limestone, glazed brick, and tile.
Its gabled roof is Spanish tile and copper. The
Student Center's massing of long parallel
blocks is also typical of early Rice buildings; the
multi-purpose room's octagonal shape expresses its use as a gathering place.

Part of the design intention was to continue
the system of expression and ornamentation
begun with our first building at Rice, Herring
Hall. Glazed brick, limestone, and glazed tile
provide several rhythms of material change,
and ornament is used in the surface of the skin
to express construction and program. Like Herring Hall, entrance treatments are layered by
cutting and folding the brick skin. This method
refers to the layered, carved stone portals of
earlier Rice buildings while remaining consistent with modern thin-wall construction.

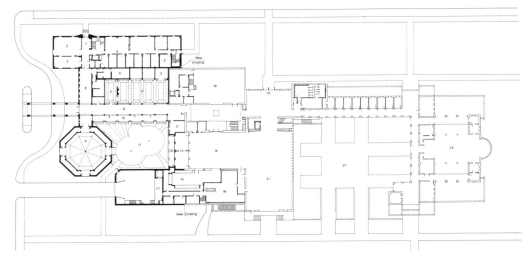

To create a new image for the entire complex,
the Student Center's main entrance was moved
from the north side of the building to the west
side of the addition, where most users arrive.
It serves as the focal point of the new wing
and the "porte cochere" affords covered
automobile drop-off.

This entrance begins a new main corridor
that acts as a unifying element linking the old
and new wings of the Student Center. The corridor opens on to all the main spaces in the
building, including a new garden courtyard that
is an outdoor living room. It also provides daylight, filtered by a covered arcade, to the main
corridor and private dining rooms.

Key

1 Lobby	12 Porch
2 Lounge	13 Private Dining Room
3 Conference	14 Existing Cafeteria
4 Student Advising	15 Servery
5 Mechanical Room	16 Existing Kitchen
6 Display	17 Loading Dock
7 Porte Cochere	18 Existing Bookstore
8 Corridor	19 North Entrance
9 Multi-purpose Room	20 Existing Grand Hall
10 Arcade	21 Existing Cloister
11 Garden	22 Existing Chapel

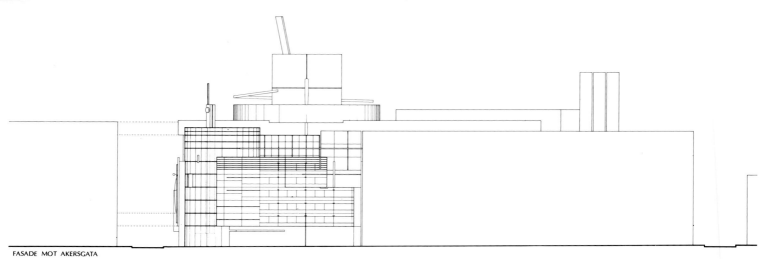

FASADE MOT AKERSGATA

Peter Pran, Carlos Zapata

for Ellerbe Becket

DITTEN PROJECT FOR SCHIBSTED GRUPPEN

Oslo, Norway
Competition, 1988
Design Team: Peter Pran, Carlos Zapata, Vatche Aslanjan, Maria Wilthew, Curtis Wagner, Wayne Fishback

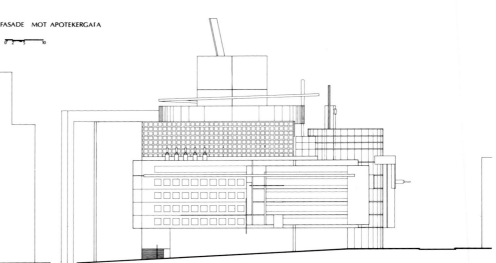

FASADE MOT APOTEKERGATA

This design of the new headquarters for "Aftenposten" and "Verdens Gang," the two largest newspapers in Norway, is the first prize winner in an international/national architecture competition. The building site is located along Akersgaten (the main newspaper street in Oslo), adjacent to the two existing newspaper buildings. The site is located across the street from three main government buildings, and two blocks away from the Parliament Building, Karl Johans Gate, and Studenterlunden (the area which in many ways constitutes the heart of the city).

The exuberant entry space and the highly articulated exterior entry celebrate and dignify the headquarters for these two important newspapers. Although the vertically shaped

cylinder entry space defines a corner entry, an asymmetrical arrangement in massing and facades relates appropriately to the two different streets it is facing. The facade toward the main street, Akersgaten, is given a rich, horizontal expression in glass and steel, respectful of the height and character of the government building across the street. The long facade facing the side street, Apotekergaten, is given a different and more complex copper-glass-stone-concrete treatment that is appropriate for the street's more intimate character. The entry

cylinder receives these two facades and pulls them together by allowing vertical and horizontal elements, and enclosed spaces, to intersect and move through it. Along Teatergaten and Munch's Gate, the building masses are pulled out as individual blocks or "walls" defining the overall complex along these streets. The separation of these two building blocks also allows them to be rented out separately from the major portion of the complex. The center of this unusual and idiosyncratic building site is defined by a large cylindrical atrium. Within this cylinder is suspended a floating cube that houses the main staff cafeteria at its top, with a magnificent view of the entire city. The cube is held up structurally by three asymmetrically placed columns, with elevators on a slant attached in tracks to one of these.

A diagonal walkway on the ground floor connects the main entries at the corner of Akersgaten/Apotekergaten and the corner of Teatergaten/Munch's Gate, while intersecting the central cylindric atrium. At the higher office floors, and particularly at the ninth floor, another diagonal walkway of a different orientation connects the main entry along Teatergaten with a bridge connection over Apotekergaten to the existing "Aftenposten" building.

The metal-glass-stone facades give the two newspapers a new image and continue the modern character of the existing ›Aftenposten‹ and ›Verdens Gang‹ buildings.

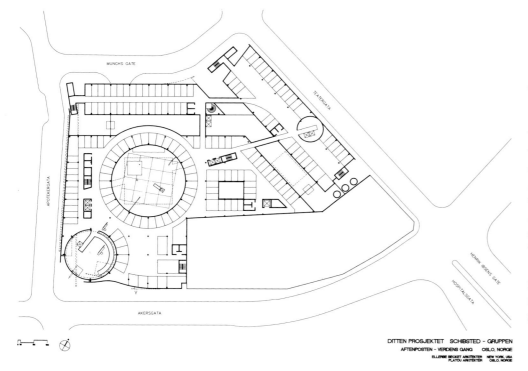

DITTEN PROSJEKTET SCHIBSTED - GRUPPEN
AFTENPOSTEN - VERDENS GANG   OSLO, NORGE
ELLERBE BECKET ARKITEKTER   NEW YORK, USA
PLATOU ARKITEKTER   OSLO, NORGE

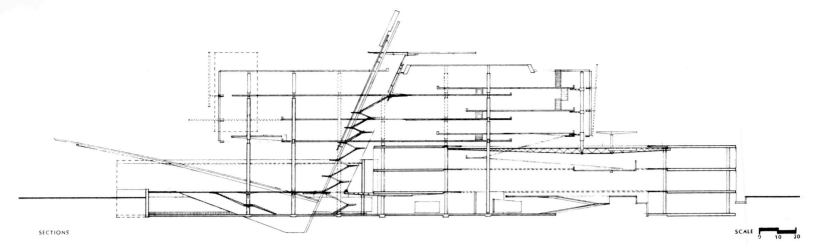

SECTIONS   SCALE [■▬] 5 10 20

Peter Pran, Carlos Zapata
for Ellerbe Becket

UNIVERSITY OF MINNESOTA
School of Architecture and
Landscape Architecture

St. Paul/Minneapolis, Minnesota, 1988–1989
Design Team: Peter Pran, Carlos Zapata,
Ed Calma, Curtis Wagner, Maria Wilthew, Frank Yu,
Vatche Aslanjan, John Gaunt, Bryan Carlson,
Tom Schneider, Don Snyder

The goal is to create an addition that responds to all major campus planning issues, meets all functional and user requirements, provides outstanding new spatial qualities, and will represent the leading edge design in contemporary architecture.

The new additions work sensitively with the existing building, while fully retaining the exist-ing building's main character and its handsome square shape. The new wing to the north and the main entry canopy to the west flow gently and respectfully over the existing building, and activate and give direction to the central atrium space. These gentle cantilevers into the central covered atrium give a clear exterior/interior orientation. The existing "mushroom"-shape roof is replaced by a new glass skylight roof that reinforces the new wing and canopy.

To provide large, major interior spaces on the site in response to the demanding require-ments of the program, and a building shape that articulates the transfer between the two major campus grids, we chose a cylindrical massing – broken to accommodate the specif-ics of the site. Inside the cylinder, the auditorium, the library, and the cafeteria are placed in a most invigorating, intersecting relationship with space. Outside the richly articulated cylinder, the interior space connects up with a clearly defined exterior landscape to the west.

The new north entry to the auditorium and the architecture school itself define a clear image. The wing to the north, which contains studios, articulates a positive tension to the cylinder below, allowing students and faculty to move freely and directly between studios above and auditorium, library, and cafeteria below.

The studios are placed on the highest floors in the new building wing. Classrooms are placed on the second floor of the existing build-ing; here, too, with certain floor portions taken out to allow visual contact between first and second floors of the existing building.

The entries to the completed building com-plex open to the west, east, and north, providing a pleasant and easy internal circulation and promenade system, which further allows the general campus population easy access and passing-through of the Architecture Building.

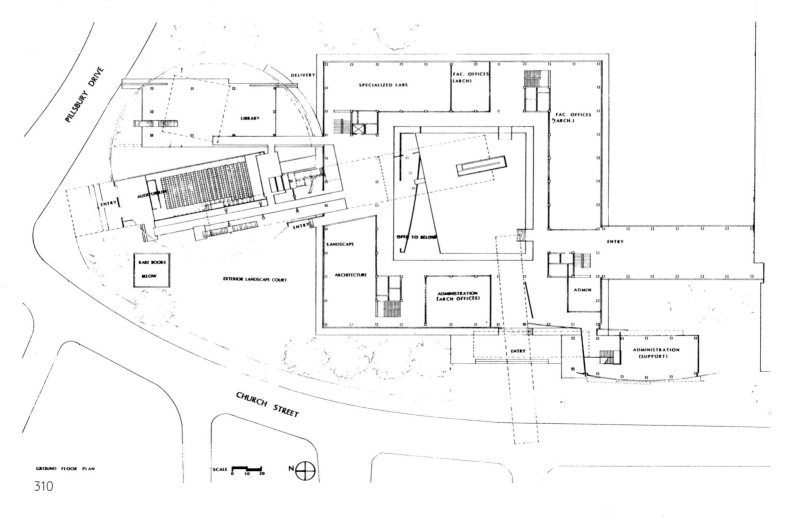

GROUND FLOOR PLAN   SCALE [■▬] 0 10 20   N⊕

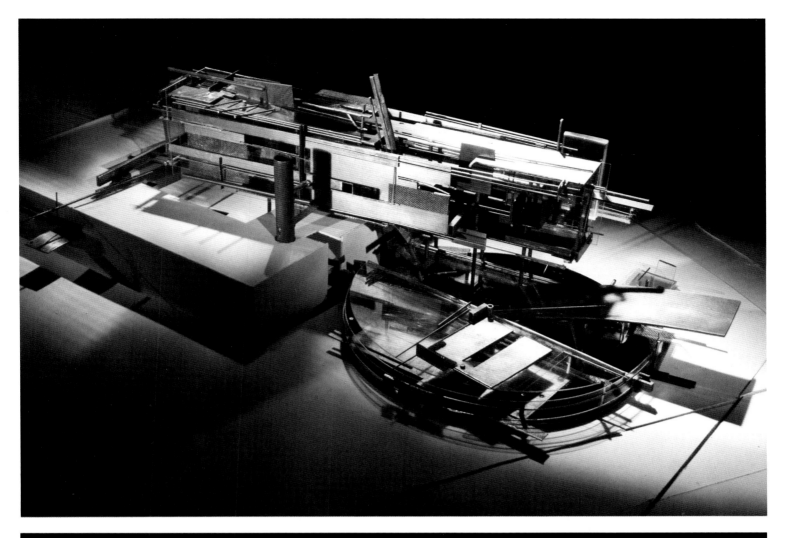

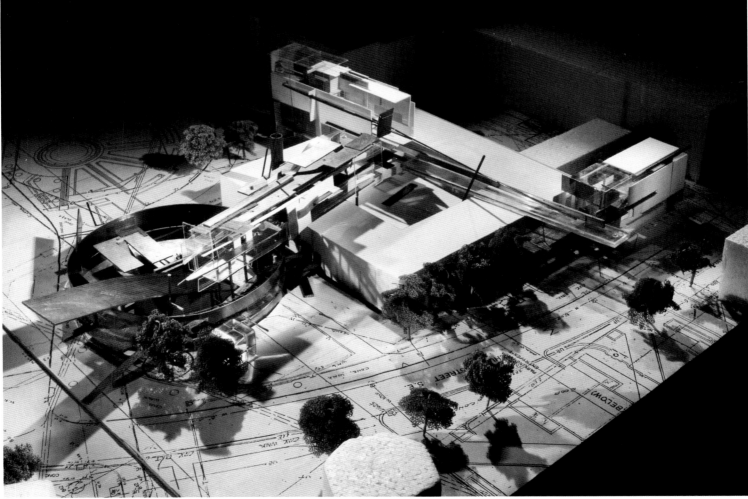

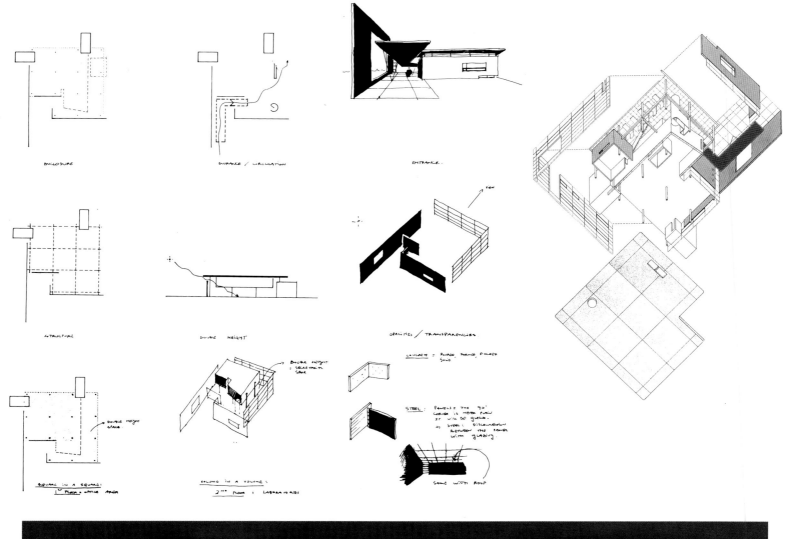

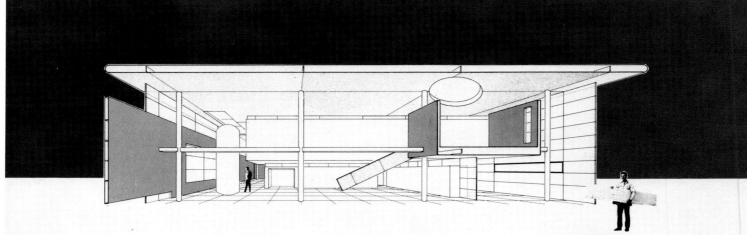

Pascal Quintard-Hofstein

PQH Projects

OFFICE BUILDING IN PHILADELPHIA

Philadelphia, Pennsylvania, 1988

Program: A mixed-use building with offices and a laboratory. The new building is to be located on a triangular site behind an existing production plant. A tight budget.

Solution: A two-story building. Offices on the ground, laboratories on the second floor. A double-height-space. An entrance bound by a wall and capped by a canopy. The double-height space is a secretarial area: a lunch room will limit that space and float, attached to the ground by a stair: spatial autonomy of the double-height space.

Geometry: The square as open figure: the 90° corners are never joined by the same material.

Materials: Steel structure. Steel floors. A concrete wall framing the entrance.

East wall and north wall: translucent material (Kalwall).

West wall and south wall: opaque material, punctured by windows.

Steel roof.

Pascal Quintard-Hofstein

PQH Projects

HOUSE # 227

California, Project, 1988
Design Team: Pascal Quintard-Hofstein with Joseph Franchina, Thierry LeGuay and Jim Wiesenfeld (structural consultant)

Program: A house for a movie director. The house should provide a small viewing room inside the house for private viewing sessions.

Proposal: A house between two walls, with a courtyard as an outdoor room.

The house is "capped" from the top, the courtyard is closed from the side. The movie screen is an opacity that closes the courtyard. The screen is an interior surface, and "projects" the house back to its interior.

The roof is the high limit of the house, and limits the roof garden. It is detached as a sail and frames the views to the sky.

The north wall is the wall of enclosure and also the corner/back wall – it organizes the views. The thick, south wall is a "techno-wall," in which all the pipes and ducts will be concealed. It provides the air and the temperature. The techno-wall is a regulator.

The ground of the house is not the earth but a grid of columns and a stair. The ground of the house is elevated sixteen feet above the datum. The house is lifted and achieves maximum autonomy.

Structure: 18 × 16-inch steel tubes, hollow in the house, solid in the courtyard.

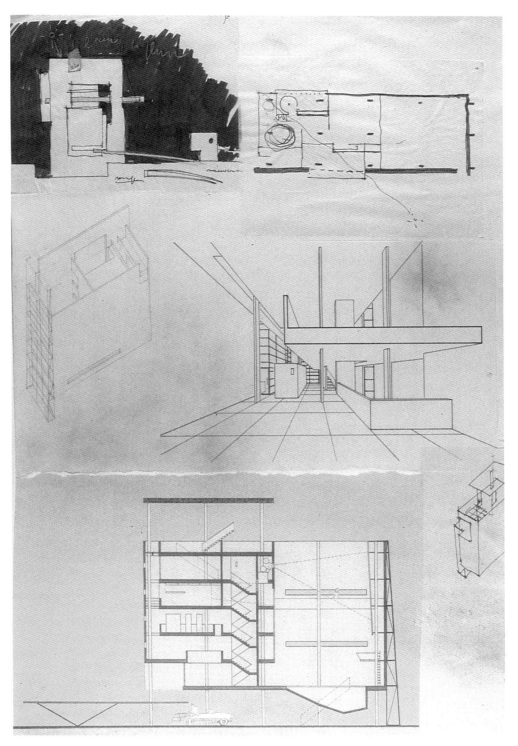

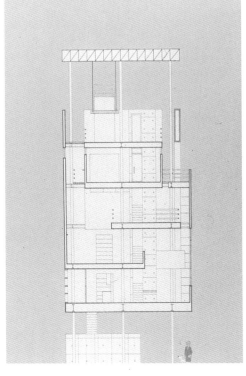

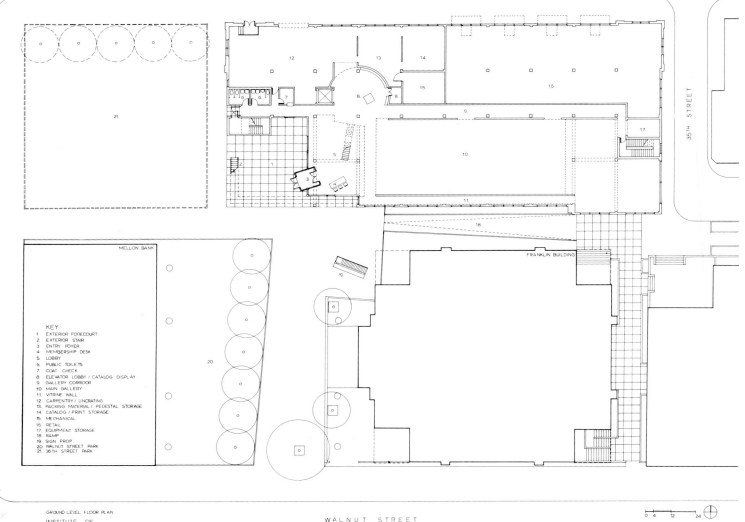

MELLON BANK

KEY
1   EXTERIOR FORECOURT
2   EXTERIOR STAIR
3   ENTRY FOYER
4   MEMBERSHIP DESK
5   LOBBY
6   PUBLIC TOILETS
7   COAT CHECK
8   ELEVATOR LOBBY / CATALOG DISPLAY
9   GALLERY CORRIDOR
10 MAIN GALLERY
11 VITRINE WALL
12 CARPENTRY / UNCRATING
13 PACKING MATERIAL / PEDESTAL STORAGE
14 CATALOG / PRINT STORAGE
15 MECHANICAL
16 RETAIL
17 EQUIPMENT STORAGE
18 RAMP
19 SIGN PROP
20 WALNUT STREET PARK
21 35TH STREET PARK

FRANKLIN BUILDING

GROUND LEVEL FLOOR PLAN
INSTITUTE OF
CONTEMPORARY ART

WALNUT STREET

Smith-Miller + Hawkinson

THE INSTITUTE OF CONTEMPORARY ART

Philadelphia, Pennsylvania
Competition, 1986
Design Team: Henry Smith-Miller, Laurie
Hawkinson, Ruri Yampolsky, Craig Konyk, Tim
McNicholas, Annette Fierro, Sam Anderson,
John Conaty, Kit Yan, George Gomez

The ICA is an arts organization devoted to new artists and artforms and has no permanent collection. Its existing building enjoys a unique position with regard to the University and the City. Our project with the addition of the four-story tower addresses the scale and formality of a major city thoroughfare (Walnut Street), serves as a "fourth wall" of a courtyard bounded by two adjacent buildings, acts as terminus for a small-scale retail development, and provides a focus for a midblock mews. The building is ideally suited for conversion to a combination of art gallery, offices, and retail spaces. Its "loft" type construction – concrete slab and steel structure, and brick exterior – is easily modified and has high live- and dead-load capacities.

We added two new gardens, one public, the other private, and built elements – a series of outbuildings and walls, to act as cognitive elements and to reinforce the existing University Campus fabric.

The program elements of the Institute were placed within the shell of the existing building to reinforce and revitalize areas on all sides of the building. By removing portions of the existing structure, we were able to alter the closed nature of the existing building and promote the idea of a building "in transition." The haptic quality of the addition of the tower, the carving away of the areas around the main entrance, the new devices, cranes and ramps – all reinforce the program of the ICA. The building proposes that the process of exhibition become architecture.

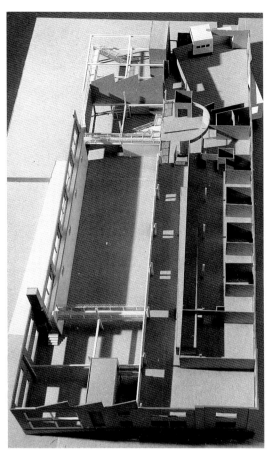

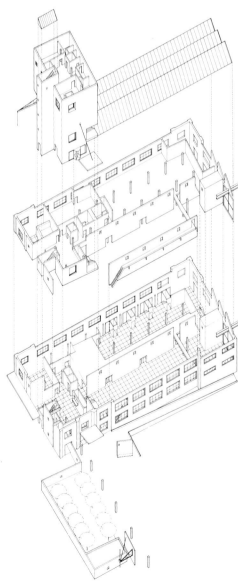

Robert A. M. Stern Architects

TWO TWENTY TWO BERKELEY STREET

222 Berkeley Street, Boston,
Massachusetts, 1986–
Design Team: Anthony Cohn, Ellen Coxe, Keller
Easterling, Tom Eisele, Tim Lenahan

Two Twenty Two Berkeley Street, a mixed-use building in Boston's Back Bay combining offices, shops, a winter garden, and space for 400 cars parked underground, is the second phase of a controversial major retail/office complex in one of the most architecturally elaborate, yet fragile, urban centers in America.

The main entrance to Two Twenty Two Berkeley occurs on Berkeley Street, where a restrained classicizing portico is the dominant feature. By orienting the building to Berkeley Street, that recently neglected street is given a renewed sense of importance. The design offers Boylston Street a continuous row of shops, interrupted at one point by a boldly scaled entrance leading to a public arcade and winter garden. The details of the Boylston Street entrance, which is flanked by paired columns carrying urns and entered through a revolving door housed in a tempietto, emphasize its public importance.

The west elevation, visible from Copley Square, is distinguished by a slender tower-like element toward the north side, complementing the tourelles of Trinity Church, and a terracing effect created by the setbacks at the top of the building. The office tower is crowned by an interpretation of an eighteenth-century orangery and of Boston's widely admired Horticultural Hall, creating a distinctive skyline silhouette that places it firmly within the American tradition of Classical skyscrapers.

The familiar Boston palette of red brick and granite has been adopted for Two Twenty Two Berkeley, adopting a vocabulary inspired by the eighteenth- and early nineteenth-century, late Georgian, architecture of Beacon Hill. It was revived in the Back Bay in the 1900s and used for one of Boston's few tall buildings of the 1920s, the Ritz Hotel. Two Twenty Two Berkeley Street varies the use of that vocabulary, both in its details and in the building's overall massing.

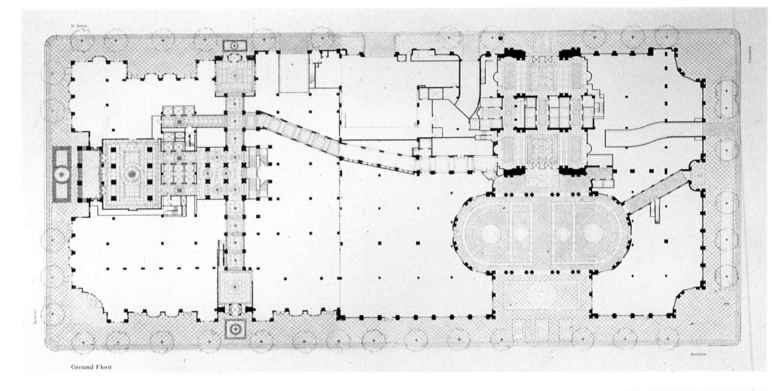

Ground Floor

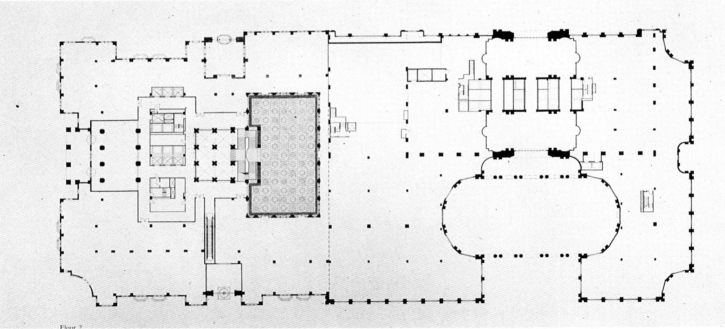

Floor 2

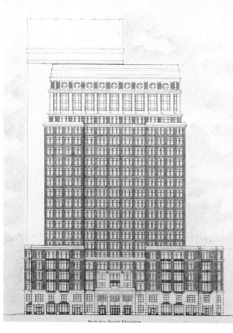

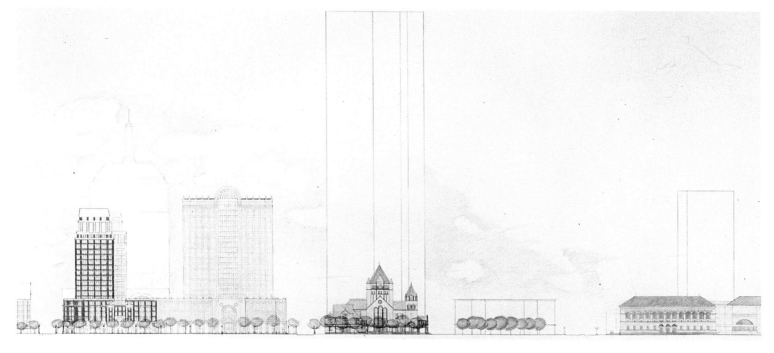

Robert A. M. Stern Architects

MEXX RETAIL SHOP

150 Peter Cornelius Hoofstrat, Amsterdam,
1986–1987
Design Team: Alex Lamis, Graham S. Wyatt

Located on Amsterdam's most fashionable shopping street this 3,000-square-foot shop represents the first venture into retailing for a young and rapidly growing international fashion company. In this shop design, not only the merchandise but also sales staff and customers are on stage. The shopfront is a proscenium arch which opens on to the drama within. Inside, a layered composition from front to back recalls the sets in a theater, and the lighting accents individual items of clothing rather than bathing the entire space in a uniform light.

The architectural forms are both young and aggressive – in keeping with the company's image. They also reinterpret and pay homage to the ebullient if idiosyncratic Amsterdam school of architecture of the 1920s; unlike the brick and wood aesthetic of that work, the finishes are hard and "cool" (glass, brushed stainless steel, and terrazzo) and the colors have been kept to black, white, and gray to show off the clothes to best effect. Small amounts of natural finish English Sycamore add a special "natural" accent and allow a broad spectrum of clothing colors to be shown to good effect.

Robert A. M. Stern Architects

INTERNATIONAL HEADQUARTERS FOR
MEXX INTERNATIONAL

Voorschoten, Netherlands, 1985–1987
Design Team:
Graham S. Wyatt, Preston Gumberich, William Nolan, Jeff Schofield, Pat Tiné

Set in a suburb of the Hague, this corporate headquarters reflects the inherent dichotomy of a tightly organized international corporation that produces seemingly impromptu, colorful, youth-oriented clothing. The design consists of an existing 25,000-square-foot, nineteenth-century silver factory renovated to accommodate corporate offices on the ground floor and fashion design studios in what were the second floor silversmiths' studios. Behind the existing structure a new, 25,000-square-foot addition provides fashion display areas, meeting rooms and further office space around three sides of a double-height, south-facing atrium.

A new employees' restaurant opens, with south- and east-facing glass doors, on to a lawn. A reflecting pool provides animated daylighting to the ceilings and curved glass walls of the atrium and restaurant.

The design strategy attempts to create a retrospective history for the entire building, as if it had grown over time from the cool Baroque Classicism of the original facility to the freewheeling shapes of the addition, which attempts to capture the lighthearted and idiosyncratic spirit of Dutch modernism.

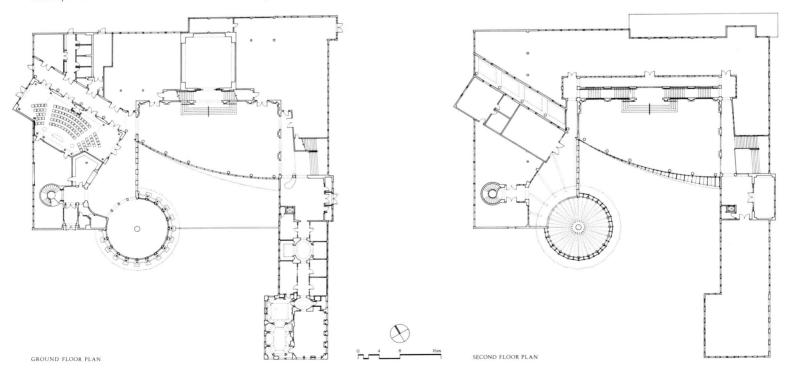

GROUND FLOOR PLAN

0   4   8   16m

SECOND FLOOR PLAN

UKZ Design, Inc.
Ungers, Kiss, Zwigard

KNEE RESIDENCE

North Caldwell, New Jersey, 1983–1986

Single family residence with living/dining room, family room, kitchen, 3 bedrooms, 3½ bathrooms, studio/office, garage, storage, and gardens. Sited on one-acre suburban lot of elongated trapezoidal shape, one-third wooded. The project has two primary elements: an L-shaped corner building and a walled garden. The living/dining area is intersected, dividing the ground floor into a formal and an informal living area. The living areas are separated by the entry in the garden wall. The master bedroom, above the family room, is separated from the children's bedrooms by a hallway integrating the studio/office area. The basement contains a two-car garage, laundry and storage facilities.

Harry C. Wolf

APLIX MANUFACTURING FACILITY

Charlotte, North Carolina, 1981-1982

This project proposes an alternative to the numerous unremarkable industrial buildings. Built on a fast-track program within a very constrained budget, it seeks to create a calm and restrained presence with simple materials carefully chosen and thoughtfully assembled.

A great circle was incised in this gently sloping site, functionally to induce drainage away from the building, visually to create a sense of place in an otherwise unremarkable site. A double row of Lombardy poplars outlines the circle. One day they will provide a unifying gesture between the building and the land.

The exterior skin of the manufacturing area is of precast 8 × 20-foot panels scored into 4-foot squares in gray concrete with a white aggregate. There is a diagonal striation in the panel and the resulting rib is fractured to expose the white aggregate. The total building height is established by the high-bay require-

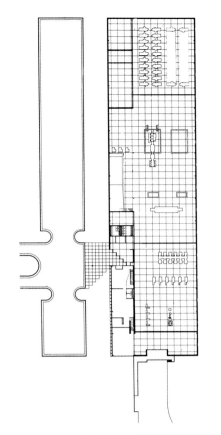

ments of the manufacturing operation and results in a height of 20 feet from the finished floor to the top of the parapet.

In the office block in the northeast corner of the building, two levels of office space were sandwiched into the 20-foot height of the manufacturing plant. By exposing the steel structure and the metal deck, an illusion of added height is created in the offices, even within the limited floor-to-floor dimensions. Green-tinted, insulated glass covers three sides of the office block. A freestanding sun screen shades the eastern side. The two-story space continues to the northeastern edge and will provide an easy means of accomplishing the projected office expansion. Also located on the northeastern side of the building is a staging area for the shipping operation.

The entire structure is carefully articulated to coordinate with the total geometry of the modularly organized building and its lighting, HVAC and sprinkler systems. The west wall of the building is removable to accommodate predicted future expansion.

Harry C. Wolf
for Ellerbe Becket

NCNB NATIONAL BANK HEADQUARTERS
OFFICE BUILDING

Tampa, Florida, 1982–1988

A cylinder, the archetype of the tower, serves as a metaphor both for a citadel guarding this entrance to the city and for a lighthouse. In stone, reflecting strength and stability, a sense of solidness, the building's natural materials stand as a softly spoken counterpoint to twentieth-century mirror-clad buildings.

An examination of the site reveals a clue to its nature. The line of the river, which is also the line of the existing Tampa Museum building, intersects the geometry of the city grid with a slope of two to five. That same rectangle, divided on its length into thirds, generates golden section rectangles, so that there is an overlay of these two integrated geometries inherent in the site.

A diagram of the building elevation, based on this ratio and with an assumed floor to floor height of 13 feet, generated five six-story-high packages of 78 feet each, in a cylinder with a 78-foot radius. Astonishingly enough, this gen-

erates a footprint of some 19,000 square feet, exactly in accord with the developer's objective of a 18,000 to 20,000 square footprint in a 30-story height.

The public banking functions requiring a span and volume greater than that available in the tower are pulled out into 78-foot cubes, which serve to mediate the scale between the street and the tower, while urbanistically holding the corner of the site.

The bank hall structure is a white steel truss with 13-foot members on center, infilled with limestone on the east and west, and, in the center, walls and roof of glass. This structure is raised 8 feet above plaza and, within its thickened walls, houses offices for loan officers who overlook the hall. The tower's reinforced concrete structure is similarly clad in limestone, with recessed bands of whiter stone every six floors reflecting the geometry.

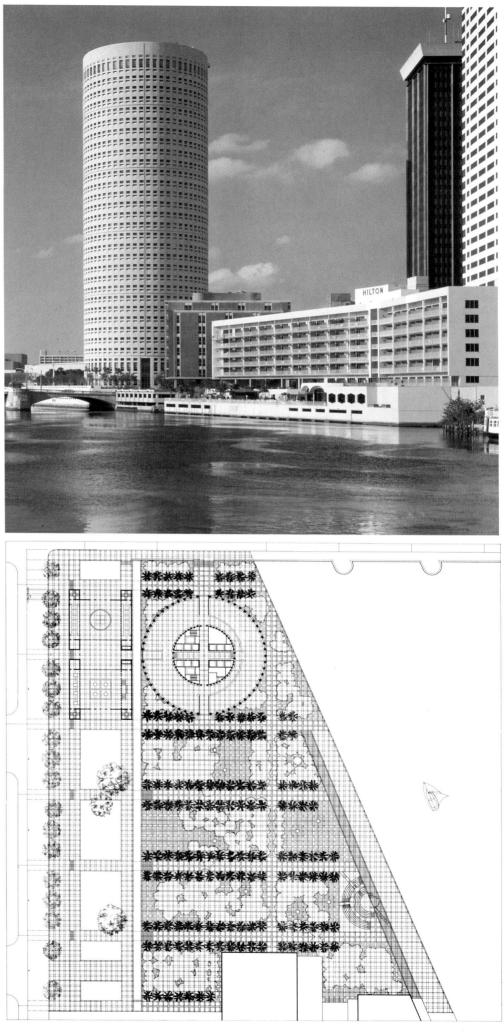

Harry C. Wolf

for Ellerbe Becket

KANSAI AIRPORT

Osaka, Japan, Competition, 1988

The Kansai Airport Competition called for the design of a passenger terminal building and related facilities ("Aerocity"), serving 25 million passengers a year, to be built on reclaimed land five kilometers offshore in Osaka Bay. The passenger terminal was to utilize three floors of a single building consisting of a main central terminal and concourse wings. The concourse, over a mile long, was to be serviced by a people-mover system.

The buildings form a tripartite composition. The crescent of Aerocity, centralized and still; the walls of the terminal; and the hypostyle hall of the concourse.

The translucent walls of the terminal lightly veil the elegant concrete structure, whose diagonals quietly echo the super-scale of the roadway arc beyond. Throughout, the careful modulation of natural light invites nature's asymmetry to counterpoint man's instinct for symmetry and order.

The aluminum roof structure over the concourse is finished in a matte surface the color of pewter. With eight hyperbolic casings arrayed around each column, the folds of the lattice surface create a complex pattern of shadow gently filtering the natural light. The large degree of repetition, the simplicity of a straight-line generator, and the overall lightness of each roof unit lend themselves to preassembly, adding to the speed and economy of construction. The hyper-paraboloid roof provides enclosure on the garden side, support for a suspended monorail system, and a spectacular 83-foot cantilever over the aircraft, recalling the scale and drama of a nineteenth-century railway station.

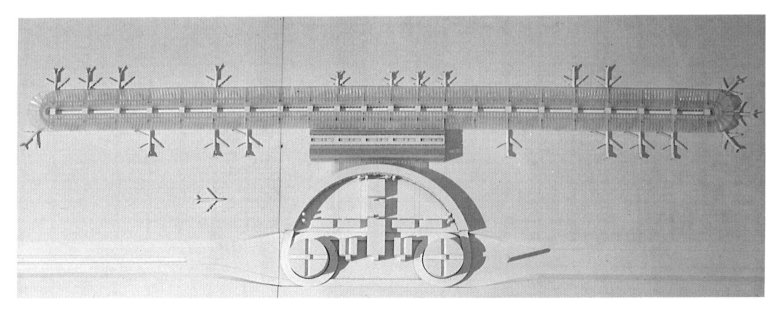

Appendix

Short Biographies of the Architects

Compiled by Petra Skiba

Agrest, Diana
Agrest & Gandelsonas

Born in Argentina.

Studied architecture and urbanism at the University of Buenos Aires; from 1967 to 1969 worked at the École Practique des Hautes Études and at the Centre de Recherche d'Urbanisme, Paris. Publications on architecture and urban planning. In 1979 founded the architectural practice Agrest & Gandelsonas, together with Mario Gandelsonas. Exhibitions and publications of their work in the USA, Europe, and South America. From 1972 to 1984 member of the Institute for Architecture and Urban Studies, New York.

Ambasz, Emilio

Born 1943 in Argentina.

Studied at Princeton University. Design curator at the Museum of Modern Art, New York, 1970 to 1976. Vice-President of the Architectural League, 1981 to 1988. He has taught at Princeton University School of Architecture and was guest professor at the Hochschule für Gestaltung in Ulm, West Germany. In 1976 took part in the Venice Biennale. Numerous exhibitions and publications in the USA, Europe, and Japan. Ambasz holds a series of patents for discoveries made in the field of industrial and mechanical design, as well as several awards and honors. In 1989 there was an exhibition of his work at the Museum of Modern Art, New York. He lives and works in New York.

Arsene, Vladimir

Born 1951 in Bucharest, Romania.

Graduated from the Institute for Architecture and Urban Studies in Bucharest in 1976. Since 1978 has been working as freelance architect in New York. Worked in the practice of Gruzen Samton Steinglass Architects and Abramovitz Harris Kingsland Architects, New York. He has taught at the Institutes of Technology in New York and New Jersey. Publications on his work in the USA, Europe, and Japan. Currently working with The Grad Partnership in Newark, New Jersey.

Barie, John Peter
Swanke Hayden Connell

Born in England.

Studied at the Architectural Association School of Architecture in London and after that studied architecture at Pennsylvania State University until 1965. Partner in the architectural firm Swanke Hayden Connell. Numerous honors and awards for office buildings, housing estates, and urban planning.

Barnes, Edward Larrabee
Edward Larrabee Barnes Associates

Born 1915 in Chicago, Illinois.

Until 1942 studied architecture with Walter Gropius and Marcel Breuer at Harvard University, Cambridge, Massachusetts. Awarded the Sheldon Travelling Fellowship, 1941–42. Since 1949 he has been director of his own practice in New York, Edward Larrabee Barnes Associates. From 1954 to 1959 Professor of Architecture and Design at the Pratt Institute, New York, and from 1957 to 1964 at Yale University, New Haven, Connecticut. Since 1983 Honorary Professor of Fine Arts at the Rhode Island School of Design, Providence. He has been strongly influenced by the Bauhaus through his teachers, although Barnes has preferred abstract compositions made up of clear, geometrical shapes with smooth surfaces. Among his best pieces of work are the Student Center of the Monterey Peninsula College, Monterey, California (1973), the Walker Art Center, Minneapolis (1974), and the IBM Tower, New York (1977).

Botta, Mario

Born 1943 in Mendrisio, Italy.

From 1958 to 1961 apprenticeship as technical drawer. Studied at the Instituto Universario di Architettura in Venice, 1964 to 1969. In 1976 guest professor at the École Polytechnique Federale in Lausanne. In 1965 Botta worked in Le Corbusier's practice, in 1969 in Louis Kahn's. After that he formed his own architectural practice in Lausanne. He has participated in numerous exhibitions in Europe, the USA, and Japan. Botta is one of the most important representatives of the so-called "Tessiner Schule."

Cederna, Ann
Masque

Born 1960.

Studied architecture and urban planning until 1982 at the University of Kentucky, Lexington, and from 1984 to 1986 at Cornell University, Ithaca, New York. Worked in the practices of Leonardo Ricci & Maria Dallerba-Ricci, Lexington, Kentucky, from 1981 to 1983, with Max Gordon and Associates from 1983 to 1985, and then with Emilio Ambasz & Associates. In 1985 she founded, with Douglas Brent Frederick, the architectural practice Masque, which in 1986 won the Architectural Projects Award for Commissioned Work, New York City Chapter of the American Institute of Architects for Le Canalou Residence. Exhibitions and publications in the USA and Italy.

Connell, Edward Sparks
Swanke Hayden Connell

Born in the USA.

Graduated in architecture from the University of Texas in 1956. Since 1970 Administrative Director of the architectural practice Swanke Hayden Connell.

Denari, Neil M.

Born 1957 in Fort Worth, Texas.

Studied architecture at the University of Houston and at Harvard University. From 1984 to 1987 participated in international exhibitions and several competitions. His predominantly conceptual projects were presented in numerous international publications. Since 1986 he has been running his own practice in Los Angeles.

Diller, Elisabeth
Diller + Scofidio

Born 1954 in Łódź, Poland

Studied at the Faculty of the Chanin School of Architecture of the Cooper Union. Little architectural practice; mainly projects which arose independently, combining architecture with performance, sculpture, and music. In 1979 went into partnership with Ricardo Scofidio, forming the architectural practice Diller + Scofidio, New York. Among other projects, they worked on an installation for the Museum of Modern Art. Exhibitions in the USA, Japan, Israel, and Europe. Numerous awards and honors – for example, from the American Academy in Rome and the National Endowment for the Arts.

Dimitriu, Livio G.
Urban Studies and Architecture Group

Born 1950 in Vršac, Yugoslavia.

Graduated from the Cooper Union School of Architecture. Graduate scholarship in the History of Modern Architecture at the Institute for Architecture in Bucharest, Romania. Worked in the architectural practices of Peter Eisenman, Rem Koolhaas, and

Colin Rowe and at the Institute for Architecture and Urban Studies. He has taught at various institutes and schools of architecture in the USA, Italy, and Japan. Numerous publications on architecture and related themes. Exhibitions and publications of his work in the USA, Europe, Asia, and South America. Dimitriu has won several national and international prizes, including, recently, the New York Chapter Honor Award of the American Institute of Architects. His office is in New York.

Dinkeloo, John
Kevin Roche John Dinkeloo and Associates

Born 1918 in Holland, Michigan. Died 1981 in Fredericksburg, Virginia.

After studying at the University of Michigan, Ann Arbor, Dinkeloo went into the Chicago practice of Skidmore, Owings and Merrill, where he was head of project planning from 1946 to 1950. In 1950 he worked for Eero Saarinen, and from 1956 went into partnership with him. After Saarinen's death he took over his practice together with Kevin Roche, transferring it from Bloomfield Hills and Birmingham, Michigan, to Hamden, Connecticut, where it was run from 1966 until Dinkeloo's death under the name Kevin Roche John Dinkeloo and Associates. Roche worked together with Dinkeloo, concentrating increasingly on the structural aspects of architecture, which played an important role in the work of both architects. Dinkeloo is responsible for introducing into architecture, among other things, synthetic caoutchouc-sections, metal-coated glass, and weatherproof steel.

Eisenman, Peter
Eisenman Architects

Born 1932 in Newark, New Jersey.

Studied at Cornell University in Ithaca, New York, at Columbia University in New York, and at the University of Cambridge, England. In 1957–58 worked in the team TAC (The Architects Collaborative). He has taught at the University of Cambridge, at Princeton University, New Jersey, and, since 1967, at the New York Cooper Union. In 1967 he founded and directed (until 1982) the Institute for Architecture and Urban Studies in New York. Co-publisher of the magazine for architectural theory *Oppositions*. Numerous awards and honors.

Elskop, Ines
1100 Architect

Born in Argentina.

Graduated in philosophy from the University of Buenos Aires in 1975, then studied economics at Fordham University. Since 1982 has worked in various architectural practices. In 1983 formed, together with David Piscuskas and Juergen Riehm, the practice 1100 Architect P. C. in New York.

Fieldman, Michael
Michael Fieldman & Partners

Born in Nokomis, Saskatchewan, Canada.

Studied mathematics, physics, and architecture at McGill University in Montreal. His practice was commissioned by the US Government to design industrial buildings for the "Operation Breakthrough" in New Jersey City and St. Louis. Exhibitions of his work in Denmark, Finland, and the USA. Fieldman has won several awards and prizes for his work, including two from the New York Institute of Architects. He works in his own practice, Michael Fieldman & Partners, in New York.

Fiorenzoli, Giuliano

Born in Florence, Italy.

Studied architecture at the University of Florence from 1963 to 1969 and, at the same time, studied at the Academy of Fine Arts in Florence. Graduated in 1971 from the Massachusetts Institute of Technology. Took part in the Venice Biennale in 1978. The most remarkable of his frequently exhibited and published projects is the Rainbow Plaza Center at Niagara Falls, which he designed in collaboration with Raimund Abraham. Fiorenzoli was awarded numerous architectural prizes, including the "American Institute of Architects, New York Chapter Unbuilt Award" in 1985. He lives and works as an independent architect with his own practice in New York.

Fort-Brescia, Bernardo
Arquitectonica

Born in 1951 in Lima, Peru.

Studied architecture at Harvard University until 1975. From 1975 to 1977 guest professor at the University of Miami, Coral Gables, Florida. In 1977 he founded, together with Laurinda H. Spear, the practice Arquitectonica in Coral Gables, Florida.

Fox, Sheldon
Kohn Pedersen Fox Associates

Graduated in architecture in 1953 from the University of Pennsylvania. Worked in the architectural practices of Kahn and Jacobs. Vice-President of John Carl Warnecke and Associates. Since 1976 in partnership with Eugene Kohn and William Pedersen. Member of the American Institute of Architects and the Architectural League of New York. He has worked extensively on hotel buildings, airports, and office buildings.

Frederick, Douglas Brent
Masque

Born 1956.

Studied architecture and town planning at Cornell University, Ithaca, New York, and at the University of Maryland, College Park, Maryland. Worked in O. M. Ungers's practice in Cologne in 1981–82 and with William Downing & Associates, Ithaca, New York, from

1985 to 1987. In 1985 founded the architectural practice Masque with Ann Cederna. In 1986 they won the Architectural Projects Award for Commissioned Work, New York City Chapter of the American Institute of Architects for the Le Canalou Residence. Exhibitions and publications in the USA and Italy. He has taught at various colleges in the USA and in Switzerland.

Freed, James Ingo
I. M. Pei & Partners

Born in Essen, West Germany.

Studied at the Illinois Institute of Technology, where he was Dean from 1975 to 1978. Teaching posts at various universities and schools of architecture in the USA. He has worked in the practices of Dandforth & Speyer, Michael Ruse, and Mies van der Rohe. He is now in partnership with I. M. Pei & Partners. Over the last few years his work has been exhibited and published throughout the world. Freed has been awarded numerous prestigious prizes, such as the American Institute of Architects Chicago Architecture Award and the Reynolds Memorial Award for Excellence in Architecture. Since 1977 he has been a member of the American Institute of Architects.

Gandelsonas, Mario
Agrest & Gandelsonas

Born in Argentina.

Studied architecture and urban construction at the University of Buenos Aires, and from 1967 to 1969 worked at the École Practiques des Hautes Études and at the Centre de Recherche d'Urbanisme in Paris. In 1979 founded the architectural practice Agrest & Gandelsonas with Diana Agrest; since 1986 director of Agrest & Gandelsonas Development Consultants. From 1971 to 1984 Fellow of the Institute for Architecture and Urban Studies. Publications in numerous international specialist magazines.

Giovannini, Joseph
Giovannini & Associates

Born in Los Angeles, California.

Studied architecture at Harvard University until 1974, then worked in the practice of Borrow Fieldman in Montreal. In 1976 returned to Los Angeles as freelance architect. Publications in "The Herald Examiner," for which he received the Pulitzer Prize in 1982. Since 1983 he has been working in his own architectural practice in New York. Numerous publications, including ones on Deconstructivism.

Giurgola, Romaldo
Mitchell/Giurgola Architects

Born 1920 in Rome, Italy.

Studied architecture at the University of Rome, 1945 to 1949. After moving to the USA, continued his studies at Columbia University, New York, from 1949 to 1951. In 1958 he founded, together with Ehrmann Mitchell, an architectural practice in Philadelphia, which was transferred to New York in 1966. Numerous exhibitions in the USA and Europe; several national and international exhibitions and prizes for his designs. Giurgola has published various papers on architectural theory with Ehrmann Mitchell.

Graves, Michael

Born 1934 in Indianapolis, Indiana.

Studied architecture at the University of Cincinatti, Ohio, and at Harvard University, Cambridge, Massachusetts. Scholarship for two years at the American Academy in Rome. In 1964 founded his own practice in Princeton, New Jersey; in 1972 appointed professor at the university there. Graves first became well known through the Book *Five Architects*, published in 1972, in which his work and that of Peter Eisenman, Charles Gwathmey, John Hejduk, and Richard Meier ("The New York Five") was presented. His work at that time was distinguished by a formal and extremely radicalized reversion to early Modernism, especially to Le Corbusier's 1920s style. He subsequently went back further in history, to, among others, Etienne-Louis Boullée and Claude-Nicolas Ledoux, although no direct references are made to their work. Characteristic examples from his early period are, apart from those presented in this book, the Fargo-Moorhead Cultural Center Bridge (1977), the Kalko House in Green Brook, New Jersey (1978), and the Public Services Building in Portland, Oregon (1980 – 82).

Gwathmey, Charles
Gwathmey Siegel & Associates Architects

Born 1938 in Charlotte, North Carolina.

Studied architecture from 1956 to 1962 at the University of Pennsylvania, Philadelphia, with Louis Kahn and Robert Venturi, as well as at Yale University in New Haven, Connecticut, with Paul Rudolph, James Stirling, and Shadrach Woods. From 1964 to 1966 Professor of Design at the Pratt Institute, New York; after that, numerous teaching posts at various universities and schools of architecture in the USA. In 1966 he founded, together with Richard Henderson, his own practice in New York; since 1968 he has also been in partnership with Robert Siegel. Gwathmey belonged in the sixties to the "New York Five," known for their formal reversion to early Modernism. Apart from numerous interior design projects, Gwathmey initially designed mainly private houses; other projects with his partners then followed. The practice has won numerous prizes, including, in 1982, The Firm Award, the highest award of the American Institute of Architects.

Hadid, Zaha

Born 1950 in Bagdad, Iraq.

Studied mathematics at the American University in Beirut, then architecture at the Architectural Association in London with Leon Krier, Jeremy Dixon, and Rem Koolhaas. From 1976 to 1978 member of the group OMA (Office for Metropolitan Architecture), then founder of his own practice in London. Teaching post at the Architectural Association in London. In 1983 he won the international competition for the "Peak" in Hong Kong.

Halsband, Frances
R. M. Kliment & Frances Halsband

Born 1943 in New York City.

Studied architecture at Swarthmore College and at Columbia University. For five years worked in the practice Mitchell/Giurgola Architects in New York. In 1972 partnership with Robert M. Kliment in New York. Member of the National Committee on Design of the American Institute of Architects, also President of the Architectural League of New York.

Hardy Holzman Pfeiffer Associates

Architectural practice founded in 1967 by Hugh Hardy, Malcolm Holzman, and Norman Pfeiffer with its main office in New York City. Apart from numerous building projects, HHPA is famous for its work in restoration and in the visual and performing arts. HHPA has designed art centers, museums, libraries, and a wide variety of other buildings throughout the USA. HHPA has received several awards and prizes, among them the Honor Awards of the American Institute of Architects and, in 1974, the Brunner Prize in Architecture of the National Institute of Arts and Letters. There are several publications on this architectural team.

Hawkinson, Lawrie
Smith-Miller & Hawkinson

Born in the USA.

Studied architecture at the Cooper Union, New York, and art at the University of California, Berkeley. Has worked in the practice of Venturi, Rauch and Scott Brown, and taught at Columbia University, Parsons School of Design, and the University of Miami, Coral Gables. Her work has been exhibited in the USA, and she has received awards in industrial design. With her partner, Henry Smith-Miller, she won the competition for the Institute of Contemporary Art in Philadelphia.

Hayden, Richard Seth
Swanke Hayden Connell

Born in the USA.

Graduated in architecture at Syracuse University in 1960. Since 1962 has worked for the architectural practice Swanke Hayden Connell. Also freelance architect in various states throughout the USA. Partly responsible for the restoration of the Statue of Liberty.

Holl, Steven
Steven Holl Architects

Born in Bremerton, Washington.

Studied architecture at the University of Washington and the Graduate School of the Architectural Association in London. He has taught at various universities and schools of architecture in the USA, and is currently Professor of Architecture at Columbia University. Exhibitions and publications in the USA, Europe, and the Far East. Among other awards, he won the American Institute of Architects Chapter Award in 1985. He has his own practice in New York with various colleagues.

Isozaki, Arata
Arata Isozaki & Associates

Born 1931 in Oita, Japan.

Graduated in architecture from the University of Tokyo in 1954. Worked with Kenzo Tange from 1954 to 1963. Since 1963 has had his own practice, Arata Isozaki & Partners, in Tokyo.

Jahn, Helmut
Murphy/Jahn

Born 1940 in Zirndorf near Nuremberg, West Germany.

Studied at the Technische Hochschule in Munich and at the Illinois Institute of Technology, Chicago. In 1967 he joined the practice of C. F. Murphy Associates, founded by C. F. Murphy in 1959. In 1973 he became partner, Vice-President, and Director of the Design Department of the practice, which was renamed Murphy/Jahn Architects in 1981. With Jahn as its leading designer, the practice moved away, in the 1970s, from the influence of Ludwig Mies van der Rohe, as can be seen from the Kemper Arena in Kansas City (1974), the central administration of the company Rust-Oleum in Vernon Hills, Illinois (1978), the Xerox Center in Chicago (1980), and the State of Illinois Center in Chicago (1981).

Keenen, John
Kennen/Riley Architecture

Born in the USA.

Studied at the Harvard Graduate School of Design until 1978, at Georgetown University, Washington, DC, until 1979, and at Columbia University, New York City, until 1983. Worked for the New York practices Agrest & Gandelsonas, Kagan and di Cosmi, Wen & Wang Architects, and for Skidmore, Owings and Merrill. Since 1984 in partnership with Terence Riley in New York City. He has received several awards and prizes for the team Keenen/Riley Architecture. Exhibitions in the USA, Japan, and Europe. Publications in various specialist magazines.

Kiss, Laszlo
UKZ Design, Inc.

Born in Oradea, Romania.

Kiss worked first of all as design architect for Skidmore, Owings and Merrill in New York. In 1980 he founded an architectural practice with Simon Ungers, which became UKZ when Todd Zwigard became the third partner in 1983.

Kliment, Robert M.
R. M. Kliment & Frances Halsband

Born 1933 in Prague, Czechoslovakia.

Studied architecture at Yale University, and received grant to study in Italy. From 1962 to 1972 he worked in the practice Mitchell/Giurgola Architects in Philadelphia and New York. In 1972 he founded a joint practice with Frances Halsband. Member of the American Institute of Architects.

Kohn, Eugene A.
Kohn Pedersen Fox Associates

Graduated in architecture from the University of Pennsylvania in 1957. Worked in the practice John Carl Warnecke and Associates. After that, he founded, with William Pedersen and Sheldon Fox, the architectural practice Kohn Pedersen Fox Associates, which has worked on many major projects. Kohn is, among other things, a Fellow of the American Institute of Architects and of the Royal Institute of British Architects. In 1985 the latter organized an exhibition of the work of Kohn Pedersen Fox. He has frequently held teaching posts at universities in the USA and England. He has served on many competition juries.

Kolatan, Sulan
Kolatan/MacDonald Studio

Born in Istanbul, Turkey.

Graduated as engineer from the Rheinisch-Westfälische Technische Hochschule in Aachen, West Germany, and continued her studies at Columbia University. Worked for O. M. Ungers and Kohn Pedersen Fox, New York. Since 1982 has run a practice with William MacDonald. Exhibitions in the USA and West Germany. Kolatan's/MacDonald's work has been published in the USA and Italy, and they won the Fifth Young Architects Forum.

Krueck, Ronald A.
Krueck & Olsen Architects

Born in the USA.

Graduated in 1970 from the Illinois Institute of Technology. In 1970–71 worked in the practice of C. F. Murphy Associates, Chicago, and, from 1971 to 1976, for Hammond Beeby and Associates, Chicago. Since 1978 partnership with Keith Olsen in the architectural practice Krueck & Olsen Architects. Teaching posts at Illinois Institute of Technology, Chicago, and at the Harvard Graduate School of Design. Numerous awards and honors, mainly from the American Institute of Architects.

Lupo, Frank
New York Architects

Born in the USA.

Studied architecture at the University of Cincinnati and at Yale University, from which he received the William Wirth Winchester Traveling Fellowship. He has taught at the Cooper Union. Worked in the practices of Gwathmey Siegel Associates and Morphis and Studio Works. In 1984 founded the practice New York Architects, together with Daniel Rowen. In 1985 took part in the Venice Biennale.

MacDonald, William
Kolatan/MacDonald Studio

Born 1956 in Milford, Massachusetts.

Studied architecture at the Architectural Association in London, at Syracuse University, and at Columbia University. Worked in New York in the practices of Eisenman/Robertson, O. M. Ungers, The Architectural Studio, and Skidmore, Owings and Merrill. Teaching posts at Columbia University and at the University of Virginia, Charlottesville. Exhibitions in the USA, West Germany, France, and Italy. Architectural practice with Sulan Kolatan in New York.

Macklowe, Harry

The Macklowe Organization, founded by Harry Macklowe, has designed and erected numerous buildings and new construction methods. A particular concern is the integration of works of art in office buildings, housing estates, and hotels. Macklowe's best-known work is the Metropolitan Tower in New York City.

Meier, Richard Alan
Richard Meier & Partners

Born 1934 in Newark, New Jersey.

Studied at Cornell University in Ithaca, New York. After that, worked in various practices, including those of Skidmore, Owings and Merrill in New York, and Marcel Breuer. Since 1963 has run his own practice in New York, Richard Meier & Partners. He has taught at several universities in the USA. He became well known through an exhibition (1969) and book (1972) on "The New York Five." His early buildings were primarily family homes, then came large housing estates. Among his best-known works are the Bronx Development Center, New York (1970–76), the Atheneum in New Harmony, Indiana (1975–79), and the Museum for Applied Arts (1979) in Frankfurt, West Germany. Since 1976 Meier has been a Fellow of the American Institute of Architects and, since 1986, of the International Academy of Architecture.

Mitchell, Ehrmann
Mitchell/Giurgola Architects

Born 1924 in Harrisburg, Pennsylvania.

Studied architecture at the University of Pennsylvania, Philadelphia, 1941 to 1948. From 1951 to 1958 worked in the practice of Bellante and Clauss, London. Since 1948 in partnership with Romaldo Giurgola, at first in Philadelphia, and from 1966 in New York. Mitchell has been president of the American Institute of Architects since 1979. Exhibitions in the USA and Europe. Numerous awards and competition prizes.

Mostoller, Michael
Michael Mostoller and Fred Travisano

Born in the USA.

Studied at Rensselaer Polytechnic Institute and at Harvard University. Since 1969 he has been working as a freelance architect. In 1985 he formed a practice with Fred Travisano based on their mutual commitment to housing and urban issues. Hereceived a prize from the American Institute of Architects for his designs for residential hotels. There have been numerous exhibitions of, and publications on, his work.

Olsen, Keith
Krueck & Olsen Architects

Born in the USA.

Studied architecture at Illinois Institute of Technology until 1970. After that, worked until 1971 for C. F. Murphy Associates, Chicago. From 1973 to 1978 he worked for Hammond Beeby Associates, Chicago. In 1978 he founded the architectural practice Krueck & Olsen Architects with Ronald A. Krueck. Numerous prizes and awards, especially from the American Institute of Architects. Publications in various specialist magazines.

OMA
(Office for Metropolitan Architecture)

Practice founded in London in 1975 by Rem Koolhaas and Elia Zenghelis. The painters Zoe Zenghelis and Madelon Vriesendrop joined it, and have been responsible for much of its work. As early as 1972 Koolhaas and Zenghelis presented their first joint project, a fantastical collage of the Berlin Wall with the title "Exodus." The conceptual designs of the early seventies have been followed by competition entries and commissioned designs that always embody a clearly intelligible design theory. Koolhaas and Zenghelis have participated in numerous international exhibitions and competitions. They have architectural practices in London and Rotterdam.

Oubrerie, José

Born in Nantes, France.

Studied at the École Nationale Supérieure des Beaux-Arts, Paris, and at the École des Beaux-Arts, Nantes. Freelance architect in the USA and Europe. He has taught in the USA, France, and Italy, and is currently Dean of the College of Architecture of the University of Kentucky, Lexington. Writer on architecture, especially on Le Corbusier, whose assistant he was for a few years. Recipient of several prizes and honors – for instance, from the French Académie d'Architecture in 1987.

Pedersen, William
Kohn Pedersen Fox Associates

Born in 1938 in St. Paul, Minnesota.

Studied architecture until 1961 at the University of Minnesota, and until 1963 at the Massachusetts Institute of Technology. In 1965 he won the Rome Prize in Architecture and studied for two years at the American Academy in Rome. Worked for I. M. Pei & Partners between 1967 and 1971. From 1971 to 1976 Vice-President of John Carl Warnecke and Associates. After that, in partnership with Eugene Kohn and Sheldon Fox. Publications in various architectural magazines. Fellow of the American Institute of Architects and of the American Academy in Rome.

Pelli, Cesar
Cesar Pelli & Associates

Born 1926 in Tucuman, Argentina.

Studied at the University in Tucuman and at the University of Illinois in Urbana. In partnership with Eero Saarinen from 1954 to 1964. He then went to Los Angeles, where he worked until 1968 as Design Director for Daniel, Mann, Johnson and Mendenhall, and from then until 1977 as a partner of Gruen Associates. Since 1977 he has been Dean of the Architecture Department at Yale University, New Haven, Connecticut. At the same time he opened a practice there, together with Fred Clark and Diana Balmori, under the name Cesar Pelli & Associates. His most famous buildings, the Town Hall in San Bernardino, California (1969), and the Pacific Design Center in Los Angeles (1971), show a sensitive interpretation of late rationalist architecture. The Hermann Park Towers, Houston, Texas (1979), and the extension and superstructures of the Museum of Modern Art, New York (1980), are two of his most recent projects.

Piscuskas, David
1100 Architect

Born in the USA.

Studied art at Brown University and architecture at the University of California at Los Angeles, where he received numerous awards and honors for his work. In Los Angeles he has produced performance events, combining dance with architecture. In 1983 he moved to New York, where, together with Juergen

Riehm and Ines Elskop, he founded the practice 1100 Architect. He has taught at the Parsons School of Design.

Polshek, James Stewart
James Stewart Polshek and Partners

Born 1930 in Akron, Ohio.

Studied at Yale University School of Architecture, the Case Western Reserve University, and the Royal Academy of Fine Arts in Copenhagen, Denmark. In 1963 he founded, with various partners, the architectural practice James Stewart Polshek & Partners. He has taught at a number of universities in the USA. From 1972 to 1987 he was Dean of Columbia University Graduate School of Architecture. Numerous prizes and honors, including the Progressive Architecture Project Award in 1969. Since 1972 he has been a Fellow of the American Institute of Architects.

Pran, Peter
Ellerbe Becket Architects

Born in Norway.

Studied at the university in Oslo, Norway, and at the Illinois Institute of Technology. He has worked for Russo & Sonder, Eli Attia, Grad Partnership, Schmitt, Garden & Erikson, and SOM. He also worked for three years for Mies van der Rohe in Chicago. Exhibitions of, and publications on, his work in the USA and Europe. Numerous awards and honors, including, together with Carlos Zapata, the Design Award of the American Institute of Architects, New York Chapter in 1986, 1987, 1988, and 1989, as well as the "Progressive Architecture" Design Award, 1989. He is Design Director and Vice-President of Ellerbe Becket and Distinguished Professor at the new York Institute of Technology.

Quintard-Hofstein, Pascal
PQH Projects

Born in Paris, France.

Studied architecture at the École Nationale Supérieure des Beaux-Arts, Paris. He worked together with Jean Nouvel in Paris. In 1982 he moved to New York, where he worked in the practice of Marcel Breuer and Associates. He later became co-director of the company Green Card. He taught at the New York Institute of Technology, Old Westbury, and at the Pratt Institute. Publications and various exhibitions of his projects. He has received several prizes, including the American Institute of Architecture Prize for Unbuilt Projects in1986.

Ranalli, George

Born 1946 in New York City.

Graduated in architecture in 1972 from the Pratt Institute and from the Graduate School of Design at Harvard University. Exhibitions of his projects in the USA and Europe. Publications of his work in international architecture magazines.

Riehm, Juergen
1100 Architect

Born in West Germany.

Graduated in architecture from the Fachhochschule Rheinland-Pfalz in Trier, West Germany, in 1977. Continued studying at the Städelschule, Frankfurt, with Peter Cook. Until 1982 he worked for various architectural practices in West Germany. In 1983 he moved to New York, where, together with David Piscuskas and Ines Elskop, he founded the practice 1100 Architect.

Riley, Terence
Keenen/Riley Architecture

Born in Italy.

Studied at the Architectural Studio in Rome, Italy, in 1975 – 76, at the University of Notre Dame, Indiana, until 1978, and at Columbia University, New York City, until 1982. From 1978 to 1980 he worked for Sabek Architects & Planners, Athens, in 1983 with Naomi Leff in New York, in 1984 with Marcel Breuer in New York, and with James Stewart Polshek and Partners. Since the end of 1984 he has been in partnership with John Keenen in New York and had numerous exhibitions in the USA, Japan, and Europe. Publications in various specialist magazines.

Roche, Kevin
Kevin Roche John Dinkeloo and Associates

Born 1922 in Dublin, Ireland.

Studied at the National University of Ireland in Dublin. Worked for Michael Scott and Partners, Dublin, and Maxwell Frey and Jane Drew, London. In 1948 he moved to the USA. In 1951 he joined Eero Saarinen's practice, where he became head of design. After Saarinen's death in 1961 he took over the practice, together with John Dinkeloo. He set up a practice in Hamden, Connecticut, called Kevin Roche John Dinkeloo and Associates. In the work of Roche and Dinkeloo the abstract geometry of Ludwig Mies van der Rohe is combined with a powerful structural expressionism and a strong physicality that is developed out of the specific situation. Among the most important works of Roche and Dinkeloo are the Oakland Museum, Oakland (1961– 68), the Administration Building of the Ford Foundation, New York (1963 – 68), the Veterans Memorial Coliseum, New Haven, Connecticut (1965 – 72), the extension to the Metropolitan Museum of Art, New York (1967 – 68), and the project for the Central Administration of the Fiat Company in Turin (1973).

Rowen, Daniel
New York Architects

Born in the USA.

Studied architecture at Brown University and at Yale University, where he now works as a lecturer. Worked in the practice of Gwathmey Siegel & Associates. At this time he received many awards. In 1984 he founded, together with Frank Lupo, the practice New York Architects. With their first joint design, for the Times Tower Competition of 1984, they won the first prize of the Municipal Arts Society.

Schwartz, Frederic
Anderson/Schwartz

Born in the USA.

Graduated in architecture from the University of California in Berkeley in 1973, and from Harvard in 1978. In 1982 he received the National Endowment for the Arts Design Fellowship. In 1984 he won the Rome Prize in Architecture. He worked for the Skidmore, Owings and Merrill practice, and was director of Venturi, Rauch and Scott Brown from 1980 to 1984. He has taught in the USA and Europe. Publications in various specialist magazines. Major prizes and honors, including the Progressive Architecture Design Award and an American Institute of Architects award.

Scofidio, Ricardo
Diller + Scofidio

Born 1935 in New York City.

Studied at the Faculty of the Chanin School of Architecture of Cooper Union. He has worked little in architectural practices, his projects mainly arising independently and combining architecture with performance, sculpture, and music. In 1979 partnership with Elisabeth Diller in the architectural practice Diller + Scofidio, New York. Among other projects, they worked on an installation for the Museum of Modern Art. Exhibitions in the USA, Japan, Israel, and Europe. Numerous awards and honors – for example, from the American Academy in Rome and the National Endowment for the Arts.

Siegel, Robert
Gwathmey Siegel & Associates

Born 1939 in New York City.

Attended the Arts Student League in New York from 1949 to 1956 and the High School of Music and Art, New York. From 1953 to 1957 holder of a scholarship from the Pratt Institute, New York. He also studied there from 1957 to 1962, and at the Harvard University Graduate School of Design in 1963. From 1968 in partnership with Charles Gwathmey and Richard Henderson. Apart from teaching, he has worked as critic, competition judge, and editor. With Gwathmey Siegel & Associates he has worked on projects for corporate and institutional buildings as well as for housing. The office has won numerous prizes, including The Firm Award in 1982, the highest honor of the American Institute of Architects.

Smith-Miller, Henry
Smith-Miller + Hawkinson

Born in the USA.

Studied architecture at the University of Pennsylvania and at Princeton University. Before working together with Lawrie Hawkinson, he was active in the practices of Richard Meier, Michael Graves, and Peter Eisenman. Exhibitions and publications in the USA and elsewhere. Awards for interior design. First prize, with Lawrie Hawkinson, in a competition organized by the Institute of Contemporary Art in Philadelphia.

Spear, Laurinda Hope
Arquitectonica

Born in the USA.

Graduated in architecture from Columbia University in 1977. In 1977 and 1979 taught at the University of Miami School of Engineering and Environmental Design, Florida. In 1977 founded the practice Arquitectonica, together with Bernardo Fort-Brescia, in Coral Gables, Florida. Numerous honors and prizes, including the Rome Prize in Architecture.

Stern, Robert A. M.
Robert A. M. Stern Architects

Born 1939 in New York City.

Studied at Columbia University, New York, until 1960, then at Yale University in New Haven until 1965. Worked for a short time in Richard Meier's practice, and after that for several years as urban planner in New York. In 1977 he formed his own firm in New York, Robert Stern Architects. Since 1977 Professor at Columbia University. In 1976 and 1980 took part in the Venice Biennale. He has published numerous articles on Post Modernism.

Stubbins, Hugh
The Stubbins Associates

Born 1912 in Birmingham, Alabama.

In 1929 – 30 studied architecture at the Georgia Institute of Technology, Atlanta, and from 1933 to 1935 at the Harvard University Graduate School of Design, Cambridge, Massachusetts, where he received a scholarship and several prizes. From 1935 to 1943 he worked as designer and draftsman in various practices. In 1940 instructor and assistant to Walter Gropius at the Graduate School of Design. From 1943 to 1945 assistant to the President of the Polaroid Corporation, Cambridge. Since 1969 architectural practice with Rex Allen in Cambridge, Massachusetts, and in San Francisco.

Travisano, Fred
Michael Mostoller and Fred Travisano

Born in the USA.

Graduated from the Cooper Union School of Architecture. After working for SOM and John Hejduk in New York, he became director of the Department for Development at the Department of Planning and Development in the city of Trenton, New Jersey. Since 1978 has had his own practice in Trenton. In 1981 he received a research grant from the American Academy in Rome. In 1985 he founded an architectural practice with Michael Mostoller, in Princeton, New Jersey. Various awards, including the HUD prize for his work in Trenton.

Tschumi, Bernard

Born 1944 in Switzerland

Studied at the Institut für Technologie in Zurich. Taught at the Architectural Association, London, from 1970 to 1979; at the Institute for Architecture and Urban Studies in New York, 1976; and at Princeton University in 1978 and 1980. He was guest professor at the Cooper Union School of Architecture in New York from 1980 to 1983. Numerous guest lectures in the USA and in Europe. Exhibitions in New York, London, Paris, Copenhagen, Madrid, Kassel, Berlin, Los Angeles, and Tokyo. His critical and theoretical texts have been published in numerous architectural and art magazines. Tschumi has won prizes in many international competitions, including those for the Parc de la Villette in 1983; La Defense, Paris, in 1983; Tokyo Opera House in 1986; and, in 1985, the Preis für progressive Architektur for the Parc de la Villette. He lives and works in New York and Paris.

Tsien, Billie
Tod Williams, Billie Tsien and Associates

Born in the USA.

Studied architecture at Brown University until 1969, at Yale University until 1971, and at U.C.L.A. until 1977. worked for Coy Howard and Company, Los Angeles, from 1975 to 1977 and, from 1977 to 1986, for Tod Williams and Associates. Since 1987 in partnership with Tod Williams. Several performance events in the USA, Japan, and Israel. Numerous publications in various specialist magazines.

Ungers, Oswald Mathias

Born 1926 in Kaiseresch, Eifel, West Germany.

From 1947 to 1950 studied architecture at the Technische Hochschule in Karlsruhe with Egon Eiermann. Since 1950 freelance architect in Cologne. From 1964 has had an office in Berlin and, since 1970, in Ithaca, New York. Professor at the Technische Universität in Berlin from 1963 to 1968 and, from 1968 to 1975, director of the Faculty of Architecture at Cornell University, Ithaca, New York. Until the mid-sixties worked on many residential buildings, and from then until the mid-seventies almost entirely on competition entries. Since then numerous prestigious projects have been carried out by his offices in Cologne, Berlin, Frankfurt, and Karlsruhe.

Ungers, Simon

Born 1957 in Cologne, West Germany.

Graduated from Cornell University in 1980. In the same year founded his first architectural practice with Laszlo Kiss. In 1983 Todd Zwigard joined the practice, which was then named UKZ Design, Inc. Until 1986 Ungers was Principal Partner of UKZ. He has lived and worked in New York City since 1987.

Venturi, Robert Charles
Venturi, Rauch and Scott Brown

Born 1925 in Philadelphia, Pennsylvania.

Studied at Princeton University, New Jersey, from 1943 to 1950. Until 1958 worked in the practices of, among others, Eero Saarinen in Bloomfield Hills, Michigan, and Louis Kahn in Philadelphia. Since 1958 he has had his own practice with various partners. In 1964 he began working with John Rauch. They were joined by Denise Scott Brown, and the practice has been called Venturi, Rauch and Scott Brown since 1980. Venturi has also been acclaimed for his papers on architectural theory. He has taught at several universities and schools of architecture in the USA.

Vignelli, Massimo
Vignelli Associates

Born 1931 in Milan, Italy.

Studied architecture in Milan and Venice. Since then has worked with his wife Lella, who is an architect specializing in interior design. In 1965 joint founder and Design Director of the Unimark International Corporation, Chicago. In 1971 founded the architectural practice Vignelli Associates and Vignelli Designs in New York. His work has been exhibited and published throughout the world and several of his works have been bought by museums. The Vignellis have received numerous honors and prizes, including, in 1973, the Industrial Arts Medal of the American Institute of Architects.

Viñoly, Rafael
Rafael Viñoly Architects

Born in Montevideo, Uruguay.

Studied at the Faculty of Architecture and Urbanism at the University of Buenos Aires, where he later worked as Associate Professor of Architecture. In 1965 Viñoly formed, together with six partners, the Estudio de Arquitectura, which received numerous major commissions in South America. Following an invitation to work at the Harvard University Graduate School of Design, Viñoly moved to the USA in 1978. In 1981 he founded the practice Rafael Viñoly Architects in New York.

Voorsanger, Bartholomew
Voorsanger & Mills Associates

Born in the USA.

Studied architecture at Princeton University and at Harvard University. After that, Voorsanger worked for three years in Montreal, with the urban planner Vincent Ponte, then for I. M. Pei and Partners. Voorsanger's work has been exhibited and published in the USA, Europe, and Japan. He has received numerous honors and prizes, including the New York City Art Commission Award for Excellence in Design for the Hostos Community College. He has served on the juries of major national and regional competitions. Since 1978 he has been in partnership with Edward I. Mills in New York. In 1985 he was appointed Fellow of the American Institute of Architects for the category design.

Williams, Tod
Tod Williams, Billie Tsien and Associates

Born 1943 in the USA.

Studied art and architecture at Princeton University and at Cambridge University in England. Williams worked for several years for Richard Meier & Partners before founding his own architectural practice in New York. There have been numerous exhibitions of, and publications on, his projects. Williams received a scholarship from the National Endowment for the Arts. In 1982 and 1986 he received honors from the American Institute of Architects.

Wolf, Harry C.
Ellerbe Becket Architects

Born in Charlotte, North Carolina.

Studied architecture at the Georgia Institute of Technology. Taught at Columbia University and Harvard. His work has been published in the USA and abroad. Over the last twenty years Wolf's projects have won more than forty major prizes, among them three Design Honor Awards from the American Institute of Architects, New York Chapter. After working for twenty years in North Carolina, Wolf moved to New York to concentrate on his chief area of interest, architecture as an art product.

Zapata, Carlos
Ellerbe Becket Architects

Born in Rubio, Venezuela.

Studied at the Pratt Institute and at Columbia University in New York, at the International Center of the University of Copenhagen, and at the International Seminar of the University of Palermo, Italy. Worked in the practices of Russo + Sonder and Eli Attia. Together with Peter Pran he has won the Design Award of the American Institute of Architects, New York Chapter in 1986, 1987, 1988, and 1989, as well as the "Progressive Architecture" Design Award. He is Senior Project. Designer and Associate Design Director in the Ellerbe Becket New York office. He is also Adjunct Assistant Professor at the New York Institute of Technology.

Zwigard, Todd
UKZ Design, Inc.

Born in the USA.

Zwigard joined Simon Ungers and Laszlo Kiss in 1983 and together they formed the architectural firm UKZ Design, Inc. He is also lecturer at the Environmental Design Department of the Parsons School of Design.

Photographic Acknowledgments

All uncredited illustrations are taken from the architects' or their office archives.

Peter Aaron   193 top, 318, 319
David Anderson   213
    and cover illustration (back)
O. Baitz, Inc.   266, 267
Berenholtz   175
Ben Blackwell   273
Steven Brooke   322 bottom left
Kenneth Champlin   197 top left
Paul Chapman   306 left
Frederick Charles   278, 279 top
Dan Cornish   118 bottom, 139 top, 202, 203, 227 center
    left, center, bottom left, bottom center
Peter K. Cowan   303
George Cserna   209 – 211
Marc C. Darley   149
Jen Fong   90 left, 92 top right, 93
Dick Frank   110 top right
Jeff Goldberg   246, 247, 249, 297 top
M. Haeselsrave   307 top
Paul Hester   306 right, 307 except top
Wolfgang Hoyt   110 –113, 194, 257, 280, 281, 297 bottom,
    300, 301
Timothy Hursley   192
Elliott Kaufman   104, 105
Nathaniel Lieberman   126, 127, 136 top, 137 bottom left
Peter Mauss   197 right
Norman McGrath   142 –145
Michael Moran   115, 117, 258, 259 bottom right, 260, 261
Bo Parker   183
Paschall/Taylor   130, 131
Jeff Perkell   193 bottom left, center right
Jack Pottle   181 bottom
Bernard Rickenbach   274, 275, 277
Cervin Robinson   103, 165, 290, 322 bottom center,
    bottom right, 323 top right, bottom left
Eric Schiller   285 center, bottom
Roland Stefanescu   pp. 100, 101, 266 – 269
Ezra Stoller   179, 299
Guy Sussman   181 top
William Taylor   132, 133
Adrian Velicescu   324, 325
Luca Vignelli   244, 245
Paul Warchol   148, 150, 151, 219, 315